i860™ Microprocessor Architecture

i860™ Microprocessor Architecture

Neal Margulis

intel®
Osborne McGraw-Hill

Osborne **McGraw-Hill**
2600 Tenth Street
Berkeley, California 94710
U.S.A.

For information on translations and book distributors outside of the U.S.A., write to Osborne **McGraw-Hill** at the above address.

A complete list of trademarks appears on page 613.

i860™ Microprocessor Architecture

1234567890 DOC 99876543210

ISBN 0-07-881645-9

CONTENTS AT A GLANCE

CONTENTS

ACKNOWLEDGEMENT

Writing a book that contains this much information is not an effort that I would attempt without help.

Mark Atkins, an Intel applications engineer and friend, made a tremendous difference to this book. Mark went beyond the job of technical editor by writing and debugging example programs, and co-writing the application example chapters on the Fast Fourier Transform and on 3-D graphics rendering.

Collecting and organizing the information for the Instruction Set Summary, "Appendix A," was done by Glenn Schuster. Glenn produced a very complete and very usable reference.

Much of what I know about the i860 I have learned from Les Kohn. Many other people have contributed to my understanding and appreciation of the i860. These include Rajeev Bharadhwaj, Kanwar Chadha, Sai-Wai Fu, Piyush Patel, Mike Rhodehamel, Hon Sit, and Lauren Stafford. Special thanks goes to the design engineers who made the i860 a reality.

Neal Margulis

INTEL FOREWORD

The i860 64-bit microprocessor brings new levels of performance and capability to the microprocessor world. Incorporating more than one million transistors and executing up to three operations per clock, the i860 processor can perform up to 80 MFlops (Millions of Floating-point Operations Per Second) and 40 MIPS (Millions of Instructions Per Second) at 40 MHz. At Intel we have been excited by the range of new products and applications being developed around this chip. The i860 microprocessor is being used in applications ranging from 3-D graphics systems to music synthesizers (my personal favorite) to desktop workstations with the computing power of a Cray 1 to large multiprocessor systems that provide performance competitive with the latest supercomputers at much lower cost.

To achieve this level of performance, we merged the high-integer capabilities of RISC processors with techniques used in the supercomputer world to achieve high floating performance and with the techniques used in high-end graphics workstations to achieve integrated 3-D visualization. Compressing all of this computing power onto a single chip wasn't trivial. Similarly, taking full advantage of the computing power of the i860 processor requires mastering some new programming concepts such as software pipelining and 3-D rendering algorithms. That is where this book comes in. *i860 Microprocessor Architecture* starts by providing an excellent introduction to the philosophy and concepts behind the i860 microprocessor. It then provides complete details on the i860 processor's architecture, including the data types, register model, integer, floating point and graphics instructions, and operating system support. Along the way it provides many programming tips and examples that will help you master i860 microprocessor programming.

Writing a book like this requires intimate knowledge of processor design and programming techniques, as well as the patience and ability to explain these concepts clearly. Neal Margulis is uniquely qualified for this challenge. I first met Neal when we were forming Intel's i860 microprocessor application group. Neal was so enthusiastic that he developed the design of a four-processor i860 system on his own time. Needless to say, he got the job. Working in this group, Neal developed much of the reference and training material and gave many presentations on the i860 processor. As an i860 processor expert, he was often called upon to help customers with specific design problems. Neal could always be counted on to answer even the most difficult questions and is well aware of the pitfalls and common misunderstandings of new i860 microprocessor users.

The i860 microprocessor creates many opportunities for application developers. With this book, and some imagination, we can look forward to many great new i860 microprocessor applications.

Les Kohn
i860 Microprocessor Chief Architect

INTRODUCTION

The i860 microprocessor is the world's first million-transistor microprocessor and Intel's first RISC processor for general-purpose computers. The i860-processor-based computer brings supercomputer performance and application to the scientific, technical, engineering, and business mainstream. Because of this flexibility, the i860 processor is being used in a variety of configurations such as accelerators, graphics subsystems, workstations, and multiprocessing and parallel processing.

By using supercomputer techniques, the i860 microprocessor achieves balanced integer, floating-point, and graphics performance. Because the i860 microprocessor is a RISC architecture, programming it is different from programming any of Intel's other processors, such as the 386 and i486 microprocessors. The i860 microprocessor is a new architecture, and it presents many new challenges.

About This Book

This book is written to help you understand the i860 microprocessor. As a new generation of computers that utilize the i860 microprocessor enters the market, new opportunities are created. There are hundreds, if not thousands, of applications awaiting the power and capabilities of the i860 processor. This book will aid you in several ways. First, it will give you valuable insights into the i860 architecture that will help you to understand the capabilities of the i860 microprocessor. Next, this book will guide you in programming your first power-packed i860 microprocessor application. Finally, this book provides the most complete reference section on i860 microprocessor instructions available anywhere. This reference, in itself, will make programming the i860 microprocessor much easier and faster. Throughout the text, isolated code fragments and more extensive application program examples reinforce programming concepts and give you a cornerstone on which to build your application.

How This Book Is Organized

i860 Microprocessor Architecture is organized to provide continuity when reading each chapter. Because of its unique organization, it can also be used as a reference guide to help you quickly find the facts you need. The book is divided into eleven chapters and three appendixes. Chapters 1 through 9 are designed so that you can read them from start to finish or skip directly to a topic of interest. Chapters 10 and 11 are application examples that tie together the information you learned from the first nine chapters. The three appendixes form a complete programmer's reference guide, including an alphabetized listing of each instruction.

Chapter 1, "i860 Microprocessor Overview," sheds light on the development of the i860 processor, originally known as the N10. Also explained is the significance of the i860 microprocessor to Intel and what it will mean to computer users.

Chapter 2, "Processor Design: A Performance-Driven Approach," details the myriad tradeoffs of designing a microprocessor. Understanding these tradeoffs is critical to understanding and evaluating *CISC* (Complex Instruction Set Computing) and *RISC* (Reduced Instruction Set Computing) processors. After reading this chapter, you will see how the design of a microprocessor affects its performance.

Chapter 3, "i860 Microprocessor Architecture Overview," takes you on a tour of the functional units that comprise the i860 microprocessor.

Also introduced are the basics of how the i860 processor performs integer, floating-point and graphics operations. The i860 processor's hardware interface to the external world is also included.

Chapter 4, "Machine Organization," teaches you the fundamental aspects of the i860 microprocessor's architecture, including the data formats, the register model, and memory addressing. These explanations establish a common vocabulary and notation that will be used throughout this book. Additional information on programming conventions is included at the end of this Introduction.

Chapter 5, "RISC Core Operations," starts the description of RISC core operations, in which the RISC core is responsible for the fundamental operation of the processor. Each class of RISC core instructions is explained along with tips for performance programming. Example programs that enforce the explanations are included.

Chapter 6, "Floating-Point Operations," presents detailed information on the operations for floating-point arithmetic and long-integer arithmetic. Floating-point addition, subtraction, multiplication and division are all explained as well as how to use floating-point pipelining so your programs can achieve the highest performance. Several example programs are included, highlighted by a vector dot product example.

Chapter 7, "Graphics Rendering Instructions," covers the i860 processor's support for 3-D graphics rendering. This chapter starts with the basics for shading and displaying 3-D objects. Then the detailed operations, and how to implement them using the i860 processor's graphics rendering instructions, are explained. Included is an example that performs shading, hidden surface elimination, and distance interpolation concurrently.

Chapter 8, "Programming for Parallelism," shows how to put the RISC core and floating-point operations together to achieve maximum performance. The i860 processor's unique dual-operation instructions and dual-instruction mode operation warrant a full chapter packed with programming hints and examples.

Chapter 9, "Operating System Support," takes a step back from the challenges of application programming to explain the i860 processor's support for operating systems. The techniques for supporting virtual memory and multitasking operating systems are unraveled, as are the details for handling traps, interrupts and task switching. Special attention is given to the i860 processor's virtual caching.

Chapter 10, "Application Example: The Fast Fourier Transform," is a complete example program that applies the i860 processor to the real-world application of the Fast Fourier Transform (FFT). The FFT is used universally in digital signal processing (DSP) applications. This chapter explains the basics of DSP and the FFT equations and shows you step by step how to optimize the FFT code for the i860 microprocessor.

Chapter 11, "Application Example: The 3-D Graphics Transform," gets started with an introduction to the 3-D coordinate system and the transform matrix. Next, the fundamentals for rotating, scaling, panning, and zooming 3-D objects are explained. Finally, this chapter analyzes the performance of the transform and explains the transform code design for the i860 microprocessor.

Appendix A, "Instruction Set Summary," is a complete alphabetical reference of each i860 microprocessor instruction. Each entry includes the instruction's operation, syntax, description, and encoding. Also included is the effect each instruction has on the processor's status flags, what exceptions the instruction can cause, and how to use the instruction for the fastest execution of program sequences.

Appendix B, "Instruction Format and Encoding," tabulates the instruction formats and encodings for each i860 processor instruction.

Appendix C, "Instruction Timing and Characteristics, " provides a tabulated reference to aid assembly-language programmers in avoiding freeze conditions and calculating delays. Also tabulated are the instruction faults, restrictions, and execution behaviors.

Conventions Used in This Book

To make this book easier to read and understand, several conventions are used throughout the text:

- Register names and instruction mnemonics are printed in a special bold typestyle; for example, **dirbase**.
- Bits, bit field names, processor pins, and signal names are printed in capital letters in an alternate typestyle to make them stand out from the text; for example, CC and BREQ.

- A pound sign following a pin name indicates that the pin is active low. For example, ADS#.
- Variables are shown in a special italic type. For example, *src1* and *idest.*
- Text type italics are used the first time a term is introduced and occasionally for emphasis.

Throughout this book, i860 processor assembly language notation will be used in the example programs and program fragments. To keep the examples simple, much of the normal error checking code is not included. You can add this later if you use the code in your own programs. Also, to keep the examples general, the mechanics of assembling and linking the programs are not covered in this book. You should refer to the documentation that comes with your language(s) and tools.

Several conventions are used in program listings and the instruction descriptions that appear throughout the book and in Appendix A:

- Program listings and other lines of code in figures and in text appear in a monospace font. For example:

```
xor r5, r6, r7
```

The operation of instructions is described with a Pascal-like notation. The symbols and notation have the following meaning:

- A <-- B indicates that the value of B is assigned to A.
- Compound statements are enclosed between the keywords of the "if" statement (IF ... , THEN ... , ELSE ... , FI) or of the "do" statement (DO ... , OD).
- The operator ++ indicates autoincrement addressing.
- The italic variables *isrc1, isrc2, idest, fsrc1, fsrc2,* and *fdest* correspond to the position field within an instruction mnemonic.
- The italic variables *src1, src2,* and *dest* correspond to the position field within the instruction encoding.

Reserved Bits and Software Compatibility

In many registers and memory layout descriptions, certain bits are marked as *reserved* or *undefined.* When bits are thus marked, it is essential for compatibility with future processors that software not utilize these bits. The i860 microprocessor has an advantage over previous Intel processors in that there is a register that software can read in order to determine the processor type and stepping number (see the discussion of **epsr** in Chapter 4). Software should follow these guidelines in dealing with reserved or undefined bits:

- Do not depend on the states of any reserved or undefined bits when testing the values of the registers that contain such bits. Mask out the reserved and undefined bits before testing.
- Do not depend on the states of any reserved or undefined bits when storing them into memory or in another register.
- Do not depend on the ability to retain information written into any reserved or undefined bits.
- When reloading a register, or loading a register for the first time, always load the reserved bits and undefined bits with the values previously stored from the register.

As warned by Intel, "Depending on the values of reserved or undefined bits makes software dependent upon the unspecified manner in which the i860 microprocessor handles these bits. Depending upon values of reserved or undefined bits risks making software incompatible with future processors that define usages for these bits. *Avoid any software dependence upon the state of reserved or undefined bits.*"

Comments, queries, and suggestions regarding this book are welcome and should be directed to the author via CompuServe (user ID 70431,431).

Other Osborne/McGraw-Hill Books of Interest to You

We hope that *i860 Microprocessor Architecture* will assist you in mastering Intel's i860 microprocessor, and will also pique your interest in learning more about other ways to better use your computer.

If you're interested in expanding your skills so you can be even more "computer-efficient," be sure to take advantage of Osborne/McGraw-Hill's large selection of top-quality computer books that cover all varieties of popular hardware, software, programming languages, and operating systems. While we cannot list every title here that may relate to the Intel i860 microprocessor and to your special computing needs, here are just a few books that complement *i860 Microprocessor Architecture.*

80386 Microprocessor Handbook, by Chris H. Pappas and William H. Murray, takes experienced programmers inside the 80386 chip and provides complete details on the 80386 instruction set, as well as the 80387/80287 coprocessor and the 82385 cache controller chip.

Written for experienced 80386 programmers, *Advanced 80386 Programming Techniques,* by James L. Turley, begins with advanced memory segmentation and proceeds to the internal four-level protection hierarchy, multitasking, demand paging, system security, 8086/80186/80286 emulation, and intertask communication.

80386/80286 Assembly Language Programming, by William H. Murray and Chris H. Pappas, is a comprehensive guide enabling experienced programmers to take full advantage of the unique design of the 80386 and 80286 microprocessors. The authors carefully detail the use of assembler pseudo-ops, macros, procedures, libraries, testing and debugging techniques, and more.

WHY THIS BOOK IS FOR YOU

If you are looking at this book on the i860 microprocessor architecture, you are probably either seeking information to help you tackle your current i860 processor programming challenge, want to learn about the i860 processor's capabilities, or want to stay current with the excitement surrounding the new RISC microprocessors. This book will meet your needs regardless of your specific concern.

i860 Microprocessor Architecture is the authoritative guide to programming the i860 microprocessor. You can save yourself countless hours of frustrating trial-and-error programming by taking advantage of Neal Margulis's expertise in programming the i860. The clear explanations and commented examples will have you writing efficient code in no time. *i860 Microprocessor Architecture* puts all the i860 processor information in one book, making it the ideal reference book that you will use again and again.

If you want to see what the i860 microprocessor can do for your microprocessor applications, skim through the table of contents. Starting with the first chapter, this book explains the i860 processor capabilities and how they can be used. Later chapters will show you how the i860 processor can perform the hottest 3-D graphics, signal processing and multimedia applications.

Perhaps you have been hearing about the new RISC processors and want to see what all the excitement is about. This book can bring you up to speed with the latest techniques microprocessors are using to achieve maximum performance.

CHAPTER 1
i860 MICROPROCESSOR OVERVIEW

On February 27, 1989, Intel surprised the computer world with the announcement of the i860 *RISC* (Reduced Instruction Set Computer) microprocessor. After three well-guarded years of development, Intel brought the i860 processor out from under wraps. Although the i860 processor was not the first RISC microprocessor, it offered capabilities and performance levels beyond those of any other processor. Billed as the first one-million transistor, 64-bit, supercomputing processor, the i860 processor quickly gained notice as a performance leader.

Intel had not been expected to break with its tradition of compatibility and announce a RISC processor for the general computer market. With industry support from IBM, Microsoft, and many others, the i860 processor became a chip to watch. Intel had made its entry into the computer world's RISC revolution.

From the N10 to the i860 Microprocessor

Even at its humble beginning in 1986 the N10 project had big plans. The goal of the project was ambitious but simple—design the highest performance processor possible. Freed from the compatibility constraints of the *X*86 processor family, a RISC architecture was the obvious choice.

The architecture called for an efficient RISC core with fast integer performance and memory management, large caches for instructions and data, and specialized floating-point hardware. Les Kohn, the project's chief architect, felt that floating-point performance for microprocessors had been treated as second-class for too long and had to be brought into balance with integer performance. Where most processors take from five to ten clock cycles to perform a floating-point operation, Kohn recognized how pipelining could reduce that to one clock cycle. With that kind of computational ability, the processor has a tremendous appetite for data. To feed the processor data, the design team chose an on-chip 4K instruction cache, an 8K data cache, and lots of wide data paths.

Kohn had tried to start a RISC project since joining Intel in 1982. After several attempts were stopped short, Kohn knew what was needed to get the project funded until completion. The N10 development was carried out under a shroud of secrecy. The processor's specifications were highly guarded, with distribution within Intel restricted to a select few in Santa Clara. Potential customers were shown the N10 details only under a strict nondisclosure agreement. Even then, the processor's code name varied from customer to customer. Kanwar Chadha, the marketing manager and an N10 evangelist, kept a database of which customers were shown the processor under which code name. It was very important to keep the N10 out of the spotlight until Intel could prove that it could be built and meet its performance goals.

Customers were excited about the N10 from the start, but some doubted that such a complex chip could work. When functional silicon appeared in September 1988 these fears proved groundless. The N10's technical details were first shown in public at a technical conference, and they were a complete surprise. Industry speculation on how Intel would promote the N10 varied, but the official product unveiling a few weeks later ended speculation. When Bill Gates, the chairman of Microsoft, referred to the i860 processor, he said, "We fully expect to see a whole new generation of high-performance systems built on i860 microprocessor technology that will challenge the current standards in that market. Although projections indicate the first use of the i860 microprocessor will be in the technical computing market, eventually we expect to see application of this chip in the personal computer market.... [This] will bring the computation power of supercomputers to PCs."

Evolution or Revolution?

Often, a new technology will be relegated to a limited scope of applications at first, only to end up applying to a much broader scope. Many revolutionary innovations are mistaken in their early development as merely evolutionary steps. Once a revolutionary innovation is recognized as such, however, there is no stopping it.

Modern transportation, for example, has undergone many evolutionary steps and a few revolutionary ones. The first modern transportation system in this country was the railroad, and the transcontinental railroad flourished until the popularization of flight. The railroad companies missed the opportunity to expand their transport options to include air travel because they were blinded by their huge investments in trains and tracks. Although today it is clear that planes offer a significant travel advantage over trains, they initially were dismissed as toys and not considered commercially feasible for transportation.

Railroad companies had their own history of technical advances; for example, the automatic coupler, air brakes, and the diesel-electric locomotive. Railroad management felt that such technological advances would continue and would allow trains to keep pace with planes. Few people recognized the transportation potential of aircraft and the early airplane industry was relegated to airmail delivery. Following World War II, however, air travel increased, and by 1957 equaled rail travel. With the advent of the jet engine, air travel more than tripled between 1960 and 1970 and then it doubled again in less than eight years, mostly at the expense of rail travel.

Computers have gone through stages of revolution and evolution. Because computers were large and expensive, they had to be housed in separate rooms and had to be fully utilized to defray their cost. The nature of the mainframe of the 1960s and 1970s required it to be used as a batch machine where computing jobs were first prepared, then submitted, with results retrieved at a later time (or date).

When a revolutionary breakthrough succeeds it is due to the breakthrough's ability to change the way a problem is perceived. The perception of what computers can do has also changed. At first, computers were mistaken for an evolutionary step in the development of the adding machine. And although computers had immediate value as replacements for adding machines, the market for high-speed adding machines was very limited. In 1954 the American Federation of Information Processing Societies (AFIPS) estimated that fifty companies in the country could eventually use computers. But when computers were applied to problems such as reservation systems and *MIS* (management information science) systems, the number of applications swelled. The ability of early mainframe computers to revolutionize the way that work is done grew out of the ways that people modified the tasks that were performed.

Microprocessor Revolution

The invention of the microprocessor was the technological spark that led to the microcomputer (or personal computer) revolution. Just as the original market for computers was severely underestimated, so too was the market for personal computers. Labeling microcomputers as more affordable mainframes also failed to recognize their ability to revolutionize the workplace. Revolution came about because of new applications for computers, not because consumers decided they needed their own MIS systems. Instead of the batch style operation used by minicomputers, personal computers encouraged interaction, increased accessibility, and relative ease of use.

The first microprocessors, the Intel 4004 and 8008, were designed for specific applications—the calculator and the computer terminal. They served to integrate and replace complex, custom-designed circuits. Later, microprocessors became the heart of the general purpose computing system we know today. The Intel *X*86 family and the Motorola 68K family both use extensive instruction sets known today as *CISC* (Complex Instruction Set Computing). CISC architectures have improved their performance in successive generations by taking advantage of increased silicon technology. The architectural advances of microprocessors closely mimicked those of their ancestors, the data processing mainframes.

In 1986, the first commercial RISC processors entered the market. With the R2000 from MIPS Computer Systems Inc., followed by SPARC from SUN Microsystems, these relatively simple chips approached the RISC performance goal of one instruction per clock cycle. As with any new architecture, the lack of an installed software base hampered initial acceptance. Still, the raw performance numbers were compelling, and Motorola entered the market with the 88K, which deliberately broke with their 68K family in terms of compatibility.

This set the stage for the introduction of the i860 microprocessor. The ability to put more than a million transistors onto a single chip of silicon, combined with the architectural advantages of RISC, allows an architecture beyond anything previous processors could achieve. Beyond satisfying the need for traditional data processing, the i860 processor satisfies the need for data throughput and data computation. The i860 processor draws on the architecture not only of mainframes, but of supercomputers like the Cray. In bringing supercomputer power to the microprocessor world, it is possible to support a new class of multimedia applications that demand interactive computing with high-performance image, sound, and display processing capabilities.

RISC processors, unconstrained by software compatibility requirements, are better able to deliver performance from today's technologies. The applications for which people use computers are evolving so rapidly that the current microprocessor standards are already being challenged. Beyond higher performance for traditional applications, RISC processors must offer new capabilities to meet the needs of an entire new class of applications. Technological innovations such as FAX machines, compact disk (CD-ROM) players, and optical scanners are expanding the applications that the right processor can satisfy. No other processor architecture is as well suited to meet the needs of this new class of applications as the i860 processor architecture.

i860 Microprocessor Architecture Summary

The i860 processor is a single chip, 64-bit microprocessor that exploits many advanced architectural concepts with the goal of providing balanced integer, floating-point, and graphics performance. The i860 processor architecture is suited for a range of systems including workstations, minicomputers, graphics and application accelerators, and parallel supercomputers.

Unlike a typical system where integer, floating-point, and graphics capabilities are spread across several chips, the i860 processor was designed from the ground up to integrate all of these features. The result is a fully defined architecture that, for most systems, eliminates the need for support chips such as floating-point accelerators, vector processors, *DSP* (Digital Signal Processing) chips, and graphics coprocessors. A fully defined architecture sets a complete software standard, makes the software developer's job easier, and results in more powerful application software. A fully defined architecture also enables greater portability of software between different i860 processor-based systems.

The major functional units of the i860 processor and the paths between them are shown in Figure 1-1. By incorporating all of the functional units on a single chip, the chip designers were able to optimize the communication channels between the units. The processor includes

- Instruction cache
- Data cache
- Bus control unit
- RISC core
- Floating-point control unit
- Pipelined floating-point adder
- Pipelined floating-point multiplier
- 3D graphics unit
- Memory management unit

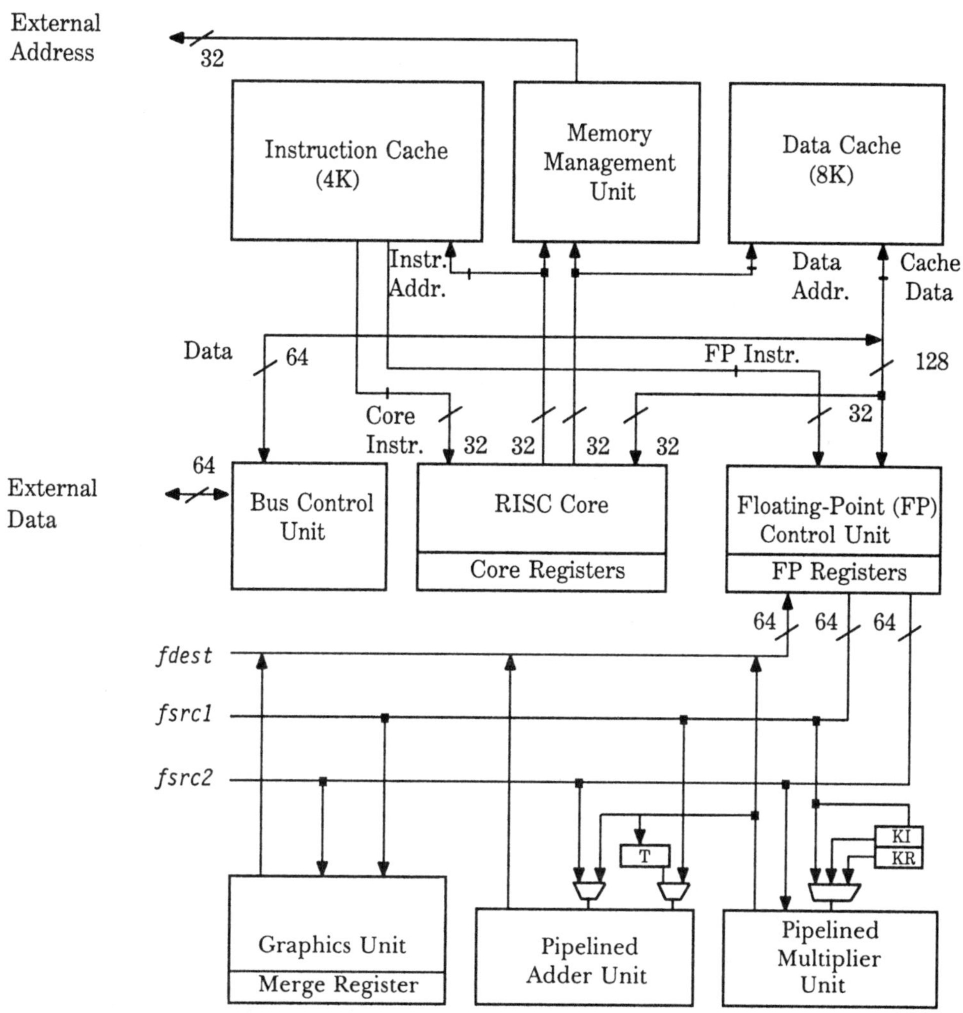

Figure 1-1. Functional units and data paths of the i860 processor

The on-chip 4K instruction cache and 8K data cache provide fast access to the most recently referenced memory locations without having to access slower off-chip memory. By including the caches on-chip, very wide buses are used to balance the data and instruction bandwidth to the processing speed of multiple execution units. Data and instructions are fetched simultaneously with the on-chip Harvard architecture, which employs separate instruction and data paths. The data cache has a 128-bit bus connecting it to the floating-point unit and a 32-bit bus connecting it to the RISC core. The instruction cache has a dedicated 64-bit bus to support two 32-bit instructions fetched simultaneously; one for execution by the RISC core, and one for execution by the floating-point unit. Externally, the processor has 32-bit addressing and a 64-bit data bus, which is used to access external memory.

The RISC core, floating-point unit, and graphics unit are pipelined. This allows a simple form of parallelism where the i860 processor overlaps execution of sequential instructions. The i860 processor also supports more sophisticated forms of parallel execution where both the RISC core and the floating-point unit can execute and produce results concurrently. Also, within the floating-point unit, the adder and multiplier units can be programmed to work together to perform common computations. By combining the floating-point architecture with the graphics unit, it is possible to support interactive visualization and display pictures and data in the form most familiar to people—three-dimensional. The on-chip *MMU* (Memory Management Unit) provides operating system support for multiuser and multitasking operating systems.

Quantifying Performance

By many measures the i860 microprocessor is the highest performance processor available today. Will another processor exceed its level of performance? Certainly, when Intel introduces the sequel to the i860 processor. In fact, Intel has gone on record that it plans to introduce a two-million-transistor successor to the i860 microprocessor in 1990, which will run the same software, but will address a higher point on the performance curve.

Although each application for microprocessors has its own standards by which to judge performance, some fundamental aspects of processor performance can be established. Chapter 2, "Processor Design: A Performance-Driven Approach," evaluates how a processor's design affects its ability to perform at a system level.

CHAPTER 2

PROCESSOR DESIGN: A PERFORMANCE-DRIVEN APPROACH

The i860 processor architecture is designed to deliver performance at a system level. Many trade-offs made at the processor level have implications for the system hardware architecture, the operating system software, and the application software. Processor design encompasses *VLSI* (Very Large Scale Integration) technology, instruction set design, and processor architecture. A performance-driven approach includes deciding what to support directly in silicon, and what to support at the software level.

Having a reduced instruction set is not the goal for any RISC processor, but the logical outcome of evaluating how to deliver performance at a system level. Although a full discussion of processor design trade-offs is beyond the scope of this book, this chapter provides an overview of processor design trade-offs so that the architecture of the i860 processor can be better understood and appreciated.

Silicon Technology

Every generation of semiconductor technology contributes faster transistors and more of them to computer designers. Figure 2-1 shows Moore's Law, which states that the number of transistors on a microprocessor doubles every couple of years. It is therefore not surprising that, regardless of architectural innovations, microprocessors have been able to increase performance with every generation. However, the market pressure to maintain software compatibility in successive generations is a mixed blessing. Although it has assured some degree of success for each new implementation (considerable success in the case of the Intel *X*86 and Motorola 68K families), it has also limited designers' ability to take best advantage of current technologies.

Both technical and nontechnical explanations have been given to explain why CISC architectures have evolved as they have, and why CISC is no longer the right way to go. Technology has advanced to the point that the basic assumptions that led to the architecture of early

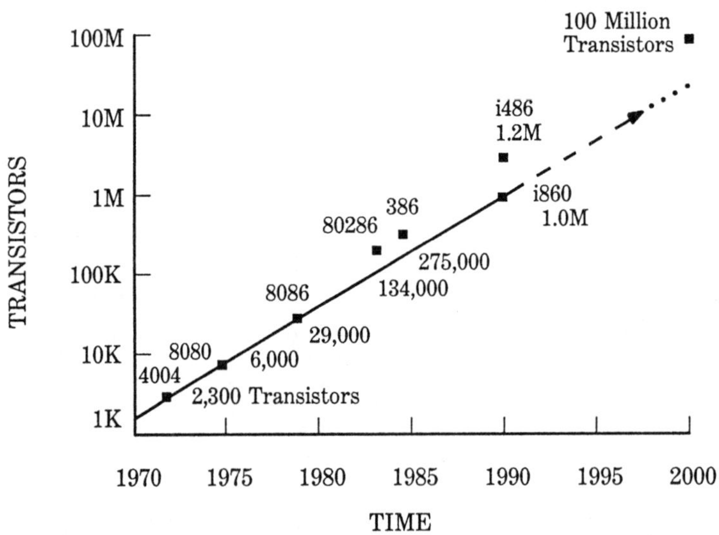

Figure 2-1. Moore's Law

CISC processors are no longer valid. Microcode (hardwired software) can be replaced with fast read/write cache memory. Cache memory has the advantage of dynamically determining which sequences of operations should be kept close to the processor, as opposed to microcode ROM where it is determined at design time. Alternative explanations of how and why CISC architectures evolved are "creeping elegance" or "it just happened." An analogy can be made with the large tail fins that "just happened" on American cars in the the 1950s.

CISC processors have continually added hardware support for less frequently used instructions with the intention of better supporting compilers and operating systems. Still, compilers and operating systems have had little success in gaining an advantage using these complex instructions. This is attributed to microcode routines not providing the precise complex routine required, and to the difficulty compilers have in recognizing the rare case when the microcode routines would suffice. Statistical analysis from programs run on CISC machines confirms the predominant use of simple instructions.

RISC Classic

RISC processors exhibit distinct attributes:

- Single-cycle execution
- Load/store architecture
- Fixed format instructions
- Hardwired control

These attributes are shared by most RISC machines and grow out of the desire to enhance processor performance. The design philosophy that leads to these commonalities can be stated as follows:

1. Analyze the target applications for statistical information on the operations performed.
2. Design for maximum efficiency in handling the frequently performed operations.

3. Move less frequent and more complex operations to software sequences.
4. Expose more of the processor's concurrency to the instruction set when there is a performance advantage to do so.
5. Include additional resources only after weighing the advantage of the added speed-up against a possible slowdown of more frequently used resources.

Applying this philosophy results in processors that have highly optimized data paths, use extensive pipelining, and pay careful attention to the memory hierarchy (including the registers and caches). The other major result is that complexity is moved from run time hardware to compile time software. In other words, don't save for run time what can be done at compile time.

Processor Performance Goals

If each instruction on a computer takes only one clock cycle, then the number of instructions executed per second is equal to the processor's clock cycle frequency. However, instructions may take more than one clock cycle to execute. A measure called the *native MIPS* rating can be calculated as follows:

$$\text{native MIPS} = \frac{instructions}{clock} * \frac{clocks}{10^{-6}\ sec}$$

The native MIPS rating can be very misleading when considering processor performance. It has been compared to the rpms (revolutions per minute) of a car: It tells you how fast the engine is going, but not how fast the car is going. Like the miles per hour rating for a car, the native

MIPS rating needs to be standardized to a metric that indicates what you really want to measure. A more meaningful measurement for processor performance—time per task—involves factoring in the strength of the instruction set to the native MIPS rating. The time per task can be calculated analytically as follows:

time/task = (*clocks/instruction*) * (*time/clock*) * (*instructions/task*)

Processor design involves trying to decrease these three parameters: clocks per instruction, time per clock, and instructions per task. Because these parameters are interrelated, reducing one of these measures often involves increasing another. For example, performance gained by reducing instructions per task and including more complex multiple clock cycle instructions will be offset by an increase in the average number of clocks per instruction. Similarly, attempting to perform too complex an operation in one clock cycle may slow down performance by increasing the time per clock for all instructions.

The time per clock is a major consideration as it affects all instructions. So, in order not to decrease the performance gains made by reducing the time per clock and the number of clocks per instruction, the instruction set must be designed to limit the increase in instructions per task. The interrelation of these three measures, combined with statistical information on the relative occurrence of specific operations, drives the processor design trade-offs.

The effort to enhance performance concentrates on reducing the average clocks per instruction. Fortunately, the most frequently executed instructions are simple ones; load from memory, register to register move, register add, update memory, branch, and other such simple operations. Because simple instructions are the predominant percentage of operations, RISC philosophy dictates that the processor design concentrate on ensuring that the simple instructions are performed as quickly as possible.

The most efficient method for decreasing the clocks per instruction, without decreasing the clock speed, is to overlap instruction execution as described in the following sections.

Pipelining

Pipelining is not a goal in itself. It is a means to a goal. *Pipelining* is a design technique where execution of multiple instructions is overlapped, with the goal of reducing the average number of clocks per instruction. Computers are not the only industry that utilizes pipelining. Manufacturing assembly lines break down the process of assembly into simple steps. For instance, if the manufacture of a product requires four steps—each performed by a different worker, and each requiring the same amount of time—four workers can overlap their efforts, resulting in a speed-up equal to the number of steps.

Modern RISC processors rely on this same concept, and break down instruction execution steps into simple stages. RISC instruction sets are designed to move efficiently through the processor's pipeline by taking only one clock cycle at each stage. If instructions were to take multiple clock cycles in any of the stages, considerable efficiency would be lost. If instructions have multiple clock cycles of execution, they cause the instructions that follow to stall. If the instruction streams allow a variety of multiclock operations at various stages of the pipeline, pipeline management quickly becomes very complex. This complexity often forces processors with multiclock instructions to use microcode to step through complex instructions serially, thus reducing the benefit of pipelining.

Even if multiclock instructions could be handled just with hardware control, the various interinstruction dependencies would make it extremely difficult for a compiler to schedule instructions to reduce or eliminate interinstruction delays. Recognizing these difficulties, RISC processors define their instructions to be easily broken up into simple execution stages that can be overlapped. Overlapping the instructions allows a new instruction to start with each clock cycle.

Figure 2-2 illustrates the resulting speed-up of overlapping instructions. With sequential (scalar) execution, each instruction passes through all stages of the pipeline before the next instruction starts. With pipelined execution, instructions start as soon as the previous instruction enters the next stage. In the same number of clock cycles that sequential execution processes three instructions, pipelined execu-

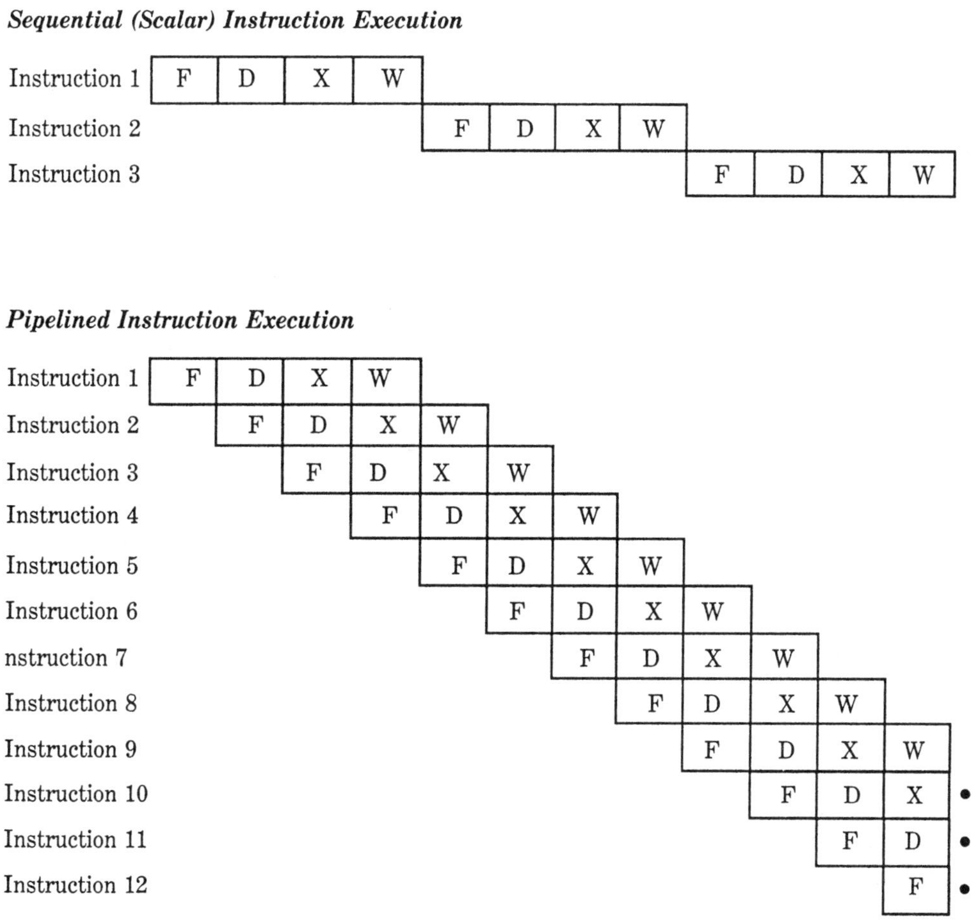

Figure 2-2. Instruction pipelining speed-up

tion processes 12 instructions, a fourfold improvement. (Nine instructions start *and* complete; six instructions start *or* complete.) When it is implemented properly, pipelining does not affect the results produced by code sequences.

Instruction Processing

In order to execute each instruction efficiently, processing is broken into four stages. Each stage performs a designated operation in one clock cycle and passes the instruction information to the next stage. The stages are the fetch, decode, execute, and write.

FETCH	DECODE	EXECUTE	WRITE

Fetch The fetch stage selects the instruction from the instruction cache and moves it into an internal storage buffer.

Decode The decode stage accesses the source registers and decodes the instruction.

Execute The execute stage performs the *ALU* (Arithmetic Logic Unit) operation. Address calculation for memory operations is done here.

Write If the instruction was not a memory operation, the results of the instruction are written to the register file during this stage. The data cache access is accessed here for memory operations.

To allow each stage of the pipeline to complete in one clock cycle, careful attention is given to the instruction set operations and the instruction format. RISC instruction sets use a fixed length instruction format where the *opcode* (instruction type field) and the register designators are in the same bit fields within each instruction's encoding. Without having to decode the length of the instruction, or take multiple clock cycles to read the instruction into the processor, the fetch stage can execute in one cycle. Because the fields within the instruction that indicates the source registers are always in the same position, the source registers' accesses can begin in the decode stage before the instruction type is known. For integer operations, the execute stage is always performed in one clock cycle. This is made possible by register-based execution where all operations are performed on data in registers. During the write stage, the result is written back into the register file.

Avoiding Pipeline Breaks

As a result of multiple instructions being operated on simultaneously, there is an increased chance of pipeline breaks. *Pipeline breaks,* also called *freeze conditions,* occur when instructions interfere with each other. To maintain performance, the pipeline must keep all of the stages active all of the time and reduce the occurrence of freeze conditions. The three general types of freeze conditions that a processor's design must combat are

- **Resource conflicts** These occur when two operations require the same resource, and one of them must freeze.
- **Data dependencies** These occur when instructions are waiting for data from a previous operation.
- **Control dependencies** These occur when branch instructions change the execution sequence.

The impact of each of these freeze conditions and how that impact can be minimized is discussed in the following sections.

Resource Conflicts

If a processor resource conflict arises frequently, then performance obviously suffers. A good example of this can be seen in the memory port. If instructions are fetched every clock cycle, the memory port is always kept busy. When a data load or store occurs, it also requires a memory reference. Since data references are approximately 30% of all instructions, a single memory port conflict would cause a substantial (greater than 10%) performance degradation. To alleviate this resource conflict, RISC processors often use a Harvard architecture where instructions and data accesses have their own memory ports.

A similar resource conflict arises for accesses to the register files. To reduce register access conflicts, register files need to have multiple ports. Usually, ports are dedicated as either read or write ports, and more than one of each is often required.

Data Dependencies

The four-stage pipeline introduces data dependencies by overlapping instructions. Consider the case where the results of one register operation are required as a source value for the next sequential operation. For example, in the sequence to take the truncated average of **r6** and **r7**:

```
add  r6, r7, r8;          r8  <-- r6 + r7
shr  1,  r8, r8;          r8  <-- (r6 + r7)/2
```

The **shr** (shift right) instruction requires the data, **r8**, that is the result of the **add** (addition) instruction. By inspecting the pipeline, we can see the difficulty that this introduces. The register **r8** is accessed during the decode stage of the **shr** instruction. Unfortunately, this occurs at the same time as the **add** instruction produces the result of **r8**.

```
add:      F        D        X(r8 produced)  W(r8 written here)
shr:               F        D(r8 needed)       X          W
```

Undetected, the pipelined execution may (or may not) use the wrong value of **r8**. This case, referred to as a *read-after-write* hazard, can be detected in hardware and avoided. Once detected, the hardware can avoid a freeze by forwarding the required data from the **add** result directly back into the ALU to be used for the **shr**. The data forwarding is done independently of the write stage where **r8** is updated in the register file.

Another possible data dependency results from a memory load instruction. Consider the sequence:

```
ld   0(r17),   r6        ; r6 <-- memory [r17]
sub  r6,  r7,  r8        ; r8 <-- r6 - r7
xor  r3,  r4,  r5        ; r5 <-- r3 xor r4
```

Because memory accesses take additional time for the data to be accessed, the data from a load instruction cannot be forwarded in time for the next instruction to use as source data. This data dependency, shown in Figure 2-3, can be avoided simply by freezing the pipeline until the data become available from memory (one or more clock cycles later). Freezing the pipeline, however, affects performance negatively by increasing the average clock cycles per instruction. RISC processors lessen the impact of data load freezes with a combination of software and hardware called a *delayed load.*

For a delayed load, the compiler "schedules" (arranges) the instructions so that the instruction following the **ld** (load data instruction) does not depend on the data being loaded. This instruction slot is called the *load-delay slot* (which the hardware allows to execute without disrupting the pipeline). The previous sequence can be reordered to avoid the freeze by placing the **xor** instruction, which does not depend on the load data, in the load-delay slot. The code sequence can be rearranged as:

```
ld   0(r17),   r6          ; r6 <-- memory [r17]
xor  r3,  r4,  r5          ; r5 <-- r3 xor r4
sub  r6,  r7,  r8          ; r8 <-- r6 - r7
```

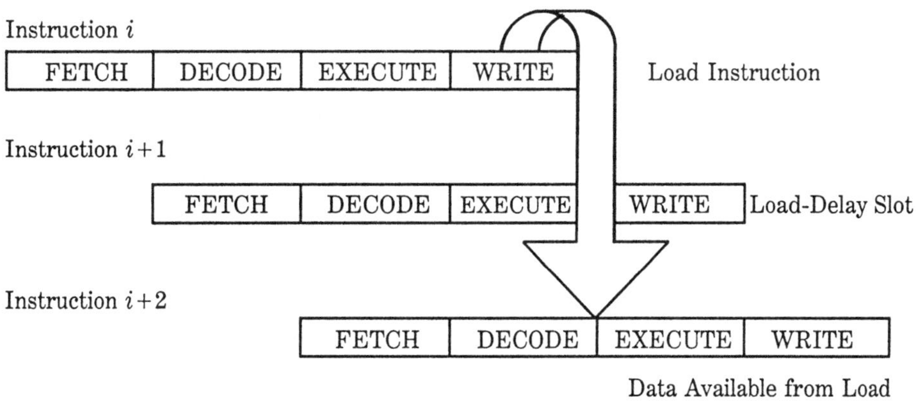

Figure 2-3. Load-delay slot

Control Dependencies

Instructions that change the sequence of program execution (*branches* and *calls*) have long been the nemesis of pipelined machines. The difficulty arises from the branch instruction calculating the new address for the instruction fetch, *after* the fetch should have happened. To prevent pipeline stalls due to branches, RISC processors use a delayed branch instruction where the instruction following the branch is executed *before* the branch takes effect. Shown in Figure 2-4, this procedure allows the processor to continue the execution of a useful instruction while it fetches the new instruction from the branch target. The instruction slot following the branch, called the *branch-delay slot*, can be filled with a useful instruction. This useful instruction can be from the block of code leading up to the branch, or the target of the branch instruction can be copied (or moved) to the delay slot and the branch target adjusted by one instruction. Both the load-delay slot and the branch-delay slot are examples of exposing the processor's operations in the instruction set to allow a compile time optimization.

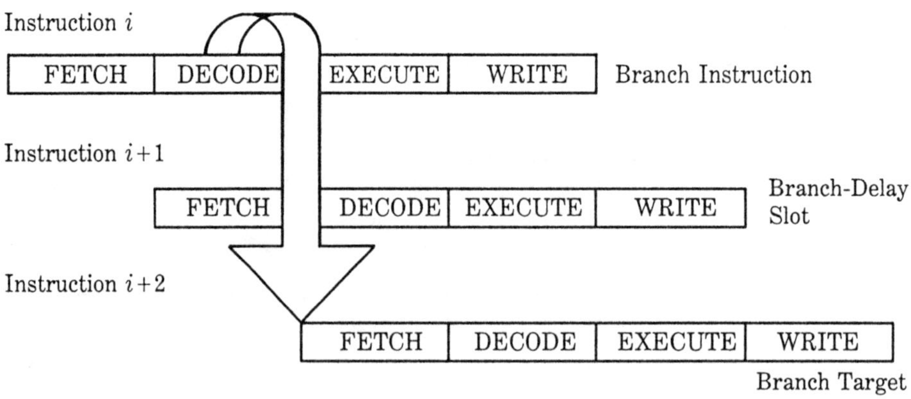

Figure 2-4. Branch-delay slot

As shown in the following sequences, the operation of delayed branches causes the execution order of code to differ from the assembly language sequence.

Assembly Language Sequence

```
          .
          .
          .
          Instruction1
          Instruction2
          Instruction3
          Delayed_branch label1
          Instruction4
          Instruction5
          .
          .
          .
label1:   Instruction6
          Instruction7
```

Execution Sequence

```
Instruction1
Instruction2
Instruction3
Instruction4
Instruction6
Instruction7
```

In addition to branch and call instructions, which always cause a change in the program sequence, there are conditional branches. The conditional branches rely on a flag or a register operation to determine if they will be taken (causing a change in program sequence) or not taken (causing no change in the program sequence). The behavior of conditional branches makes filling the delay slot with a useful instruction more difficult. To optimize instruction sequences better, many RISC processors include versions of conditional branches with and without delay slots.

Adding additional hardware to avoid resource conflicts is justified only if the conflict occurs often enough to justify the additional expense.

Added hardware must not be included at the expense of slowing down other more frequent operations. Both the load delay slot and the branch delay slot illustrate the exposure of processor operations to enhance the processor performance. This approach, combining software and hardware, is more efficient than a hardware-only solution.

Floating Point

Floating-point instruction flow follows a pipeline structure similar to the integer pipeline. It is impractical for floating-point operations, however, to complete their full execution in one cycle. Instead, floating-point operations contain multiple execution stages that can be arranged in two ways. In the first method, called *scalar* or *run-on floating point,* a floating-point instruction is issued and passes through the multiple stages of execution. This is illustrated in Figure 2-5a.

The second method is to pipeline the multiple stages of the floating-point units so that a new instruction can start before the previous operation completes. Varied degrees of pipelining can be supported from instruction overlapping to explicit pipelining. With explicit pipelining, each instruction advances the execution pipeline one stage as illustrated in Figure 2-5b.

Pipelined floating point has several advantages over scalar execution. One is that a new instruction can be issued every clock cycle without complex dependency detection hardware. Also, explicit pipelining allows software greater control over the floating-point operations, and coordinates multiple operations before the results are stored to registers.

If scalar floating-point hardware contains many independent execution units, some similar advantages of concurrent operations could be realized by overlapping execution of these independent units. Most processors, however, contain only two (multiplier and adder) or three (multiplier, adder, and divider) independent units, and only minimum speedup can be realized. Overlapping their execution requires hardware to mediate resource accesses because the add, multiply, and divide units all use the same registers for sources and results. If all of the scalar floating-point execution units are busy, a resource conflict restricts further instructions from being issued. If floating-point instructions can be issued every clock cycle, as in superscalar processing discussed later in this chapter, the case for pipelined floating point hardware is even stronger.

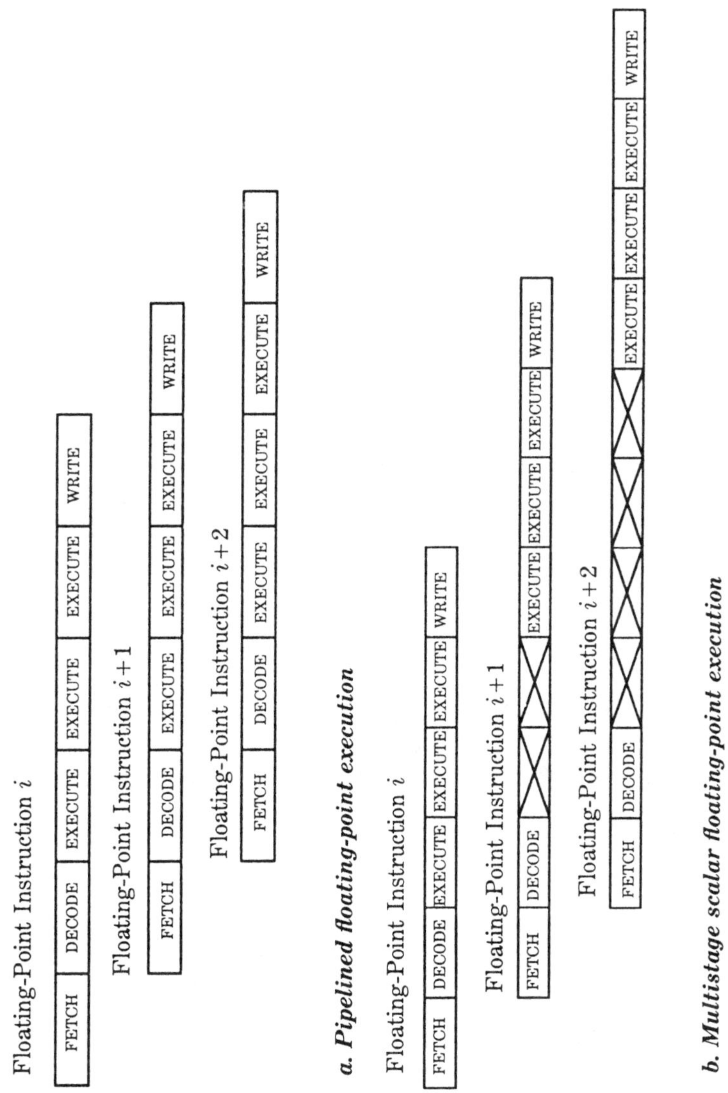

Figure 2-5. Types of floating-point execution

Registers

With a sufficient number of registers, and a compiler that makes efficient use of them, the number of memory load and store operations can be substantially reduced. For performance, register-based execution must have fast register access times and the needed data must be in the registers. Register accesses are faster than memory accesses because a register file is smaller than memory (registers contain a few dozen bytes, memory contains millions of bytes). Caching of memory locations, even when done on-chip, is not as fast as register accesses. The register access time is fast because the hardware knows where in the instruction format the registers are designated as opposed to using a computed address as with memory accesses.

Compile time software is responsible for ensuring that the data operands being used are allocated to registers when needed. *Register allocation* is performed at compile time to optimize both within a function (procedure, subroutine, and so on), and between functions. *Register coloring* is a technique to allocate registers to the most commonly used variables and parameters within a function. Registers can be reallocated to new variables when the need to reuse an older variable expires. Register operations can be arranged to allow a destination register to be specified that does not overwrite a source operand, and results can be used as sources for subsequent operations. This eliminates the need to shuffle values in registers, thus reducing the number of instructions needed for a task.

A common method for passing parameters to functions is a memory-based stack. Stack memory accesses can be avoided by passing parameters in registers. Register-based parameter passing is faster as it avoids the stack memory accesses by the calling routine before and after the function call, and by the function. Register-based parameter passing is accomplished efficiently through software conventions.

Multiple Instruction Issue

Reducing the average clock cycles per instruction to less than one requires the processor to issue multiple instructions in one clock cycle.

Processors that issue, execute, and return results from multiple instructions in each basic clock cycle, where the instructions could otherwise be executed sequentially, are known as *superscalar machines.*

Because of the added rate of execution, superscalar machines place greater demands on the processor hardware, especially the aspects intended to combat hardware resource conflicts and data dependencies. Also, considering that the number of instructions in a *basic code block* (a sequence of instructions that does not include any control transfer instructions, such as branch, call, or return) is small, only a limited number of simultaneous issues is needed to exploit the available parallelism. To achieve further dramatic improvements requires the machine design to confront the more difficult problem of exploiting parallelism beyond the basic code blocks.

When we examine the functional units and resources of a typical processor, we see that with a minimum of additional hardware, an integer and a floating-point instruction can operate in parallel. Executing floating-point instructions in parallel with integer instructions increases the performance of almost all applications that include operations performed by the floating-point unit. The floating-point unit may be limited to floating-point data operations, or include support for some other operations such as integer arithmetic using the floating-point register file.

Figure 2-6 shows the pipelined execution of a superscalar processor that executes an integer and a floating-point instruction concurrently. Consider such a processor and what is required to support this concurrency for all stages of the processor that are pipelined. First, the processor must have a wider fetch path to be able to fetch two instructions at once. Next, the processor must be able to decode two instructions at a time. Because the processor already has separate execution units for integer and floating-point operations, executing the instructions in parallel is easily supported. However, the integer and floating-point register sets must be separate, or have additional ports to support reading and writing the values simultaneously.

To match the execution units available on a machine, the compiler must be able to schedule the instruction sequences efficiently to allow the hardware maximum concurrent execution. Several trade-offs must be made in how the concurrent fetching and decoding is supported. One method, called *transparent issue,* involves the processor doing run time checking of the stream of instructions in order to decide which instructions can be issued simultaneously. This run time method requires substantial hardware for dependency and hazard checking. To achieve

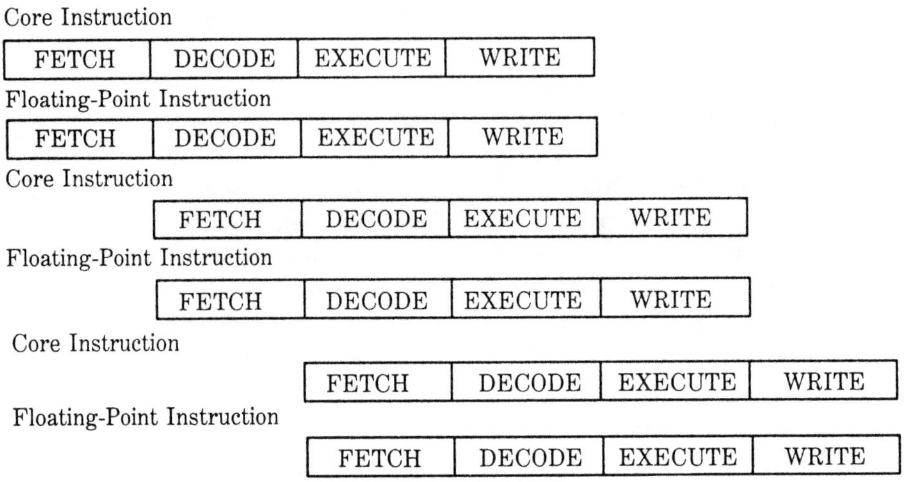

Figure 2-6. Superscalar execution

a performance benefit from the additional execution units, even with transparent issue, the compiler must arrange the code to avoid freeze conditions.

A second method for issuing multiple instructions can significantly simplify the run time hardware support needed. As with transparent issue processing, at compile time the instruction sequences are arranged into instruction groups or pairs that can be issued simultaneously. For nontransparent issue machines, the compiler goes one step further by inserting "hints" to the processor regarding the parallelism of code blocks. These hints can include meeting alignment requirements, and even indicating the explicit pairing within the instruction encoding.

By providing this software assistance, the hardware needed to issue multiple instructions can be faster and simpler, resulting in overall higher performance. If the programming model is too rigid, it may require many null operations to be inserted, which will decrease the code density. To avoid this drawback, a machine must make the transition easily from issuing multiple instructions to issuing only one instruction.

Operating System Support

Enhanced performance at a system level must consider the processor's support for the operating systems. Different operating systems have different specific needs from the processor. Where one system may need extensive virtual memory support, another may be more concerned with interrupt response time. Following the RISC design philosophy, the processor should efficiently implement the underlying primitives that are most often used, and permit more complex and infrequent features to be implemented in the software.

Operating systems have a basic need to support virtual memory, interrupts, and traps, and may require special-function instructions. The processor's overall approach must not add complexity to the hardware unless the frequency of use makes it necessary. In general, operating system execution performs the same type of operations and is able to use the same instructions already included in the processor for application software.

Virtual Memory

In order to ease the application programmer's job, and shield programs from the make-up of physical memory, a technique called *virtual memory* is used. Virtual memory allows multiple programs to coexist without dedicating a full address space to each program, even if the programs are larger than the amount of physical memory in a machine. A solution for virtual memory support must encompass relocation and protection.

The preferred basis for virtual memory support is paging with fixed-size virtual pages that are mapped to physical pages. The translation speed is greatly enhanced by including the mapping information in an on-chip *TLB* (Translation Look-a-Side Buffer) where *translation* means the table contains pairs of virtual and real addresses, much like bilingual dictionary entries; *Look-a-Side* means the table access is done in parallel with another operation so as not to require any additional pipeline stages; and *buffer* means a small fast array for temporary storage.

Instead of providing some arbitrarily large number of protection levels, two levels usually are sufficient. A trusted level for kernel code, and an untrusted level for user code provide the basics where more elaborate schemes can be implemented in kernel software if required. This is the standard protection in almost all RISC processors as well as IBM and DEC CISC processors.

Interrupt and Task Support

Some processors provide an arbitrary number of different interrupt and trap vectors where the processor hardware chooses where to execute code when an interrupt occurs, based on the cause of the interrupt. For example, a floating-point error may cause the CPU to branch to a different location than an external hardware interrupt would. However, it is simpler both for software and hardware to provide only one vector, with the software responsible for the determination and processing.

Full hardware mechanisms to save and restore the machine state are also unnecessary and usually are not included in RISC processors. In addition to being difficult to implement without excessive hardware support, these mechanisms are only marginally faster than using software sequences of already avaliable simple instructions to perform the save or restore. Even when included in a processor, such mechanisms often are not used because they do not perform exactly what is required.

This chapter has discussed many of the trade-offs in processor design for enhanced performance. These trade-offs will help you to understand and appreciate the i860 RISC processor.

CHAPTER 3
i860 MICROPROCESSOR ARCHITECTURE OVERVIEW

The i860 processor is a single chip, 64-bit microprocessor that makes use of many advanced architectural concepts. It is designed for balanced integer, floating-point, and graphics performance. Using Intel's one-micron, double-metal CMOS technology, this one-million transistor microprocessor measures 10 mm × 15 mm. The i860 processor architecture is suited for applications such as workstations, minicomputers, graphics and application accelerators, and parallel supercomputers.

Unlike a typical system where integer, floating-point, and graphics capabilities are spread across several chips, the i860 processor was designed from the ground up to integrate all of these features. The result is a fully defined architecture that, for most systems, eliminates the need for support chips such as floating-point accelerators, vector processors, DSP chips, and graphics coprocessors. A fully defined architecture sets a complete software standard, makes the software developer's job easier, and results in more powerful application software. A fully defined architecture also enables greater portability of software between different i860 processor-based systems.

Processor Pieces

The major functional units of the i860 processor and the paths between them are shown in Figure 3-1. By incorporating all of the functional units on a single chip, the chip designers were able to optimize the communication channels between the units. The processor includes:

- RISC core
- Memory management unit
- Floating-point control unit
- Pipelined floating-point adder
- Pipelined floating-point multiplier
- 3D Graphics unit
- Instruction cache
- Data cache
- Bus control unit

A 4K instruction cache and an 8K data cache on-chip allow wide internal buses to balance data and instruction bandwidth to the processing speed of multiple execution units. Data and instructions are fetched simultaneously with the on-chip Harvard architecture. The data cache has a 128-bit bus connecting it to the floating-point unit and a 32-bit bus connecting it to the RISC core. The instruction cache has a dedicated 64-bit bus to support two instructions fetched simultaneously; one for execution by the RISC core, and one for execution by the floating-point unit. Externally the processor has a single 64-bit data bus. The MMU supports 4 gigabytes of both virtual and physical memory with an on-chip TLB and an external 32-bit address bus.

The functional units can operate concurrently and are extensively pipelined. Instruction processing uses the RISC core's four-stage pipeline, while the floating-point adder and multiplier each have separate

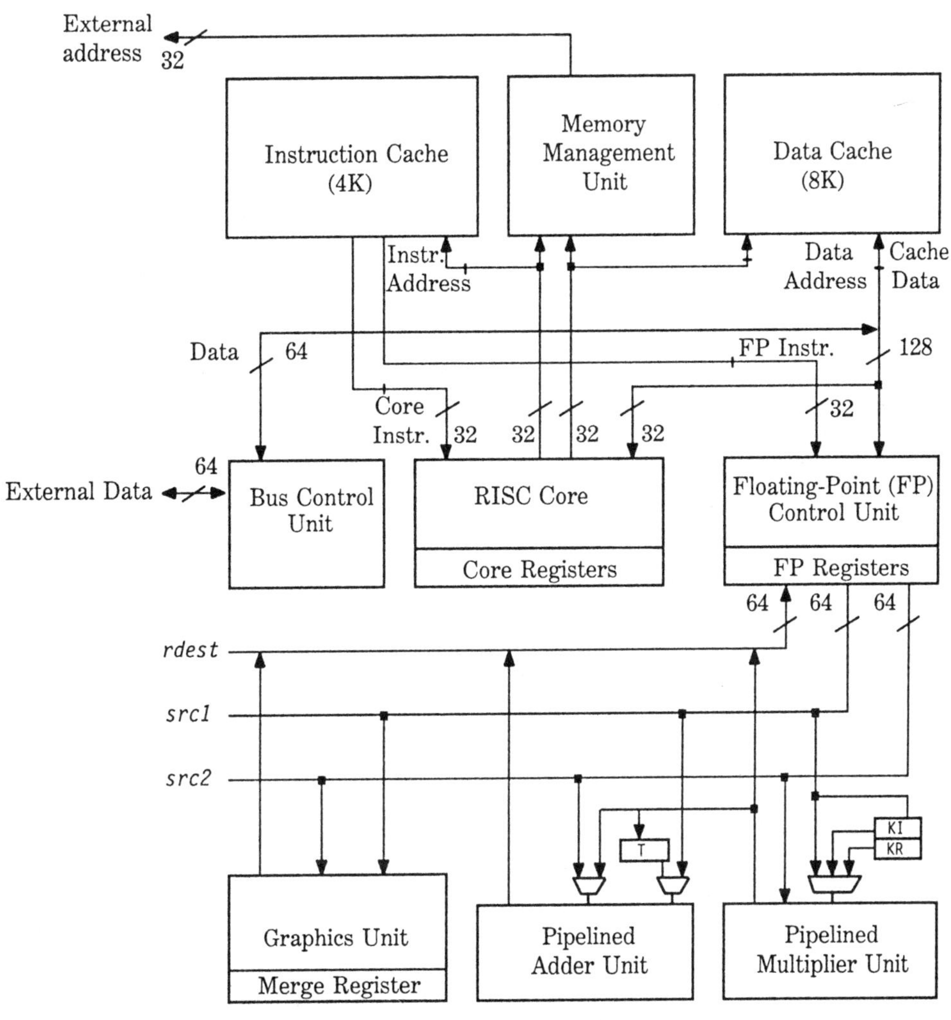

Figure 3-1. Functional units and data paths of the i860 microprocessor

three-stage execution pipelines. The bus control supports a three-stage pipeline for loading floating-point values, and matches it with an external bus that supports up to three overlapping accesses. The graphics unit has a one-stage execution pipeline.

Parallelism

The i860 processor can behave like traditional microprocessors and execute instructions as they appear in the instruction stream. This is called *single-instruction mode,* and on each clock cycle the processor can execute either a RISC core operation or a floating-point operation. This single-instruction mode allows multiclock scalar floating-point operations to be overlapped with continued core execution. Although single-instruction mode does allow both a RISC instruction and a floating-point instruction to have overlapped execution, it does not allow the simultaneous issue of instructions. Using single-instruction mode, the best possible performance a processor can achieve is one instruction per clock.

To further decrease the number of clocks per instruction, the processor must issue more than one instruction per clock. To accomplish this, the i860 processor supports a dual-instruction mode where both an integer and a floating-point instruction are issued in parallel. When performing this, the RISC core fetches two 32-bit instructions per clock using the 64-bit wide instruction cache. Of the instructions fetched, one is executed by the RISC core and one by the floating-point unit. This parallelism is supported by the separate register files for integer and floating-point operations. The RISC core keeps the data flowing to the floating-point processing units by fetching and storing information to the floating-point registers, while the floating-point execution units are operating on data.

To take advantage of dual-instruction mode, the floating-point hardware can accept new instructions each clock cycle by pipelining the floating-point execution units. Beyond the instructions to perform an add or multiply, instructions that initiate both an add and a multiply, called *dual-operation instructions,* are provided. Combining the dual-instruction mode with the dual-operation floating-point instructions permits the programmer to exploit the i860 processor's peak execution rate of one integer and two floating-point operations per clock cycle.

Being able to control the hardware to this extent vastly increases the programmer's ability to get maximum performance from the i860 processor. With this parallelism, the architecture can support traditional vector processing where the inner loops of the software vector routines operate up to the peak floating-point hardware rate of 80 MFlops (Millions of FLoating-Point Operations Per Second) at 40 Mhz. Consistent with a RISC philosophy, the i860 processor achieves the performance of hardware vector instructions without the complex control logic of hardware vector machines. The accessible software pipelining is more general than found on traditional vector machines, and can also be used for many algorithms that cannot be vectorized.

Register Model and Data Support

The i860 microprocessor has separate register files for the integer and floating-point units. Figure 3-2 shows these registers and the remaining user-visible registers, six control registers and the four special-purpose registers.

The RISC core contains the integer register file of thirty-two 32-bit registers, designated `r0` through `r31`, that can contain addresses or data. The floating-point control unit contains a separate set of thirty-two 32-bit floating-point registers designated `f0` through `f31`, which can be addressed individually as thirty-two 32-bit registers, sixteen 64-bit registers, or eight 128-bit registers.

The i860 microprocessor allows integer and floating-point data types, as well as pixel data formats for graphics operations. Integer data are supported as signed or unsigned, and floating-point data can be either single- or double-precision. The floating-point data follow the ANSI /IEEE standard formats, which are described in Chapter 4, "Machine Organization."

The RISC Core

The RISC core instructions are shown in Figure 3-3. In order to process instructions efficiently, the RISC core breaks down each instruction's execution into four stages. As discussed in Chapter 2, each stage

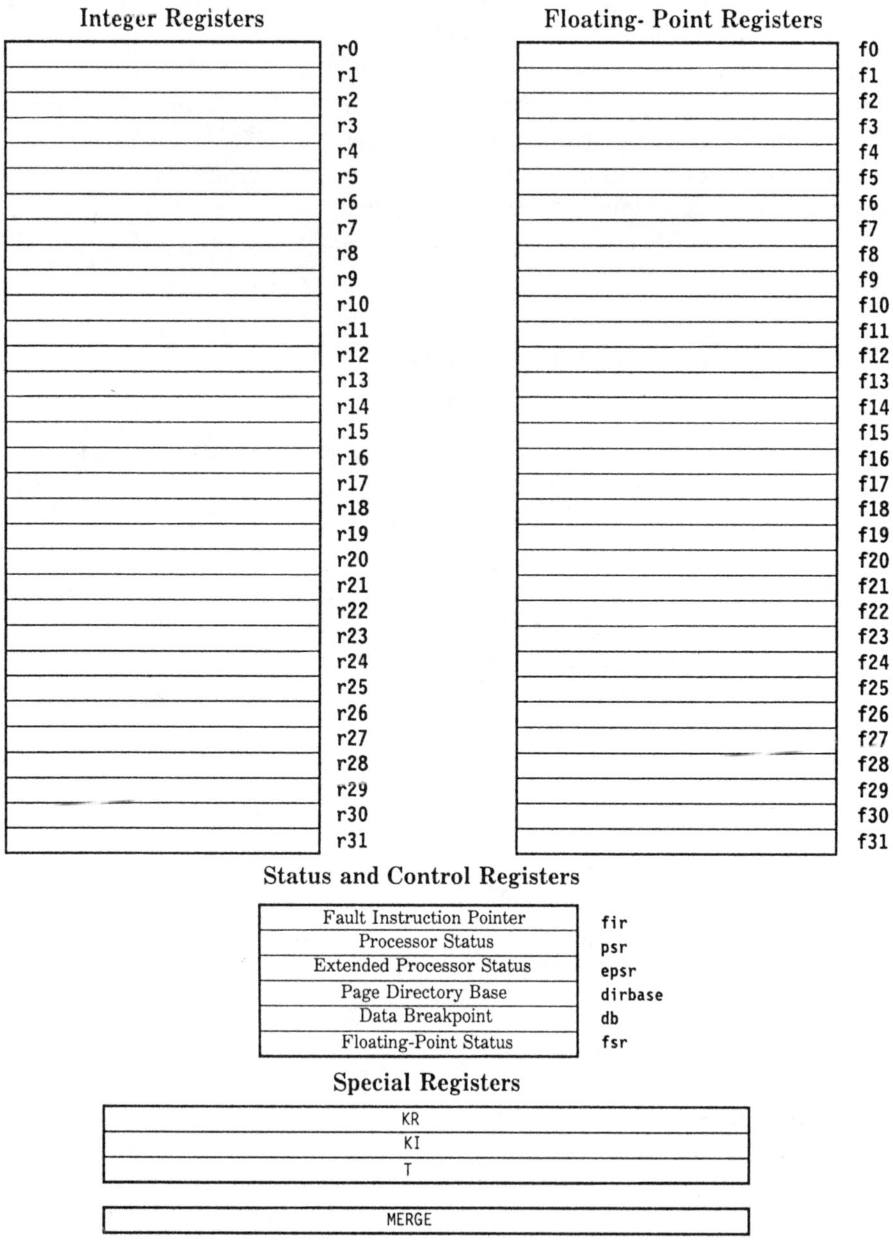

Figure 3-2. Processor's register set

Core Unit	
Mnemonic	Description
Load and Store Instructions	
`ld.x`	Load integer
`st.x`	Store integer
`fld.y`	Floating-Point load
`pfld.z`	Pipelined Floating-Point load
`fst.y`	Floating-Point store
`pst.d`	Pixel store
Register to Register Move	
`ixfr`	Transfer integer to F-P register
Integer Arithmetic Instructions	
`addu`	Add unsigned
`adds`	Add signed
`subu`	Subtract unsigned
`subs`	Subtract signed
Shift Instructions	
`shl`	Shift left
`shr`	Shift right
`shra`	Shift right arithmetic
`shrd`	Shift right double
Logical Instructions	
`and`	Logical AND
`andh`	Logical AND high
`andnot`	Logical AND NOT
`andnoth`	Logical AND NOT high
`or`	Logical OR
`orh`	Logical OR high
`xor`	Logical exclusive OR
`xorh`	Logical exclusive OR high

Figure 3-3.* *RISC core instruction set

Control-Transfer Instructions	
`trap`	Software trap
`intovr`	Software trap on integer overflow
`br`	Branch direct
`bri`	Branch indirect
`bc`	Branch on CC
`bc.t`	Branch on CC taken
`bnc`	Branch on not CC
`bnc.t`	Branch on not CC taken
`bte`	Branch if equal
`btne`	Branch if not equal
`bla`	Branch on LCC and add
`call`	Subroutine call
`calli`	Indirect subroutine call
System Control Instructions	
`flush`	Cache flush
`ld.c`	Load from control register
`st.c`	Store to control register
`lock`	Begin interlocked sequence
`unlock`	End interlocked sequence

Figure 3-3. RISC core instruction set **(continued)**

performs a designated operation in one clock cycle and passes the instruction to the next stage. As you will recall, the stages are fetch, decode, execute, and write.

FETCH	DECODE	EXECUTE	WRITE

Fetch The fetch stage selects the instruction from the instruction cache and moves it to an internal storage buffer.

Decode The decode stage accesses the source registers and decodes the instruction.

Execute The ALU operation is performed in the execute stage. Address calculation for memory operations is done here.

Write The results of instruction execution are written to the register file during the write stage. If the instruction was a memory operation, the data cache access is performed in the write stage.

To allow each stage of the pipeline to complete in one clock cycle, careful attention is given to the instruction format. Figure 3-4 shows the general format for all of the register-based RISC core instructions. All instructions are 32-bits long with designated fields for the opcodes and registers. The *opcode field* is six bits and includes the instruction identifier and the immediate I-bit used for interpreting `src1`. The register fields `src2`, `dest`, and `src1` are each five bits and can designate any of the 32 integer registers. If the I-bit is set, `src1` is interpreted as a 16-bit immediate value using the five bits from the `src1` field and the lowest 11 bits. For load/store and control instructions the specific formats will vary, but will maintain the simple structure.

This simple instruction format has several advantages over a complex instruction set. For simple instruction sets, the fetch stage can execute in one cycle, without having to decode the length of the instruction, or take multiple cycles to read the instruction into the processor. In the decode stage, the source register accesses can begin before the instruction type is known. This is possible because the field within the instruction format indicating the source registers used is always in the same place. By allowing only instructions that can be executed in one stage, the execute stage is always performed in one cycle. During the write stage, the result is written back into the register file. Each of these advantages combined with the four-stage pipeline allows instructions to be overlapped and allows a new instruction to start with each clock cycle.

Load/Store Architecture

The only memory operations permitted on the i860 processor are loads and stores. All other operations are performed directly on the values in

31	25	20	15	10	0
opcode/I	`src2`	`dest`	`src1`	immediate, offset, or null	

Figure 3-4. General instruction format for core operations on registers

the registers. The load/store architecture simplifies the design of the processor and allows the programmer to hide the delay caused by memory accesses.

Loads from memory always have at least a one clock delay, even if the data is in the onboard cache. The delay occurs because the load pipeline, unlike the alu or shift pipeline, has 5 stages. Figure 3-5 shows an instruction sequence for a load instruction and two subsequent instructions. The data from the load operation is available at the end of

```
ld.l    0(r17), r5     ; r5 <-- mem.l[r17]
addu    r5, r6, r7     ; r7 <-- r5 + r6
or      r8, r9, r10    ; r10 <-- r8 OR r9
```

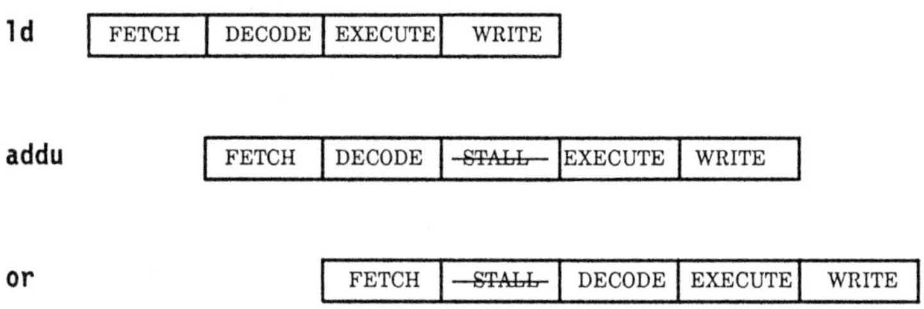

a. Load-delay-slot stall

```
ld.l    0(r17), r5     ; r5 <-- mem.l[r17]
or      r8, r9, r10    ; r10 <-- r8 OR r9
addu    r5, r6, r7     ; r7 <-- r5 + r6
```

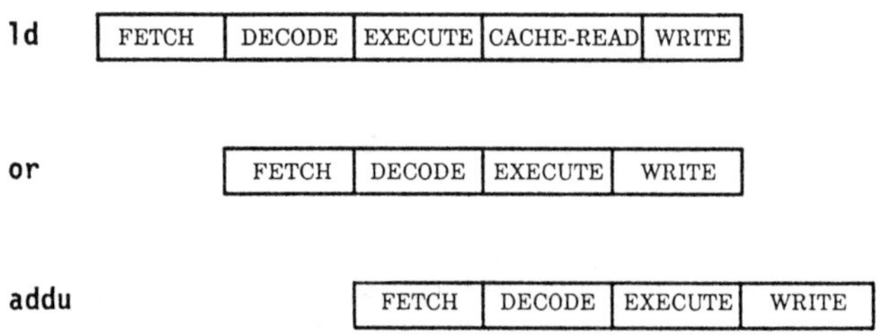

b. No load-delay-slot stall

Figure 3-5. Filling the load-delay slot to avoid stalls

the load instruction's cache-read stage. This is too late for the instruction immediately following the load to use the data as a source operand. The instruction slot following a load is the load-delay slot. If the instruction in the load-delay slot attempts to use the data, the processor will stall for one clock cycle (assuming a cache hit) as shown in Figure 3-5a.

The i860 processor gives the programmer two options for the load-delay slot. The most beneficial option is to rearrange the sequence of instructions so that a useful instruction, which does not depend on the load data, is placed in the load-delay slot. This case is shown in Figure 3-5b where the load instruction takes only one clock cycle and causes no disruption to the pipeline. The second option, if no suitable instruction for the load-delay slot can be found, is simply to order the instructions sequentially. When the register operation attempts to read the data from the register being loaded, the processor will freeze for one clock cycle and then proceed as shown in Figure 3-5a. The i860 processor keeps track of which register has a load pending by way of a scoreboard. Although most loads will be cache hits, the scoreboard technique has further utility in the case of a cache miss. Instructions can proceed following a cache miss load until an instruction specifies the pending register. Programs can benefit by placing the load instructions as early as possible before instructions that operate on the data.

The store instructions write data from a register to memory. For the i860 processor, this can result in a write to the cache or a write to main memory. In both cases, the processor's pipeline does not have to wait for the write to complete. For cache hits, the new data is updated in the cache. For cache misses, the data is written to the on-chip write buffers, and the bus control unit carries out the memory write.

Two types of floating-point loads are available, **fld** (floating-point load) and **pfld** (pipelined floating-point load). The **fld** instruction loads the floating-point register from the cache, or loads the data from memory and fills the cache line if the data is not in the cache. To better match the data rate needed for execution, up to four floating-point registers can be loaded from the 128-bit wide data cache in one clock cycle. For accessing data structures too large to fit into the on-chip cache, the **pfld** instruction transfers data directly from memory to the floating-point registers without disturbing the cache. The **pfld** instruction uses a three-stage pipeline, discussed in Chapter 5, to hide the memory latency for successive off-chip accesses.

Core Integer Operations

Once data have been loaded into the integer registers, any of the integer operations can be performed. These register operations are performed in one clock cycle, and the result can be used as a source in the instruction that immediately follows. The i860 processor includes arithmetic, shift, and logical instructions and uses the form **operation** *isrc1, isrc2, idest.*

The three operand instructions allow the operation to specify *two* source registers (or a source register *src2* and an immediate for *src1*) and to store the result to a third register without destroying either of the source values. This saves the program from copying a source value to a temporary register before the operation.

The i860 processor's arithmetic operations perform addition and subtraction for both signed and unsigned 32-bit values. The logical instructions include the **and**, **andnot**, **or**, and **xor** operations and can be used to implement bit operations. The third class of integer operations is the shift instructions. The i860 processor can barrel-shift up to 31 bit positions in one clock cycle and has a double-shift instruction that concatenates two registers and shifts them into a third register.

Branches

Several types of branch instructions are included in the core instruction set. The unconditional branch and call instructions have a delay slot where the processor always executes the next sequential instruction before the branch takes effect, while the conditional branch instructions have variations with and without a delay slot. The conditional branches **bc** and **bnc** branch if the *CC* (Condition Code) bit is set or cleared, and include the delayed versions **bc.t** and **bnc.t**. Having both delayed and nondelayed variations of branch instructions allows the compiler to optimize the code for when a branch is likely to be taken. The nondelayed compare and branch instructions **bte** (branch if equal) and **btne** (branch if not equal) compare two source operands and branch if they are equal or not equal.

The final branch instruction, **bla** (branch-on-LCC and add), is a single-cycle loop instruction that performs three operations relying on its own *LCC* (Loop-Condition-Code). The instruction performs a Branch-on-LCC, an add operation, and than sets the LCC bit based on a comparison of the values being added. The mnemonic is intentionally strange (taken from blah), and more obviously would be called a loop instruction.

Floating Point

The floating-point unit includes its own set of floating-point registers, a pipelined adder unit, and a pipelined multiplier unit. Floating-point unit instructions support both single-precision and double-precision floating-point data types and follow the ANSI/IEEE 754 standard. The i860 processor's floating-point hardware implements all four modes of IEEE rounding. The special values *infinity, NaN,* and *denormal* generate a trap when encountered, and the trap-handler software must produce an IEEE-standard result. The double-precision floating-point data occupy two adjacent floating-point registers with bits 31. . .0 stored in an even-numbered register and bits 63. . .32 stored in the adjacent higher odd-numbered register.

The floating-point adder and multiplier perform the instructions listed in Figure 3-6. To save silicon area, a floating-point divide unit was not included. Instead, floating-point divide and square root are performed in software using Newton-Rhapson algorithms. (See "Reciprocals and Series Expansion" in Chapter 6, "Floating-Point Operations.") The processor does provide an 8-bit seed (or "guess"), to prime the software algorithm. Full IEEE rounding can be implemented by using the **fmlow** instruction that returns the low-order bits of a floating-point multiply. Programs can take the best advantage of the hardware by performing the calculations only to the required precision. For example,

Floating-Point Unit	
Mnemonic	Description
Floating-Point Multiplier Instructions	
fmul.p	F-P multiply
pfmul.p	Pipelined F-P multiply
pfmul3.dd	3-Stage pipelined F-P multiply
fmlow.dd	F-P multiply low
frcp.p	F-P reciprocal
frsqr.p	Floating-Point reciprocal square root
Floating-Point Adder Instructions	
fadd.p	F-P add
pfadd.p	Pipelined F-P add
fsub.p	F-P subtract
pfsub.p	Pipelined F-P subtract
pfgt.p	Pipelined F-P greater than compare
pfeq.p	Pipelined F-P to equal compare
pfle.p	Pipelined F-P less than or equal
famov.r	F-P adder move
pfamov.r	Pipelined F-P adder move
fix.p	F-P to integer conversion
pfix.p	Pipelined F-P to integer conversion
ftrunc.p	F-P to integer truncation
pftrunc.p	Pipelined F-P to integer truncation
Dual-Operation Instructions	
pfam.p	Pipelined F-P add and multiply
pfsm.p	Pipelined F-P subtract and multiply
pfmam.p	Pipelined F-P multiply with add
pfmsm.p	Pipelined F-P multiply with subtract

Figure 3-6. Floating-point instruction set

16-bit reciprocals used for graphics calculations will not require the full IEEE rounding and can be performed very quickly.

The Scalar Model Versus the Pipelined Model

The pipelined floating-point adder and multiplier support two computation models; scalar and pipelined. Scalar mode allows interdependent sequences of operations to complete quickly (scalar meaning non-repeated calculations), with each operation typically depending on the result of the previous operation. Scalar floating-point add and subtract operations take three clock cycles to complete, while scalar floating-point multiply takes three clock cycles for single-precision and four clock cycles for double-precision. Before starting, scalar instructions wait for any previous scalar instructions currently in progress to complete. Once initiated, scalar instructions pass through all stages of their execution.

Pipelined mode instructions perform the same operations as scalar mode instructions do, but they operate differently. Pipelined operations are useful for performing repetitive operations that do not depend on the result of the previous operation. Vector processing is one example where pipelined instructions can be used effectively. Pipelined instructions advance the execution pipeline one stage, and the pipeline does not advance further until the next appropriate instruction is encountered. Instructions other than the ones that affect the pipeline being used may proceed without affecting the pipeline's intermediate states. Also, the destination specified as part of a pipelined floating-point instruction is the result of an operation that was started earlier. Although programming in pipelined mode is more difficult, there is a considerable performance advantage for doing so. With pipelined instructions, the adder can produce a result every clock cycle, and the multiplier can produce a result every clock cycle for single-precision, and every other clock cycle for double-precision.

Figure 3-7 shows both the scalar and pipelined versions of a code sequence to add five pairs of numbers. The scalar example in Figure 3-7a is straightforward. Each **fadd** (floating-point **add**) takes three clock cycles to execute; then the next **fadd** may begin. The sequence of five **fadd**s takes 15 clock cycles to execute. Because the floating-point values are single-precision they can each be stored in one floating-point register.

The use of pipelined instructions is illustrated with the adder pipeline example in Figure 3-7b. Here, the adder begins by adding the numbers in **f2** and **f7**. Because this is the first instruction of the series, the pipeline is not yet full and the result coming out of the adder is not needed. Therefore, the result is sent to **f0**, which is always zero and is used as a null destination. On each successive clock cycle, a **pfadd** instruction is issued to advance the pipeline. When the sum of the first **pfadd** becomes available at the result stage, it is stored to the destination specified by the fourth instruction.

```
fadd.ss     f2, f7, f12      ; f12 <-- f2 + f7
fadd.ss     f3, f8, f13      ; f13 <-- f3 + f8
fadd.ss     f4, f9, f14      ; f14 <-- f4 + f9
fadd.ss     f5, f10, f15     ; f15 <-- f5 + f10
fadd.ss     f6, f11, f16     ; f16 <-- f6 + f11
```

a. Scalar floating-point addition

	x		y		z
f2	2.0	**f7**	7.0	**f12**	x
f3	3.0	**f8**	8.0	**f13**	x
f4	4.0	**f9**	9.0	**f14**	x
f5	5.0	**f10**	10.0	**f15**	x
f6	6.0	**f11**	11.0	**f16**	x

Instruction Sequence		**add** Pipeline			Destination
pfadd.ss	**f2,f7,f0**	2+7	?	?	None
pfadd.ss	**f3,f8, f0**	3+8	2+7	?	None
pfadd.ss	**f4,f9, f0**	4+9	3+8	2+7	None
pfadd.ss	**f5,f10,f12**	5+10	4+9	3+8	**f12** ← 9.
pfadd.ss	**f6,f11,f13**	6+11	5+10	4+9	**f13** ← 11.
pfadd.ss	**f0,f0,f14**	0	6+11	5+10	**f14** ← 13.

b. Pipelined floating-point addition

Figure 3-7. Floating-point add *example*

In this example, three instructions after the **f2** plus **f7** starts, the result is stored to **f12** by the instruction that is initiating the addition of **f5** and **f10**. Once all of the desired **pfadd** instructions have started, three extra **pfadd**s may be necessary at the end of a sequence in order to "flush" the desired results through the pipeline. When adding a long series of numbers, the overhead of filling and flushing the pipeline is negligible. When performing only one or two adds, scalar mode can be used to minimize pipeline overhead.

Dual-Operation Floating Point

Pipelined mode is also used for "dual-operation instructions" where the add and multiply pipelines are both advanced in parallel. Figure 3-8 shows the adder unit, the multiplier unit, the special registers, and the dual-operation data paths. Six operands are required for dual-operation instructions, two inputs and one output for both the adder and multiplier: Three are provided from the register file and the remaining three from the special registers and bypasses. The instruction encodings specify the source and destination paths for the units.

For single-precision, both the adder and multiplier units can produce one result per clock cycle for a peak rate of 80 MFlops at 40 Mhz. For

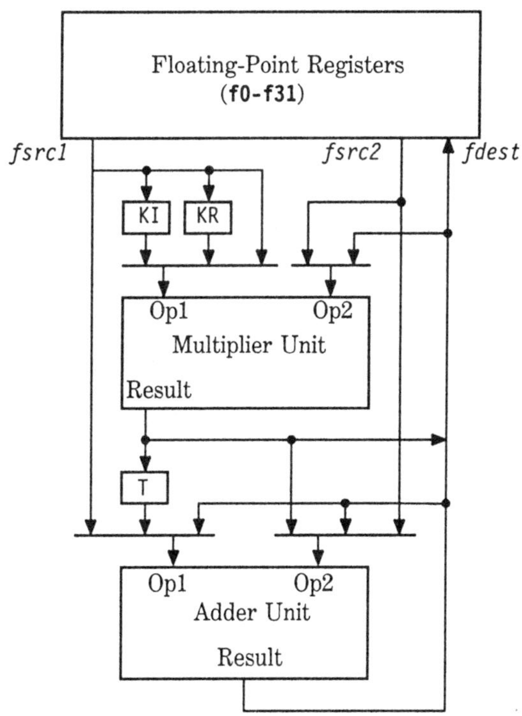

Figure 3-8. Floating-point unit and dual-operation data paths

double-precision, the multiplier can produce a result every other clock cycle, and the adder produces a result every clock cycle, for a peak rate of 60 MFlops. However, if your algorithm has an even distribution of multiplications and additions, the double-precision peak number is 40 MFlops. Reducing the double-precision multiply rate saved significant silicon area and is consistent with the external bus data bandwidth available for double-precision operations.

The following example illustrates the speed-up using pipelined dual-operation instructions. A series of 100 numbers is to be multiplied by a constant, added to a second series of 100 numbers, then stored;

```
      DO 10, I=1, 100
10    X[i]= A[i] * C + B[i]
```

If the addition and multiplication are executed in scalar mode, a result is produced every six clock cycles. For example:

```
fmul C, A[i], temp              ; temp  <--  C * A
fadd temp, B[i], X[i]           ;  X   <--  temp + B
```

First the multiplication is performed and the result stored in a temporary register. Then, the addition is performed with the temporary register, and the result stored. Each multiply and add takes three clock cycles and the six-clock-cycle sequence is repeated 100 times for a total of 600 clock cycles of floating-point execution time.

With pipelined dual-operation instructions, the add and multiply are performed in parallel and a new result is produced each clock cycle. For example:

```
r2p1 B[i-3], A[i], X[i-6]       ;  X  <--  A * KR + B
```

This illustrates the **pfam** (pipelined floating-point add and multiply) dual-operation instruction variation specified as

r2p1 *fsrc1*, *fsrc2*, *fdest*

The instruction specifies that the multiplication is initiated with the "Konstant" register KR and *fsrc2* as the operands, that the addition is initiated with the result from the multiply and *fsrc1* as the operands, and that the result from an earlier add is stored to *fdest*. Because the three stages of the add and multiply pipelines are chained in series, the result comes from the operation that began six clock cycles previously. This is shown graphically in Figure 3-9. By overlapping the multiply and add, the loop of 600 clock cycles in scalar mode is reduced to 100 clock cycles of floating-point execution time. How to perform floating-point computations is explained in much greater detail in Chapter 6, "Floating-Point Operations," with additional examples given in Chapter 8, "Programming for Parallelism."

Dual-Instruction Mode

The i860 microprocessor can provide its fast floating-point hardware with the necessary data bandwidth to achieve peak performance for the inner loops of common routines. The dual-instruction mode allows the RISC core to perform loads and stores to the floating-point registers at the same time as floating-point operations. Figure 3-10 shows the sequence for entering and exiting dual-instruction mode. While in dual-

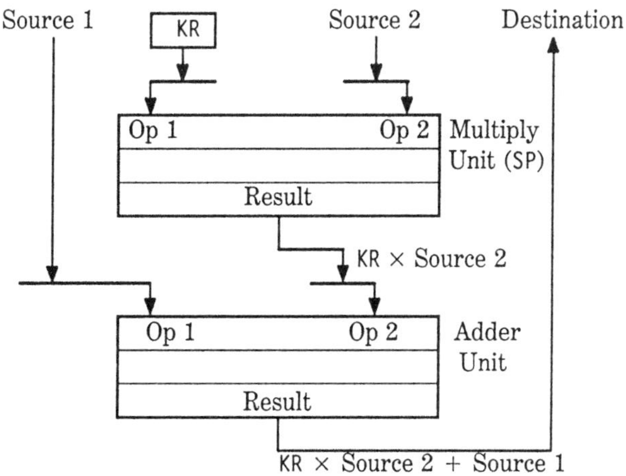

Figure 3-9. Dual-operation example

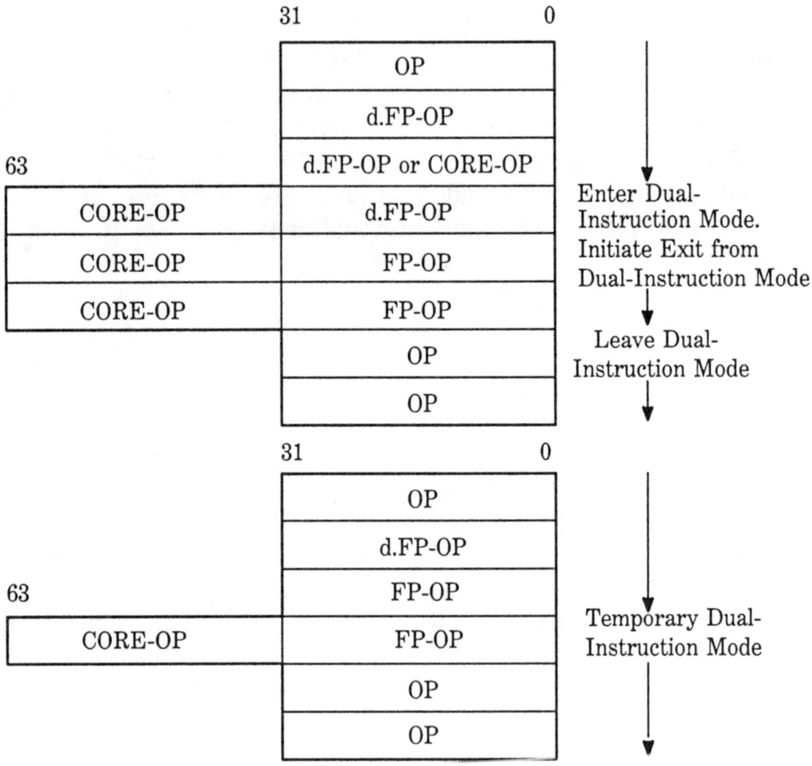

Figure 3-10. Dual-instruction mode transitions

instruction mode, each clock cycle of execution consists of instruction pairs of a floating-point and an integer instruction. The floating-point instruction may be one of the dual-operation instructions, for a total of three operations per clock cycle.

Additional ports are required in the register file to support floating-point register accesses for both floating-point operations and for memory loads and stores. The five-port register file prevents contention for ports of the floating-point registers. There are two read ports and one write port to support the floating-point operations, and another read and write port for the RISC core to use in loading and storing data.

Graphics

Displaying pictures by computer involves several steps. In general, pictures are approximated by a database of points. Each point can be represented by pairs or triplets of numbers depending on whether the data is two- or three-dimensional. Points can be arranged to represent vertices of edges or polygons. Displaying a picture involves determining a specific view of the database. The view to be displayed is formed by rotating, translating, scaling, and performing various projections of the data. The floating-point hardware of the i860 processor efficiently performs the 4 × 4 transforms used as the basic calculation for orienting the points before display. Any high-level lighting model calculations can also be performed by floating-point hardware.

Once these steps are performed, displaying the picture requires the use of integer operations for shading and hidden surface removal. The graphics unit of the i860 processor speeds these final rendering operations by utilizing the floating-point registers and data paths in parallel with the core. Graphics instructions take advantage of the 64-bit data paths and can operate on multiple pixels simultaneously, resulting in a speed-up ten times greater than using the RISC core to perform shading. Instructions support 8-, 16-, and 24- or 32-bit pixels, operating respectively on 8, 4, or 2 pixels simultaneously.

Consider a solid cube where each side is a polygon and the vertices of each polygon make up the cube's database. During the transform step, new positions for the vertices of the cube are calculated. As shown in Figure 3-11a, a simple wire frame display of the cube will show all of the lines, even the ones that should be hidden from view. For a more sophisticated display of the object, where polygons overlap, only the polygon closest to the viewer should be displayed. By removing the

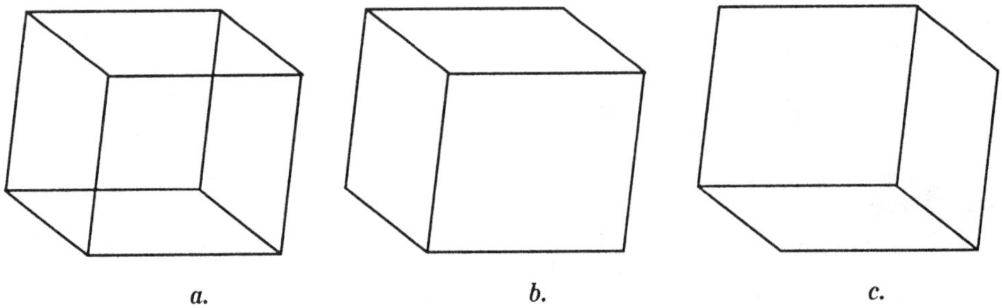

Figure 3-11. a. Wire frame display
b. and c. Display with hidden lines removed

hidden edges, as in Figures 3-11b and c, the intended view of the cube is clear.

In graphics calculations, the Z value represents the distance of the object from the viewer. For overlapping points, the Z values of different polygons can be checked and only the pixel data of the polygon closest to the viewer displayed. Although the depth of each polygon's vertices is known, to overlay polygons not on a vertex, the depth must be interpolated from the bordering vertices. This step is called *Z interpolation.* With Z interpolation, the depth of all the points of a polygon can be determined.

The i860 processor's graphics unit includes both Z interpolation instructions, and a Z compare instruction for determining which polygon's point is closer to the viewer and should be displayed.

To show shaded images, the surface of the polygons must be displayed. From the database, the locations and color intensities of the vertices of the polygons are known, but points between these vertices must be calculated. Instead of shading the polygon one constant color, the color can be changed gradually along its surface. The i860 processor supports intensity interpolation to allow smooth linear changes in pixel intensity and color between vertices. This provides a smoother appearance than flat (constant) shading of the polygons. The more data bits per pixel, the smoother the interpolation can be. One technique, called *Gouraud shading,* interpolates intensities along the scan lines. Figure 3-12 illustrates pixel interpolation for Gouraud shading of a triangle. The intensity level across the scan line is interpolated from 30 to 27.

The RISC core operates in parallel with the graphics unit to execute a pixel store instruction. The pixel store instruction conditionally updates the display with the pixel values for the polygon closest to the viewer. The **pst** instruction updates 64-bits worth of pixel data in a single instruction.

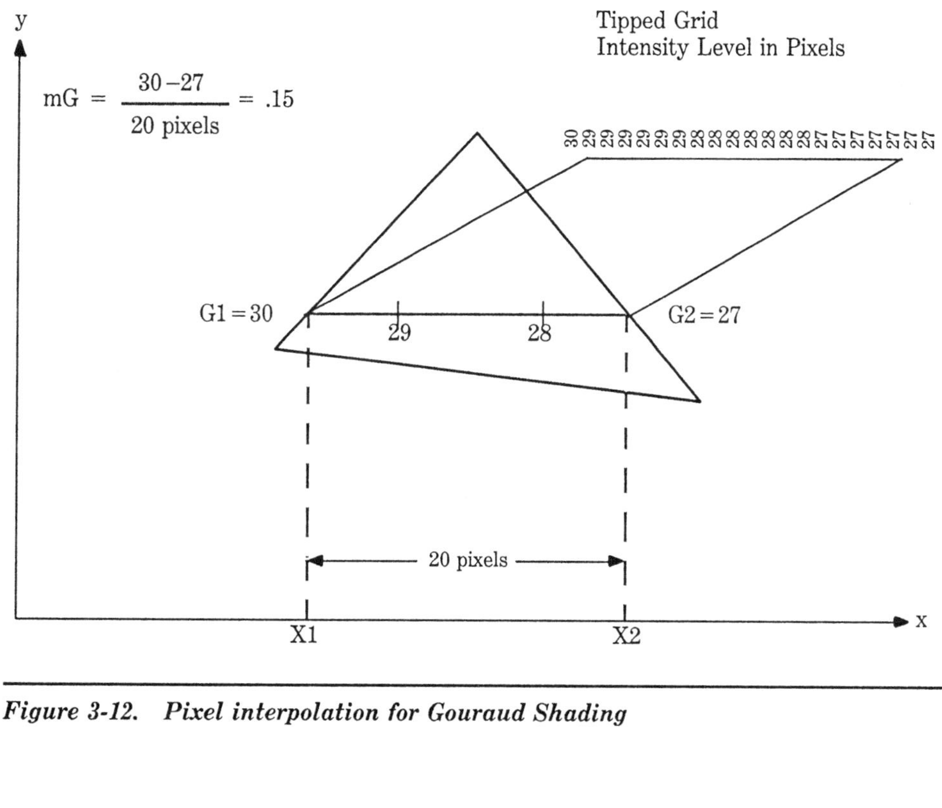

Figure 3-12. Pixel interpolation for Gouraud Shading

Memory Management

The i860 microprocessor's on-chip MMU implements the basic features needed for paged virtual memory management. The memory management technique is intentionally the same as the 386 and i486 microprocessors' paging. This allows the two processors to exist easily in a common operating environment. It is also useful for reusing paging and virtual memory software written in a high level language such as C.

While paging is enabled, the processor translates a virtual address to a physical address as shown in Figure 3-13. Like the IBM 370, VAX, and other mainframe computers, the i860 processor stores the translation information in page tables that are arranged in a two-level hierarchy as shown in Figure 3-14. The *page directory* is pointed to by the DTB *(Directory Table Base)*, which is part of the **dirbase** register. This directory is one-page long (4K) and contains address entries for 1024 *page tables*. The page tables are also one-page long and describe 1024 pages.

The paging tables are created and stored in memory by the operating system. If the processor had to access these page tables in memory each time that a memory load or store was executed, performance would suffer greatly. To save the overhead of the page table look-ups, the processor automatically caches mapping information for the 64 recently

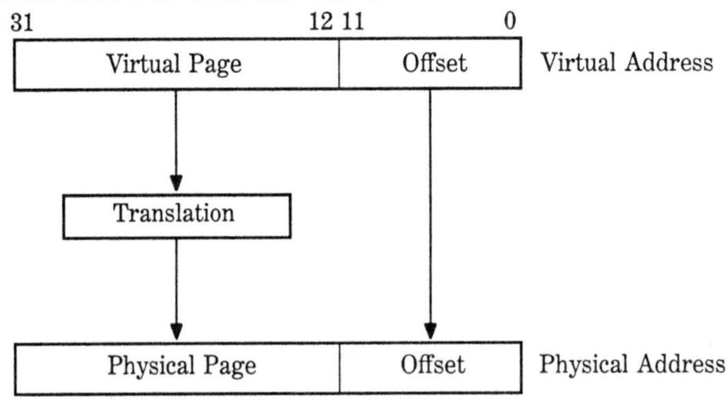

Figure 3-13. Virtual-to-physical address translation

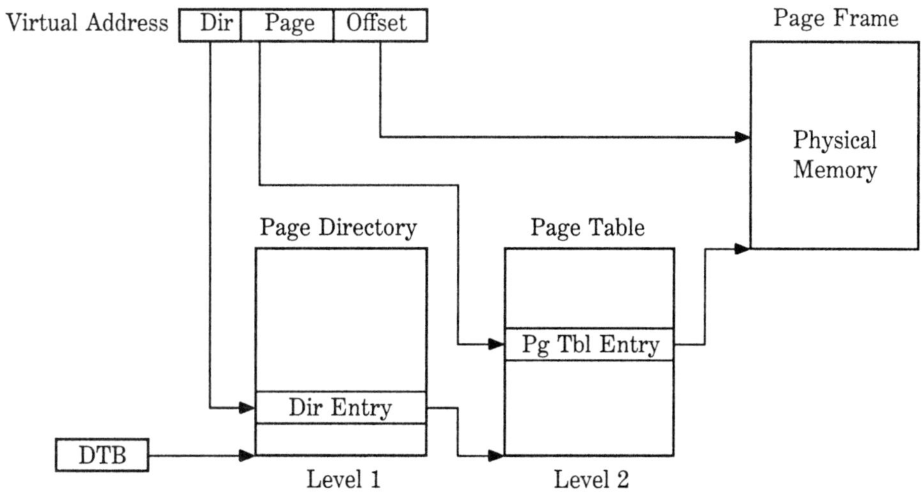

Figure 3-14. Two-level paging scheme

used pages in an on-chip, four-way set associative TLB (Translation Look-a-Side Buffer). The processor's bus hardware automatically copies page table entries from memory into the TLB when required.

Caches

The i860 processor's CPU has a 4K instruction cache and an 8K data cache. Each cache has its own address and data paths to support concurrent accesses. The data cache supports up to 128-bit accesses on each clock cycle and the instruction cache supports up to 64-bit accesses. The aggregate bandwidth at 40 Mhz is 960 MB per second. Both caches are two-way set-associative and have a 32-byte line size as shown in Figure 3-15.

The data cache uses write-back caching. Write-back caching allows data that has been read into the processor's cache to be written without immediately updating the contents of main memory. If the only modified copy of the data is in the cache, that cache entry is said to be "dirty."

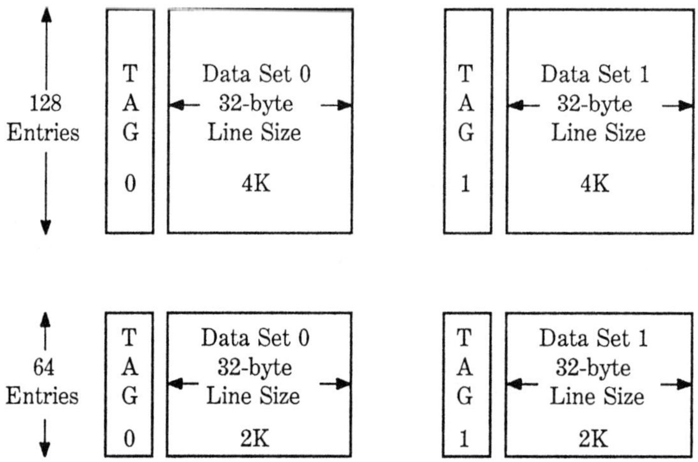

Figure 3-15. Data (top) and instruction (bottom) cache organizations

The caching strategy is called write-back because memory will be updated when a new read displaces an entry, and the dirty data is written back to memory. Writes that occur to locations not in the cache (write misses) are buffered in on-chip write buffers, then written to memory. These write misses do not allocate cache entries. Program execution is significantly enhanced with the high-speed caches. For example, the Fast Fourier Transform program in Chapter 10, "Application Example: The Fast Fourier Transform," runs six times slower if the caches are disabled.

The instruction and data caches map their contents with respect to the processor's virtual address. This is done in the design to avoid a *critical path* in the cache access time ("critical path" is the term used by designers for logic or circuitry that is the limiting factor in the cycle time of the processor). The virtual address mapping avoids having to perform a TLB translation before the cache access. As discussed in Chapter 9, "Operating System Support," operating systems for i860 processor-based systems must comprehend this cache-addressing behavior for proper operation.

Cache Model

The cache can be used effectively for both traditional applications and for vector computations. A convenient software model to manage the data cache for vector computations on large matrices is to treat the data cache as a *vector register set.* Vectors that are being reused are kept in the onboard cache by referencing with the normal floating-point load instruction (**fld**). The vectorization process analyzes nested loops to determine which vectors are reusable in the second loop level. *Vector memory* references use the pipelined **pfld** instruction to stream the data from memory directly into the registers and not disturb the cache. Using the data cache as a vector register set is more flexible than using a small fixed length vector register. This cache programming model has the advantages of providing a vector register set for vector computations while still having the flexibility of a data cache for scalar computations.

With the two-clock-cycle transfer rate, the external bus can supply one memory operand for every double-precision add/multiply pair, or two contiguous single-precision operands for every two single-precision add/multiply pairs. The other two vector operands for an add/multiply pair must come from the onboard data cache.

The Bus Interface

The i860 processor's external bus interface is designed to sustain high CPU performance and ease system design. The bus performs a 64-bit transfer every two clock cycles to allow for the design of a practical TTL (*Transistor-Transistor Logic*) system even at 50 Mhz. The bus can interface either to a second level cache or directly to a DRAM memory system, and allows optional pipelining for increasing the access time without decreasing the bandwidth. The full bus bandwidth can be realized from one bank of DRAMs; however, the latency will be greater than if fast external SRAM memory or a fast external second level SRAM cache is used.

Figure 3-16 shows the i860 processor's bus signals. The microprocessor's external interface is synchronous with a demultiplexed address and data bus. A synchronous bus means that all bus timings are specified with respect to clock signal edges. This eases the design of external tracking and control logic. The bi-directional data bus is 64-bits wide and can accept or drive new data on every other clock cycle. This results in bandwidth of 160 MB per second at 40 Mhz. The bus interface pins A31-A3 and BE7#-BE0# are used to access 4 gigabytes of address space.

The address lines select the 8-byte word and the byte enables select the byte within the word. For read accesses to cacheable memory, the processor will cache the entire data bus so the system may ignore the byte enable pins. For write operations, the byte enables are used to determine which bytes in memory are to be updated. The 64 bi-

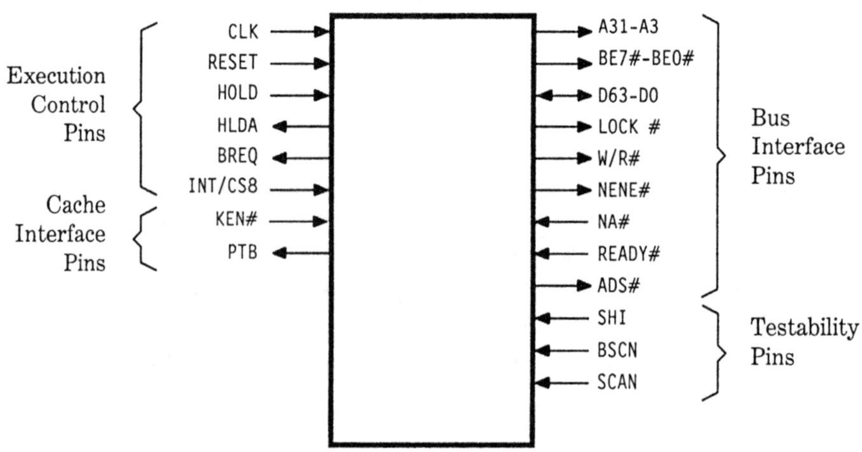

Figure 3-16. Processor bus organization

directional data pins can transfer 8-, 16-, 32- or 64-bit quantities; BE0# corresponds to data lines D7-D0 and BE7# corresponds to data lines D63-D56.

A summary of the processor's pins is given in Table 3-1. The processor is clocked with a single-frequency level clock. An optional mode for executing out of a single 8-bit wide ROM can be entered at reset by activating the INT/CS8 pin. In this mode, code is fetched from the ROM with the byte enable signals BE2#-BE0# redefined as address lines A2-A0.

The ADS# output is asserted during the first clock cycle of each bus cycle to indicate the start of a cycle and can be sampled by the system at the next rising clock cycle edge. Write and read bus cycles are distinguished by the W/R# signal. The processor makes no distinction for memory and I/O accesses. It is left up to the system hardware to "memory map" I/O devices to specific address locations.

The i860 processor has support for page mode and static column mode DRAMs with the Next Near (NENE#) output signal. NENE# indicates to the DRAM controller whether the current address is in the same DRAM page as the previous cycle. This is done by a comparison of the upper address bits of each access. If a NENE# access occurs, the memory controller can perform a fast page mode or static column mode access from the DRAM. The NENE# output is programmable for different page sizes.

The bus optionally allows for two levels of bus pipelining selected on a cycle-by-cycle basis. When pipelining, a new cycle is started before the completion of the outstanding cycles. Two levels of pipelining allow three cycles to be in operation at one time. Fast TTL latches can be used on the address and data bus. This latching isolates the memory array from the processor's pin timings, allowing easy scalability and providing the maximum time for memory accesses. With pipelining, the maximum processor data bus bandwidth can be sustained even if the system requires six processor clock cycles of access time.

The NA# input to the CPU controls pipelining. NA# can be asserted before the current cycle ends. When the processor samples NA# active, it can start driving the next bus cycle's address and bus-cycle definition. As shown in Figure 3-17, NA# can be asserted two times before returning data for any of the cycles.

While NA# controls the address and bus-cycle definition signals, READY# controls the data operations. When READY# is sampled active for

Table 3-1. Processor Pin Summary

Pin Name	*Function*	*Active State*	*Input/Output*
	Execution Control Pins		
CLK	CLock		I
RESET	System reset	High	I
HOLD	Bus hold	High	I
HLDA	Bus hold acknowledge	High	O
BREQ	Bus request	High	O
INT/CS8	Interrupt, code-size 8	High	I
	Bus Interface Pins		
A31-A3	Address bus	High	O
BE7#-BE0#	Byte Enables	Low	O
D63-D0	Data bus	High	I/O
LOCK#	Bus lock	Low	O
W/R#	Write/Read bus cycle	Hi/Low	O
NENE#	NExt NEar	Low	O
NA#	Next Address request	Low	I
READY#	Transfer Acknowledge	Low	I
ADS#	ADdress Strobe	Low	O
	Cache Interface Pins		
KEN#	Cache ENable	Low	I
PTB	Page Table Bit	High	O
	Testability Pins		
SHI	Boundary Scan Shift Input	High	I
BSCN	Boundary Scan Enable	High	I
SCAN	Shift Scan Path	High	I

A # after a pin name indicates that the signal is active when at the low voltage level.

Table 3-1. Processor Pin Summary (continued)

Pin Name	*Function*	*Active State*	*Input/Output*
	Intel-Reserved Configuration Pins		
CC1-CC0	Configuration	High	I
	Power and Ground Pins		
V_{CC}	System Power		
V_{SS}	System ground		

A # after a pin name indicates that the signal is active when at the low voltage level.

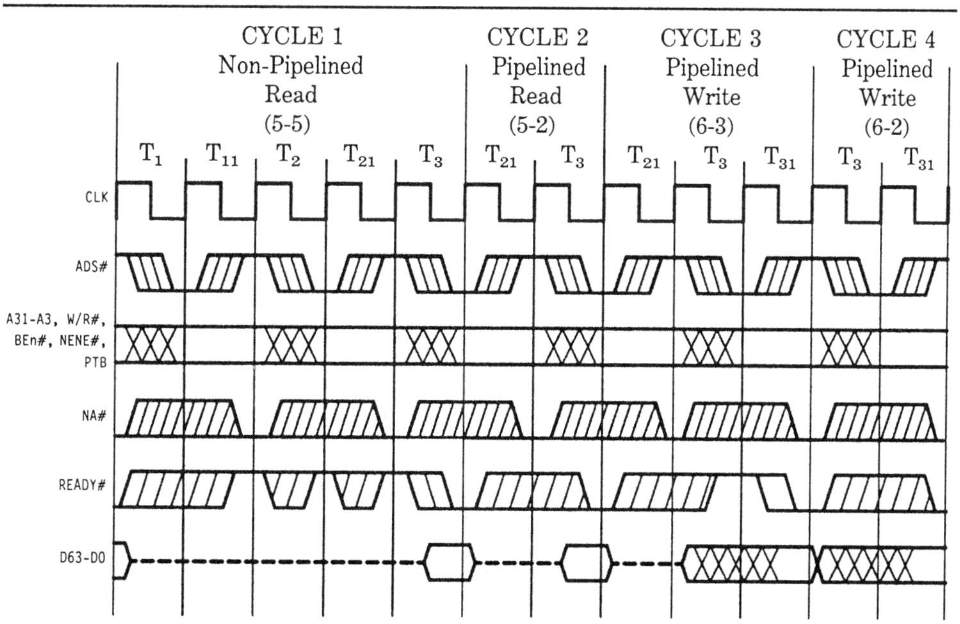

Figure 3-17. Two-Level Pipelining

a read, the processor latches the data from the data bus. When READY# is sampled active for a write, the processor stops driving the data from that cycle. READY# also serves to end a bus cycle.

The processor samples the KEN# input to determine if the data for the current read cycle is cacheable. This is useful for marking areas of the system address space as noncacheable. Address space that is used for I/O devices can be decoded to deassert KEN# during processor accesses. Software can also mark areas of memory as noncacheable using paging. If the software has not disabled caching of the page, and KEN# is active for a read cycle, the processor will generate three additional 64-bit bus cycles to fill the 32-byte cache block.

The signals HOLD, HLDA, and BREQ are used for arbitration of the processor's local bus. When a *DMA* (Direct Memory Access) controller, or another processor, needs access to the local bus of the CPU, it asserts HOLD. When the CPU completes all of its outstanding bus cycles, it floats the bus interface pins and returns HLDA active high. The CPU will remain in this state with HLDA active until HOLD is deasserted. The CPU can continue processing from instructions and data already in the on-chip caches even while in HOLD. When the processor wants an external bus cycle, it asserts the BREQ output signal. Intelligent arbitration logic can sample the BREQ signal to efficiently arbitrate a shared bus.

The bus LOCK# signal output is used to provide atomic (indivisible) read-modify-write sequences. LOCK# prevents the processor from breaking up indivisible sequences if an interrupt occurs (via the CS8/INT pin). LOCK# can be activated with software by using the **lock** instruction and deactivated with the corresponding **unlock** instruction. LOCK# is also activated automatically by the TLB for address transition memory accesses that perform a read-modify-write sequence.

By utilizing a 64-bit architecture, the i860 processor delivers balanced MIPS, MFlops, and graphics performance. The one-million transistor budget allows for integrating the RISC core, dedicated fast floating-point hardware, graphics capabilities, and cache memories on a single chip. The design allows maximum parallelism between the functional units while achieving a balance between computation speed and data bandwidth.

Proper programming techniques are essential to take advantage of the processor's parallelism and pipelined execution units. Before getting started on the programming challenges, take time to read the next chapter, which explains the processor's most basic machine model. Knowing a CPU's basic register model, addressing model, and data type support is essential for programming.

CHAPTER 4
MACHINE ORGANIZATION

The basic architecture of a computer can be described by the data formats it comprehends, the user-visible registers, and the way it addresses memory. This chapter discusses the basic machine organization of the i860 microprocessor and establishes a common vocabulary and notation that will be used throughout this book. First, the data types supported and their representations are explained, followed by the register model and the memory representation of data. Additional information on programming conventions is included at the end of this chapter.

Data Representations

Digital computers operate on binary digits, also called bits, where each bit is either a one or a zero. Binary-represented numbers are different from ordinary numbers. Consider your fingers as binary digits that can each be a one or a zero. Counting on your fingers, you are likely to count to ten with ten fingers, whereas a computer could count to 1,023 on ten fingers (computers call them bits).

Computers obtain input, process it, and produce output. Input can take many forms, for example, characters from a keyboard or pictures from a digitizing video camera. By the time input gets to the CPU, it is in binary form. The CPU or processor follows a sequence of instructions called a program. The program specifies where the input comes from and what operation is to be performed on it. Memory is used to store the program as well as storing data.

Integer Data

Unfortunately, the ordinary decimal numbering system that people use does not easily convert to the binary numbering that computers use. Similarly, long sequences of ones and zeros are difficult for people to understand. As a compromise, binary number representation is compressed into hexadecimal representation. For example, the binary representation 10110111b (b is for binary) is converted to B7H (the H is for hexadecimal), by grouping four binary digits starting at the right as shown in Table 4-1. The conversion from binary to decimal is more difficult. Table 4-2 gives the decimal equivalents for powers of two. Performing conversions from the binary powers of 2, you see that

$$1\times2^7 + 0\times2^6 + 1\times2^5 + 1\times2^4 + 0\times2^3 + 1\times2^2 + 1\times2^1 + 1\times2^0 = 183.$$

A simpler conversion can be performed using the hexadecimal notation and powers of 16, $B\times16^1 + 7\times16^0 = 183$. Table 4-3 gives the decimal equivalents for powers of 16. Hexadecimal constants also are written, according to the C language convention, with the prefix "0x." For example, B7H in a C or assembly language program would be represented by 0xB7.

As shown in Figure 4-1, integer data may be represented as signed integers or as unsigned ordinals. A 32-bit ordinal can represent the range 0 to 4,294,967,295 ($+2^{32}-1$). For signed values, the i860 processor uses two's complement form and can represent the range

Table 4-1. Binary, Hexadecimal, and Decimal Equivalents

Value	*Binary*	*Hexadecimal*	*Decimal*
Zero	0000	0	0
One	0001	1	1
Two	0010	2	2
Three	0011	3	3
Four	0100	4	4
Five	0101	5	5
Six	0110	6	6
Seven	0111	7	7
Eight	1000	8	8
Nine	1001	9	9
Ten	1010	A	10
Eleven	1011	B	11
Twelve	1100	C	12
Thirteen	1101	D	13
Fourteen	1110	E	14
Fifteen	1111	F	15

−2,147,483,648 (-2^{31}) to 2,147,483,647 ($+2^{31}-1$). The i860 processor also has limited support for 64-bit long integers and 64-bit long ordinals.

The left-most significant bit, bit 31 of integer data, is the sign bit. In the case of the i860 processor, arithmetic operations on the integer registers always occur on all 32-bits, thus byte and short-word data are automatically sign extended when they are loaded. For example, if you want to add −1, which is stored in memory as byte data, and 5, which is also in memory, you need to properly sign extend the data when they are loaded. In memory, byte data −1 is represented as 11111111b and extended to 11111111111111111111111111111111b when loaded. If you just counted to see that there are 32 bits, you will appreciate the HEX representation FFFFFFFFH. Adding FFFFFFFFH plus 0000005H gives the correct result of 00000004H. Unsigned operation on data may produce the same numeric result, but the effect on the processor's flags is different.

Table 4-2. Decimal Equivalents of Powers of Two

Powers of 2	*Decimal Equivalents*
2^{31}	2,147,483,648
2^{30}	1,073,741,824
2^{29}	536,870,912
2^{28}	268,435,456
2^{27}	134,217,728
2^{26}	67,108,864
2^{25}	33,554,432
2^{24}	16,777,216
2^{23}	8,388,608
2^{22}	4,194,304
2^{21}	2,097,152
2^{20}	1,048,576
2^{19}	524,288
2^{18}	262,144
2^{17}	131,072
2^{16}	65,536
2^{15}	32,768
2^{14}	16,384
2^{13}	8,192
2^{12}	4,096
2^{11}	2,048
2^{10}	1,024
2^{9}	512
2^{8}	256
2^{7}	128
2^{6}	64
2^{5}	32
2^{4}	16
2^{3}	8
2^{2}	4
2^{1}	2

Table 4-2. Decimal Equivalents of Powers of Two (continued)

Powers of 2	*Decimal Equivalents*
2^{0}	1.0
2^{-1}	0.5
2^{-2}	0.25
2^{-3}	0.125
2^{-4}	0.0625
2^{-5}	0.03125
2^{-6}	0.015625
2^{-7}	0.0078125
2^{-8}	0.00390625
2^{-9}	0.001953125
2^{-10}	0.0009765625
2^{-11}	0.00048828125
2^{-12}	0.000244140625
2^{-13}	0.0001220703125
2^{-14}	0.00006103515625
2^{-15}	0.000030517578125

Table 4-3. Decimal Equivalents of Hexadecimal Numbers

Hex	*Dec*	*Hex*	*Dec*	*Hex*	*Dec*	*Hex*	*Dec*	*Hex*	*Dec*
1	1	10	16	100	256	1000	4,096	10000	65,536
2	2	20	32	200	512	2000	8,192	20000	131,072
3	3	30	48	300	768	3000	12,288	30000	196,608
4	4	40	64	400	1,024	4000	16,384	40000	262,144
5	5	50	80	500	1,280	5000	20,480	50000	327,680
6	6	60	96	600	1,536	6000	24,576	60000	393,216
7	7	70	112	700	1,792	7000	28,672	70000	458,752
8	8	80	128	800	2,048	8000	32,768	80000	524,288
9	9	90	144	900	2,304	9000	36,864	90000	589,824
A	10	A0	160	A00	2,560	A000	40,960	A0000	655,360
B	11	B0	176	B00	2,816	B000	45,056	B0000	720,896
C	12	C0	192	C00	3,072	C000	49,152	C0000	786,432
D	13	D0	208	D00	3,328	D000	53,248	D0000	851,968
E	14	E0	224	E00	3,584	E000	57,344	E0000	917,504
F	15	F0	240	F00	3,840	F000	61,440	F0000	983,040

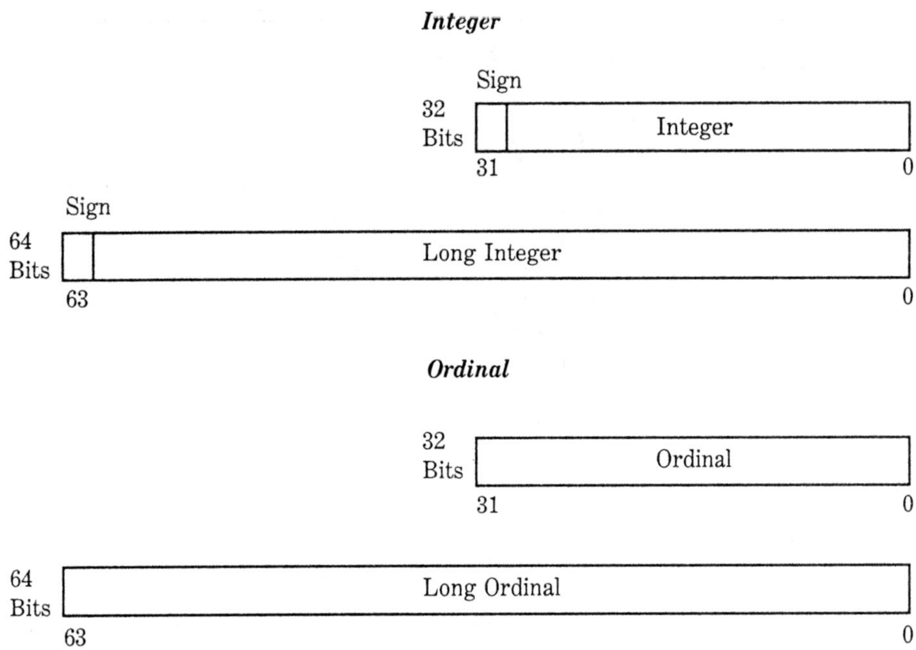

Figure 4-1. Integer and ordinal data

Real Data

Not all numbers are represented easily by integers. For example, to represent very big or very small numbers in decimal form, scientific notation is used: The speed of light, in meters per second, can be expressed as:

2.997925×10^8 m/sec

This notation has three components: the implied sign +, the significand 2.997925, and the exponent. The significand is also called the mantissa or fraction. Note that the same number can be represented by many different notational variants:

29.97925×10^7
299.7925×10^6
$0.02997925 \times 10^{10}$

and so on. However, scientific numbers are normalized so the value has only one significant digit to the left of the decimal point.

In binary, the maximum range of numbers that can be represented by two's complement numbers is 2^{32} or 4 gigabytes. This is not sufficient for all types of data. Fortunately, binary numbers can also be used to represent very big or very small real numbers. Floating point is the data type used to represent a subset of all real numbers.

The i860 processor supports single- and double-floating-point precision formats. The single-precision floating-point data type uses a 32-bit binary floating-point number, and the double-precision floating-point data type uses a 64-bit binary floating-point number. The value range for a set of numbers may dictate using the double-precision representation. The downside to double precision is that calculations tend to be slower because more bits are being operated on and moved around.

Floating-Point Representation

The format of the two representations for binary floating-point data is shown in Figure 4-2. Similar to scientific notation, there are three components to binary floating-point numbers: the sign, the exponent, and the significand. The sign field indicates whether the floating-point number is positive or negative. As with two's complement numbers, a 1 in this field indicates a negative number, and a 0 indicates a positive number.

Similar to decimal notation where the exponent field specifies the powers of 10 to multiply the significand by, in binary notation, the exponent specifies the powers of 2 to multiply the significand by. To allow designation of negative exponents, the binary number in the exponent field is the sum of the actual exponent and a positive constant called a bias. Thus, the exponent field always contains a positive number, and a zero in the exponent field represents the most negative exponent.

For example, if the exponent field of a single-precision floating-point number is 11000000b, decimal 192, the actual exponent value is 192 minus the bias. For single-precision, the bias is 127. Thus, a value of 192 in the exponent field represents an exponent of 65.

The significand field indicates the fractional portion of the number. As in scientific notation, binary floating-point representation uses a

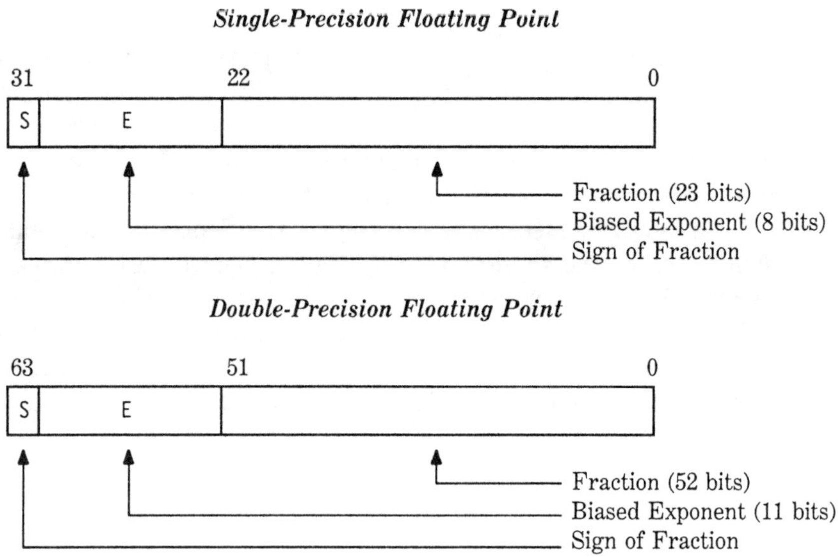

Figure 4-2. Single- and double-precision floating-point representations

normalized significand. Because the significand is in binary, an invisible 1 to the left of the decimal point can be used for the normalization. This saves a bit in the representation; and all of the significand bits are used to represent digits to the right of the radix point. For example, if the significand bits of a floating-point number are specified as 0001011. . .10, the actual significand is 10001011. . .10 with the radix point after the first (from the left) bit.

Binary bits to the right of the radix point represent fractional numbers. The further to the right, the less significant the number. Referring back to Table 4-2, you see that the first digit to the right of the radix point is 2^{-1} which is equal to 1/2 or 0.5. The next digit to the right is 2^{-2} or 1/4 which is equal to 0.25 and so on.

Single-precision numbers have a 23-bit significand and an 8-bit exponent. In base 10, this guarantees a range from 10^{-37} to 10^{38} with a precision of at least 6 significant digits. The formula for deciphering single-precision floating-point numbers can be expressed as:

$$(-1)^{sign} * (1.F_1F_2F_3F_4F_5...F_{23}) * 2^{(E-127)}$$

Where sign is the 1 or 0 stored in the sign bit, F_1-F_{23} are the bits of the significand fields, and E is the unsigned value stored in the exponent field.

Figure 4-3 shows you a full example for deciphering a single-precision floating-point value. First, you see the value is positive because the sign bit is a 0. Second, you calculate the actual exponent value by taking the exponent field value, 155, and subtracting 127. The actual exponent, 28, is the power of two that the significand must be multiplied by. Third, you rewrite the significand to show the hidden 1 and the normalizing point. To convert from binary to integer, it is easier to perform the exponent multiplication before the conversion. Because the exponent is in factors of two, the multiplication can be performed by shifting the significand. Because the exponent is positive, in the fourth step you shift the point to the right by 28 bits, filling in zeros at the low-order bits. This final form represented in binary and hexadecimal is converted to a decimal equivalent in step five.

Note that in the example, an extra 12 meters per second have been added to the speed of light. This is due to the precision of the number being too great to represent exactly in single-precision. If this small inexactness would cause some problem in your calculation, the number could be represented in double-precision.

Double-precision floating-point values have a 52-bit significand and an 11-bit exponent. The bias for the double-precision exponent is 1023. In base 10, the double-precision floating-point numbers are guaranteed to represent from 10^{-307} to 10^{308} with 15 significant digits. The representation formula, with the same notation explained above, can be expressed as:

$$(-1)^{sign} * (1.F_1F_2...F_{52}) * 2^{(E-1023)}$$

The representations described here and used by the i860 processor are in accordance with the ANSI/IEEE standard 754. The standard also specifies rounding and error handling. In order to facilitate this, the i860 processor generates traps when certain numbers are encountered in a floating-point operation. The trap-handler software must implement the IEEE-standard result. Table 4-4 shows the encoding for these special values.

Given the floating-point hexadecimal notation 4D8EF3C4H, determine what single-precision floating-point number it represents.

1. Represent in Binary Notation

   0100 1101 1000 1110 1111 0011 1100 0100

   Broken into the representation fields.

S	Exp.	Significand
0	10011011	00011101111001111000100

   Sign bit equals 0: Therefore, the significand is positive.

2. Determine the Exponent

   Exponent Field:

   $10011011 = 2^7 + 2^4 + 2^3 + 2^1 + 2^0 = 128 + 16 + 8 + 2 + 1 = 155$

   Bias equal 127: Therefore, the actual exponent is 28 calculated from $155 - 127$.

3. Determine value of significand

   The significand field 00011101111001111000100 is rewritten to show the hidden 1 and the normalized binary point:

   1.00011101111001111000100

4. Show in final binary form

   Shift the point of the significand to the right by the exponent value 28. Fill in five zeros to the right where the representation runs out of bits.

   10001110111100111100010000000

   Represented in Hex:

   1 0001 1101 1110 0111 1000 1000 0000

   11DE7880H

5. Convert from binary to decimal

   $= 2^{28} + 2^{24} + 2^{23} + 2^{22} + 2^{20} + 2^{19} + 2^{18} + 2^{17} + 2^{14} + 2^{13} + 2^{12} + 2^{11} + 2^7$

   $= 299{,}792{,}512$

Figure 4-3. Converting from floating-point to integer

Table 4-4. Floating-Point Encodings

Class			Sign	Biased Exponent	Significand ff–ff*
POSITIVES	NANS	Quiet	0	11..11	11..11
			0	11..11	10..00
		Signaling	0	11..11	01..11
			0	11..11	00..01
	Infinity		0	11..11	00..00
	REALS	Normals	0	11..10	11..11
			0	00..01	00..00
		Denormals	0	00..00	11..11
			0	00..00	00..01
		Zero	0	00..00	00..00
NEGATIVES	REALS	Zero	1	00..00	00..00
		Denormals	1	00..00	00..01
			1	00..00	11..11
		Normals	1	00..01	00..00
			1	11..10	11..11
	Infinity		1	11..11	00..00
	NANS	Signaling	1	11..11	00..01
			1	11..11	01..11
		Quiet	1	11..11	10..00
			1	11..11	11..11
			Single:	< 8 bits>	<23 bits>
			Double:	<11 bits>	<52 bits>

*Integer bit is implied and not stored

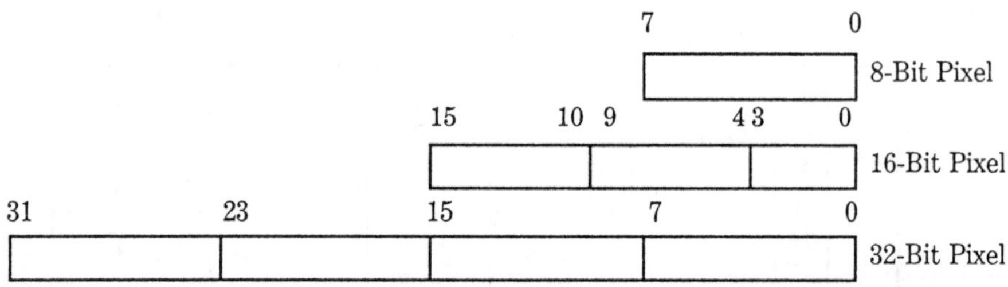

Figure 4-4. Pixel formats

Pixel Data

The i860 processor supports pixel data of 8, 16, and 32 bits. Both pixel store and pixel add operations are available, with the processor operating on 64 bits of pixel data with each instruction. The pixel formats are defined as shown in Figure 4-4 but the meaning of each field is left up to the user.

Figure 4-5 shows one possible assignment of the pixel fields for each format. The number of intensity bits determines the dynamic range of intensities supported, and can be converted to color variations. For example, with 16-bit pixels, the 6-bit red intensity field allows for 64 red color variations, the 6-bit green intensity field allows for 64 green color variations, and the 4-bit blue intensity field allows for 16 blue color variations, giving a total of 64K of different colors. To increase the number of colors available to the intensity fields, the intensity bits can be fed into a color lookup table (called a *pallet*) as part of a graphics

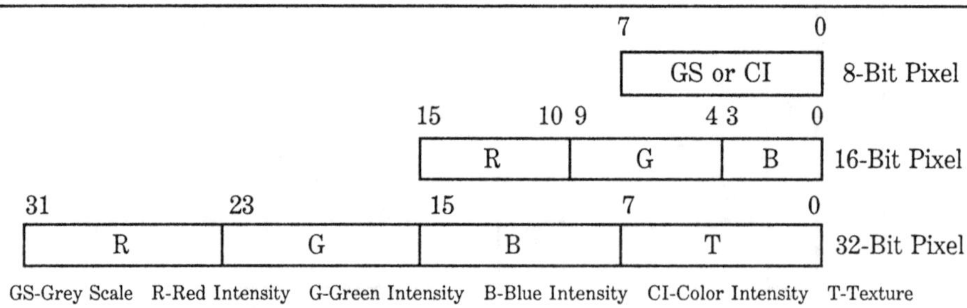

Figure 4-5. Pixel field assignment example

system. Note that this does not increase the number of colors available simultaneously.

Register Model

As Figure 3-2 in the last chapter shows, the i860 microprocessor has the following registers:

- An integer register file
- A floating-point register file
- Four special-purpose registers (KR, KI, T, and MERGE)
- Six control registers (**psr**, **epsr**, **db**, **dirbase**, **fir**, and **fsr**)

The control registers are accessible only by load and store control-register instructions; the integer and floating-point registers are accessed by arithmetic operations and load and store instructions. The special-purpose registers KR, KI (Konstant), T (Temporary), and MERGE are used by a few specific floating-point instructions.

The instructions that operate on the data in the integer and floating-point registers are explained in Chapter 5, "RISC Core Operations," and Chapter 6, "Floating-Point Operations," respectively. Instructions that operate on the special registers KR, KI, and T are also included in Chapter 6. The graphics instructions and the operation of the MERGE register are explained in Chapter 7, "Graphics Rendering Instructions." Many of the control registers' bits are used by the operating system software for memory management and trap handling, which is explained fully in Chapter 9, "Operating System Support."

Integer Register File

There are 32 integer registers, each 32 bits wide, referred to as **r0** through **r31**, which are used for address computation and scalar integer computations. Register **r0** always returns zero when read, independently of what is stored in it. This special behavior of **r0** makes it useful for modifying the function of certain instructions. For example, specifying **r0** as the destination of a subtract (thereby effectively discarding the result) produces a compare instruction. Similarly, using **r0** as one source operand of an **or** instruction produces a test-for-zero instruction.

Floating-Point Register File

There are 32 floating-point registers, each 32 bits wide, referred to as **f0** through **f31**, which are used for floating-point computations. Registers **f0** and **f1** always return zero when read, independently of what is stored in them. The floating-point registers are also used for some integer arithmetic operations and graphics operations.

The floating-point registers act as buffer registers in vector computations, while the data cache performs the role of the vector registers of a conventional vector processor. When accessing 64-bit floating-point or integer values, the i860 microprocessor uses an even/odd pair of registers. When accessing 128-bit values, it uses an aligned set of four registers (**f0, f4, f8, . . . , f28**). The instruction must designate the lowest register number of the set of registers containing 64- or 128-bit values, as shown in Figure 4-6; that is, the least significant bits of the significand for floating point. The highest numbered register of a pair would contain the sign and exponent.

Control Registers

There are six control registers accessible in the i860 processor. They are

processor status register (**psr**)
extended processor status register (**epsr**)
data breakpoint register (**db**)
directory base register (**dirbase**)
fault instruction register (**fir**)
floating-point status register (**fsr**)

The control registers are accessed via the load control (**ld.c**) and store control (**st.c**) instructions. To check specific bits of the control register you first transfer the control register contents to an integer register by using the **ld.c** instruction. Similarly, you can perform bit manipulation of control-register data in an integer register, then transfer to the appropriate control register using **st.c**. The following section describes what each control register is used for and what each bit indicates.

a. Double-Precision Register Model

63 32	31 0	
f1	f0	f0
f3	f2	f2
f5	f4	f4
f7	f6	f6
f9	f8	f8
f11	f10	f10
f13	f12	f12
f15	f14	f14
f17	f16	f16
f19	f18	f18
f21	f20	f20
f23	f22	f22
f25	f24	f24
f27	f26	f26
f29	f28	f28
f31	f30	f30

b. Registers as accessed by **pfd.q** *and* **fst.q**

127 96	95 64	63 32	31 0	
f3	f2	f1	f0	f0
f7	f6	f5	f4	f4
f11	f10	f9	f8	f8
f15	f14	f13	f12	f12
f19	f18	f17	f16	f16
f23	f22	f21	f20	f20
f27	f26	f25	f24	f24
f31	f30	f29	f28	f28

Figure 4-6. Floating-point register model

Processor Status Register The *processor status register* (**psr**) contains miscellaneous state information for the current process. Figure 4-7 shows the format of the **psr**. Fields marked by an asterisk in the figure can be changed only in supervisor mode.

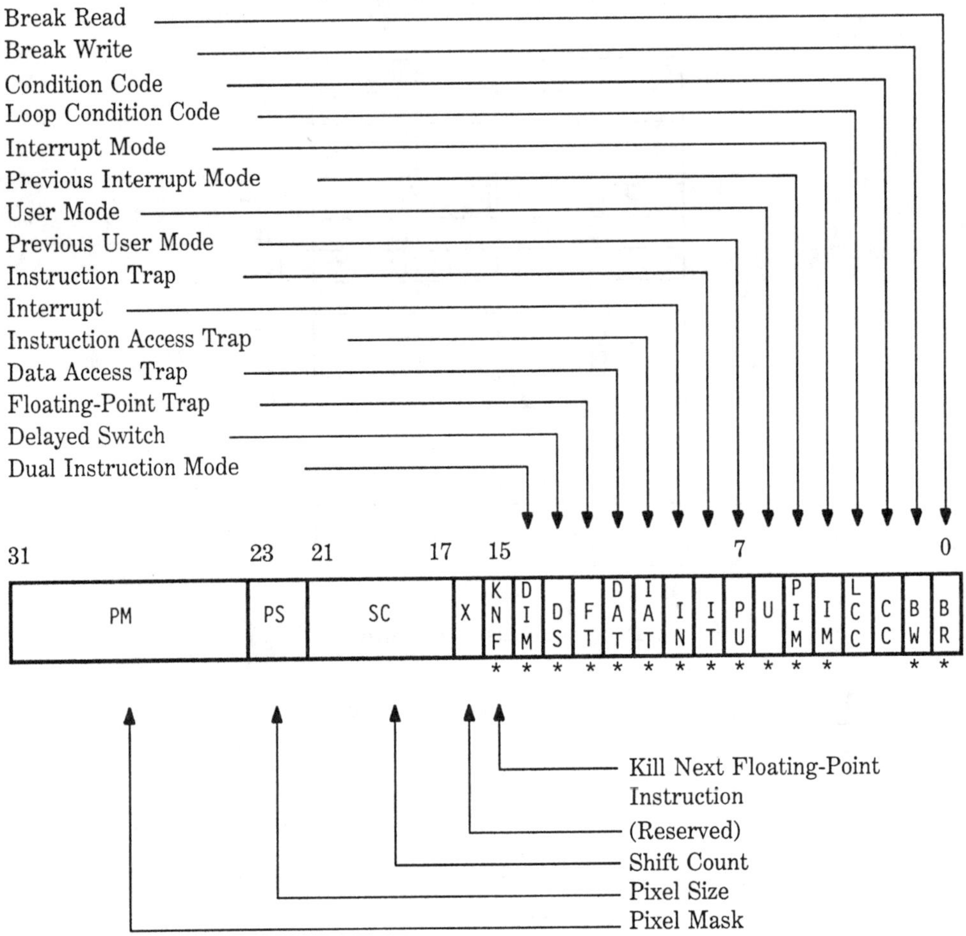

*Can be changed only from supervisor level

Figure 4-7. Processor status register

BR and BW BR (Break Read) and BW (Break Write) enable a data access trap when the operand address matches the address in the **db** register and a read or write (respectively) occurs.

CC Various instructions affect the CC (Condition Code) according to the value of their result. The conditional branch instructions test CC.

LCC The **bla** instruction described in Chapter 5, "RISC Core Operations," sets and tests LCC (Loop-Condition Code).

IM IM (Interrupt Mode) enables external interrupts if set; disables interrupts if clear. (Chapter 9, "Operating System Support," covers interrupts.)

PIM and PU PIM (Previous Interrupt Mode) and PU (Previous User Mode) save the corresponding status bits (IM and U) on a trap, because those status bits are cleared by the CPU when a trap occurs. They are restored into their corresponding status bits when returning from a trap handler with a branch indirect instruction when a trap flag is set in the **psr**.

U U (User Mode) is set when the i860 microprocessor is executing in user mode; it is clear when the i860 microprocessor is executing in supervisor mode. In user mode, writes to some control registers are inhibited.

IT IT (Instruction Trap), IN (Interrupt), IAT (Instruction Access Trap), DAT (Data Access Trap), and FT (Floating-Point Trap) are trap flags. They are set when the corresponding trap condition occurs. The trap handler examines these bits to determine which condition or conditions have caused the trap.

DS DS (Delayed Switch) is set if a trap occurs during the instruction before dual-instruction mode is entered or exited. If DS is set and DIM (Dual-Instruction Mode) is clear, the i860 microprocessor switches to dual-instruction mode one instruction after returning from the trap handler. If DS and DIM are both set, the i860 microprocessor switches to single-instruction mode one instruction after returning from the trap handler.

DIM When a trap occurs, the i860 microprocessor sets DIM if it is executing in dual-instruction mode; it clears DIM if it is executing in single-instruction mode. If DIM is set, then the i860 microprocessor resumes execution in dual-instruction mode after returning from the trap handler.

Table 4-5. Values of PS

Value	*Pixel Size in Bits*	*Pixel Size in Bytes*
00	8	1
01	16	2
10	32	4
11	(Undefined)	(Undefined)

KNF When KNF (Kill Next Floating-Point Instruction) is set, the next floating-point instruction is suppressed (except that its dual-instruction mode bit is used). A trap handler sets KNF if the trapped floating-point instruction should not be re-executed. KNF is useful for returning from a trap that occurred in dual-instruction mode, because it permits the core instruction to be executed while the floating-point instruction is suppressed. KNF is automatically reset by the i860 microprocessor after the instruction has been successfully bypassed. It is possible that the core instruction may cause a trap when the floating-point instruction is suppressed. In this case, KNF remains set, permitting a retry of the core instruction.

SC SC (Shift Count) stores the shift count used by the last right-shift instruction. It controls the number of shifts executed by the double-shift instruction.

PS and PM PS (Pixel Size) and PM (Pixel Mask) are used by the pixel-store instruction and by the graphics instructions. The values of PS control pixel size as defined in Table 4-5. The bits in PM correspond to pixels to be updated by the pixel-store instruction **pst.d**. The low-order bit of PM corresponds to the low-order pixel of the 64-bit source operand of **pst.d**. The number of low-order bits of PM that are actually used is the number of pixels that fit into 64 bits, which depends upon PS. If a bit of PM is set, then **pst.d** updates the corresponding pixel in memory.

Extended Processor Status Register The *extended processor status register* (**epsr**) contains additional state information for the current process beyond that stored in the **psr**. Figure 4-8 shows the format of the **epsr**. Fields marked by an asterisk in the figure can be changed only in supervisor mode.

The processor type is one for the i860 microprocessor. The stepping number has a unique value that distinguishes among different revisions of the processor. These are readable by user programs and can be used for conditionally executing different programs on different versions of the processor.

IL `IL` (Interlock) is set if a trap occurs after a **lock** instruction but before the load or store following the subsequent **unlock** instruction. `IL` indicates to the trap handler that a locked sequence has been interrupted.

WP `WP` (Write Protect) controls the semantics of the `W` bit of page table entries. A clear `W` bit in either the directory or the page table entry

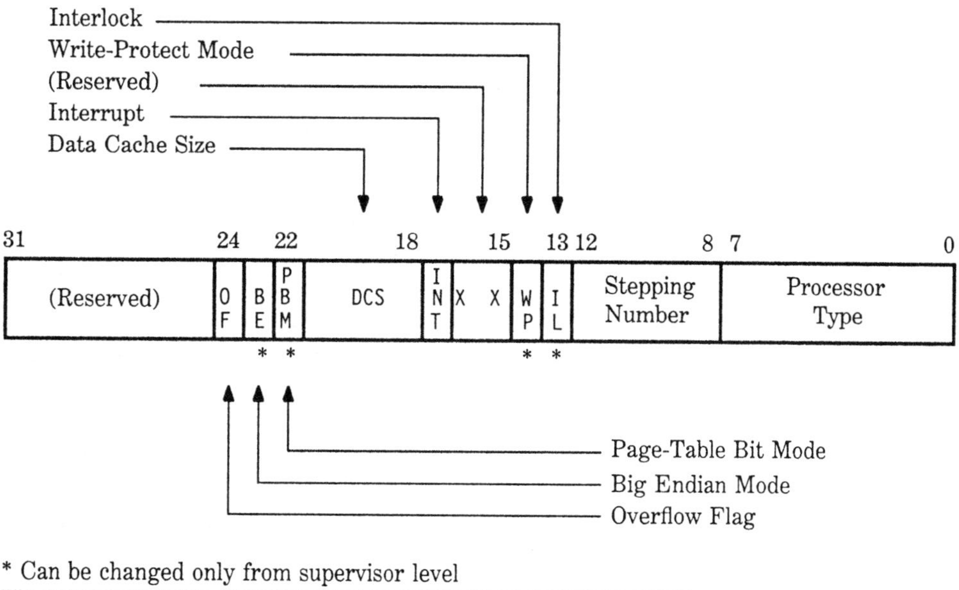

Figure 4-8. Extended processor status register

causes writes to be trapped. When WP is clear, writes are trapped in user mode, but not in supervisor mode. When WP is set, writes are trapped in both user and supervisor modes.

INT INT (Interrupt) is the value of the INT input pin. It is a read-only field.

DCS DCS (Data Cache Size) is a read-only field that tells the size of the on-chip data cache. The number of bytes actually available is $2^{12+\mathrm{DCS}}$; therefore, a value of zero indicates 4K, one indicates 8K, and so on. For the i860 processor, DCS = 1.

PBM PBM (Page-Table Bit Mode) determines which bit of page-table entries is output on the PTB pin. When PBM is clear, the PTB signal reflects bit CD of the page-table entry used for the current cycle. When PBM is set, the PTB signal reflects bit WT of the page-table entry used for the current cycle.

BE BE (Big Endian) controls the ordering of bytes within a data item in memory. Normally, for example, when BE is clear, the i860 microprocessor operates in little endian mode, in which the addressed byte is the low-order byte. When BE is set (big endian mode), the low-order three bits of all load and store addresses are complemented, then masked to the appropriate boundary for alignment. This causes the addressed byte to be the most significant byte. More information on byte ordering is given later in this chapter.

OF OF (Overflow Flag) is set by **adds**, **addu**, **subs**, and **subu** when integer overflow occurs. For **adds** and **subs**, OF is set if the carry from bit 31 is different than the carry from bit 30. For **addu**, OF is set if there is a carry from bit 31. For **subu**, OF is set if there is no carry from bit 31. Under all other conditions, it is cleared by these instructions. OF controls the function of the **intovr** instruction.

Data Breakpoint Register The *data breakpoint register* (**db**) is used to generate a trap when the i860 microprocessor accesses an operand at the address stored in this register. The trap is enabled by BR and BW in

psr. When comparing, a number of low-order bits of the address is ignored, depending on the size of the operand. For example, a 16-bit access ignores the low-order bit of the address when comparing to **db**; a 32-bit access ignores the low-order two bits. This ensures that any access that overlaps the address contained in the register will generate a trap. The trap occurs before the register or memory update by the load or store instruction.

Directory Base Register The *directory base register* (**dirbase**), shown in Figure 4-9, controls address translation, caching, and bus options.

ATE ATE (Address Translation Enable), when set, enables the virtual-address translation algorithm described in Chapter 9 "Operating System Support." The data cache must be flushed before changing the ATE bit.

DPS DPS (DRAM Page Size) controls how many bits to ignore when comparing the current bus-cycle address with the previous bus-cycle

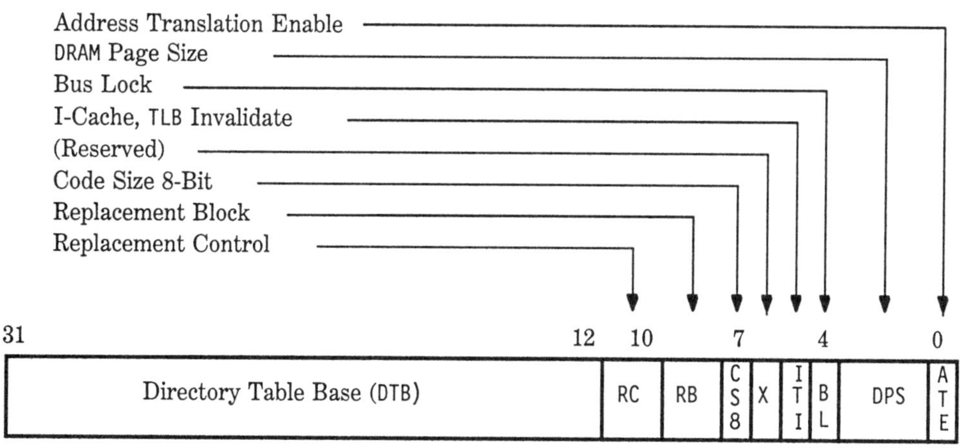

Figure 4-9. Directory base register

address to generate the NENE# signal. This feature allows for higher-speed memory accesses when using static column or page-mode DRAMs and consecutive reads and writes occur to the same column or page. The comparison ignores the low-order 12 + DPS bits. A value of zero is appropriate for one bank of 256K by n RAMs, one for 1M RAMs, and so on.

BL When BL (Bus Lock) is set, external bus accesses are locked. The LOCK# signal is asserted on the next bus cycle whose internal bus request is generated after BL is set. It remains set on every subsequent bus cycle as long as BL remains set. The LOCK# signal is deasserted on the next bus cycle whose internal bus request is generated after BL is cleared. A trap that occurs during a locked sequence immediately clears BL and the LOCK# signal and sets IL in **epsr**. In this case, the trap handler should resume execution at the beginning of the locked sequence. The **lock** and **unlock** instructions control the BL bit (refer to Chapter 9, "Operating System Support").

ITI ITI (Instruction-Cache, TLB Invalidate), when set in the value that is stored in **dirbase**, causes the instruction cache and address-translation cache (TLB) to be flushed. The ITI bit does not remain set in **dirbase.** ITI always appears as zero when read from **dirbase**. The data cache must be flushed before invalidating the TLB (except for the case of setting the D- or P-bit in a PTE that is not itself in the data cache).

CS8 When CS8 (Code Size 8-Bit) is set, instruction cache misses are processed as 8-bit bus cycles. When this bit is clear, instruction cache misses are processed as 64-bit bus cycles. This bit cannot be set by software; hardware sets it at initialization time. It can be cleared by software (one time only) to allow the system to execute out of 64-bit memory after bootstrapping from 8-bit ROM. A nondelayed branch to code in 64-bit memory should directly follow the **st.c** instruction that clears CS8, in order to make the transition from 8-bit to 64-bit memory occur at the correct time. The branch must be aligned on a 64-bit boundary.

RB RB (Replacement Block) identifies the cache block to be replaced by cache replacement algorithms. The high-order bit of RB is ignored by the instruction and data caches. RB conditions the cache flush instruction. Table 4-6 explains the values of RB.

RC RC (Replacement Control) controls cache replacement algorithms. Table 4-7 explains the significance of the values of RC. RC and RB are used to implement data cache flushing.

DTB DTB (Directory Table Base) contains the high-order 20 bits of the physical address of the page directory when address translation is enabled. The low-order 12 bits of the address are zeros (therefore the directory must be located on a 4K boundary).

Fault Instruction Register When a trap occurs, the **fir** register contains the address of the instruction that caused the trap. Reading **fir** anytime except the first time after a trap occurs yields the address of the **ld.c** instruction. This register is read-only.

Floating-Point Status Register The *floating-point status register* (**fsr**) contains the floating-point trap and rounding-mode status for the current process. Figure 4-10 shows its format.

Table 4-6. Values of **RB**

Value	*Replace* TLB *Block*	*Replace Instruction and Data Cache Block*
00	0	0
01	1	1
10	2	0
11	3	1

Table 4-7. Values of RC

Value	*Meaning*
00	Selects the normal replacement algorithm where any block in the set may be replaced on cache misses in all caches.
01	Instruction, data, and TLB cache misses replace the block selected by RB. The instruction and data caches ignore the high-order bit of RB. This mode is used for instruction cache and TLB testing.
10	Data cache misses replace the block selected by the low-order bit of RB.
11	Disables data cache replacement.

FZ If FZ (Flush Zero) is clear and underflow occurs, a result-exception trap is generated. When FZ is set and underflow occurs, the result is set to zero, and no trap due to underflow occurs.

TI If TI (Trap Inexact) is clear, inexact results do not cause a trap. If TI is set, inexact results cause a trap. The sticky inexact flag (SI) is set whenever an inexact result is produced, regardless of the setting of TI.

RM RM (Rounding Mode) specifies one of the four rounding modes defined by the IEEE standard. Given a true result b that cannot be represented by the target data type, the i860 microprocessor determines the two representable numbers a and c that most closely bracket b in value ($a < b < c$). The i860 microprocessor then rounds (changes) b to a or c according to the mode selected by RM as defined in Table 4-8. Rounding introduces an error in the result that is less than one least-significant bit.

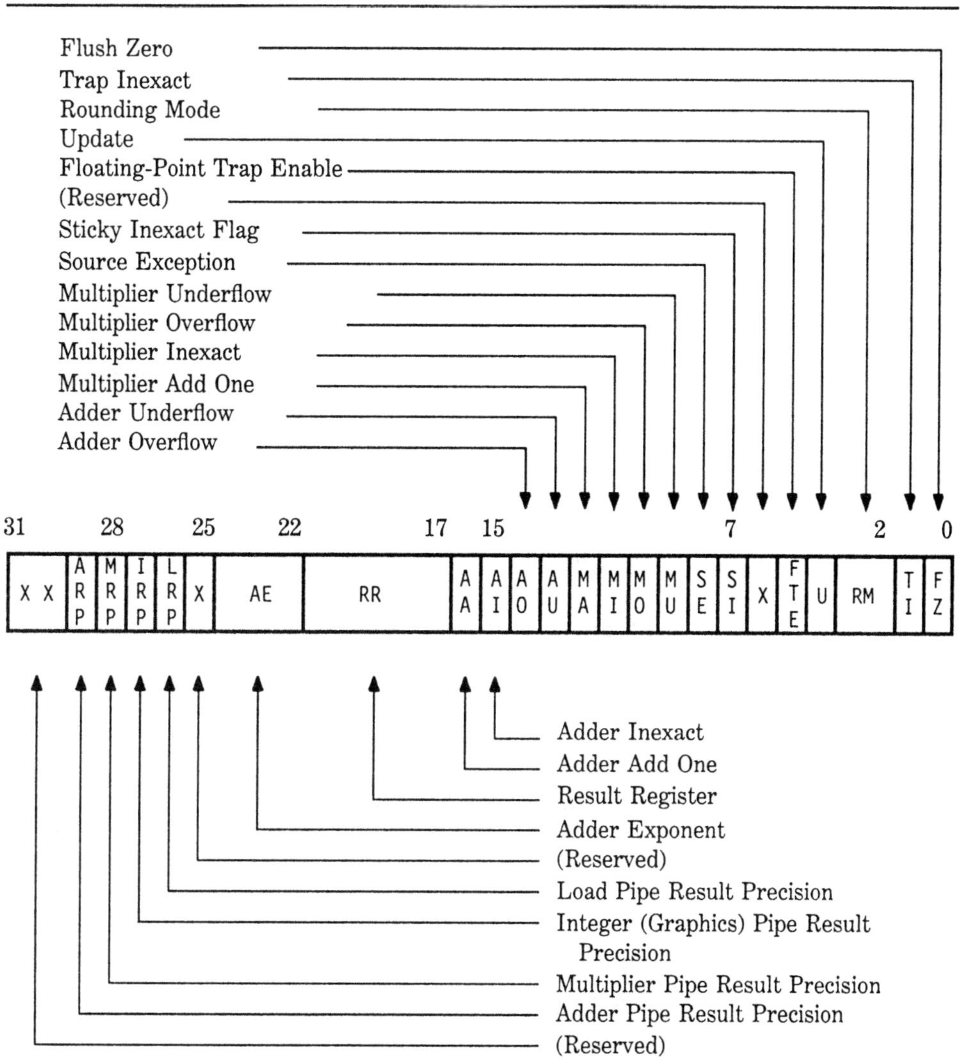

Figure 4-10. Floating-point status register

U-bit The U-bit (Update Bit), if set in the value that is stored in **fsr** by a **st.c** instruction, enables updating of the result-status bits (AE, AA, AI, AO, AU, MA, MI, MO, and MU) in the first stage of the floating-point adder

Table 4-8. Values of RM

Value	*Rounding Mode*	*Rounding Action*
00	Round to nearest or even	Closer to *b* of *a* or *c*; if equally close, select even number (the one whose least significant bit is zero).
01	Round down (toward $-\infty$)	*a*
10	Round up (toward $+\infty$)	*c*
11	Chop (toward zero)	Smaller in magnitude of *a* or *c*.

and multiplier pipelines. If this bit is clear, the result-status bits are unaffected by a **st.c** instruction; **st.c** ignores the corresponding bits in the value that is being loaded. An **st.c** always updates **fsr** bits 21...17 and 8...0 directly. The U-bit does not remain set; it always appears as zero when read. A trap handler that has interrupted a pipelined operation sets the U-bit to enable restoration of the result-status bits in the pipeline.

FTE The FTE (Floating-Point Trap Enable) bit, if clear, disables all floating-point traps (invalid input operand, overflow, underflow, and inexact result). Trap handlers clear the bit while saving and restoring the floating-point pipeline state and to produce NaN, infinite, or denormal results without generating traps.

SI SI (Sticky Inexact) is set when the last-stage result of either the multiplier or adder is inexact, for example, when either AI or MI is set. SI is "sticky" in the sense that it remains set until reset by software. AI and MI, on the other hand, can be changed by the subsequent floating-point instruction.

SE SE (Source Exception) is set when one of the source operands of a floating-point operation is invalid; it is cleared when all the input operands are valid. Invalid input operands include denormals, infinities, and all NaNs (both quiet and signaling). Trap-handler software can implement IEEE-standard results for operations on these values.

MA, MI, MO, MU, AA, AI, AO, AU, and AE When read from the **fsr**, the result-status bits MA, MI, MO, and MU (Multiplier Add One, Inexact, Overflow, and Underflow, respectively) describe the last-stage result of the multiplier.

When read from the **fsr**, the result-status bits AA, AI, AO, AU, and AE (Adder Add One, Inexact, Overflow, Underflow, and Exponent, respectively) describe the last-stage result of the adder. The high-order three bits of the 11-bit exponent of the adder result are stored in the AE field. The trap handler needs the AE bits when either overflow or underflow occurs with double-precision inputs and single-precision output.

After a floating-point operation in a given unit (adder or multiplier), the result-status bits of that unit are undefined until the point at which result exceptions are reported.

When written to the **fsr** with the U-bit set, the result-status bits are placed into the first stage of the adder and multiplier pipelines. When the processor executes pipelined operations, it propagates the result-status bits of a particular unit (multiplier or adder) one stage for each pipelined floating-point operation for that unit. When they reach the last stage, they replace the normal result-status bits in the **fsr**.

In a floating-point dual-operation instruction, for example add-and-multiply or subtract-and-multiply, both the multiplier and the adder may set exception bits. The result-status bits for a particular unit remain set until the next operation that uses that unit.

AA (Adder Add One), when set, indicates that the absolute value of the fraction of the result of an adder operation was increased by one, due to rounding. AA is not influenced by the sign of the result.

MA (Multiplier Add One), when set, indicates that the absolute value of the fraction of the result of a multiplier operation was increased by one, due to rounding. MA is not influenced by the sign of the result.

RR RR (Result Register) specifies which floating-point register (**f0-f31**) was the destination register when a result-exception trap occurred due to a scalar operation.

LRP, IRP, MRP, and ARP LRP (Load Pipe Result Precision), IRP (Integer (Graphics) Pipe Result Precision), MRP (Multiplier Pipe Result Precision), and ARP (Adder Pipe Result Precision) aid in restoring the pipeline state after a trap or process switch. Each defines the precision of the last-stage result in the corresponding pipeline. One of these bits is set when the result in the last stage of the corresponding pipeline is double-precision; it is cleared if the result is single-precision. These bits cannot be changed by software.

Memory Organization

Memory is a collection of sequential locations, each with a unique address and each capable of storing data. For modern computers, the amount of information at each unique address is eight bits, also called a byte. If data require more than one byte of storage, it can reside in multiple continuous bytes. Short words of two bytes, words of four bytes, double words of eight bytes, and quad words of 16 bytes are used to represent multibyte data values. Note that the i860 processor differs in vocabulary from *X*86 processors where two bytes represent a word, and four bytes a double word.

How multibyte values are represented in memory is an issue. Memory extends from the lowest address, zero, to the highest address, 4 gigabytes. The two ways possible to represent a multibyte data value for a word are illustrated in Figure 4-11. On the left is the big endian method where the high-order byte of the word is stored at the lowest byte address of the word. On the right is the little endian method where the high-order byte of the word is stored at the highest byte address of the word. Arguing which is the better method is like staring at the moon and arguing which end is the top.

Intel *X*86 processors operate entirely in a little endian mode, and Motorola 68K processors operate in a big endian mode. The i860 processor is primarily a little endian processor, but it includes a mode for

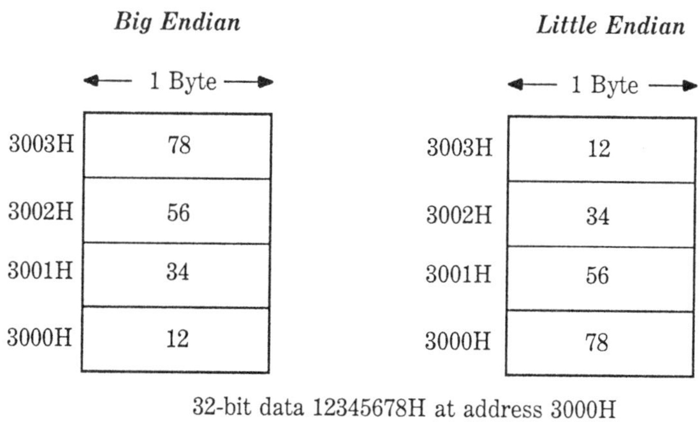

Figure 4-11. Big and little endian data representations

operating on big endian data. Big endian mode may be entered from supervisor mode by setting the BE bit of the **epsr** register. Big endian mode affects only data accesses. Instructions and page tables (during TLB processing) are accessed as little endian data regardless of the endian mode of the processor.

Big Endian Data on the i860 Microprocessor

To implement big endian addressing, the i860 processor complements the three lowest logical address bits, A2, A1, and A0. Complementing these three address bits alters what data are loaded into registers, and where data are stored from the registers, for 8-, 16-, and 32-bit accesses. By complementing the address bits, big endian mode affects which byte enable signals and which data lines are active during memory accesses. None of the other address bits are affected by big endian addressing.

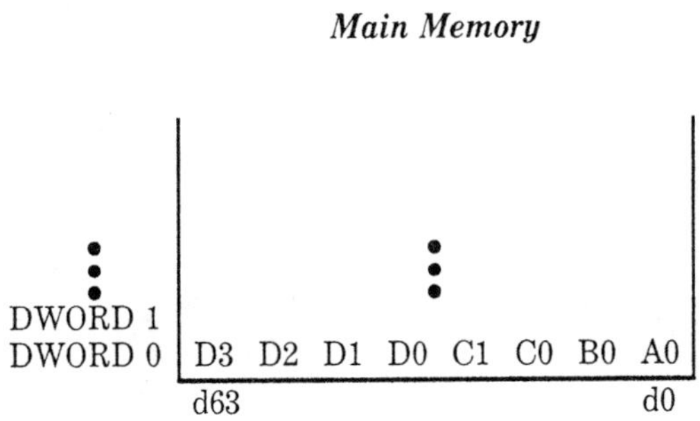

Figure 4-12. Memory data

Consider the 64-bit word stored at location 0 shown in Figure 4-12. The system memory is connected to the processor so that data lines D63 through D0 correspond to the bit positions indicated in the Figure. For a byte load from location 0, one byte will be loaded from memory into the lower eight bits of the destination register. The question remaining is—will it be the high-order byte D3H or the low-order byte A0H that is loaded into the register?

In little endian mode, the Byte Enables BE0# through BE7# are activated corresponding to locations at memory address 0 through 7. Therefore, a byte load from location 0 will activate BE0#, and the data will be read from data lines D7-D0. Big endian accesses complement the lower three address bits and the byte enables are activated inversely to the address accessed. So for a byte load from 0, address lines A2, A1 and A0 will be complemented to ones, and BE7# will be activated with data returned on data lines D63-D56. Referring to Figure 4-13, byte loads from location 0 load the lower eight bits of register **r16** with A0H for little endian accesses, and with D3H for big endian accesses. This is consistent with the earlier definition of big endian which stated that the high-order byte of the word is stored at the lowest address of the word.

Instruction	Little Endian Byte Enables (BE#)	Little Endian Data Bus (d63 … d0)	Little Endian r16 (d31 … d0)	Big Endian Byte Enables (BE#)	Big Endian Data Bus (d63 … d0)	Big Endian r16 (d31 … d0)
`ld.b 0(r0), r16`	0	A0	A0	7	D3	D3
`ld.b 1(r0), r16`	1	B0	B0	6	D2	D2
`ld.b 2(r0), r16`	2	C0	C0	5	D1	D1
`ld.b 3(r0), r16`	3	C1	C1	4	D0	D0
`ld.b 4(r0), r16`	4	D0	D0	3	C1	C1
`ld.b 5(r0), r16`	5	D1	D1	2	C0	C0
`ld.b 6(r0), r16`	6	D2	D2	1	B0	B0
`ld.b 7(r0), r16`	7	D3	D3	0	A0	A0
`ld.s 0(r0), r16`	1:0	B0 A0	B0 A0	7:6	D3 D2	D3 D2
`ld.s 2(r0), r16`	3:2	C1 C0	C1 C0	5:4	D1 D0	D1 D0
`ld.s 4(r0), r16`	5:4	D1 D0	D1 D0	3:2	C0 C1	C1 D0
`ld.s 6(r0), r16`	7:6	D3 D2	D3 D2	1:0	B0 A0	B0 A0
`ld.l 0(r0), r16`	3:0	C1 C0 B0 A0	C1 C0 B0 A0	7:4	D3 D2 D1 D0	D3 D2 D1 D0
`ld.l 4(r0), r16`	7:4	D3 D2 D1 D0	D3 D2 D1 D0	3:0	C1 C0 B0 A0	C1 C0 B0 A0

***Figure 4-13.** Little endian and big endian data loads (sign extension not shown)*

Figure 4-13 shows the byte enables activated, the data bus, and the register contents for byte, half-word, and word loads for both little endian and big endian accesses. All of the valid loads that correspond to the lowest 64 bits of memory are shown. Note that the bytes within a data item are never swapped. This relates to the byte ordering significance between the two modes being the same. Instead of being swapped, the bytes are shifted when passing between the register and the data bus.

For 64- and 128-bit values, little and big endian accesses are identical. For read accesses that are cached in the on-chip data cache, the entire 64 bits of data are read into the cache for each of the four cache reads. The data in the cache mirrors that of main memory. The shifting for big and little endian accesses occurs at the registers. For 8-, 16- and 32-bit I/O devices that are connected to the lowest bits of the data bus, big and little endian accesses can both access the device, but do so at different addresses. For example, an 8-bit I/O device connected to data lines D7-D0, which is accessed at address 06000H for little endian mode, will be accessed at address 06007H for big endian mode.

Writes occur from the register to the data bus and activate the byte enables to correspond to which data lines have valid data. In both big and little endian modes, the lower 8, 16, or 32 bits from the register are driven onto the data bus during writes. The data lines that the write data are output on, and the corresponding byte enables that are activated, follow the same pattern as in the read example shown earlier.

Although the mechanics of big and little endian mode are simple, managing the two modes at the program and operating system level is considerably more difficult. The operating system must ensure that data are always read and written in the same mode. Also, programs that operate on big endian data should read the operands at their corresponding operand length. This is necessary to avoid any improper byte swapping. For example, single-precision floating-point data should be accessed with **fld.l** when in big endian mode, rather than **fld.d** or **fld.q**.

Notations and Conventions

Throughout this book, i860 processor assembly language notation will be used in the example programs or program fragments. Each instruction's operation will include comments. Appendix A provides the full instruction set listed alphabetically and describes the instructions' operation fully.

Each instruction's operation is described with a Pascal-like notation. The symbols and notation have the following meanings:

- A <-- B indicates that the value of B is assigned to A.
- Compound statements are enclosed between the keywords of the "if" statement (IF . . . , THEN . . . , ELSE . . . , FI) or of the "do" statement (DO . . . , OD).
- The operator + + indicates autoincrement addressing.
- Register names and instruction mnemonics are printed in text in a bold typestyle to make them stand out; for example, **dirbase**. The programming languages may require the use of lowercase letters.

Reserved Bits and Software Compatibility

In many registers and memory layout descriptions, certain bits are marked as *reserved* or *undefined.* When bits are thus marked, it is essential for compatibility with future processors that software not utilize these bits. The i860 processor has an advantage over previous Intel processors in that there is a register that software can read in order to determine the processor type and stepping number (see **epsr**). Software should follow these guidelines in dealing with reserved or undefined bits.

- Do not depend on the states of any reserved or undefined bits when testing the values of the registers that contain such bits. Mask out the reserved and undefined bits before testing.
- Do not depend on the states of any reserved or undefined bits when storing them into memory or in another register.
- Do not depend on the ability to retain information written into any reserved or undefined bits.
- When reloading a register, or loading a register for the first time, always load the reserved bits and undefined bits with the values previously fetched from the register.

Caution: As warned by Intel, "Depending on the values of reserved or undefined bits makes software dependent upon the unspecified manner in which the i860 microprocessor handles these bits. Depending upon values of reserved or undefined bits risks making software incompatible with future processors that define usages for these bits. *Avoid any software dependence upon the state of reserved or undefined bits.*"

CHAPTER 5
RISC CORE OPERATIONS

The RISC core is responsible for the fundamental operation of the processor. In addition to fetching integer and floating-point instructions, the core executes load, store, arithmetic, logical, and branch instructions. It performs all of the memory load and store operations including those to the floating-point registers.

This chapter explains how the core instructions operate. Each class of instructions is described along with tips for maximum performance programming. Example program sequences are included to reinforce the explanations. The core instructions used for specific operating system-related features are explained in Chapter 9, "Operating System Support."

Load/Store Architecture

All data operations are performed on operands that are in the processor's registers. Thus, the only memory operations provided are load and store instructions. This is referred to as a load/store architecture and has the advantages described earlier in Chapter 3, "i860 Processor Architecture Overview." Figure 5-1 shows each of the load and store instructions. The pixel store instruction, **pst**, will be described in Chapter 7, "Graphics Programming."

Integer Loads and Stores

The integer load and store instructions access memory with one addressing mode that implements several common ones. The basic load

Mnemonic	*Description*	*Operation*	*Syntax*
fld.y	F-P Load	*fdest <--* *mem[src1 + src2]*	**fld.y** *isrc1(isrc2),fdest* **fld.y** *#const(isrc2),fdest* **fld.y** *isrc1(isrc2)++,fdest* **fld.y** *#const(isrc2)++,fdest*
fst.y	F-P Store	*mem[src1 + src2]* *<-- freg*	**fst.y** *freg,isrc1(isrc2)* **fst.y** *freg,#const(isrc2)* **fst.y** *freg,src1(isrc2)++* **fst.y** *freg,#const(isrc2)++*
ld.x	Load Integer	*idest <--* *mem[src1 + src2]*	**ld.x** *isrc1(isrc2),idest* **ld.x** *#const(isrc2),idest*
pfld.z	Pipelined F-P Load	*fdest <--* *mem[third previous* **pfld's** *(src1 +src2)*]	**pfld.z** *isrc1(isrc2),fdest* **pfld.z** *#const(isrc2),fdest* **pfld.z** *isrc1(isrc2)++,fdest* **pfld.z** *#const(isrc2)++,fdest*
pst.d	Pixel Store		**pst.d** *freg,#const(isrc2)* **pst.d** *freg,#const(isrc2)++*
st.x	Store Integer	*mem[const + src2]* *<-- isrc1*	**st.x** *isrc1,#const(isrc2)*

Figure 5-1. Load and store instructions

instruction format uses *isrc2* as a base address register, and adds an offset to determine the full address. The register fields *isrc1, isrc2,* and *idest* can be any of the 32 integer registers, while *const* is a 16-bit offset embedded as an immediate field in the instruction.

The integer register **r0** always contains the value 0. This aids in implementing instruction and addressing variations without having separate instructions. The following load examples show the basic available addressing modes: immediate, register indirect, register indirect with immediate offset, and register indirect with index addressing.

```
ld.x    64(r0), r15        ; r15 <-- memory.x [64]
ld.x    0(r14), r15        ; r15 <-- memory.x [r14]
ld.x    8(r14), r15        ; r15 <-- memory.x [8 + r14]
ld.x    r13(r14), r15      ; r15 <-- memory.x [r13 + r14]
```

Store instructions can implement the first three of the four addressing modes shown here. Remember that the store instruction reads a value out of the integer register file. Because the integer register file has only two read ports, a store using register indirect with index addressing mode is not possible, as it would require accessing a third register's read port.

The integer load and store instruction can specify data of 8-, 16-, and 32-bit values. For 8- and 16-bit values, the operation occurs with the lower bits of the register. Loads of 8 and 16 bits are sign extended to fill the 32 bits. This allows the integer addition or subtraction to always operate on the full 32 bits of the register without concern for how the data was represented in memory.

Data must be aligned in memory to correspond to the effective address boundary, for example, 16-bit values at even addresses and 32-bit values on quad-aligned address boundaries. If an access to non-aligned data is attempted, a data access trap will occur.

Load instructions have at least a one-clock delay before the loaded data can be accessed. For best performance, the instruction following the load (called the load-delay-slot) should not use the destination of the load as a source operand. Note that for maximum performance, a load instruction should not directly follow a store that is expected to hit in the cache.

Floating-Point Loads and Stores

The i860 processor's RISC core is also responsible for performing the memory operations for the floating-point registers. There are two separate types of floating-point memory instructions. The first is the **fld** and **fst** instructions, and the second is a pipelined floating-point load instruction, **pfld**.

The **fld** and **fst** instructions use the four addressing modes of the load instruction, and have an additional autoincrement addressing mode designated by the **++**. Autoincrement addressing adds *isrc1* to *isrc2* to calculate the address for the memory access. The result of the addition is stored into *isrc2*. This addressing mode supports accessing arrays of data by avoiding a separate instruction for address computation. The increment value can be adjusted for any size data stride. For example, to access every fourth entry of an array of single-precision floating-point values, an increment value of 16 would be used (every fourth entry of an array of four byte elements).

The **fld** and **fst** load and store operations can specify 32-, 64-, or 128-bit values. Each floating-point register is 32 bits wide. When accessing 64-bit values, the i860 processor uses an even/odd pair of registers, and 128-bit accesses use a set of four registers. The **fld** or **fst** instruction must designate the lowest register number of the set.

The multiregister loads and stores can be performed independent of the data type being accessed. The 128-bit data cache path allows the RISC core to load or store up to four 32-bit registers in a single clock cycle. The 128 bits of data may represent four single-precision values, two double-precision values, 16 single byte values, or any sequential stored values. If the data is not in the cache, then the processor will access main memory to retrieve the requested data. The processor's bus control will break the 128-bit access into two 64-bit processor bus accesses.

Pipelined Floating-Point Load

The pipelined floating-point load instruction, **pfld**, loads the floating-point registers from external memory without the data being placed in the cache. This allows data that will be referenced only once to be loaded from external memory with the pipelined load, while data that is being reused can be accessed with the nonpipelined load and kept in the onboard cache. The pipelined load instruction allows each of the addressing modes that the regular floating-point load instruction does, but restricts the data widths to 32- and 64-bit loads.

The **pfld** uses a three-stage load pipeline that serves to hide the memory latency. Hiding the latency is especially important for **pfld** instructions as they are designed to access data from off-chip memory, not from the cache. Each **pfld** initiates a memory access, advances the load pipeline one stage, and stores the result from the load address that was started three instructions previously. Therefore, the first three **pfld** instructions (that are not returning requested data) specify **f0**, which is always zero, as the destination. The **pfld** instruction can specify 32- or 64-bit data where 64-bit data uses an even/odd register pair.

Figure 5-2 illustrates the **pfld** three-stage pipeline. Here, register indirect with index addressing is used to access 64-bit quantities from memory. The **pfld** instructions each place an address on the processor's

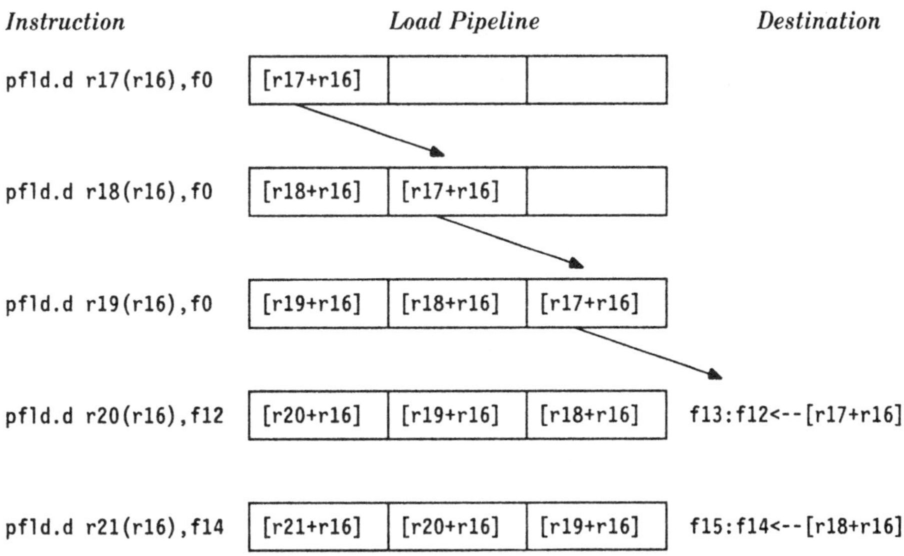

Figure 5-2. Pipelined floating-point load three-stage pipeline

external bus, advance the load pipeline one stage, and store the last stage of the load pipeline into the destination register. Figure 5-2 uses the memory address expressed by the contents of registers to represent the data moving through the pipeline. As a result of the pipelining, the data from the first instruction's memory access is not stored to the destination register until the fourth instruction. The destination register in the instruction specifies only **f12**, but the double-precision value is stored to the **f13:f12** register pair.

The processor's external bus is designed to support the three outstanding cycles possible with successive **pfld** instructions. Because the returned data will not be cached, the processor loads the requested data and does not wait for any additional cache miss processing to fill the cache line. If a **pfld** instruction attempts to load from an address stored in the on-chip cache, the memory cycle will not appear on the bus, and the cache will supply the data, although at a two-clock penalty.

Figure 5-3 shows the **pfld** operation along with autoincrement addressing. Autoincrement addressing increments the base register before

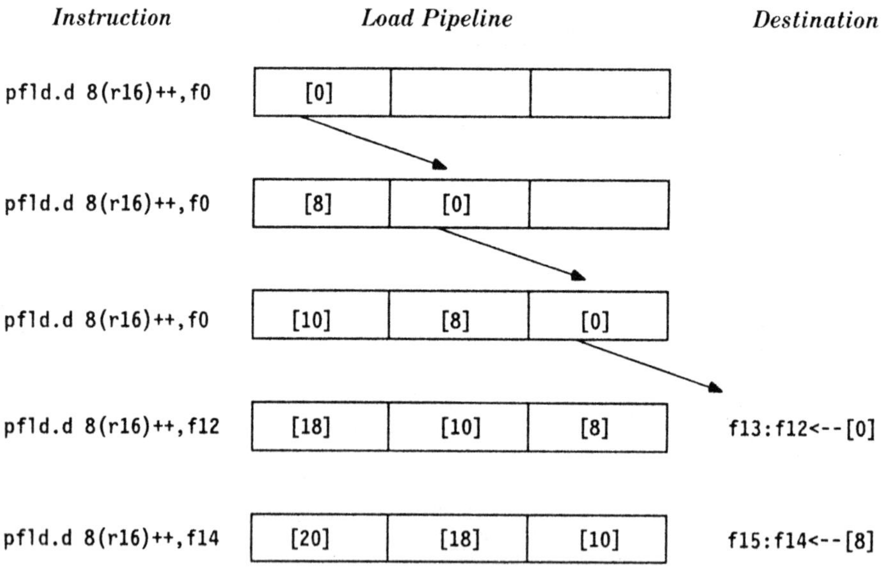

Figure 5-3. Pipelined floating-point loads with autoincrement addressing

each load. In this example, the base register **r16** starts at –8. Each **pfld** instruction increments **r16** by a constant, 8 in this case, so that a new address is formed. This is useful to access arrays of floating-point data, or, combined with store operations, to implement an efficient block memory move. Figure 5-3 uses the memory address expressed in hexadecimal to represent the data moving through the pipeline.

The **fld** instruction does not affect the **pfld** pipeline, or interfere with **pfld** instructions in progress. The pipelined and nonpipelined loads can be intermixed as shown in Figure 5-4. In this example, register **r18** designates the base of a data array of values that will be reused in a computation, and **r17** designates the base of a data array where the values will be used only once. Accesses to the **r18** array are expected to

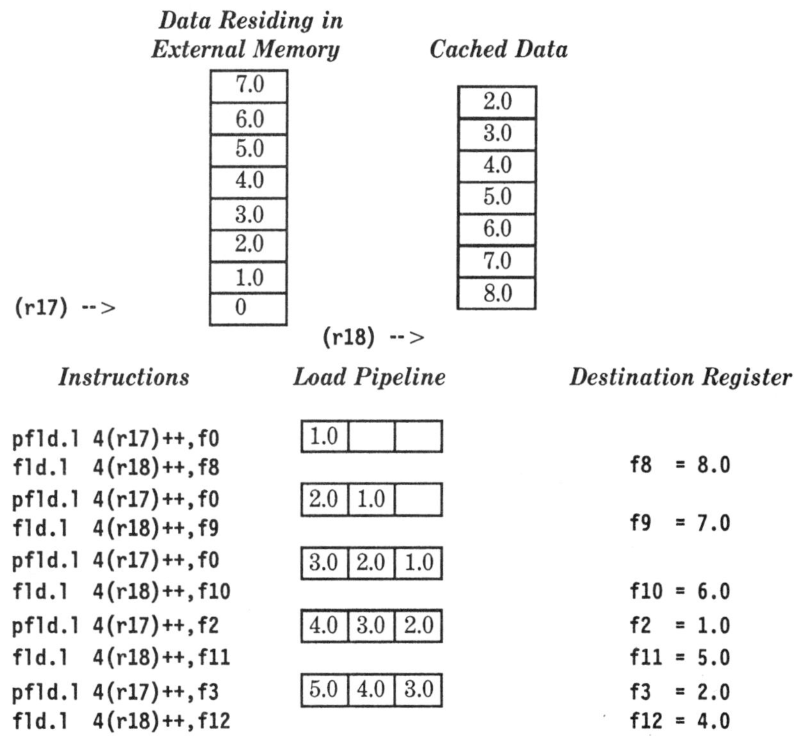

Figure 5-4. Mixing pipelined floating-point loads with standard floating-point loads

hit in the cache, while the **r17** array accesses should go to main memory. Note that this example illustrates single-precision data values moving through the pipeline. This pattern of intermixing cached and noncached memory accesses is common for matrix operations.

The **pfld** instruction transfers data from the head of the load pipeline into the destination register, advances the load pipeline, and sends out the address for the next data to be loaded. Because the instruction is updating the destination register from an on-chip load pipeline, the instruction can operate in one clock cycle. The **fld** instruction transfers the data from the cache into the data registers. If a **fld** instruction misses the cache, memory operations for the cache line fill will occur between the two **pfld** memory loads. When **fld** instructions do not find the requested data in the cache, the processor stops execution and waits for the data to be returned from external memory.

Where there is one load-delay-slot following integer register loads, there are two load-delay-slots following floating-point register loads. Therefore, for maximum performance, the destination of a **fld** or **pfld** instruction should not be referenced as a source operand in either of the next two instructions. As with the integer register loads, a **fld** instruction should not follow a store that is expected to hit in the data cache. However, there is no performance impact for a **pfld** instruction following a store hit; since the **pfld**, although it always checks the cache, is not expected to find the data it is accessing in the cache. If the **pfld** instruction does hit in the data cache, there will be a two-clock penalty.

The external bus of the i860 processor returns data every two clock cycles. Therefore, sequences of many **pfld** instructions, which each take one clock to execute, will cause the RISC core execution to wait for data accesses to complete on the processor's bus. However, the processor can support three **pfld** instructions issued in successive clock cycles without stalling.

In addition to load and stores from the registers, the core unit has an **ixfr** instruction that transfers data from the integer registers to the floating-point registers. Like other floating-point register loads, the **ixfr** instruction has two delay slots following its execution. The counterpart instruction for transferring data from the floating-point registers to the integer registers is the **fxfr** instruction, which is carried out by the graphics unit.

Register Operations

Once data has been loaded into the integer registers, the RISC core can perform any of the integer register operations. These register operations are performed in one clock cycle, and the result can be used as a source in the instruction that immediately follows. The i860 processor includes arithmetic, logical, and shift instructions of the form

operation *isrc1, isrc2, idest*

The three operands per instruction allow the operation to specify two source registers (or a source register and an immediate for *isrc1*), and to store the result to a third register without destroying the source values. Either of the source registers can be designated as the destination register if the source data is not going to be reused.

Arithmetic Operations

The i860 processor performs the addition and subtraction instructions as listed in Figure 5-5. For subtractions, note that the immediate value can be used as the subtrahend or the minuend. For example:

r6 = 2 − **r5**	is encoded as	**subs** 2, **r5**,**r6**
r6 = **r5** − 2	is encoded as	**adds** −2, **r5**,**r6**

The subtrahend can also be a negative number where the instruction

```
subs -1, r5, r6          ;  r6  <--  -1 - r5
```

yields the one's complement of **r5**.

There are both signed and unsigned versions of the add and subtract instructions. Of course, the arithmetic instructions affect the Condition Code flag (CC) and the Overflow Flag (OF). The signed and unsigned instruction versions differ only in the setting of the flags. Both instruction versions sign extend the immediate value if one is used.

Instruction	*Description*	*Operation*	*Syntax*
adds	Add signed	*dest* <-- *src1* + *src2*	**adds** *isrc1,isrc2,idest* **adds** *#constA,isrc2,idest*
addu	Add unsigned	*dest* <-- *src1* + *src2*	**addu** *isrc1,isrc2,idest* **addu** *#constA,isrc2,idest*
subs	Subtract signed	*dest* <-- *src1* – *src2*	**subs** *isrc1,isrc2,idest* **subs** *#constA,isrc2,idest*
subu	Subtract unsigned	*dest* <-- *src1* – *src2*	**subu** *isrc1,isrc2,idest* **subu** *#constA,isrc2,idest*

Figure 5-5. Integer arithmetic instructions

If **r0** is specified as the destination register, the result is discarded, and the instruction implements the compare function. For example: **subs r4, r5, r0** will set the Condition Code (CC) if the contents of **r5** are greater than those of **r4**. The CC is used for the conditional branch instructions that are discussed later.

The Overflow Flag (OF) can be checked with the instruction **intovr**. If the OF bit is set, the **intovr** instruction causes a trap. Compilers can use this instruction for languages that check for overflow. Many programming languages, such as C, do not check for overflow.

Logical Instructions

The logical instructions include the **and**, **andnot**, **or**, and **xor** operations as listed in Figure 5-6. The operations are performed bitwise on all 32 bits. The functions of the logical operations are shown in Figure 5-7. The logical operations are performed on two source registers with the results going to a result register (the result register may be one of the source registers). Also, one of the source registers can be replaced by an immediate value. Immediate values are zero-extended to 32 bits. Note

Instruction	*Description*	*Operation*		*Syntax*
and	and	*dest* <-- *src1* **AND** *src2*	**and**	*isrc1,isrc2,idest*
			and	*#constL,isrc2,idest*
andh	and high	*dest* <-- *(#const << 16)* **AND** *src2*	**andh**	*#constL,isrc2,idest*
andnot	and not	*dest* <-- **NOT** *(src1)* **AND** *src2*	**andnot**	*isrc1,isrc2,idest*
			andnot	*#constL,isrc2,idest*
andnoth	and not high	*dest* <-- **NOT** *(~(#const << 16))* **AND** *src2*	**andnoth**	*#constL,isrc2,idest*
or	or	*dest* <-- *src1* **OR** *src2*	**or**	*isrc,isrc2,idest*
			or	*#constL,isrc2,idest*
orh	or high	*dest* <-- *(#const << 16)* **OR** *src2*	**orh**	*#constL,irsc2,idest*
xor	exclusive or	*dest* <-- *src1* **XOR** *src2*	**xor**	*isrc1,isrc2,idest*
			xor	*#constL,isrc2,idest*
xorh	xor high	*dest* <-- *(#const << 16)* **XOR** *src2*	**xorh**	*#constL,isrc2,idest*

Figure 5-6. Logical instructions

that the **andnot** instruction is not a nand (not-and) function—it inverts the *src1* value before **and**ing, but leaves *isrc2* intact.

Each logical instruction includes a "high" variation, designated by the **h** in the instruction, where the immediate field is used as the high-order 16 bits, and zeros are used as the low-order 16 bits. This allows logical operations to be performed on the upper half of the register while using a 16-bit immediate value. Be careful using the **andh** instruction—since the low 16 bits generated by the processor will be zero, the low half of the result will be cleared.

Because an instruction format contains 32 bits, a full 32-bit immediate value cannot be embedded in a single instruction. Moving a 32-bit immediate value into a register can be done with the logical instruction **orh**. For example, to move the 32-bit hex value 12345678H into **r5**, first

and

X	Y	Z
0	0	0
0	1	0
1	0	0
1	1	1

or

X	Y	Z
0	0	0
0	1	1
1	0	1
1	1	1

xor

X	Y	Z
0	0	0
0	1	1
1	0	1
1	1	0

andnot

X	Y	Z
0	0	0
0	1	1
1	0	0
1	1	0

Figure 5-7. Bitwise logical operations

load the lower half of the register, then use the **orh** instruction to modify the upper half of the register as shown here:

```
or   0x5678, r0, r5 ;    r5 <-- 5678H
orh  0x1234, r5, r5 ;    r5 <-- 12345678H
```

Bit operations can be implemented using logical operations. By using an immediate constant that contains a one in the bit position to be operated on and zeros elsewhere, the bit operations shown in Figure 5-8 can be performed in one instruction. The **h** version of the instructions allows a bit in any of the upper 16 positions to be operated on, while the non-**h** version manipulates the lower 16.

Clearing a bit is performed with the **andnot** instruction where *src1* has a one in the bit position to be cleared (use the **h** version if the bit is in the upper half of the register). Although this could also be done by **and** with all ones and a zero as the mask bit position, it would take multiple instructions. For example, setting up a mask of all ones and a zero in the mask bit takes one or two instructions to perform; then performing the **and** operation is an additional instruction.

Some masking operations can be performed in one instruction. For example, if a byte is loaded from memory, it will be sign extended automatically. To convert the byte back to its unsigned form requires masking-out the high-order bits as shown here (assume the byte's

Bit Operation	*Equivalent Logical Operation*
Set bit	**or**
Clear bit	**andnot**
Complement bit	**xor**
Test bit	**and** (CC set if bit is clear)

Figure 5-8. Bit operations

address is already in **r19**):

```
ld.b  0(r19), r20         ;  r20 <-- memory [r19]
and   0x00FF, r20, r20    ;  r20 <-- r20 & 0x000000FF
```

In addition to performing the designated operation, the logical instructions set the CC bit if the operation result is zero. This process can be used for the conditional branch instructions that are explained later in this chapter.

Shift Instructions

The final class of integer operations is the shift instructions listed in Figure 5-9. The i860 processor can barrel-shift up to 31 bit positions in one cycle. The instructions include shift left (**shl**), shift right (**shr**), shift right arithmetic (**shra**), and shift right double (**shrd**).

For the **shl**, **shr**, and **shra** instructions, the number of bit positions to shift is specified in *src1.* Left shifting is identical for arithmetic and logical shifts. The **shl** instruction fills right-most bits with zeros while the **shr** instruction fills the left-most bits with zeros. The **shra** instruction duplicates the sign bit, bit 31, to the right for the number of bits shifted.

Instruction	*Description*	*Operation*	*Syntax*
shl	Shift left	*dest <-- src2 << {src1 bits}*	**shl** *isrc1,isrc2,idest* **shl** *#constA,isrc2,idest*
shr	Shift right	*dest <-- src2 >> {src1 bits}*	**shr** *isrc1,isrc2,idest* **shr** *#constA,isrc2,idest*
shra	**shr** arithmetic	*dest <-- src2 >> {arith. src1 bits}*	**shra** *isrc1,isrc2,idest* **shra** *#constA,isrc2,idest*
shrd	**shr** double	*dest <-- src1:src2 >> {(SC) bits}*	**shrd** *isrc1,isrc2,idest*

Figure 5-9. Shift instructions

Shift instructions can be used to sign extend 8- or 16-bit integers that are generated internally (values loaded from memory are automatically sign extended). The sign extension is performed first by left-justifying the value, then right-justifying the value, duplicating the sign bit in the upper bit positions. As an example of sign extending, an 8-bit integer already in **r16** is programmed as:

```
shl   24, r16, r16   ; r16 <--  [r16] << {24}
shra  24, r16, r16   ; r16 <--  [r16] >> {24}
```

In this example, if the data in **r16** starts as 000000C4H, the shift left by 24 results in **r16** equaling C4000000H. The arithmetic shift right duplicates the sign bit, and **r16** becomes FFFFFFC4H, thus completing the sign extension of byte C4H.

In addition to the normal shifting operation, the **shr** instruction loads the *src1* value into the SC (Shift Count) field in the **psr** control register. This field is used by the **shrd** instruction, which concatenates two registers and shifts them into a third register. For example, if **r1** contains 55555555H and **r2** contains 66666666H, the following example results in **r3** containing 55556666H. The **shrd** operation is illustrated in Figure 5-10.

```
shr   0x10, r0, r0    ;  SC <-- 16
shrd  r1, r2, r3      ;  r3 <-- [shift right by 16] r1::r2
```

```
shr   Count r0,r0    //Load SC in PSR
shrd  r1,r2,r3       //Shift r1:r2 Right by SC
```

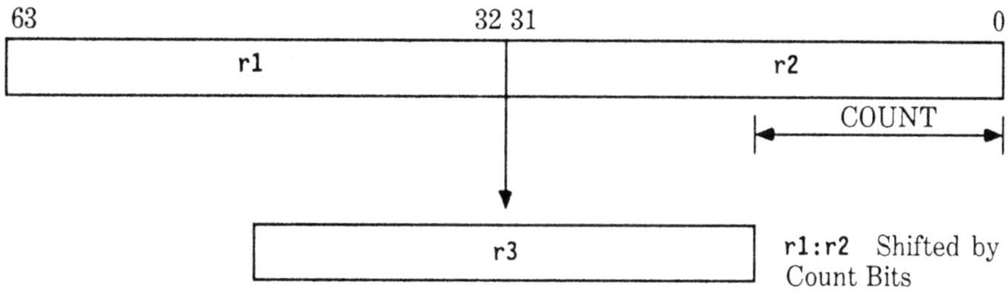

Figure 5-10. Double shift example

The **shrd** instruction is also used to implement a rotate function. By specifying the same register for both *isrc1* and *isrc2*, the value is rotated to the right by the number in SC, and stored in *rdest*.

Because the shift instructions do not affect the flags, they are used to implement the **nop** instruction and the integer register-to-register move pseudo-instruction. The assembler allows you to specify the move instruction **mov r3, r4,** which is coded and implemented as **shl r0, r3, r4.** An integer **nop** is coded and implemented as **shl r0, r0, r0** while a floating-point **nop, fnop,** is **shrd r0, r0, r0.** By using an integer instruction for **fnop**, the floating-point pipelines and registers are not disturbed. The need for **fnop** is explained in Chapter 8, "Programming for Parallelism," along with dual-instruction mode.

Branch and Call Instructions

Branch instructions change the sequential execution of a program. Call instructions also change sequential execution, but they also save an address to return to when the call is completed. In order to prevent breaks in the processor's pipeline, most of the branch and call instructions execute the next immediate instruction, referred to as the branch-delay-slot, before the branch takes effect. The control transfer instructions available on the i860 processor are shown in Figure 5-11.

Unconditional

The i860 processor includes four unconditional delayed branches; **br, bri, call,** and **calli.** The **br** (branch) and **call** are direct transfers where a 26-bit offset is specified as part of the instruction. The offset is in units of instructions, not bytes, allowing a 256 MB range. The **bri** (branch indirect) and **calli** (call indirect) are indirect transfers and use the contents of a register as the target, thus allowing a full 32-bit address specification.

In addition to changing the instruction flow, the **call** and **calli** instructions save the address of the second instruction after the **call** or **calli** (the one directly after the **call** or **calli** being the delay instruction) in register **r1**. This is used as the return address for the subroutine by specifying **bri r1**.

Because the instruction following branch and call instructions is always executed, the processor begins fetching the instruction from the branch target while the instruction immediately following the branch is executed. Figure 5-12 illustrates how the processor's pipeline is kept full for the unconditional delayed branch and delayed call instructions. To make use of the branch-delay slot, an instruction that is from the code block leading up to the branch may be moved into the delay slot. Alternatively, the destination of the branch or call can be copied into the

Inst.	*Description*	*Operation*	*Syntax*
bc	Branch on CC	*If CC goto offset*	**bc** *lbroff*
bc.t*	**bc** taken	*If CC goto offset*	**bc.t** *lbroff*
bla*	Branch on LCC w/add	*If LCC goto offset and add. Set LCC conditionally*	**bla** *isrc1,isrc2,sbroff*
bnc	Branch on not CC	*If not CC goto offset*	**bnc** *lbroff*
bnc.t*	**bnc** taken	*If not CC goto offset*	**bnc.t** *lbroff*
br*	Branch direct	*goto offset*	**br** *lbroff*
bri*	Branch indirect	*goto mem[src1]*	**bri** *isrc1*
bte	Branch if equal	*If src1 = src2 goto offset*	**bte** *isrc1,isrc2,sbroff* **bte** *#sconst,isrc2,sbroff*
btne	Branch if not equal	*If src1 ≠ src2 goto offset*	**btne** *isrc1,isrc2,sbroff* **btne** *#sconst,isrc2,sbroff*
call*	Subroutine call	*goto offset, save return*	**call** *lbroff*
calli*	Call indirect	*goto mem[src1], save return*	**calli** *isrc1*
intovr	Trap on Overflow	*If PSR(OF) = 1, goto 0xFFFFFF00*	**intovr**
trap	Software trap	*goto 0xFFFFFF00*	**trap** *isrc1,isrc2,idest*

Figure 5-11. Control transfer instructions (*indicates a delayed branch)

branch-delay-slot, and the target adjusted by one instruction. If no useful instruction can be found for the delay slot, a **nop** may be inserted.

Conditional

In addition to the branch instructions that always change the sequence of execution, there are variations that check a condition or comparison before deciding to change from sequential execution. Optimal programming for sequences that contain conditional branches is more difficult than with unconditional branches. To support this, the i860 processor includes branch instructions with and without the delay slots. By examining the program, the compiler can predict if the branch is more likely to be taken, or not taken during execution.

Program Instruction Sequence

```
            .
            .
            .
      shl
      br    LABEL
      addu
      xor
            .
            .
            .

LABEL: subu
      and
```

Processor Execution Sequence

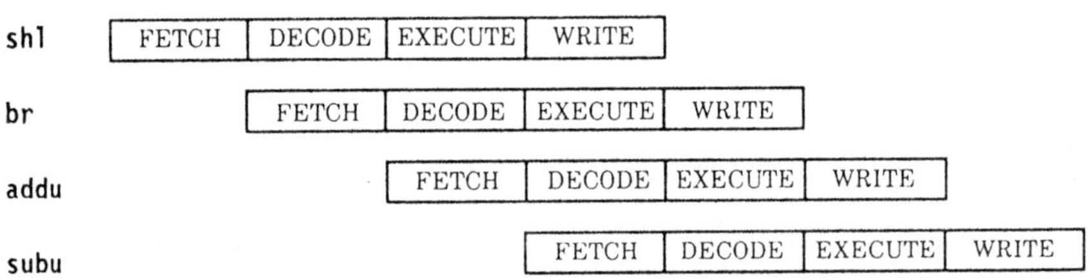

Figure 5-12. Delayed branching—unconditional branch

The conditional branches that rely on the CC bit are the **bc** (branch on condition) and the **bnc** (branch on not condition) and include both delayed and nondelayed versions. The delayed version is indicated with a **.t**. Conditional branches that are most often taken benefit from the branch-delay slot. Conditional branches that are most often not taken are better coded with the nondelayed branch version.

If a conditional branch instruction is more likely to be taken, such as at the bottom of a loop, the delayed form should be used. This allows the program to execute a useful instruction in the branch-delay slot while program execution is transferring to the beginning of the loop. As shown in Figure 5-13a, the pipeline remains full when the delayed branch is taken. When the conditional branch is not taken, the loop takes the fall-through path, and execution continues at the instruction beyond the branch-delay slot. As shown in Figure 5-13b, although the instruction in the branch-delay slot has already been fetched, its execution is not performed during the not taken delayed conditional branch. This is called *squashing* the instruction.

When the branch is not taken for a conditional delayed branch instruction, squashing causes a one-clock delay in the pipeline. This is because the instruction in the delay slot is fetched before the processor knows it is going to be squashed. If the branch is to be taken more times than not taken, the one-clock squash penalty is encountered in less than half of the branch execution occurrences. Squashing the instruction following the not taken conditional delay branch instruction allows the instruction at the branch target to be "moved" (or "copied" if other parts of the program expect to see the instruction at the original target) to the delay slot, with the target adjusted by one instruction.

For those cases where the branch is likely to not be taken, the nondelayed version allows more efficient coding. As shown in Figure 5-14a, when the nondelay conditional branch is not taken, no pipeline disruptions are caused in the pipeline and execution continues sequentially. Figure 5-14b shows the one-stage penalty that the pipeline incurs when a nondelay conditional branch is taken. This causes the next sequential instruction, which has already been fetched, to be squashed. Having both the delayed and nondelayed versions of conditional branches available reduces the number of pipeline stalls that occur due to conditional branching.

Many of the needed branch idioms can be implemented by choosing an arithmetic or a logical operation followed by a **bc** or a **bnc** instruction. Figure 5-15 shows the arithmetic operations that can be implemented with a constant, a variable, and an associated conditional branch instruction. To maximize performance, an unrelated instruction, which does not affect the CC bit, should be inserted between an arithmetic and condi-

Program Instruction Sequence

```
                .
                .
                .
          shl
          bc.t   LABEL
          addu
          xor
          and
                .
                .
                .
   LABEL:  subu
```

Processor Execution Sequence

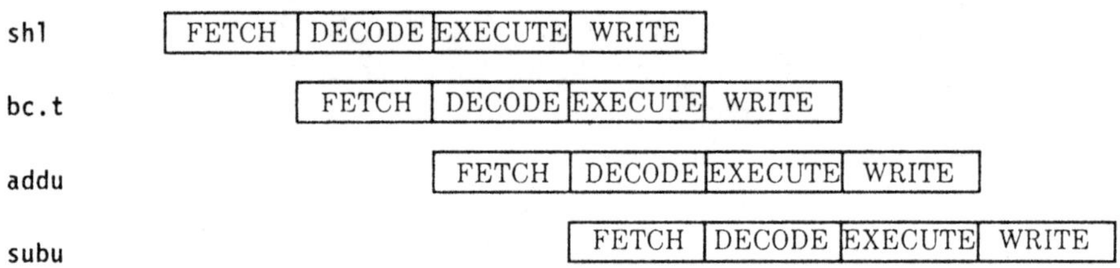

(a) Delayed branch taken

Processor Execution Sequence

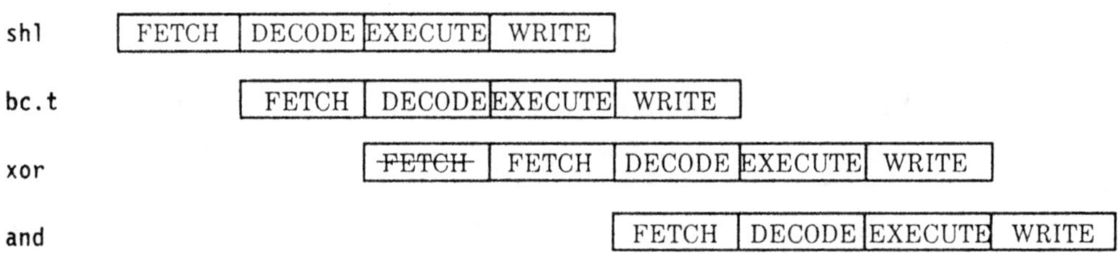

(b) Delayed branch not taken

Figure 5-13. Branch prediction with delayed branch instructions

tional branch instruction. This is because modification of the CC bit by arithmetic operations will delay a conditional branch decision in the instruction directly following the arithmetic operation. For logical

Program Instruction Sequence

```
            .
            .
            .
        shl
        bc    LABEL
        addu
        xor
        and
            .
            .
            .
LABEL:  subu
        shr
```

Processor Execution Sequence

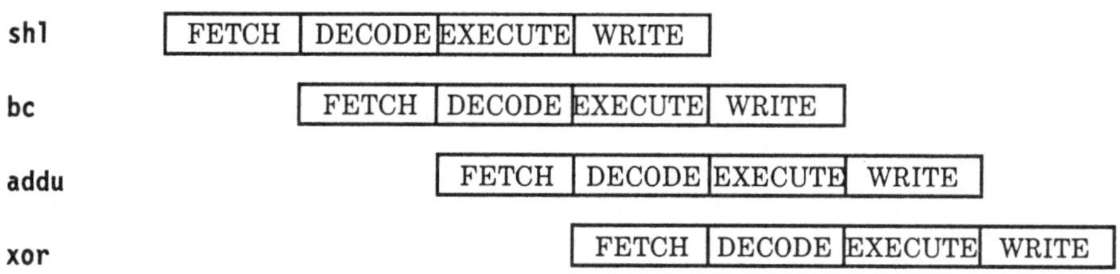

(a) Nondelayed branch not taken

Processor Execution Sequence

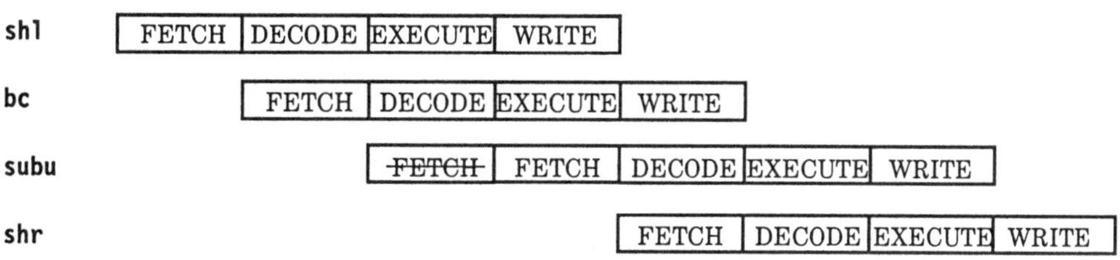

(b) Nondelayed branch taken

Figure 5-14. Branch prediction with nondelayed branch instructions

Condition	*Encoding*	*Branch When True* *Signed*	*Unsigned*
var ≤ *const*	**subs** *const, var*	bnc	
	subu *const, var*		bc
var < *const*	**adds** *-const, var*	bc	
	addu *-const, var**		bnc
var ≥ *const*	**adds** *-const, var*	bnc	
	addu *-const, var**		bc
var > *const*	**subs** *const, var*	bc	
	subu *const, var*		bnc

*Valid only when *const* > 0

Figure 5-15. Arithmetic compare and branch idioms

operations, there is no delay for affecting the CC bit and a conditional branch instruction may directly follow. Logical operations set the CC bit if the result of their operation is zero, and clear the CC bit otherwise.

There is also a nondelay branch instruction that branches on a *compare-for-equality* operation. The **bte** (branch and test equal) and **btne** (branch and test not equal) operations do register-to-register comparisons (or a register compare with a 5-bit immediate). Where appropriate, the equality branches can replace a two-instruction sequence (arithmetic/logical instruction and conditional branch sequence). Although still sufficient for most branches, note that the offset is reduced to 16 bits (which is 64K instructions, or 256 KB).

Branch-loop-and-add (Bla)

Finally, there is a loop control instruction, called **bla**, that uses its own Condition Code in the **psr** called Loop-Condition-Code (LCC). The **bla** instruction is a delayed branch that performs a conditional branch-on-LCC, an **add**, and updates the LCC in the same instruction. Because **bla** tests LCC before modifying it, an extra **bla** is needed to initialize the LCC before the **bla** that performs the looping. Loops that use **bla** must avoid any call or branch to routines that also use **bla**, thus modifying the LCC value.

```
// Write zeros to an array of 16 single-precision numbers
// Starting address of array is already in r4

      adds  -1,   r0,          r5    // r5 <-- loop increment
      or    15,   r0,          r6    // r6 <-- loop count -1
      bla   r5,   r6,   CLEAR_ LOOP  // One time to initialize LCC
      addu  -4,   r4,          r4    // Start one lower to
                                     //  allow for autoincrement
CLEAR_LOOP:
      bla   r5,   r6,   CLEAR_LOOP   // Loop for the 16 times
      fst.l f0,   4(r4)++            // Write and autoincrement
                                     //  to next word
                                     // Store executed in bla delay slot
```

Figure 5-16. Example of **bla** *usage*

To implement a loop counter, *src1* is set to −1, and *src2* to the loop count. Before the loop is entered, a **bla** is performed to initialize the LCC. LCC will be set to one unless *src1* plus *src2* results in a negative number. Because the target of the first **bla** is the sequential instruction following the delay slot, the execution flow does not vary due to the initial LCC setting. Another **bla** instruction placed as the next-to-last instruction of the loop can test for loop completion and update the loop counter. The total number of iterations is the value of *src2* before the first **bla** instruction, plus one. The example in Figure 5-16 illustrates this use of **bla**.

Putting It Together

Now that you have looked at the processor, the basic instructions, and instruction sequences, you can examine some simple yet revealing examples. The examples are written in C programming language, with the compiler output shown. The first example, shown in Figure 5-17, is a conversion routine, called *hours.c*, that converts days and hours into total hours.

The first optimization is that the parameters days and hours are passed in the registers **r16** and **r17** instead of being passed on the stack. This avoids having a pointer frame, or any entry or exit code. Second, the multiply by 24 is implemented as two shifts and a subtract. The first shift left by two implements a multiply by four, and the subtract reduces it to a multiply by three. The second shift left by three implements a multiply by eight, giving the total multiply of 24 (three times eight). Note that the first shift left takes advantage of the three operand instruction format, not destroying the original value in **r16**. This eliminates copying **r16** into a temporary register at the start of the routine, and allows the original contents of **r16** to be used as the source register in the subtract instruction that immediately follows. The final optimization is the **add** being performed in the branch-delay-slot. The **bri r1**

```
/* convert days and hours into hours */
/* C code */

int convert(days, hours)
     register unsigned int days, hours;
{
     unsigned int total;
     total = days * 24 + hours;

     return (total);
}



/* Compiler generated assembly code */
     .file  "hours.c"

_convert::

     shl    2,r16,r28
     subs   r28,r16,r16
     shl    3,r16,r16

     bri    r1
      adds  r17,r16,r16

//_total    r16    local
//_days     r16    local
//_hours    r17    local
```

Figure 5-17. Example 1: hours.c

```
main()
{ int  sum,summer(),n,a[];
 sum= summer(a,8);
}

     int summer (a,n) /* return the sum of the "n" integers */
     int *a,n;        /* of the array "a" */
{    int i,sum=0;

     for (i = n-1; i >=0 ; i--)
          sum = sum + a[i];
     return(sum);

}

     .file     "sum.c"
     mov  r7,r16
     call _summer
      or  8,r0,r17
     mov  r16,r17

_summer:
     mov  r0,r18
     adds -1,r17,r17
     shl  2,r17,r28
     adds r16,r28,r28
     adds 1,r17,r17
     adds -1,r0,r20
     bla  r20,r17,.L65
      mov r28,r16
 .L65:
     bla  r20,r17,.L43
      nop
     br   .L42
      nop
 .L43:
     ld.l 0(r16),r19
     adds -4,r16,r16
     bla  r20,r17,.L43
      adds     r19,r18,r18
 .L42:
     bri  r1
      mov r18,r16
//_a r16  local
//_n r17  local
```

Figure 5-18. Example 2: summer

returns control to the calling routine with the result of the call returned in **r16**.

The second example, shown in Figure 5-18, is a subroutine called summer that adds a series of integers. Because the number of integers to be summed may be too numerous to fit in the register set, a pointer to the address in memory for the numbers to be summed is passed in **r16**. The other parameter, passed in **r17**, is the number of integers in the series. The example shows a loop where the data must be retrieved from memory. Also shown in the figure is the calling sequence.

The setup prior to the loop initializes LCC (with the **bla** instruction), checks that at least one loop iteration occurs, and moves zero into the sum register **r18**. Although the setup portion of the program may be slightly less than ideal, the routine's performance is clearly dominated by the loop portion. The loop loads the data from memory, decrements the pointer to the next integer, performs the loop control, and accumulates the sum of the integers. These four instructions are arranged to avoid any freeze conditions, because the data from the load is not operated on until the branch-delay-slot. The use of **bla** replaces two instructions that would be required for loop control (a subtract and then a **bnc**).

Although the compiler has done a good job of arranging the inner loop as a four-clock loop, it is not ideal. It is possible to use a loop index directly as the memory pointer and reduce it to a three-clock loop. An even more aggressive approach would be to unroll the loop to perform more loads and additions for each pass through the loop. This amortizes the loop overhead over a greater number of useful instructions.

The i860 processor has floating-point hardware included on-chip and available to the programmer. As an extension to this last example, the processor's dual-instruction mode allows the load and loop control to be overlapped with the summation that may be performed in the floating-point registers. This is shown in Chapter 8, "Programming for Parallelism."

CHAPTER 6
FLOATING-POINT OPERATIONS

The floating-point unit of the i860 processor includes a pipelined adder, a pipelined multiplier, a set of floating-point registers, and three special purpose registers. The graphics unit is closely tied to the floating-point unit, and uses the same register file and data paths. This chapter explains all of the floating-point instructions, and the nongraphics specific instructions that are performed with the floating-point registers. The 3D graphics instructions are discussed in Chapter 7, "Graphics Rendering Instructions."

Floating-Point Instruction Format

Loading the floating-point registers is performed by RISC core instructions, and all floating-point operations are performed on operands that reside in the floating-point registers. The format for floating-point instructions is even simpler than the core instructions. Each instruction specifies two source registers and a destination register. Unlike the RISC core instructions, the floating-point instructions do not permit an immediate operand as part of the encoding (as standard floating-point data encodings require at least 32-bits).

Figure 6-1 shows the general instruction encoding for the floating-point instructions. The high-order six-bit field used by the RISC core opcode is fixed at 010010 for all floating-point instructions. (In hexadecimal notation, such instructions are recognized as beginning with 48H, 49H, 4AH, or 4BH.) To encode the floating-point operation, the floating-point instructions use the seven low-order bits of the instruction. The interpretation of each valid combination of these lower bits in shown in Table 6-1. The three register designator fields, `src2`, `dest`, and `src1`, are used to specify any of the 32-bit floating-point registers. The `S` and `R` bits determine the precision of the operands, while the `P` bit is used to specify scalar or pipelined execution mode. The `D` bit is used by the processor for dual-instruction mode, (described in Chapter 8, "Program-

31 26	21	16	11	9		7	6 0
0 1 0 0 1 0	*src2*	*dest*	*src1*	P	D	S	R	opcode

src1, *src2* — Source; one of 32 floating-point registers
dest — Destination register
(instructions other than **fxfr**): one of 32 floating-point registers
(**fxfr**): one of 32 integer registers

P Pipelining
1 — Pipelined instruction mode
0 — Scalar instruction mode

D Dual-Instruction Mode
1 — Dual-instruction mode
0 — Single-instruction mode

S Source Precision
1 — Double-precision source operands
0 — Single-precision source operands

R Result Precision
1 — Double-precision result
0 — Single-precision result

Figure 6-1. General format of floating-point instructions

Table 6-1. Floating-Point Opcodes

Mnemonic	Operation	6	5	4	3	2	1	0
pfam	Add and Multiply*	0	0	0	DPC			
pfmam	Multiply with Add*							
pfsm	Subtract and Multiply*	0	0	1	DPC			
pfmsm	Multiply with Subtract*							
(p)fmul	Multiply	0	1	0	0	0	0	0
fmlow	Multiply Low	0	1	0	0	0	0	1
frcp	Reciprocal	0	1	0	0	0	1	0
frsqr	Reciprocal Square Root	0	1	0	0	0	1	1
pfmul3.dd	3-Stage Pipelined Multiply	0	1	0	0	1	0	0
(p)fadd	Add	0	1	1	0	0	0	0
(p)fsub	Subtract	0	1	1	0	0	0	1
(p)fix	Convert to Integer	0	1	1	0	0	1	0
(p)famov	Adder Move	0	1	1	0	0	1	1
pfgt/pfle**	Greater Than Compare	0	1	1	0	1	0	0
pfeq	Equal Compare	0	1	1	0	1	0	1
(p)ftrunc	Truncate to Integer	0	1	1	1	0	1	0
fxfr	Transfer to Integer Register	1	0	0	0	0	0	0
(p)fiadd	Long-Integer Add	1	0	0	1	0	0	1
(p)fisub	Long-Integer Subtract	1	0	0	1	1	0	1
(p)fzchkl	Z-Check Long	1	0	1	0	1	1	1
(p)fzchks	Z-Check Short	1	0	1	1	1	1	1
(p)faddp	Add with Pixel Merge	1	0	1	0	0	0	0
(p)faddz	Add with Z Merge	1	0	1	0	0	0	1
(p)form	OR with MERGE Register	1	0	1	1	0	1	0

* **pfam** and **pfsm** have P-bit set; **pfmam** and **pfmsm** have P bit clear
** **pfgt** has R bit cleared; **pfle** has R bit set.

ming for Parallelism") where a floating-point unit instruction is executed simultaneously in parallel with a RISC core instruction.

Specifying Data Precision

Depending on the precision of the operation to be performed, the register designator may indicate one register for single-precision, or a register pair for double. Both source operands must be of the same precision.

Most i860 processor floating-point instructions allow the result to be the same or greater precision than the input operands. As shown in Table 6-2, the source and result precision are specified by a two-letter suffix to the instruction mnemonic. The instruction list designates a **.p** or **.r** suffix that is replaced by the appropriate two-letter suffix from the table.

Pipeline and Scalar Instructions

The pipelined floating-point adder and multiplier support two computation models: scalar and pipelined. Pipelined and scalar instructions are distinguished by the P bit in the instruction encoding. The computation model used depends on the type of calculation being performed. Although scalar instructions are simpler to use and can be used for all types of calculations, pipelined instructions can achieve much higher performance.

Scalar mode allows interdependent sequences of operations to complete quickly. Scalar means nonrepeated calculations, with each operation typically dependent on the result of the previous operation. Scalar floating-point add and subtract operations take three clock cycles to complete, while scalar floating-point multiply operations take three clock cycles for single-precision and four clock cycles for double-precision. Before starting, scalar instructions wait for any previous scalar instructions currently in progress to complete. Once initiated, scalar instruc-

Table 6-2. Source and Destination Precision Encodings

Suffix	*Source Precision*	*Result Precision*
.ss	single	single
.sd	single	double
.dd	double	double
.ds	double	single

.p = **.ss**, **.sd**, or **.dd**
.r = **.ss**, **.sd**, **.dd**, or **.ds**

tions pass through all stages of their execution and store the calculation result.

Pipelined mode instructions can perform the same operations as scalar mode instructions, but operate differently. Pipelined operations are useful to perform repetitive operations that do not depend on the result of the previous operation. Vector processing is one example of where pipelined instructions can be used most effectively.

Pipelined instructions advance the execution pipeline one stage, and the pipeline does not advance further until the next appropriate instruction is encountered. Instructions other than those that affect the pipeline being used proceed without affecting the pipeline's intermediate states. Also, the destination specified as part of a pipelined floating-point instruction is the result of an operation that was started earlier. Although programming in pipelined mode is more difficult, there is considerable performance advantage for doing so. With pipelined instructions, the adder can produce a result every clock cycle, and the multiplier can produce a result every clock cycle for single-precision, and every other clock cycle for double-precision.

Figure 6-2 shows both the scalar and pipelined versions of a code sequence to add five pairs of numbers. The scalar example in Figure 6-2a is straightforward. Each **fadd** takes three clock cycles to execute; then the next **fadd** may begin. The five **fadd**s take 15 clock cycles to execute.

The use of pipelined instructions is illustrated with the adder pipeline example shown in Figure 6-2b. Here, the adder begins by adding the numbers in **f6** and **f7**. Because this is the first instruction of the series, the pipeline is not yet full and the result coming out of the adder is not needed. Therefore, the result is sent to **f0**, which is always zero and is used as a null destination. On each successive clock cycle, an add instruction is issued to advance the pipeline. When the sum of the first add becomes available at the result stage, it is stored to the destination specified by that instruction.

In this example, three instructions after the **f6** plus **f7** starts, the result is stored to **f18:f19** by the instruction that is initiating the addition of **f12** and **f13**. Once all of the desired add instructions have started, three extra adds may be necessary at the end of a sequence in order to flush the desired results through the pipeline. When adding a long series of numbers, the overhead of flushing the pipeline is negligible. When performing only one or two adds, scalar mode can be used to

Operations:

```
f18:f19 <--  f6 + f7
f16     <--  f2 + f3
f17     <--  f5 - f4
f22     <--  f12 - f13
f20:f21 <--  f18:f19 - f10:f11 (where f18:f19=f6+f7)
```

Scalar instruction example:

```
fadd.sd  f6, f7, f18;          f18:f19   <--  f6 + f7
fadd.ss  f2, f3, f16;          f16       <--  f2 + f3
fsub.ss  f5, f4, f17;          f17       <--  f5 - f4
fsub.ss  f12, f13, f22;        f22       <--  f12 - f13
fsub.dd  f18, f10, f20;        f20:f21   <--  f18 - f10
```

a. Mixed-precision adder unit scalar operations

Instruction		Adder Pipeline Result			
		Stage 1	Stage 2	Stage 3	
pfadd.sd	f6, f7, f0	[f6+f7]	?	?	0
pfadd.ss	f2, f3, f0	[f2+f3]	[f6+f7]	?	0
pfsub.ss	f5, f4, f0	[f5-f4]	[f2+f3]	[f6+f7]	0
pfsub.ss	f12, f13, f18	[f12-f13]	[f5-f4]	[f2+f3]	f18:f19 <--[f6+f7]
pfsub.dd	f18, f10, f16	[f18-f10]	[f12-f13]	[f5-f4]	f16 <--[f2+f3]
pfadd.ss	f0, f0, f17	0	[f18-f10]	[f12-f13]	f17 <--[f5-f4]
pfadd.ss	f0, f0, f22	0	0	[f18-f10]	f22 <--[f12-f13]
pfadd.ss	f0, f0, f20	0	0	0	f20:f21<--[f18-f10]

b. Mixed-precision adder unit pipelined operations

Instruction Adder Pipeline Result					
		Stage 1	Stage 2	Stage 3	
pfadd.sd	f6, f7, f0	[f6+f7]	?	?	0
pfadd.ss	f2, f3, f0	[f2+f3]	[f6+f7]	?	0
pfsub.ss	f5, f4, f0	[f5-f4]	[f2+f3]	[f6+f7]	0
pfsub.dd	f18, f10, f18	[f18-f10]	[f5-f4]	[f2+f3]	f18:f19 <--[f6+f7]
pfsub.ss	f12, f13, f16	[f12-f13]	[f18-f10]	[f5-f4]	f16 <--[f2+f3]
pfadd.ss	f0, f0, f17	0	[f12-f13]	[f18-f10]	f17 <--[f5-f4]
pfadd.ss	f0, f0, f20	0	0	[f12-f13]	f20:f21<--[f18-f10]
pfadd.ss	f0, f0, f22	0	0	0	f22 <--[f12-f13]

c. Mixed-precision adder unit pipelined operations with feedback

Figure 6-2. Adder scalar and pipeline instruction examples

minimize pipeline overhead. Later in this chapter we will look at more of the details of Figure 6-2 and explain the example in Figure 6-2c.

To allow pipelined operations to treat the adder and multiplier as independent units, there are separate instructions for advancing the adder unit and the multiplier unit, and for advancing both units together. Each time a pipelined operation is performed, the input operands *fsrc1* and *fsrc2* are transferred to the first stage of the pipeline, the pipeline is advanced one stage, the status of the last stage becomes available in **fsr**, and the result of the last stage of the pipeline is stored in the destination register *fdest*.

Both scalar and pipelined instructions can update *fdest* and then access the new value from the *fdest* register in the next instruction. Pipelined instructions have the additional flexibility of using the new value of *fdest* as a source operand at the same time *fdest* is updated.

Pipeline Status

The precision specified as part of a pipelined operation is carried with the instruction throughout its execution. Therefore, the precision of *fdest* is determined by the instruction that initiates the operation, not by precision of the instruction that completes the operation.

When a scalar mode instruction is executed, it passes through all stages of the adder or multiplier unit and will destroy any unstored results. Because pipelined instructions do not automatically complete the operation they initiate, dummy pipelined instructions are sometimes needed to extract results from the pipeline. Because of this behavior, scalar and pipelined floating-point operations are not conveniently intermixed.

The results that scalar operations leave in the affected pipeline unit's stages (except the last stage) are undefined. However, no spurious result-exception traps result when the undefined values are subsequently stored by pipelined operations. The values should not be referenced as source operands. Also, for best performance when changing between the two modes, a scalar operation should not immediately precede a pipelined operation whose destination is not **f0** or **f1** (the zero registers). This is because the scalar instructions do not store the result until the write stage, and the scalar instruction's store would collide with the store of the next pipelined instruction where the write occurs earlier in the execute stage.

Another aspect of pipelined operations is that the various pipeline stages contain both intermediate data and state information. When a

Instruction	*Description*	*Operation*	*Syntax*	
fadd.p	F-P add	*dest<-- src1+src2*	**fadd.p**	*fsrc1,fsrc2,fdest*
famov.r	F-P adder move	*dest<-- src1*	**famov.r**	*fsrc1,fdest*
fix.p	F-P to Int convert	*dest<-- (integer src1)*	**fix.p**	*fsrc1,fdest*
fsub.p	F-P subtract	*dest<-- src1 - src2*	**fsub.p**	*fsrc1,fsrc2,fdest*
ftrunc.p	F-P to Int truncate	*dest<-- (truncate scr1)*	**ftrunc.p**	*fsrc1,fdest*
pfadd.p	Pipelined **fadd**	*dest<-- (src1+src2)**	**pfadd.p**	*fsrc1,fsrc2,fdest*
pfamov.r	Pipelined **famov**	*dest<-- (src1)**	**pfamov.r**	*fsrc1,fdest*
pfeq.p	Pipe = compare	*dest<-- (src1+src2)**	**pfeq.p**	*fsrc1,fsrc2,fdest*
pfgt.p	Pipe > compare	*dest<-- (src1+src2)**	**pfgt.p**	*fsrc1,fsrc2,fdest*
pfix.p	Pipelined **fix**	*dest<-- (Integer src1)**	**pfix.p**	*fsrc1,fdest*
pfle.p	Pipe ≤ compare	*dest<-- (src1+src2)**	**pfle.p**	*fsrc1,fsrc2,fdest*
pfsub.p	Pipelined **fsub**	*dest<-- (src1-src2)**	**pfsub.p**	*fsrc1,fsrc2,fdest*
pftrunc.p	Pipelined **ftrunc**	*dest<-- (Truncate src1)**	**pftrunc.p**	*fsrc1,fdest*

* = *dest* gets third-stage adder result; first-stage adder gets the input shown.

Figure 6-3. Floating-point adder instructions

process is preempted or when a trap handler performs pipelined operations using the same pipeline, both the intermediate data and the intermediate state information must be saved and later restored when resuming the interrupted code. Further details and example code for saving and restoring the pipeline are included in Chapter 9, "Operating System Support."

The Floating-Point Adder

The floating-point adder performs floating-point addition, subtraction, and comparison operations, conversion between floating-point precisions, and conversion to integer formats. The floating-point adder instructions, including their syntax and operation, are listed in Figure 6-3. Single- and double-precision adder unit operations each have three stages. Both scalar mode **fadd** and **fsub** and pipelined mode **pfadd** and **pfsub** instructions are available. With three stages, scalar operations require three clock cycles to complete, and pipelined operations update their *fdest* with the results of the third previous instruction. Because the adder pipeline is the same depth for both single- and double-precision calculations, the adder unit can mix precisions with no added complexity.

Figure 6-2 (previously shown) gives an example of performing single- and double-precision addition and subtraction. Figure 6-2a shows the five operations performed and the scalar mode floating-point instructions required to perform the calculations. In scalar mode, each floating-point adder instruction takes three clock cycles to execute. Several changes are necessary to convert the scalar code example to use the faster pipeline mode instructions. In addition to using the pipelined version of the instructions, the destination specified is for the third previous instruction. For the pipelined example in Figure 6-2b, the first three instructions are used to fill the pipeline, and the remaining five instructions are used to calculate and store the results. Although the pipelined code takes a total of eight instructions, each instruction takes only one clock cycle.

The example calculation mixes single- and double-precision calculations. As indicated with the **.sd** encoding, the first instruction,

```
pfadd.sd  f6, f7, f0
```

specifies two single-precision source operands and a double-precision result. Remember that the i860 processor keeps track of the precision specified for the operation's result as part of the pipeline status. This allows the fourth instruction

```
pfsub.ss  f12, f13, f18
```

to store the double-precision result of the first instruction while specifying a single-precision result for its own calculation.

The example code in Figure 6-2c demonstrates using the adder result as an input operand at the same time that it is stored. In this example, the instruction

```
pfsub.dd f18, f10, f18
```

stores the result into **f18** and uses the new **f18** value as an input for the addition. Of course when *fdest* is fed back as an *fsrc* operand, the precision of the result must match the precision of the new instruction's source. In this case, **f18** was specified as a double-precision result with the

```
pfadd.sd  f6, f7, f0
```

instruction, and as a double-precision source operand with the

```
pfsub.dd  f18, f10, f18
```

instruction. For the adder unit, the result can be fed back either as *fsrc1* or *fsrc2*, or both.

Compare Instructions

The floating-point compare instructions are used to set or clear the CC (Condition Code) bit of **psr**. This is useful so that the RISC core, which controls execution, can perform conditional branch instructions based on floating-point values. There are three variations of compares: **pfgt** (Pipelined floating-point greater-than compare), **pfle** (Pipelined floating-point less-than compare), and **pfeq** (Pipelined floating-point equal compare).

The **pfgt** instructions should be used for $A > B$ and $A < B$ comparison, where CC is set when *src1* > *src2*. The **pfle** instructions should be used for $A \geq B$ and $A \leq B$ comparison, where CC is cleared when *src1* ≤ *scr2*. The only difference between these two instructions is the encoding of the R bit (normally used for specifying the result precision) of the instruction. As described in Chapter 9, "Operating System Support," the trap handler examines the R bit to help determine whether a compare should set or clear CC to conform with the IEEE standard for ordered compares. The third and final compare instruction is the **pfeq**, which sets the CC if *src1* is equal to *src2*, and clears it otherwise.

The compare instructions can be used with either a sequence of scalar or pipelined instructions. As the compares are used to affect the CC bit and not to produce a mathematical result, only pipelined versions of the compare instruction are available. As with pipelined instructions, the compare operation advances the adder pipeline one stage, and stores the result of the last stage to the *fdest* specified within the compare instruction.

Within a sequence of scalar floating-point instructions, a pipelined compare is a one clock cycle instruction. The scalar floating-point instructions before and after a compare will hide the instruction's pipelined nature. Within a sequence of pipelined adder instructions, the compare will store the results stage to the destination register and advance the adder pipeline one stage. The value that the compare places into the first stage of the adder is undefined. However, no result-exception trap will occur if it is flushed through the adder result stage. Like all floating-point instructions, the compare will trap on invalid input operands.

Data Precision Conversions

The adder unit allows moving values between floating-point registers while performing precision conversions. The instructions **famov** and **pfamov** use the adder's ability to handle different precision inputs and outputs. Precision conversions are performed with the **.ds** (double to single) or **.sd** (single to double) instruction suffixes. The **famov** and **pfamov** differ from the standard **add** instructions

```
fadd.p fsrc1, f0, fdest
```

and

```
pfadd.p fsrc1, f0, fdest
```

as **(p)famov** will preserve the value of a negative zero. The **pfamov** is also used by the trap handler for restoring the pipeline states. For floating-point register moves that do not require a precision conversion, the **fmov** and **pfmov** pseudo instructions should be used because they are faster. The assembler automatically converts **fmov.ds** to **famov.ds**, and so on. This is discussed in more detail later in this chapter.

In addition to performing floating-point precision conversions, the adder performs floating-point to integer conversion. The obvious question when converting from floating-point to integer representation is what to do with the fractional portion of the number. For example, does the floating-point number 9.5 convert to the integer number 9 or 10?

The scalar instruction **fix** and pipelined version **pfix** round a floating-point source into a double-register result where the low-order 32 bits of the result contain the integer portion of the source. The rounding mode is determined by consulting the RM bits in the **fsr**. The RM bits allow the i860 processor the choice of the four IEEE rounding modes. The **ftrunc** and **pftrunc** instructions perform a conversion, but instead of checking RM, always truncate (that is, delete) the fractional portion of the floating-point value.

The results for the conversion instructions are two's complement form. If the integer part of the value being converted is bigger than can be represented as a 32-bit two's complement integer, an overflow trap will occur. Traps will never occur for underflow and inexact results. More programming sequences are available, because both pipelined and scalar (nonpipelined) versions of the conversion instructions exist.

For one or two conversions, the scalar instructions will be faster at three clock cycles each. However, if more than two conversions are being performed, the pipelined instructions should be used to produce one result per clock. Also, pipelined conversion instructions can be mingled with other pipelined instructions without incurring any performance penalties.

The Floating-Point Multiplier

The multiplier supports floating-point and integer multiplication, as well as floating-point reciprocal and reciprocal square root operations. The multiplier instructions along with their syntax and operations are shown

Instruction	*Description*	*Operation*		*Syntax*
fmlow.dd	F-P Mult.Low	*dest<--src1 X src2*	**fmlow.dd**	*fsrc1,fsrc2,fdest*
fmul.p	F-P Multiply	*dest<--src1 X src2*	**fmul.p**	*fsrc1,fsrc2,fdest*
frcp.p	reciprocal	*dest<--1/src2*	**frcp.p**	*fsrc2,fdest*
frsqr.p	reciprocal square root	*dest<--1/(src2)*$^{-0.5}$	**frsqr.p**	*fsrc2,fdest*
pfmul.p	Pipelined F-P Mult	*dest<--(src1 X src2)**	**pfmul.p**	*fsrc1,fsrc2,fdest*
pfmul3.dd	3 stage **pfmul**	*dest<--(src1 X src2)**	**pfmul3.dd**	*fsrc1,fsrc2,fdest*

**dest* <-- last stage of multiplier; first stage of multiplier <-- *src1* src2*

Figure 6-4. Floating-point multiplier instructions

in Figure 6-4. The multiplier has both a scalar and a pipelined version of the floating-point multiply instruction. The multiplier unit is designed with three pipeline stages; however, double-precision operations must pass through the first stage twice. As a result, single-precision scalar multiplication produces a result in three clock cycles, and double-precision produces a result in four clock cycles.

Pipelined multiplies operate in the same manner as pipelined adds, where each instruction specifies a result register for a previous operation. Figure 6-5 shows a sequence of pipelined multiplies for single-precision values. Since the pipeline is three-stages deep, the result stored is from the third previous operation. Figure 6-6 shows a sequence for double-precision values. Although the visible pipeline depth is reduced to two stages for double-precision, each stage takes two clock cycles of execution. Because the lengths of the pipelines differ with precision, it is complicated to mix single- and double-precision operations without first clearing the pipeline.

If there is a compelling need to mix precision, follow these rules:

- **For single to double transitions** When a pipelined multiplier operation with double-precision inputs is executed, and the previous multi-

Operations:
```
f20 <-- f4*f5
f21 <-- f6*f7
f22 <-- f8*f9
```

Scalar instruction example:
```
fmul.ss  f4, f5, f20;    f20 <-- f4*f5
fmul.ss  f6, f7, f21;    f21 <-- f6*f7
fmul.ss  f8, f9, f22;    f22 <-- f8*f9
```

Pipeline instruction example:

Instruction	Multiply Pipeline			Result
pfmul.ss f4, f5, f0	[f4*f5]	?	?	?
pfmul.ss f6, f7, f0	[f6*f7]	[f4*f5]	?	?
pfmul.ss f8, f9, f0	[f8*f9]	[f6*f7]	[f4*f5]	?
pfmul.ss f10, f11, f20	[f10*f11]	[f8*f9]	[f6*f7]	f20 <-- f4*f5
pfmul.ss f12, f13, f21	[f12*f13]	[f10*f11]	[f8*f9]	f21 <-- f6*f7
pfmul.ss f14, f15, f22	[f14*f15]	[f12*f13]	[f10*f11]	f22 <-- f8*f9

Figure 6-5. Single-precision floating-point multiplication example

Operations:
```
f21:f20 <-- f5:f4 * f7:f6
f23:f22 <-- f9:f8 * f11:f10
f25:f24 <-- f13:f12 * f15:f14
```

Scalar instruction example:
```
fmul.dd  f4, f6, f20;    f21:f20 <-- f5:f4 * f7:f6
fmul.dd  f8, f10, f22;   f23:f22 <-- f9:f8 * f11:f10
fmul.dd  f12, f14, f24;  f25:f24 <-- f13:f12 * f15:f14
```

Pipeline instruction example:

Instruction	Multiply Pipeline		Result
pfmul.dd f4, f6, f0	[f5:f4 * f7:f6]	?	
pfmul.dd f8, f10, f0	[f9:f8 * f11:f10]	[f5:f4 * f7:f6]	
pfmul.dd f12, f14, f20	[f13:f12 * f15:f14]	[f9:f8 * f11:f10]	f21:f20<--[f5:f4 * f7:f6]
pfmul.dd f0, f0, f22	0	[f13:f12 * f15:f14]	f23:f22<--[f9:f8 * f11:f10]
pfmul.dd f0, f0, f24	0	[0]	f25:f24<--[f13:f12 * f15:f14]

Figure 6-6. Double-precision floating-point multiplication example

plier operation was pipelined with single-precision inputs, the third previous (last stage) result is stored, and the previous operation (first stage) is advanced to the second stage (now the last stage). The second previous operation (old second stage) is discarded. The next pipelined multiplier operation stores the single-precision result.

- **For double to single transitions** When a pipelined multiplier operation with single-precision inputs is executed, and the previous multiplication was pipelined with double-precision inputs, the previous multiplier operation is advanced to the second stage, and a single- or double-precision zero is placed in the last stage of the pipeline. The single-precision multiplication in this case stores the result of the multiplication preceding the last double-precision multiplication. The next pipelined multiplier operation stores zero instead of the result of the prior operation, and the `MRP` bit of **`fsr`** for that next operation.

Reciprocals

The multiplier includes **`frcp`** (floating-point reciprocal) and **`frsqr`** (floating-point reciprocal square root) instructions. The **`frcp`** instruction computes the reciprocal (reciprocal of x equals 1/x) of a floating-point value with an error significand of less than 2^{-7}, that is, with 8 bits of accuracy. The **`frsqr`** instruction computes the reciprocal of the floating-point value's square root to the same accuracy. A Newton-Raphson iteration algorithm must be used to increase the accuracy of a calculation beyond 2^{-7}.

The floating-point multiplies and the reciprocal operations assist in performing other mathematical functions such as divide. The examples in Figures 6-7 and 6-8 compute $Z = X / Y$ for single- and double-precision variables. The algorithm begins by using the reciprocal instruction **`frcp`** to obtain an initial guess for the value of $1/Y$. The **`frcp`** instruction gives a result that can differ from the true value of $1/Y$ by as much as 2^{-8}. The algorithm then continues to make guesses based on the prior guess, refining each guess until the desired accuracy is achieved. This can be expressed mathematically as

$$G_{new} = G_{old}\,(2 - G_{old} * Y)$$
$$E_{new} = 2(E_{old})^2$$

```
//      The dividend X is in f6
//      The divisor Y is in f2
//      The result Z is left in f3
//      f5 contains single-precision floating-point 2

     frcp.ss      f2,  f3       // first guess has 2**-8 error
     fmul.ss      f2,  f3,  f4  // guess * divisor
     fsub.ss      f5,  f4,  f4  // 2 - guess * divisor
     fmul.ss      f3,  f4,  f3  // second guess has 2**-15 error
     fmul.ss      f2,  f3,  f4  // avoid using f3 as srcl (prevent delay)
     fsub.ss      f5,  f4,  f4  // 2 - guess * divisor
     fmul.ss      f6,  f3,  f5  // second guess * dividend
     fmul.ss      f4,  f5,  f3  // result = second guess * dividend
```

Figure 6-7. Single-precision floating-point divide example

```
//      The dividend X is in f2
//      The divisor Y is in f4
//      The result Z is left in f8

     frcp.dd  f4,  f6       // first guess has 2**-8 error
     fmul.dd  f4,  f6,  f8  // guess * divisor
     fld.d    flttwo,   f10 // load double-precision floating 2
//   The fld.d is free.  It completely overlaps the preceding fmul.dd
     fsub.dd  f10, f8,  f8  // 2 - guess * divisor
     fmul.dd  f6,  f8,  f6  // second guess has 2**-15 error
     fmul.dd  f4,  f6,  f8  // avoid using f6 as srcl
     fsub.dd  f10, f8,  f8  // 2 - guess * divisor
     fmul.dd  f6,  f8,  f6  // third guess has 2**-29 error
     fmul.dd  f4,  f6,  f8  // avoid using f6 as srcl
     fsub.dd  f10, f8,  f8  // 2 - guess * divisor
     fmul.dd  f6,  f2,  f6  // guess * dividend
     fmul.dd  f8,  f6,  f8  // result = third guess * dividend
```

Figure 6-8. Double-precision floating-point divide example

where G represents a guess, and E represents the error, that is, the difference between G and the true value of $1/Y$. These formulas self-correct an initial guess and a solution with the desired accuracy can be reached iteratively. The two example programs included here produce results with a worst-case error of two least-significant bits. If the result is referenced by the next instruction, the single-precision calculation takes 22 clock cycles and the double-precision calculation takes 38 clock cycles.

Similar Newton-Raphson approximations can be used to calculate a result for many different functions. The general form of the method is:

$$X_{new} = X_{old} - F(X_{old})/F'(X_{old})$$

Where $F'(X_{old})$ is the derivative of $F(X_{old})$. Consider the square root function and use the Newton-Raphson method to calculate the square root X of a given positive number Y. Expressed mathematically,

$$X = SQRT(Y), \text{ hence } F(X) = X^2 - Y = 0 \text{ and } F'(X) = 2X.$$

Expressed in the general form,

$$X_{new} = \frac{X_{old} - X_{old}^2 - Y}{2X_{old}} = \frac{1}{2}\left(X_{old} + \frac{Y}{X_{old}}\right)$$

As an example, calculate the square root where $Y = 2$, and the initial guess is 1. Substituting 1 into the formula for X_{old} gives an X_{new} of 1.5, which can then be resubstituted into the formula. Repeating the substitutions gives results of 1.41446, 1.414216, and 1.414214 where the actual result is approximately 1.414213562. As you can see, each successive approximation is more and more accurate. Note how the formula self-corrects for any initial guess. Calculations of approximations can be performed until the difference between successive approximations equals zero or some other acceptable error.

Integer Operations

In addition to floating-point multiplication, the floating-point multiplier is used for performing integer multiplication. The **fmlow** instruction multiplies two integers contained in floating-point registers. The **fmlow** instruction operates on 64-bit register pairs (the integer value occupies the low-order register). The **fmlow** result is stored to the floating-point destination register pair, with the integer multiply result found in the low-order register. Although contained in the floating-point registers, the integer operands will not cause a floating-point trap—that is, the **fmlow** instruction does not check for source- or result-exception traps. Similarly, the **fmlow** instruction does not update the result-status bits of **fsr**. Unfortunately, **fmlow** does not produce the true 64-bit integer product, but just the lowest 53 bits.

Integer arithmetic operations are supported by the graphics unit and can be performed on the floating-point registers. This is useful for adding and subtracting integer values produced with the **fmlow** integer multiply instruction. The instructions supported include **fiadd.w** (long-integer add), **pfiadd.w** (pipelined long-integer add), **fisub.w** (long-integer subtract), and **pfisub.w** (pipelined long-integer subtract) which can operate on 32- or 64-bit integer values. The operation is performed on two floating-point registers (32-bits each) or on two register pairs (64-bits each). The instructions perform only the arithmetic operation and do not affect CC nor cause traps due to overflow.

Because the graphics pipeline is one-stage deep, the pipelined instructions store the result of the previous instruction. Both scalar and pipelined graphics instructions take one clock cycle to execute. So why bother to write pipelined instructions for the graphics unit? The simple rule is that pipelined graphics unit instructions should be used if pipelined floating-point instructions are being used. The reason is to avoid the performance penalty that occurs when mixing scalar and pipelined instructions: where a pipelined operation will take an extra clock cycle to execute if the previous instruction was a scalar operation whose destination was not **f0** or **f1**. The penalty occurs because scalar instructions store their results later in the instruction execution pipeline than pipelined instructions, and the pipelined instruction must wait before it may store its result.

The **fiadd** and **pfiadd** are used to implement the **fmov** and **pfmov** pseudo-instructions by performing an add with **f0** as *src2*. However, only single register (**.ss**) and register pair (**.dd**) moves are performed by the graphics unit. If the assembly language pseudo-instruction with **.sd** or **.ds** suffixes is specified, the assembler will automatically convert them to the floating-point adder instruction version:

fmov.sd becomes **famov.sd**
fmov.ds becomes **famov.ds**
pfmov.sd becomes **pfamov.sd**
pfmov.ds becomes **pfamov.ds**

While this is fine for nonpipelined move instructions, it does introduce a complication for the pipelined move instructions.

If the one-stage graphics unit is assumed for a pipelined **pfmov.sd** or **pfmov.ds** instruction, only to have the assembler perform the three-stage adder unit precision conversion move (**pfamov.sd** or **pfamov.ds**), incorrect results will ensue. Therefore, extra care should be taken when using the different move instructions. Specifying an **famov** or **pfamov** instruction will ensure that the adder unit will carry out the operation, regardless of the precision combination indicated.

The graphics unit also executes the floating-point register to integer register transfer instruction **fxfr**. The transfer specifies one 32-bit floating-point register and one 32-bit integer register, and the register contents are transferred directly—regardless of the data type represented. If a floating-point value is to be converted to an integer value, the conversion should be performed in the floating-point registers (with the **fix**, **pfix**, **ftrunc**, or **pftrunc**) prior to the **fxfr**.

Figure 6-9 shows the code sequence for performing an integer multiply on values that initially are in the integer registers. The example first transfers the values to the floating-point registers, then performs the multiplication, and finally transfers the result back to an integer register. If several additions or subtractions need to be performed, along with the integer multiplications, the overhead of transferring between integer and floating-point registers can be lessened by using the integer addition and subtraction instructions performed on the floating-point registers. For multiplications by constants, it is usually faster to replace the multiply with a combination of shifts and adds in the integer registers, as discussed earlier in Chapter 5, "RISC Core Operations."

For certain calculations, the integer values should be transferred to the floating-point registers and converted to floating-point representation. The example in Figure 6-10 transfers and converts a signed integer value stored in **r4** to a double-precision floating-point value in **f7:f6**. The strategy shown moves the bits of the integer directly to the significand portion of the double-precision number. Then, it does a normalization to yield a floating-point format (of 52 significand bits with an implied "1" most significant bit). The conversion must account for the two's

```
//        The multiplier is in r4
//        The multiplicand is in r5
//        The product is left in r6. Assumed 32 bits or less.
//        The registers f2, f4, and f6 are used as temporaries.

      ixfr  r4,           f2
      ixfr  r5,           f4
//  Two core instructions can be inserted here without penalty.
      fmlow.dd       f4,   f2,   f6
//  Two core instructions can be inserted here without penalty.
      fxfr  f6,           r6
//  One core instruction can be inserted here without penalty.
//  Note that if the integer product exceeds 32 bits, more
//  Code will be needed to calculate the upper bits.
```

Figure 6-9. Integer multiplication example

```
// CONVERT SIGNED INTEGER TO DOUBLE

//        The integer is in r4
//        The double-precision floating-point result is left in f7:f6
//        The register f5:f4 contains BN+BC = 0x4330 0000 8000 0000
     xorh     0x8000, r4, r4  // Complement sign bit (equivalent to adding BC).
     ixfr     r4,    f6       // Construct low half.
     fmov.ss  f5,    f7       // Set exponent in high half(includes BN)
//   One instruction can be inserted here without penalty.
     fsub.dd  f6,    f4, f6   // (x + BN + BC) - (BN + BC) = x
//   Two core instructions can be inserted here without penalty.
```

Figure 6-10. Conversion from signed integer to double-precision floating-point example

complement integer representation and normalize the converted value. This is accomplished by using two biases:

BC	A bias that compensates for the fact that the signed integer is stored in two's complement format. The value of this bias is 2^{31}.
BN	A bias that produces a normalized number, so that the algorithm does not cause a floating-point exception. The value of this bias is 2^{52} and is encoded into the exponent bias field of the floating-point representation.

If the desired value is x, then the constructed value is x + BC + BN. By later subtracting BC + BN, the value x is left in double-precision format and properly normalized.

The value of BC + BN is $2^{52} + 2^{31}$ (0x4330_0000_8000_0000).

Refer back to Chapter 4, "Machine Organization," for the complete representation of the floating-point values. This conversion can be combined with the floating-point divide example of Figure 6-5 to give the integer divide example of Figure 6-11. The full integer divide requires 62 clock cycles or 59 clock cycles without the remainder calculation.

Conversion from signed integer to single-precision floating-point cannot be performed as easily as in the double-precision case. This is because the 32-bits of integer will not fit in the fraction field of the single-precision representation which contains only 23 bits. Instead, the conversion can be performed by the same method as with double-precision, followed by a **famov.ds**.

Dual-Operation Instructions

In addition to the pipelined instructions that perform an add or multiply, there is a class of dual-operation instructions, called *dual-ops* for short, that perform an add and a multiply. Along with advancing both pipelines, these dual-ops specify the input and output paths for the adder and multiplier—all in one 32-bit instruction. Dual-ops are useful for calculations that require both additions and multiplications, and can be used along with the pipelined instructions that advance only one of the pipelines.

```
//        The denominator is in r4
//        The numerator is in r5
//        The quotient is left in r6
//        The remainder is left in r7
//        The registers f2 through f11 are used as temporaries.
// Convert Denominator and Numerator
fld.d two52two31, f6          // load constant 2**52 + 2**31 (BC + BN)
xorh      0x8000,  r4,    r19 //
ixfr      r19,     f4         //
fmov.ss   f7,      f5         //
xorh      0x8000,  r5,    r20 //
fsub.dd   f4,      f6,    f4  //
ixfr      r20,     f2         //
fmov.ss   f7,      f3         //
fsub.dd   f2,      f6,    f2  //
// Do Floating-Point Divide
fld.d     fdtwo,   f10        // load floating-point two
frcp.dd   f4,      f6         // first guess has 2**-8 error
fmul.dd   f4,      f6,    f8  // guess * divisor
fsub.dd   f10,     f8,    f8  // 2 - guess * divisor
fmul.dd   f6,      f8,    f6  // second guess has 2**-15 error
fmul.dd   f4,      f6,    f8  // avoid using f6 as src1
fsub.dd   f10,     f8,    f8  // 2 - guess * divisor
fmul.dd   f6,      f8,    f6  // third guess has 2**-29 error
fmul.dd   f4,      f6,    f8  // avoid using f6 as src1
fsub.dd   f10,     f8,    f8  // 2 - guess * divisor
fmul.dd   f6,      f2,    f6  // guess * dividend
fmul.dd   f8,      f6,    f8  // result = third guess * dividend
// Convert Quotient to Integer
fld.d  onepluseps,f10         // load value 1 + 2**-40
fmul.dd   f8,      f10,   f8  // force quotient to be bigger than integer
ixfr      r4,      f10        // get denominator for remainder computation
ftrunc.dd f8,             f8  // convert to integer
// Compute Remainder
fmlow.dd  f10,     f8,    f10 // quotient * denominator
fxfr      f10,     r4
fxfr      f8,      r6         // transfer quotient
subs      r5,      r7,    r7  // remainder = numerator - quotient *
                              //denominator
```

Figure 6-11. Signed integer divide example

There are four basic dual-op instruction types: **pfam**, **pfsm**, **pfmam**, and **pfmsm**. Each of these instructions specifies the precision of the operands and operation of the adder (add or subtract), advances the adder pipeline, advances the multiplier pipeline, and specifies which unit supplies the result for the *fdest* destination register. The **pfam** and **pfsm** store the results of the adder to the *fdest,* while the **pfmam** and **pfmsm** store the results of the multiplier.

Figure 6-12 shows the dual operation data paths and the special registers KR, KI, and T. The special registers may be used to store and subsequently supply data for the dual-operation instructions. KR and KI can store the value of *src1* and later supply that value to the multiplier as a Konstant (constant). Having two constant registers eases calculations that involve complex math where both a real (KR) and an imaginary

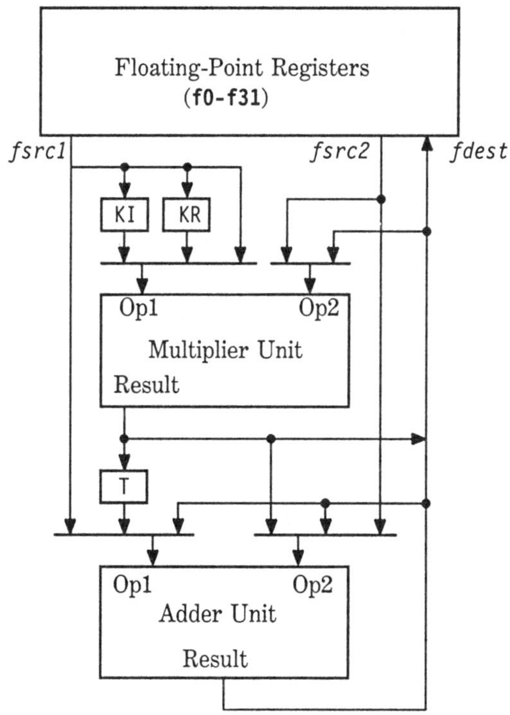

Figure 6-12. Floating-point unit including registers, data paths, adder, and multiplier

(KI) operand are used. Except for being referenced by different instructions, KR and KI are treated the same. The third special register is the T (Temporary) register, which can store the result of the multiplier pipeline and later supply that value to the adder pipeline.

In addition to data for the units' inputs coming from floating-point registers or special registers, results from each unit can be fed back and used as inputs. A four-bit *DPC* (data path control field) in the instruction's opcode field specifies the input operands and controls the loading of the special registers. The DPC encoding allows the following specifications:

1. Operand-1 of the multiplier can be KR, KI, or *src1*.
2. Operand-2 of the multiplier can be *src2*, the last-stage result of the multiplier pipeline, or the last-stage result of the adder pipeline.
3. Operand-1 of the adder can be *src1*, the T register, the last-stage result of the multiplier pipeline, or the last-stage result of the adder pipeline.
4. Operand-2 of the adder can be *src2*, the last-stage result of the multiplier pipeline, or the last-stage result of the adder pipeline.

The instruction types, combined with the DPC codes, make up the available dual-operation instructions. As shown in Tables 6-3a and 6-3b, each mnemonic specifies the required operands: two multiplier inputs and an output, two adder inputs and an output. The effect on the special registers is also specified as part of the instructions. Note that the instructions **pfam**, **pfsm**, **pfmam**, and **pfmsm** themselves are not valid instruction mnemonics, as they do not fully describe the data paths for the operands. Instead, the mnemonics from within the table, which include the DPC encoding, are used.

Table 6-3a includes the **pfam** and **pfsm** instruction types, which store the result of the adder unit to the destination register. The result from the multiplier unit may be stored to the special T register or used as Op2 for the adder unit. The **pfmam** and **pfmsm** instruction types in Table 6-3b store the result of the multiplier into the floating-point destination register. When used, the **pfmam** and **pfmsm** instructions advance the adder unit pipeline and discard the result. Instructions from both tables

Table 6-3. DPC Encodings *a.* `pfam` *and* `pfsm` *instructions*
b. `pfmam` *and* `pfmsm` *instructions*

a.

DPC	pfam Mnemonic	pfsm Mnemonic	M-Unit Op1	M-Unit Op2	A-Unit Op1	A-Unit Op2	T Load	K Load*
0000	**r2p1**	**r2s1**	KR	*src2*	*src1*	M result	No	No
0001	**r2pt**	**r2st**	KR	*src2*	T	M result	No	Yes
0010	**r2ap1**	**r2as1**	KR	*src2*	*src1*	A result	Yes	No
0011	**r2apt**	**r2ast**	KR	*src2*	T	A result	Yes	Yes
0100	**i2p1**	**i2s1**	KI	*src2*	*src1*	M result	No	No
0101	**i2pt**	**i2st**	KI	*src2*	T	M result	No	Yes
0110	**i2ap1**	**i2as1**	KI	*src2*	*src1*	A result	Yes	No
0111	**i2apt**	**i2ast**	KI	*src2*	T	A result	Yes	Yes
1000	**rat1p2**	**rat1s2**	KR	A result	*src1*	*src2*	Yes	No
1001	**m12apm**	**m12asm**	*src1*	*src2*	A result	M result	No	No
1010	**ra1p2**	**ra1s2**	KR	A result	*src1*	*src2*	No	No
1011	**m12ttpa**	**m12ttsa**	*src1*	*src2*	T	A result	Yes	No
1100	**iat1p2**	**iat1s2**	KI	A result	*src1*	*src2*	Yes	No
1101	**m12tpm**	**m12tsm**	*src1*	*src2*	T	M result	No	No
1110	**ia1p2**	**ia1s2**	KI	A result	*src1*	*src2*	No	No
1111	**m12tpa**	**m12tsa**	*src1*	*src2*	T	A result	No	No

b.

DPC	pfmam Mnemonic	pfmsm Mnemonic	M-Unit Op1	M-Unit Op2	A-Unit Op1	A-Unit Op2	T Load	K Load*
0000	**mr2p1**	**mr2s1**	KR	*src2*	*src1*	M result	No	No
0001	**mr2pt**	**mr2st**	KR	*src2*	T	M result	No	Yes
0010	**mr2mp1**	**mr2ms1**	KR	*src2*	*src1*	M result	Yes	No
0011	**mr2mpt**	**mr2mst**	KR	*src2*	T	M result	Yes	Yes
0100	**mi2p1**	**mi2s1**	KI	*src2*	*src1*	M result	No	No
0101	**mi2pt**	**mi2st**	KI	*src2*	T	M result	No	Yes
0110	**mi2mp1**	**mi2ms1**	KI	*src2*	*src1*	M result	Yes	No
0111	**mi2mpt**	**mi2mst**	KI	*src2*	T	M result	Yes	Yes
1000	**mrmt1p2**	**mrmt1s2**	KR	M result	*src1*	*src2*	Yes	No
1001	**mm12mpm**	**mm12msm**	*src1*	*src2*	M result	M result	No	No
1010	**mrm1p2**	**mrm1s2**	KR	M result	*src1*	*src2*	No	No
1011	**mm12ttpm**	**mm12ttsm**	*src1*	*src2*	T	M result	Yes	No
1100	**mimt1p2**	**mimt1s2**	KI	M result	*src1*	*src2*	Yes	No
1101	**mm12tpm**	**mm12tsm**	*src1*	*src2*	T	M result	No	No
1110	**mim1p2**	**mim1s2**	KI	M result	*src1*	*src2*	No	No
1111	"Reserved"							

* If K-load is set, KR is loaded when operand-1 of the multiplier is KR; KI is loaded when operand-1 of the multiplier is KI.

are included to store the operand into special registers, supply data from a special register for use as an input, or both to store data into and to supply data from a special register. For instructions that store data into and supply data from one special register, the data supplied from the special register is data that was loaded with a previous instruction.

The total of 64 variations of dual-operation floating-point instructions is represented in the 32 diagrams of Figure 6-13 (the add and subtract versions use the same diagram). Although no one will claim that it makes the mnemonics easy to memorize, Figure 6-14 explains how the mnemonics for the instructions are derived. An initial **m** before the encoding indicates that the multiplier result is stored and the adder result is lost. However, a leading **m12** refers to the multiplier unit source operands, not the results.

The many combinations of dual-operation instructions provide enough flexibility that most algorithms may be efficiently coded. One added restriction is that when the multiplier uses *src1* for Op1, KR or KI, *src1* must not be the same as *fdest*. In all other cases, *src1* and/or *src2* may be the same as *fdest*, and the newly produced result will be used as the source.

In addition to observing the rules for mixing precision within the multiplier pipeline described earlier, care must be taken with the temporary registers. During operations that load special registers, all 64 bits of the special register are updated. The 32-bit single-precision values are padded to 64 bits during the special register load. Three zero bits are appended to the upper exponent field, and zeros are padded to the lower 29 fraction bits. Before switching precision, a program that will use KR, KI, or T should first clear them. This will prevent the possible traps that might occur if a valid single-precision value is interpreted as a double-precision operand, or a valid double-precision value is interpreted as a single-precision operand. KR, KI and T can be initialized to zero with three single-precision

```
r2apt.ss f0, f0, f0
```

and one

```
i2apt.ss f0, f0, f0
```

instructions. Because the sequence loads all zeros, it is effective for initialization before either single- or double-precision calculations because all zeros are valid for both formats.

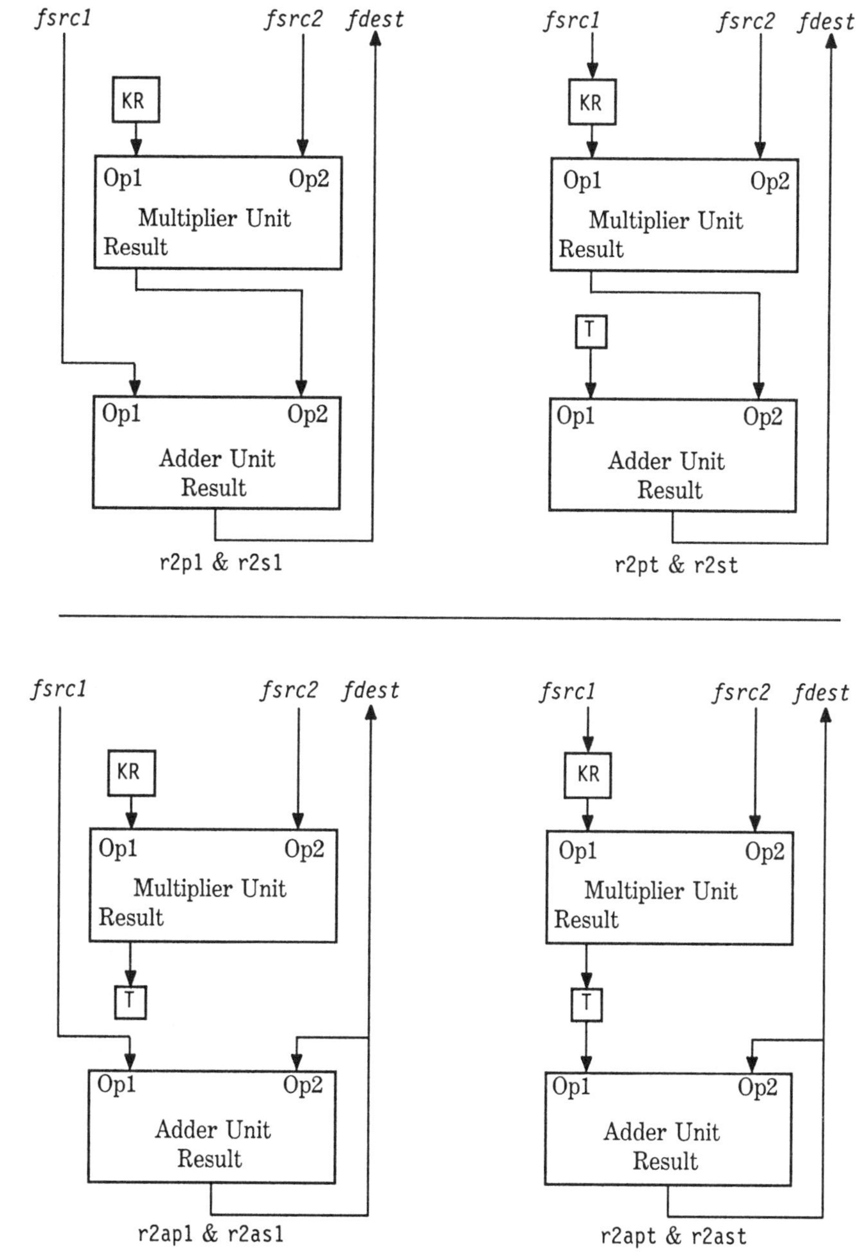

Figure 6-13. Data paths by instruction

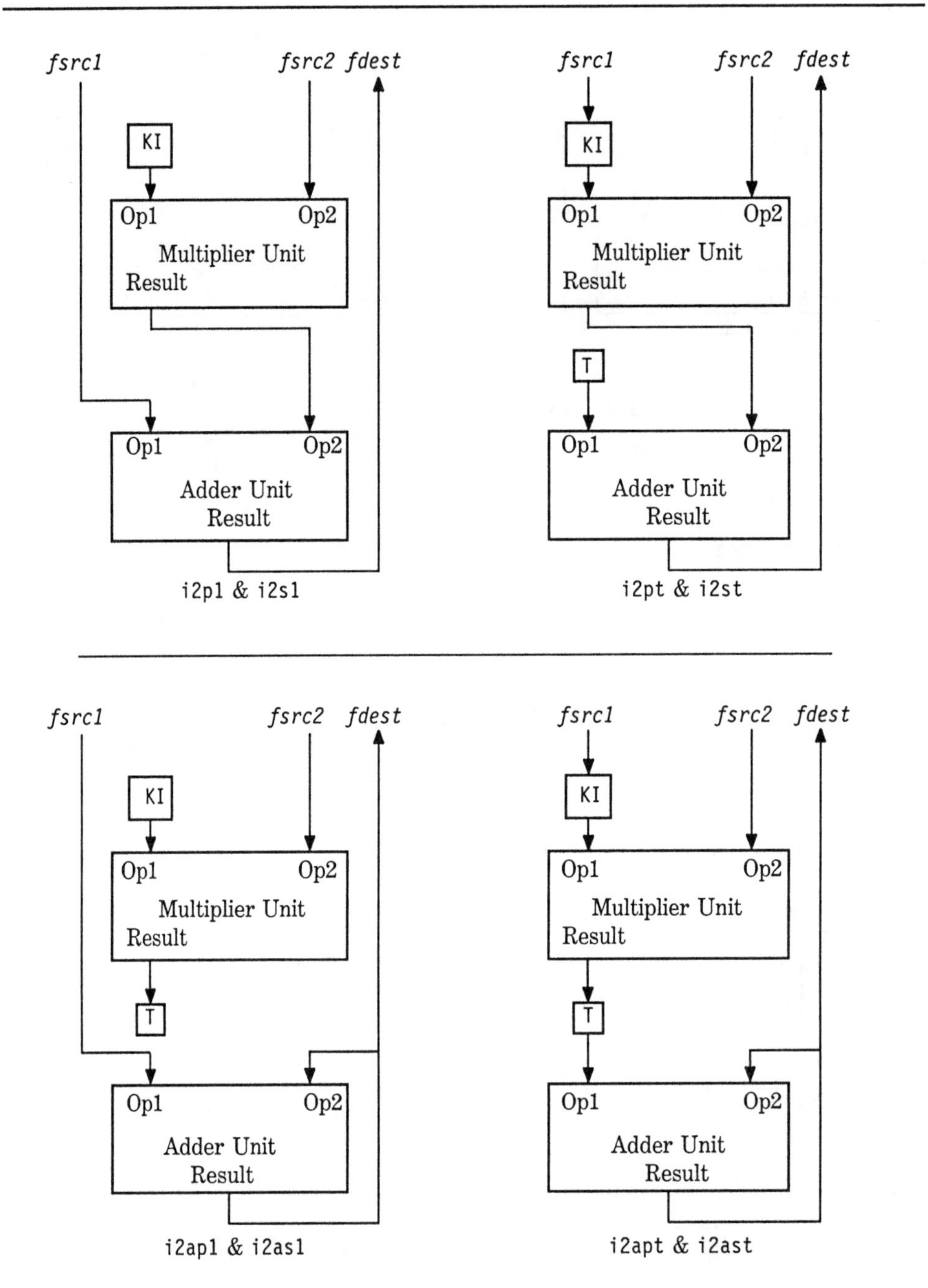

***Figure 6-13. Data paths by instruction** (continued)*

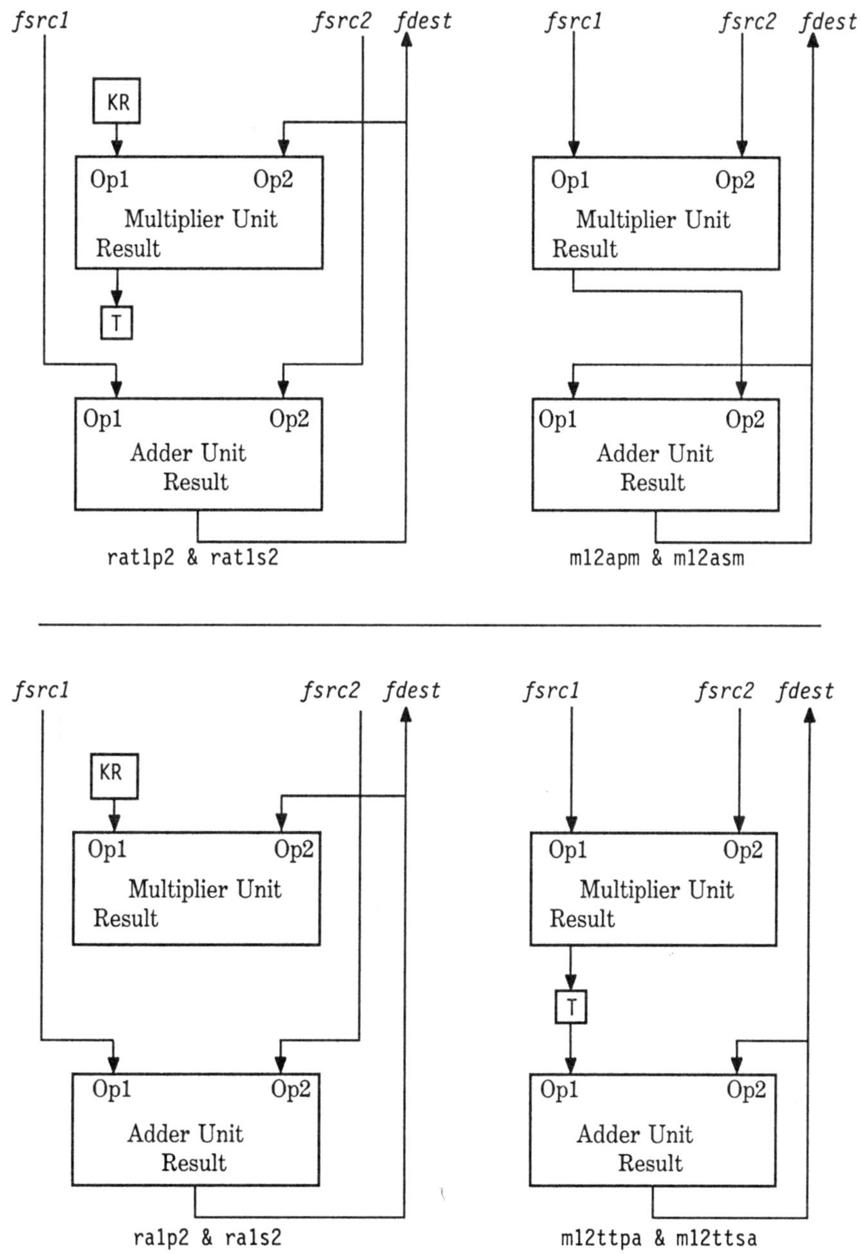

Figure 6-13. Data paths by instruction *(continued)*

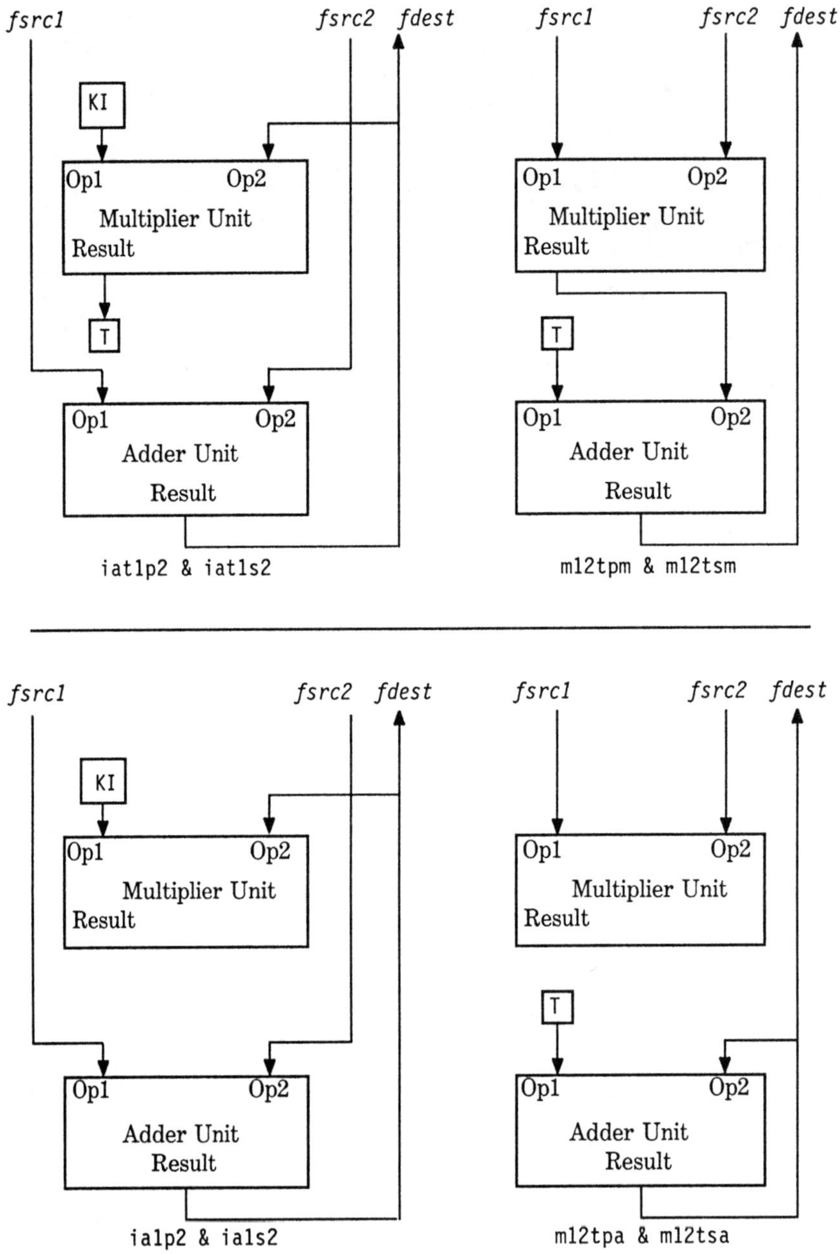

Figure 6-13. Data paths by instruction *(continued)*

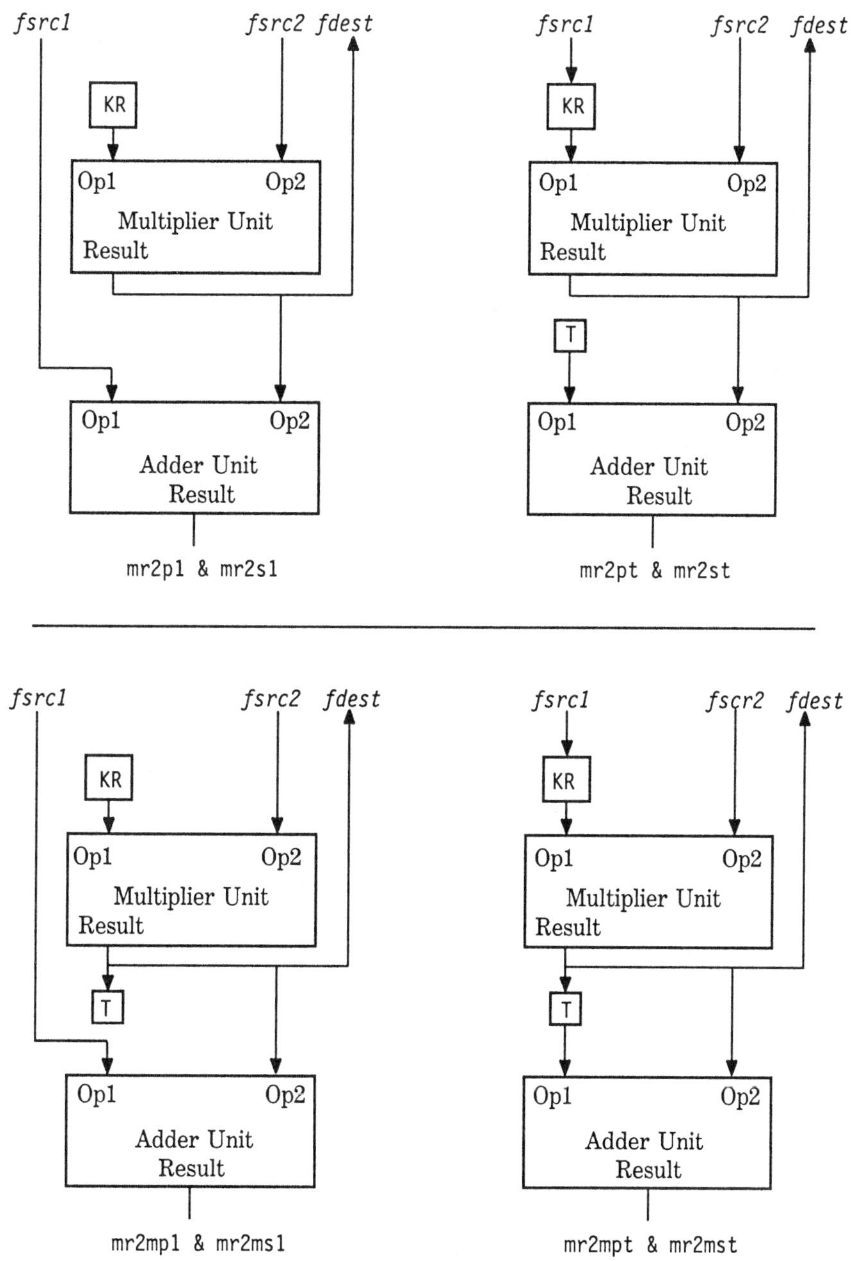

Figure 6-13. Data paths by instruction *(continued)*

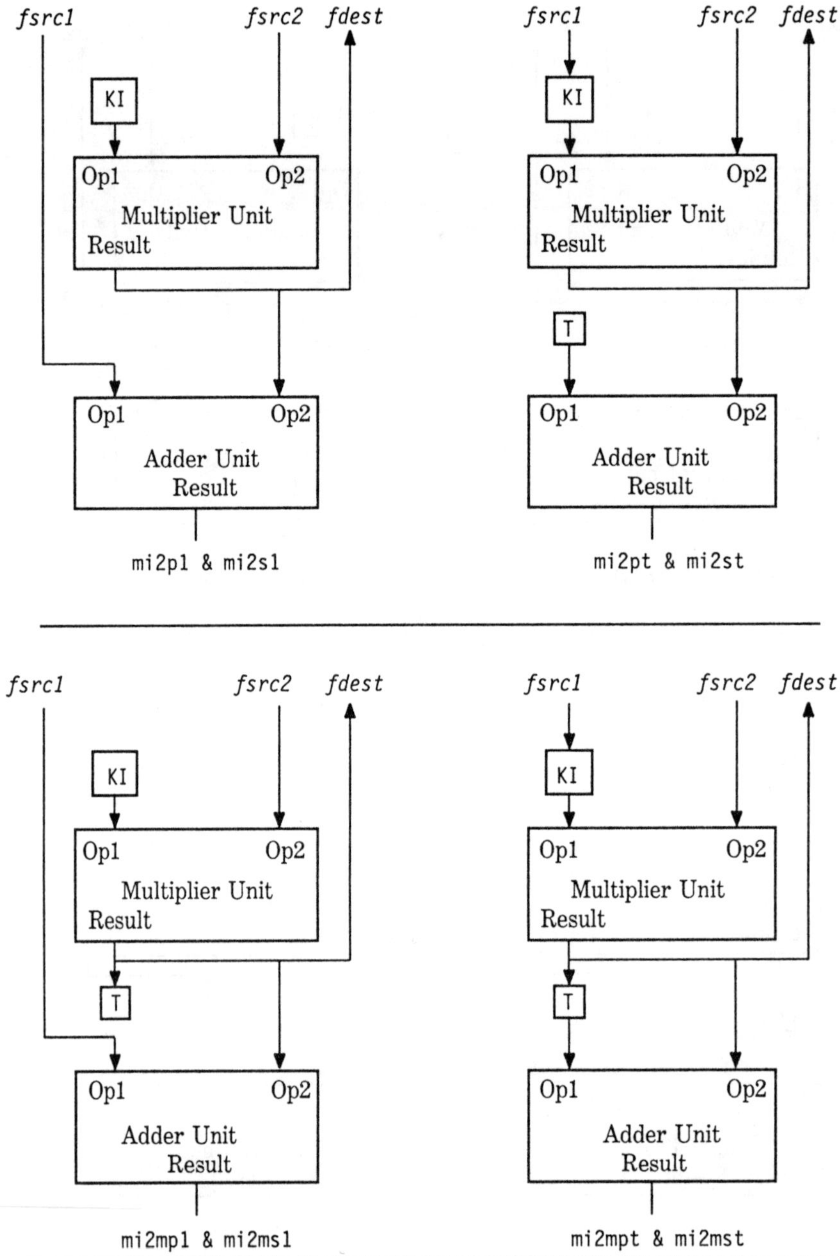

Figure 6-13. Data paths by instruction *(continued)*

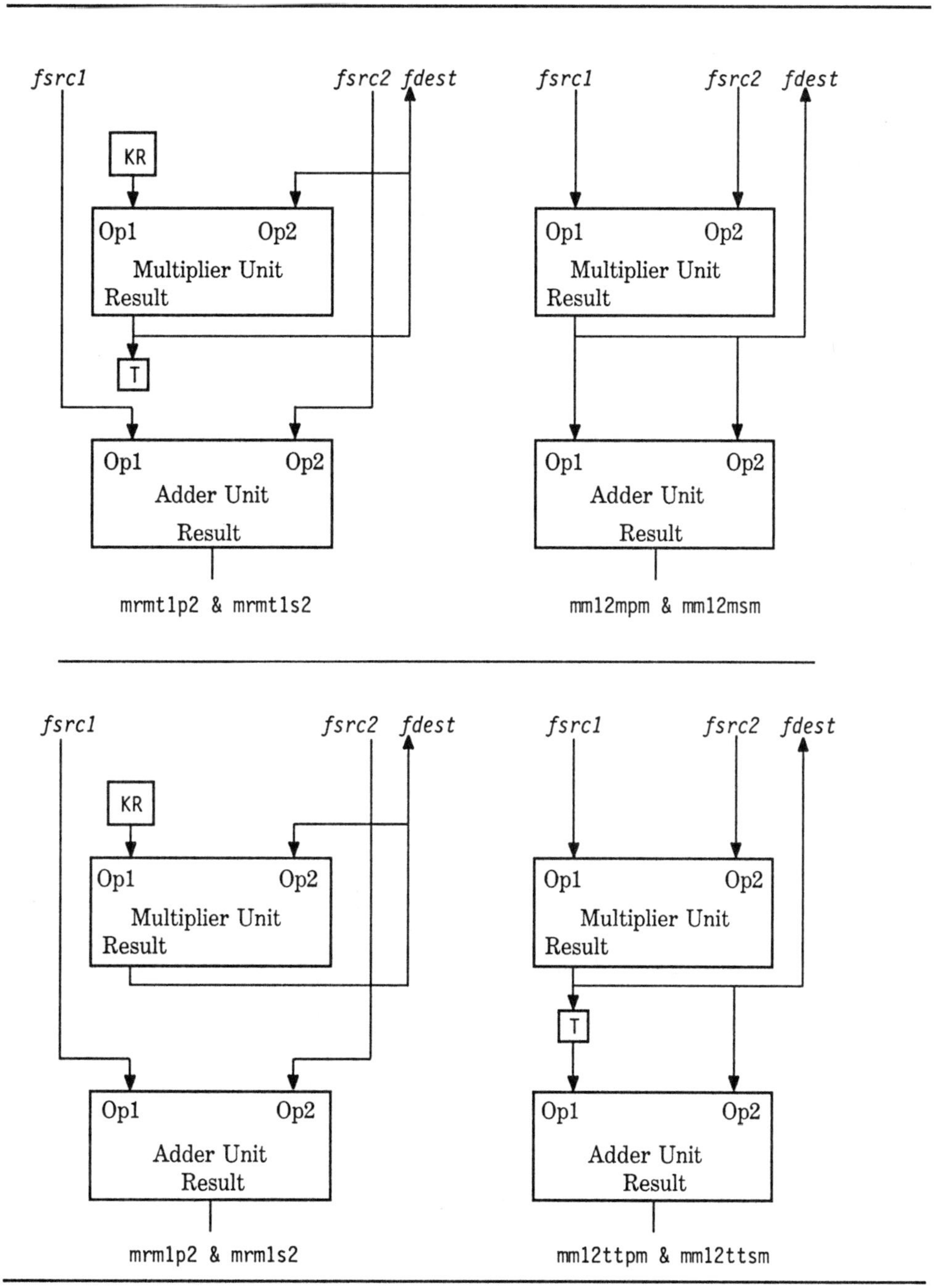

Figure 6-13. Data paths by instruction *(continued)*

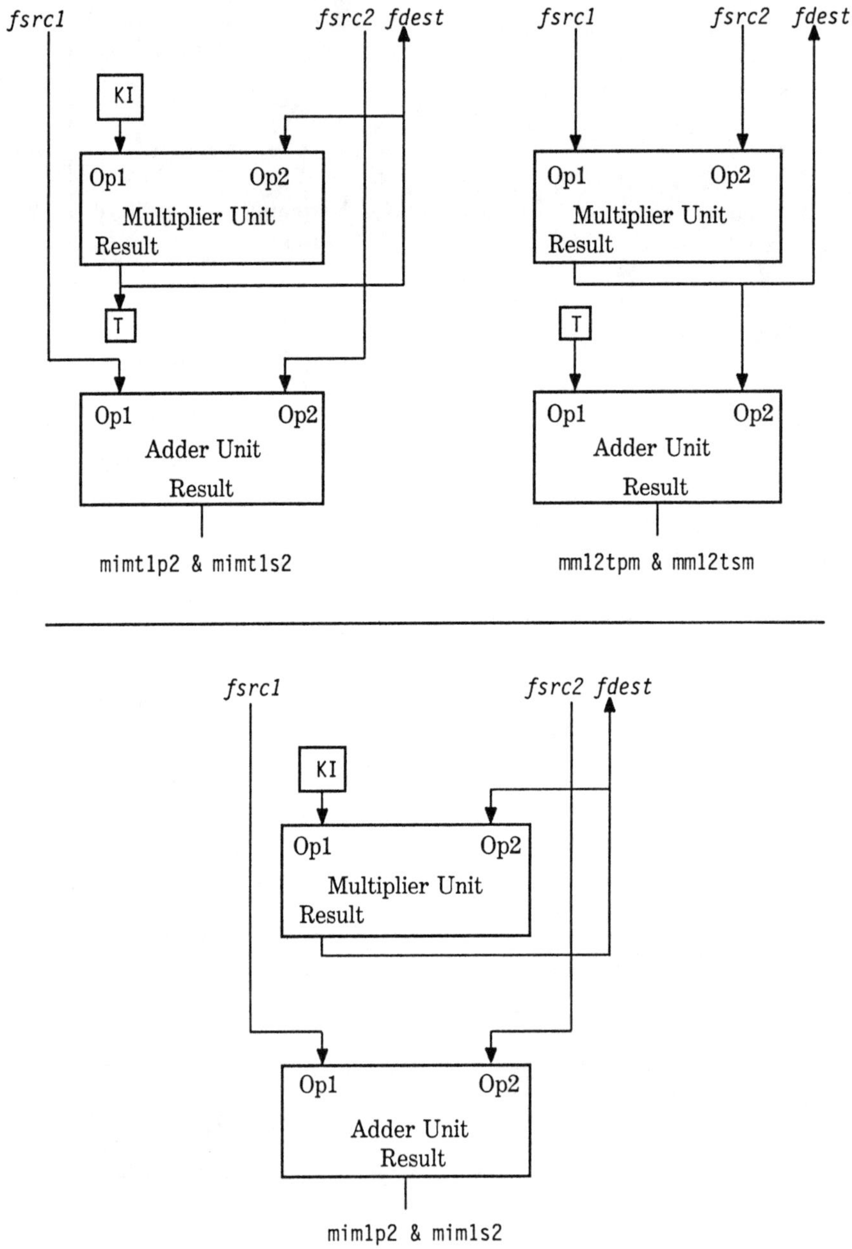

***Figure 6-13. Data paths by instruction** (continued)*

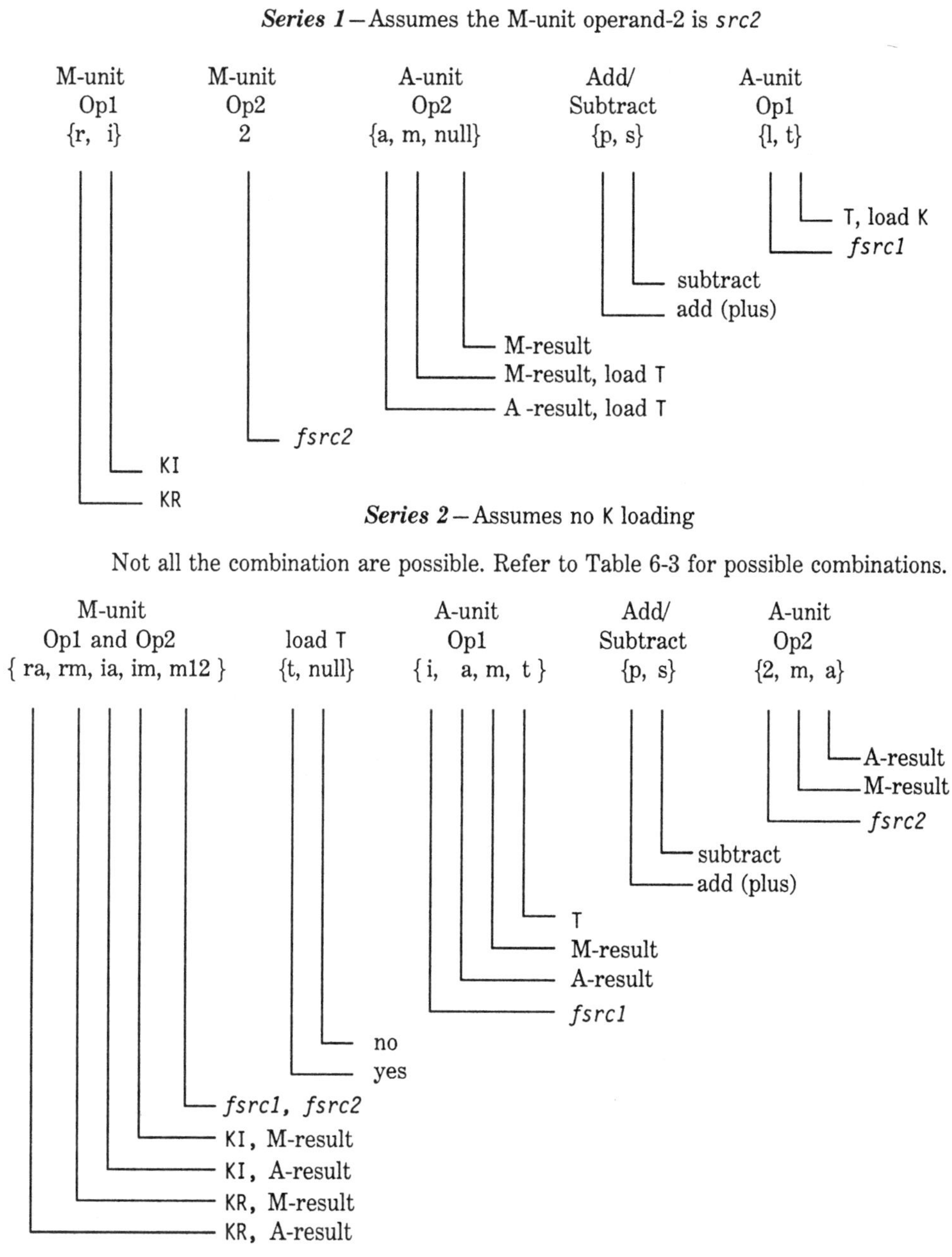

Figure 6-14. Data path mnemonics

Instruction	KI	KR	Multiplier Stages			T	Adder Stages			rdest
			1	2	3		1	2	3	

(a) Single-precision floating-point stages

Figure 6-15. Floating-point stage forms

Instruction	KI	KR	Multiplier 1	Multiplier 2	T 3	Adder Stages 1	Adder Stages 2	Adder Stages 3	rdest

(b) Double-precision floating-point stages

Figure 6-15. Floating-point stage forms

The use of dual-operation instructions has varying degrees of complexity depending on the calculation being performed. Calculations that use several different variations of dual-ops can be difficult to visualize. The blank worksheets shown in Figures 6-15a and 6-15b may be useful for tracking the intermediate stages and results of the adder and multiplier units. The first worksheet is for single- and the second for double-precision.

When developing an algorithm, it is sometimes helpful to use the pipelined operations that advance only the adder or the multiplier pipelines along with the dual-ops for implementing certain calculations. However, if a calculation requires an approximately equal number of adds and multiplies, the dual-ops can be used exclusively. One example of such a calculation is the dot product. Dot-product calculations follow a very regular structure and only one type of dual-op, **m12apm**, is required for the continuous operation portion of the calculation. This is shown in the following example where two eight-element vectors are multiplied.

Dot-Product Example

Consider performing the dot product of an eight-element vector *A* with another vector *B*. For the purpose of tracking the values through the pipelines, assume that the vectors are already loaded into the registers with the values shown in Figures 6-16 and 6-16b.

The calculation to perform is a series of multiplications followed by additions of the form:

```
1.0*8.0 + 2.0*7.0 + 3.0*6.0 + 4.0*5.0 + 5.0*4.0 + 6.0*3.0 + 7.0*2.0 + 8.0*1.0
```

a. ***Single-precision values for the example in Figure 6-17***

```
A:   f4  =  1.0
     f5  =  2.0
     f6  =  3.0
     f7  =  4.0
     f8  =  5.0
     f9  =  6.0
     f10 =  7.0
     f11 =  8.0

B:   f12 =  8.0
     f13 =  7.0
     f14 =  6.0
     f15 =  5.0
     f16 =  4.0
     f17 =  3.0
     f18 =  2.0
     f19 =  1.0
```

b. ***Double-precision values for the example in Figure 6-18***

```
A:   f4  =  1.0
     f6  =  2.0
     f8  =  3.0
     f10 =  4.0
     f12 =  5.0
     f14 =  6.0

B:   f16 =  6.0
     f18 =  5.0
     f20 =  4.0
     f22 =  3.0
     f24 =  2.0
     f26 =  1.0
```

Figure 6-16. Register values and assignments for dot-product examples

The code, shown in Figure 6-17, is broken into three phases: priming, continuous operation, and flushing. The priming phase loads the multiplier stages with the first three calculations, discards the results, then clears the adder pipeline with three **pfadd** instructions. The continuous operation phase uses the instruction **m12apm** to perform the multiply, feed the intermediate results to the adder, and perform the add operation. The flushing phase of the dot-product example retrieves the intermediate results and produces the final dot-product result.

Figure 6-18 is the dot product performed for double-precision values. The code is arranged as with the single-precision example. The distinguishing difference for the double-precision example is that the multiply

```
// Pipelined Dual-Operation Instruction (single-precision)

//                                  Multiplier           Adder
//                                    Stages             Stages
//                                  1    2   3      1      2      3        Result

// Priming phase
     m12apm.ss f4, f12,f0  //      1*8  ??   ??    ??     ??     ??        Discard
     m12apm.ss f5, f13,f0  //      2*7  1*8  ??    ??     ??     ??        Discard
     m12apm.ss f6, f14,f0  //      3*6  2*7  8     ??     ??     ??        Discard

     pfadd.ss  f0, f0 ,f0  //                      0      ??     ??        Discard
     pfadd.ss  f0, f0 ,f0  //                      0      0      ??        Discard
     pfadd.ss  f0, f0 ,f0  //                      0      0      0         Discard

// Continuous operation phase
     m12apm.ss f7, f15,f0  //      4*5  3*6  14   8+0     0+0    0         Discard
     m12apm.ss f8, f16,f0  //      5*4  4*5  18   14+0    8+0    0         Discard
     m12apm.ss f9, f17,f0  //      6*3  5*4  20   18+0    14+0        8    Discard
     m12apm.ss f10,f18,f0  //      7*2  6*3  20   20+8    18+0   14        Discard
     m12apm.ss f11,f19,f0  //      8*1  7*2  18   20+14   20+8   18        Discard
// For larger matrices, include more instructions here

// Flushing phase
     m12apm.ss f0, f0, f0  //      0*0  8*1  14   18+18   20+14  28        Discard
     m12apm.ss f0, f0, f0  //      0*0  0*0  8    14+28   18+18  34        Discard
     m12apm.ss f0, f0, f0  //      0*0  0*0  0     8+34   14+28  36        Discard

// Sum the partial results
     pfadd.ss  f0, f0, f20 //                      0+0    8+34   42        f20=36
     pfadd.ss  f20,f21,f21 //                     42+36   0+0    42        f21=42
     pfadd.ss  f0, f0, f20 //                      0+0    42+36  0         f20=42
     pfadd.ss  f0, f0, f0  //                      0+0    0+0    78        Discard
     pfadd.ss  f0, f0, f21 //                      0+0    0+0    0         f21=78
     fadd.ss   f20,f21,f20 //                                              f20=120
```

Figure 6-17. Dot-product example (single-precision)

pipeline is two stages instead of three, where each stage takes two clocks to execute. The algorithm uses dual-operation instructions because an almost equal number of add and multiply operations is required.

This simple dot-product example serves as the basis for the two-dimensional matrix multiply examples in Chapter 8, "Programming for

Parallelism." The Chapter 8 examples also cover the memory operations for loading and storing operands. A more elaborate dual-operation example that makes use of the temporary registers is shown with the FFT application example in Chapter 10, "Application Example: The Fast Fourier Transform."

```
// Pipelined Dual-Operation Instruction  (Double-Precision)

//                                Multiplier          Adder
//                                 Stages             Stages
//                                1    2         1      2     3    Result

// Priming phase
     m12apm.dd f4,  f16,f0  //    1*6  ??        ??     ??    ??   Discard
     m12apm.dd f6,  f18,f0  //    2*5  1*6       ??     ??    ??   Discard

     pfadd.dd  f0,  f0 ,f0  //                    0     ??    ??   Discard
     pfadd.dd  f0,  f0 ,f0  //                    0      0    ??   Discard
     pfadd.dd  f0,  f0 ,f0  //                    0      0     0   Discard

// Continuous operation phase
     m12apm.dd f8,  f20,f0  //    3*4  2*5       6+0     0     0   Discard
     m12apm.dd f10,f22,f0   //    4*3  3*4      10+0    6+0    0   Discard
     m12apm.dd f12,f24,f0   //    5*2  4*3      12+0   10+0    6   Discard
     m12apm.dd f14,f26,f0   //    6*1  5*2      12+6   12+0   10   Discard
// For larger vectors,  include more instructions here

// Flushing phase
     m12apm.dd f0,  f0,  f0  //   0*0  6*1      10+10  12+6   12   Discard
     m12apm.dd f0,  f0,  f0  //   0*0  0*0       6+12  10+10  18   Discard
//  Three partial sums are now in the adder pipeline.
     pfadd.dd  f0 ,f0 ,f28 //                     0     6+12  20   f28 = 18
     pfadd.dd  f28,f30,f30 //                   18+20    0    18   f30 = 20
     pfadd.dd  f0 ,f0 ,f28 //                     0    18+20   0   f28 = 18
     pfadd.dd  f0 ,f0 ,f0  //                     0      0    38   Discard
     pfadd.dd  f0 ,f0 ,f30 //                     0      0     0   f30 = 38
      fadd.dd  f28,f30,f30 //                                      f30 = 56
```

Figure 6-18. Dot-product example (double-precision)

CHAPTER 7
GRAPHICS RENDERING INSTRUCTIONS

Displaying pictures on a computer can be done in many different ways. In this chapter we consider the display of pictures that are approximated by a database (display list) of points. In the database, each point can be represented by pairs or triplets of numbers, depending on whether the data is two- or three-dimensional. Points can be arranged to represent line endpoints, or vertices of polygons. Displaying a picture involves determining a specific view of the database. The displayed view is formed by rotating, translating, scaling, and performing various projections of the data. Using a database of points is more convenient and efficient than storing the entire picture bit by bit. The integer and floating-point instructions of the i860 processor efficiently perform the basic calculations for orienting the points before display, including any high-level lighting model calculations.

Once these steps are performed, displaying the picture requires the use of special integer operations for shading, distance interpolation, and hidden surface elimination. The i860 processor has five special operations designed to speed these final display rendering operations. Four of these operations are executed by the graphics unit:

- Z-buffer check
- Add with Z merge
- Add with pixel merge
- **OR** with MERGE register

The fifth operation, pixel store, is executed by the RISC core. This chapter discusses the function each of these instructions performs and how to use them to boost the performance of graphics applications.

3-D Rendering Overview

Consider a solid object that may be approximated by a large number of polygons where the vertices of the polygons comprise the object's database. Storing all of the pixels would consume too much memory and take too much time to manipulate so the vertices are used as an approximation of the object. There are several steps, referred to as the *graphics pipeline,* that must be performed before an object's database can be displayed as pixels. These steps have considerable variation between systems. In general, the steps include translating the coordinate system of the object to the coordinates of the display system, clipping, projecting the object onto the projection plane, transforming the view of the object, performing any high-level light source calculations, and finally coloring and drawing the object's pixels to the display system.

During the transform step, new positions for the vertices of the polygons are calculated. Chapter 11, "Application Example: The 3-D Graphics Transform," contains an application example for performing the 3-D graphics transformation. Following the transform, the locations and color intensities of the vertices of the polygons are known, but the points between these vertices must be calculated. These points, along with their associated data, are called pixels (pixture elements). If an

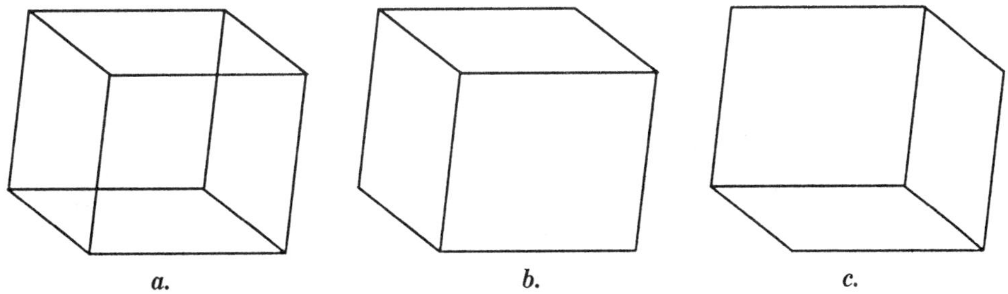

Figure 7-1. Wire frame display and display with hidden lines removed

object is displayed with only the vertices and simple line drawing of its edges, it will appear as a wire frame.

Wire frame display can create ambiguity in the interpretation of the object. This is illustrated in the wire frame drawing of a cube in Figure 7-1a. Here, the cube can be interpreted in one of two orientations; either from above and to the left, or from below and to the right. The ambiguity occurs because the edges that would not be seen on the cube are shown in the wire frame display. By removing the hidden edges, as shown in Figures 7-1b and 7-1c, the intended view of the cube becomes clear.

To show 3-D images, hiding vertices, edges, and volumes is required as the surface of the polygons in view must be displayed. Where polygons overlap, the polygon closest to the viewer must be displayed. Consider the two polygons of Figure 7-2 shown with the three-dimensional coordinates x, y, and z. The rectangle is perpendicular to the z axis and is penetrated by the triangle. Figure 7-2b shows the two polygons from the view at infinity along the positive z axis. In graphics calculations, the Z value represents the distance from the viewer. The i860 processor's graphics instructions include Z interpolation for determining Z values of points not on a vertex and Z-buffer checking to determine which pixel data should be displayed.

Once it is known which pixels will be displayed, the values for all of the pixels must be determined from the known values at the vertices.

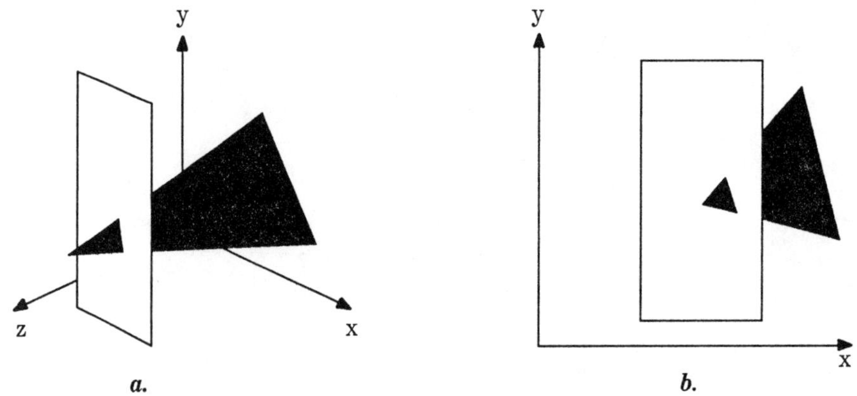

Figure 7-2. ***a. Two polygons with the three-dimensional coordinates x, y, and z***
b. Two polygons viewed from along the positive z axis

Pixel interpolation allows smooth linear changes in pixel intensity and color between vertices. The actual sequence for Z-buffer checking and pixel interpolation is usually reversed. This is because, as you will see later in this chapter, the pixel interpolation is an iterative process and not easily accomplished for nonsequential pixel regions.

Graphics Hardware

The graphics unit of the i860 processor utilizes the floating-point registers and data paths, as well as a dedicated MERGE register and bits within the **psr** (processor status register) control register. Graphics instructions take advantage of the 64-bit data paths and can operate on multiple pixels simultaneously. The processor supports 8-, 16-, and 32-bit pixels, operating respectively on 8, 4, or 2 pixels simultaneously. The pixel field formats are shown in Figure 7-3. The Z-buffer resolution can be either 16 or 32 bits. The core instruction **pst.d** (pixel store) can operate in parallel with the graphics unit instructions via dual-instruction mode.

The **psr** fields for graphics operations are shown in Figure 7-4. There are two PS (Pixel Size) bits to control the pixel size as defined in

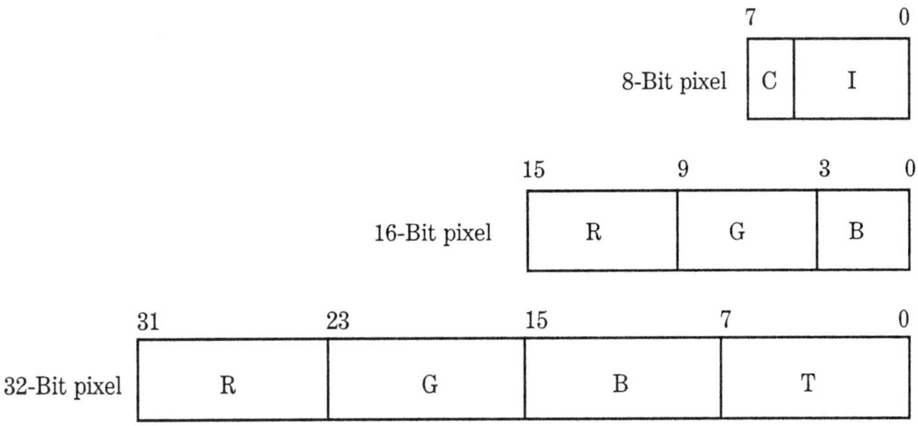

I—Intensity, R—Red Intensity, G—Green Intensity, B—Blue Intensity, C—Color, T—Texture

These assignments of specific meanings to the fields of pixels are for illustration purposes only. Only the field sizes are defined, not the specific use of each field.

Figure 7-3. Pixel formats

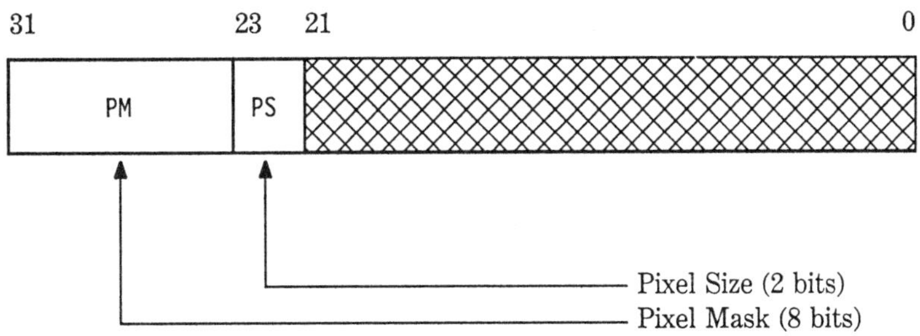

Figure 7-4. `psr` ***fields for graphics operations***

Table 7-1. The eight PM (Pixel Mask) bits are used by the **pst.d** instruction and correspond to which pixels are updated. Depending on the pixel size, only some of the PM bits will be used. For example, with 16-bit pixels only the lower four PM bits are used with the low-order bit corresponding to the low-order (lowest address) pixel. The PM bits can mask-out which pixels are stored by the **pst.d** instruction. If the PM bit is cleared, the corresponding pixel will not be stored. (This is accomplished by controlling the Byte Enable (BE7#-BE0#) pins of the chip during the store cycle.) The PM bits are set by the Z-buffer checking instruction, to be explained later in this chapter. The basic idea is that the PM bit mask allows the pixels nearer to the viewer to update the display while hidden pixels are masked-out.

The graphics instructions and the pixel store instruction primarily use the floating-point registers for holding the data values. There is also a special 64-bit MERGE register. The MERGE register is used for both distance interpolation and intensity interpolation. The MERGE register is convenient for these operations because the instructions automatically shift and merge multiple pixel values into the register. Unfortunately, the MERGE register cannot be directly accessed by the store instruction. Instead, the **form.dd** (**OR** with MERGE register) is used to transfer, with an optional **OR** operation, the MERGE register contents to a floating-point register. The floating-point register can then be accessed with the store instruction.

Because the graphics unit utilizes the floating-point registers and data path, it can operate in parallel with the RISC core. This is useful

***Table 7-1. PS (Pixel Size) Field Encoding for* psr**

Value	*Pixel Size in Bits*	*Pixel Size in Bytes*
00	8	1
01	16	2
10	32 (or 24)	4 (or 3)
11	(undefined)	(undefined)

for overlapping **pst.d** instructions with the Z and pixel value calculations. The graphics unit has a one-stage pipeline, and each of the four graphics unit instruction types has both a scalar and pipelined version. Because the graphics unit pipeline is only one stage, both the scalar and pipelined instructions are executed in one clock cycle. The pipelined graphics instructions are provided so that, if desired, they can be conveniently intermixed with the pipelined floating-point instructions. This avoids the interlock that occurs when mixing scalar and pipelined instructions as discussed in Chapter 6, "Floating-Point Operations." Most graphics code can use the scalar version without any performance loss.

Graphics Instructions

After this overview of 3-D rendering and of the graphics hardware, it is now time to explain each of the four types of graphics unit instructions and the pixel store instruction. Table 7-2 lists each of the graphics unit instructions. Although there are ten instructions listed, five are pipelined versions of the other five, and the Z-buffer check instructions **fzchks** and **fzchkl** are functionally similar but differ in the assumed Z value precision—16- (short) or 32-bit (long).

Table 7-2. Graphics Instruction Mnemonics and Descriptions

Mnemonic	*Description*
fzchks	16-bit Z-buffer check
pfzchks	Pipelined 16-bit Z-buffer check
fzchkl	32-bit Z-buffer check
pfzchkl	Pipelined 32-bit Z-buffer check
faddp	Add with pixel merge
pfaddp	Pipelined add with pixel merge
faddz	Add with Z merge
pfaddz	Pipelined add with Z merge
form	**OR** with MERGE register
pform	Pipelined **OR** with MERGE register

Z-Buffer Check Instruction

The Z-buffer stores the depths of the pixels currently being displayed. This is then used in performing hidden surface elimination. Before updating the pixel data at a given location, the new pixel's depth is compared to the depth of the pixel currently being displayed. If the new pixel is closer to the viewer than the currently displayed pixel, the point is updated with the new pixel value. If the new value is not closer, then

```
Fzchks  16-Bit Z-Buffer Check
Operation:  Consider fsrc1, fsrc2, and fdest each consisting
of four 16-bit fields. Field (0) is the least significant.

PM <-- PM shifted right by 4 bits.
FOR i = 0 to 3
DO
  PM[i + 4] <-- (fsrc2(i) ≤ fsrc1(i)) (unsigned).
  fdest(i) <-- smaller of fsrc2(i) and fsrc1(i).
OD
MERGE <-- 0.

Syntax:  fzchks  fsrc1,fsrc2,fdest


Pfzchks  Pipelined 16-Bit Z-Buffer Check

Operation:  Consider fsrc1, fsrc2, and fdest each consisting
of four 16-bit fields.

PM <-- PM shifted right by 4 bits.
FOR i = 0 to 3
DO
  PM[i + 4] <-- fsrc2(i) ≤ fsrc1(i) (unsigned).
  fdest(i) <-- last stage graphics result.
  Last stage graphics pipeline <-- smaller of fsrc2(i) and fsrc1(i).
OD
MERGE <-- 0.

Syntax:  pfzchks  fsrc1,fsrc2,fdest
```

Figure 7-5. Operation and syntax for fzchks *and* pfzchks *instructions*

the old pixel remains displayed. The Z-buffer check instructions (**fzchks**, **fzchkl**) compare newly formed pixels' Z values to the old values already in the Z-buffer. If the new pixel is closer to the viewer, the corresponding bit in the pixel mask register is set. Also, the instructions aid in updating the Z-buffer value to reflect the newly displayed pixel's Z value.

The i860 processor supports Z-buffers with either 16 or 32 bits of precision. The Z-buffer precision is independent of the pixel size. The Z-buffer precision is determined by whether the 16-bit **fzchks** (Z check short) or the 32-bit **fzchkl** (Z check long) instruction is used. In either case, 64 bits of data are operated on at once. The operation and syntax of the 16-bit **fzchks** and **pfzchks** instructions are shown in Figure 7-5. Because these instructions are for 16-bit Z precisions, four Z checks are performed in parallel. Four unsigned integer (ordinal) compares are

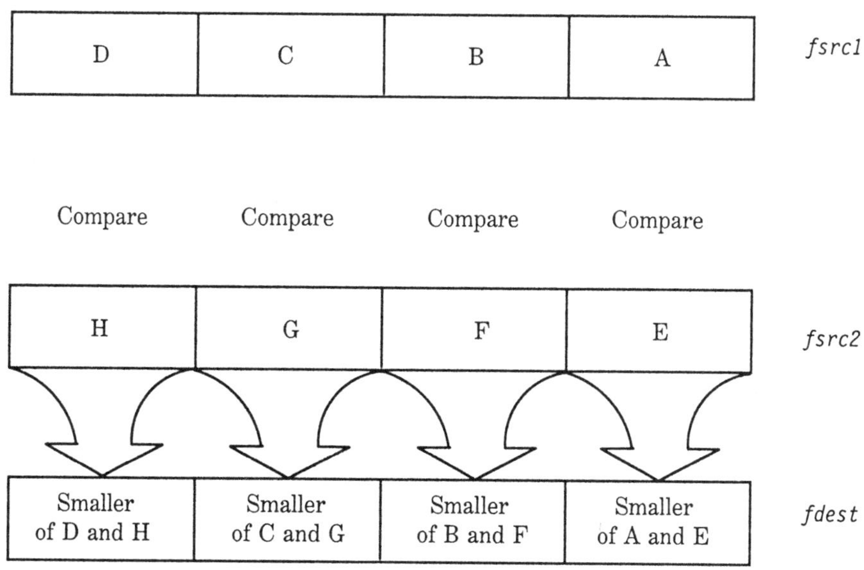

Figure 7-6. **fzchks** *compare and update*

performed on each of the four fields of *fsrc1* and *fsrc2*. The smaller of the two ordinals for each of the four fields is written to *fdest*. This is shown graphically in Figure 7-6. Because **pfzchks** is a pipelined instruction, the value stored to *fdest* is the result from the previous instruction. The operation and syntax for the **fzchkl** and **pfzchkl** instructions are shown in Figure 7-7. These are very similar to **fzchks** instructions, but perform the comparison and floating-point register update for two 32-bit values.

Both the 16- and 32-bit instruction variations set or clear the appropriate PM bits. Note that the current value in the PM field of the **psr** is

```
Fzchkl  32-Bit Z-Buffer Check

Operation:  Consider fsrc1, fsrc2, and fdest each consisting
of two 32-bit fields.

PM <-- PM shifted right by 2 bits.
FOR i = 0 to 1
DO
  PM[i + 6] <-- (fsrc2(i) ≤ fsrc1(i)) (unsigned).
  fdest(i) <-- smaller of fsrc2(i) and fsrc1(i).
OD
MERGE <-- 0.

Syntax:  fzchkl  fsrc1,fsrc2,fdest


Pfzchkl  Pipelined 32-Bit Z-buffer Check

Operation:  Consider fsrc1 fsrc2, and fdest each consisting
of two 32-bit fields.

PM <-- PM shifted right by 2 bits.
FOR i = 0 to 1
DO
  PM[i + 6] <-- (fsrc2(i) ≤ fsrc1(i)) (unsigned).
  fdest(i) <-- last stage graphics result.
  Last stage graphics pipeline <-- smaller of fsrc2(i) and fsrc1(i).
OD
MERGE <-- 0.

Syntax:  pfzchkl  fsrc1,fsrc2,fdest
```

Figure 7-7. Operation and syntax for fzchkl *and* pfzchkl *instructions*

first shifted right by four or two, and the new PM bits are written into the upper four or two bits. This preserves the previously calculated PM bits and allows the PM bits to be accumulated. To update all eight PM bits requires four **fzchkl** instructions or two **fzchks** instructions. However, because the pixel size varies, the number of PM bits used by the **pst.d** instruction at once will vary. You will see how this works in the following description of the pixel store instruction.

The Pixel Store Instruction

The RISC core executes the pixel store instruction shown in Figure 7-8. The pixel store instruction selectively updates the pixels in a 64-bit memory location. The floating-point register to be stored contains either eight 8-bit pixels, four 16-bit pixels, or two 32-bit pixels as determined by the PS field of the **psr**. The pixels to be stored must have their corresponding bit set in the PM field of the **psr**. Each bit in the PM field corresponds to one pixel with the low-order bit corresponding to the pixel at the lowest address. The bits of the PM field are right shifted following the **pst.d** instruction. Assuming all of the PM field bits were previously set up, successive **pst.d** instructions automatically manage the PM bits. For example, code using 32-bit pixels and a 16-bit Z-buffer

```
Pst.d   Pixel Store

Operation:      For pixels enabled in PM: mem.d[ #constA  + isrc2 ] <-- freg.

Shift PM right by 8/(PS+1) bits.
IF( Autoincrement )
then
isrc2  <-- #constA  + isrc2.
FI


Syntax: pst.d   freg,#constA(isrc2)    Normal
        pst.d   freg,#constA(isrc2)++  Auto increment
```

Figure 7-8. Operation and syntax for the pst.d *instruction.*

would manipulate four Z values (64 bits of Z data) at once. This means using one **fzchks** instruction and two **pst.d** instructions. Actually, a second **fzchks f0,f0,f0** is required to shift the PM into place before the first **pst.d**.

The **pst.d** instruction, combined with the **fzchks** or **fzchkl** instruction, forms the basis for implementing Z-buffer hidden-surface elimination. Only when a pixel represents the point closer to the viewer than the current point for that x and y location, will the new pixel data be stored. In order to keep the Z values in the Z-buffer current, if a pixel is updated, the new Z value must update the buffer. Fortunately, the **fzchks** and **fzchkl** instructions store the smaller Z value into the floating-point destination register as part of their pixel mask update operation.

The **pst.d** instruction stores the pixel data from a floating-point register. The pixel data is actually constructed in the MERGE register with the **faddp** or **pfaddp** instruction, then transferred to a floating-point register with a **form** or **pform** instruction.

Distance Interpolation Instruction

Although the coordinates, including the Z value of each polygon's vertices, are known, the Z value for points not on a vertex are not part of the polygon's description. The Z value for the non-vertex points must be interpolated from the bordering vertices. This step is called *Z interpolation.* With Z interpolation, the depth of all points of a polygon can be determined.

The i860 processor's graphics unit includes the linear distance interpolation instructions **faddz** and **pfaddz** for determining the Z value for points between vertices. These instructions, combined with the Z compare instructions, can determine which polygon's point is closer to the viewer and should be displayed. Consider distance interpolation along a scan line parallel to the x axis (that is, y is constant, but x and z are not). The polygon will have a start point X1 and an end point X2. The depth of z has a start value Z1 and an end value Z2. To calculate the slope of z, we take the change in z over the change in x:

$$mZ = \frac{(Z2-Z1)}{(X2-X1)} = \frac{dZ}{dX}$$

Because the calculation will be performed multiple times, it is more efficient to take the reciprocal of dX (RdX= 1/dX) and perform multiplications than to perform divisions by dX. The slope of z is

```
mZ = (Z2-Z1) * RdX
```

Letting Z(Xn) be the Z value at pixel Xn:

```
Z(X1) = Z1
Z(X1 + 1) = Z1 + mZ
Z(X1 + 2) = Z1 + 2*mZ
   .
   .
   .
Z(X1 + N) = Z1 + N*mZ
   .
   .
   .
Z(X1 + dX) = Z1 +dX*mZ = Z(X2)
```

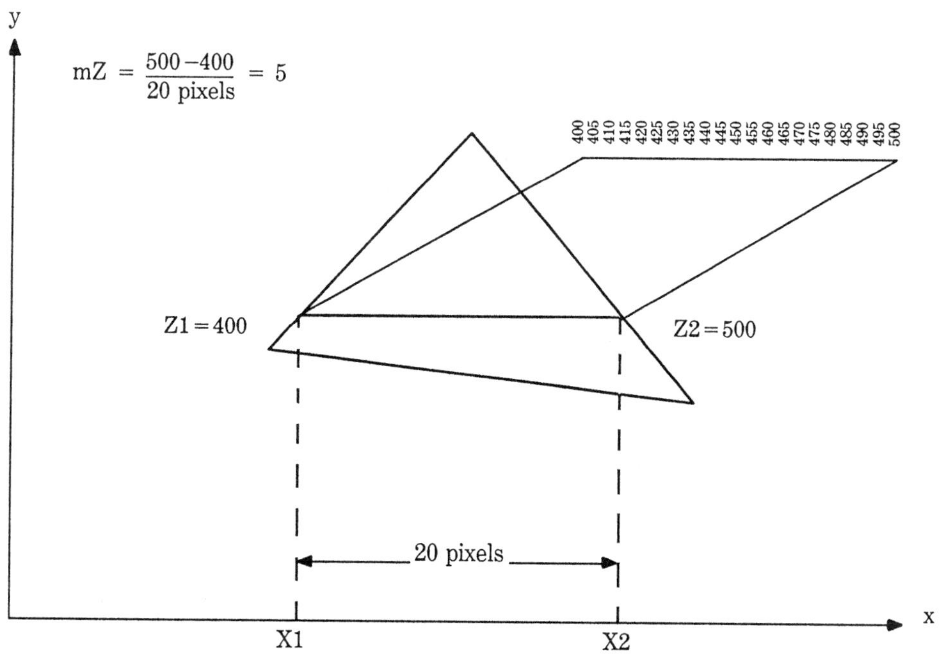

Figure 7-9. Z-buffer value interpolation

Figure 7-9 shows this Z-value interpolation for a triangle. Note that because the polygon is a plane, all scan lines that intersect the polygon will have the same value mZ, in this case 5. Therefore, it only need be calculated once for each polygon. The value added to each successive Z value is called the *interpolant* (represented by mZ in the equations above). Successive Z values are calculated by adding the interpolant. In this example, the value at Z1 equals 400 and at Z2 equals 500. For each of the 20 pixels between these points the Z value is increased by the interpolant 5.

The **faddz** and **pfaddz** instructions, shown in Figure 7-10, perform interpolating addition on two 32-bit values of a 64-bit register pair. For a 16-bit Z-buffer the lower 16 bits are treated as a fraction. The 32 bits of each are added, then loaded into the MERGE register following a 16-bit right shift of the MERGE register. This is shown graphically in Figure 7-11. Because the MERGE register is shifted, normally it is convenient to

---

Faddz Add with Z Merge

Operation: *fdest* <-- *fsrc1* + *fsrc2*
Shift the MERGE register right 16 bits and load MERGE register bits 63:48 and 31:16 with bits 63:48 and 31:16 of (*fsrc1* + *fsrc2*).

Syntax: **faddz** *fsrc1,fsrc2,fdest*

Pfaddz Pipelined Add with Z Merge

Operation: *fdest* <-- last stage graphics result.
Last stage graphics pipeline <-- *fsrc1* + *fsrc2.*
Shift the MERGE register right 16 bits and load MERGE register bits 63:48 and 31:16 with bits 63:48 and 31:16 of (*fsrc1* + *fsrc2*).

Syntax: **pfaddz** *fsrc1,fsrc2,fdest*

Figure 7-10. Operation and syntax for* faddz *and* pfaddz *instructions

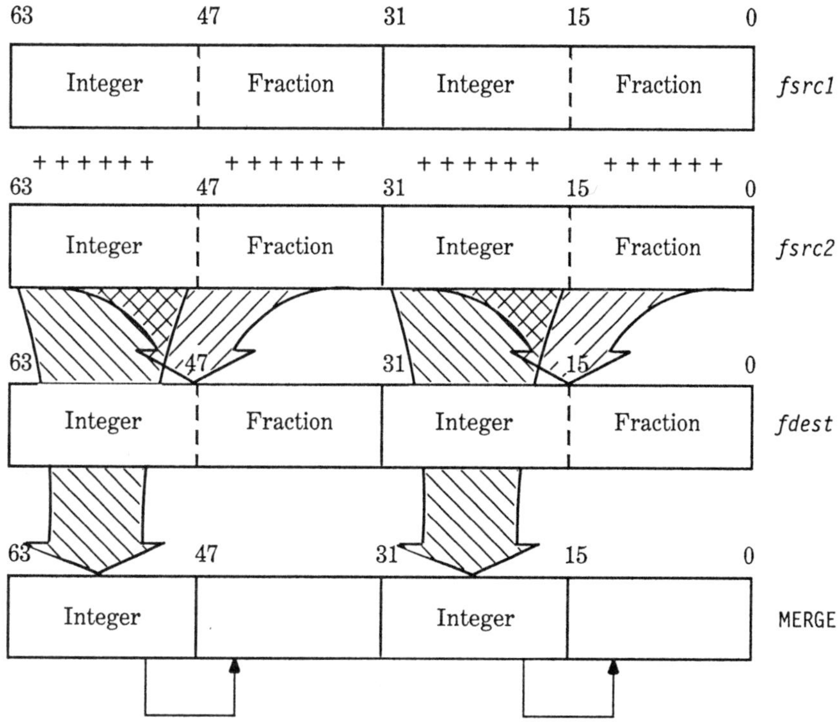

Figure 7-11. **faddz** *with 16-Bit Z-Buffer*

perform two consecutive **faddz** instructions accumulating the result. To have the two instructions construct the Z values for four adjacent pixels in the proper order, even and odd pixel pairs should be operated on with successive **faddz.**

32-bit Z-buffers using 32-bit interpolation do not use the **faddz** special instructions. The 32-bit additions can be performed in pairs using the 64-bit integer **add** instruction **fiadd**, with no fractional parts. Although the lower 32-bit addition may carry a bit to the upper addition, it will not be significant enough to distort the interpolation. For 32-bit Z-buffers with more accurate 64-bit interpolation, two 64-bit **fiadd.dd**

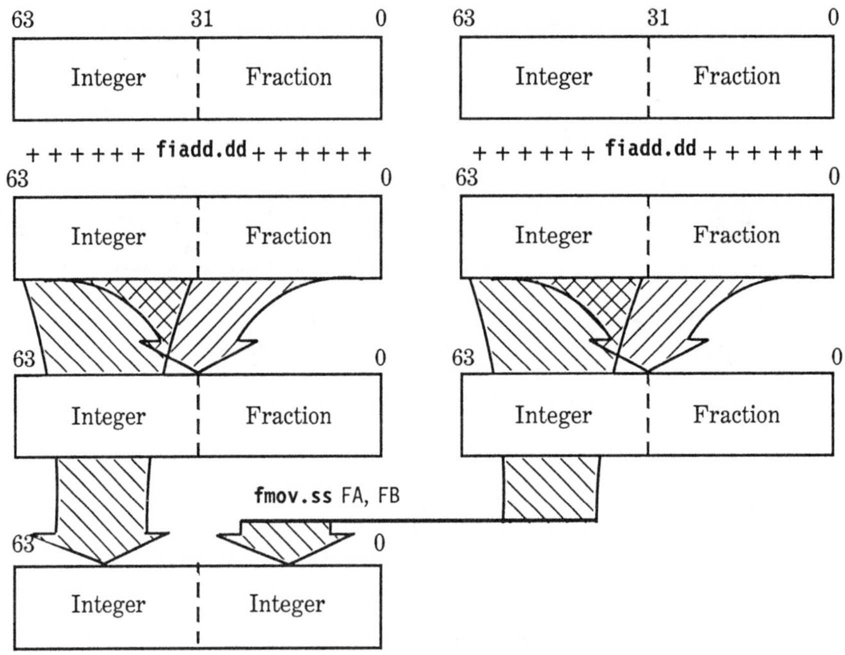

Figure 7-12. 64-bit distance interpolation

instructions are used. This is shown in Figure 7-12 with the final **fmov.ss** instruction to merge the results. Note that such 32-bit Z values don't use the MERGE register and don't need to use the **form** instruction. However, the **faddz** and **pfaddz** instructions store their results to the MERGE register. The **form** or **pform** instruction is used to transfer the MERGE register into a floating-point register. The **form** instructions may also perform an OR operation on the value. This is useful when combined with the pixel value interpolation instructions that are described in the following section.

Pixel Interpolation

To show shaded images, the surface of the polygons must be displayed. From the database, the locations and color intensities of the vertices of the polygons are known, but points between these vertices must be calculated. Instead of shading the polygon one constant color, the color can be changed gradually along its surface. The i860 processor supports intensity interpolation to allow smooth linear changes in pixel intensity and color between vertices. This provides a smoother appearance than flat (constant) shading of the polygons. The more data bits per pixel, the smoother the interpolation can be. This type of linear interpolation, called Gouraud shading, in which each successive pixel has the same amount more or the same amount less intensity as its left-hand neighbor.

The concept of pixel interpolation is very similar to the Z interpolation described in the preceding section. An object has a color value C1 at X1 and value C2 at X2. The generic term color (C) is used here to describe the red (R), green (G), and blue (B) composition of a pixel (for 16-bit and 32-bit pixels). Pixel interpolation calculates the slope of C over the line X. C is increased from X1 by the increment mC, so that at point X2 the value equals C2. Shown formally, the slope of C is

$$mC = \frac{(C2 - C1)}{(X2 - X1)} = \frac{dC}{dX}$$

We use the same RdX reciprocal value calculated for the Z interpolation to perform multiplications for colors. The slope of C is

$$mC = (C2 - C1) * RdX$$

Letting C(Xn) be the color value at pixel Xn:

$$\begin{aligned}
C(X1) &= C1 \\
C(X1 + 1) &= C1 + mC \\
C(X1 + 2) &= C1 + 2*mC \\
&\vdots \\
C(X1 + N) &= C1 + N*mC \\
&\vdots \\
C(X1 + dX) &= C1 + dX*mC = C(X2)
\end{aligned}$$

Figure 7-13 illustrates pixel interpolation for Gouraud shading of a triangle. The color, in this case green, is interpolated across the scan

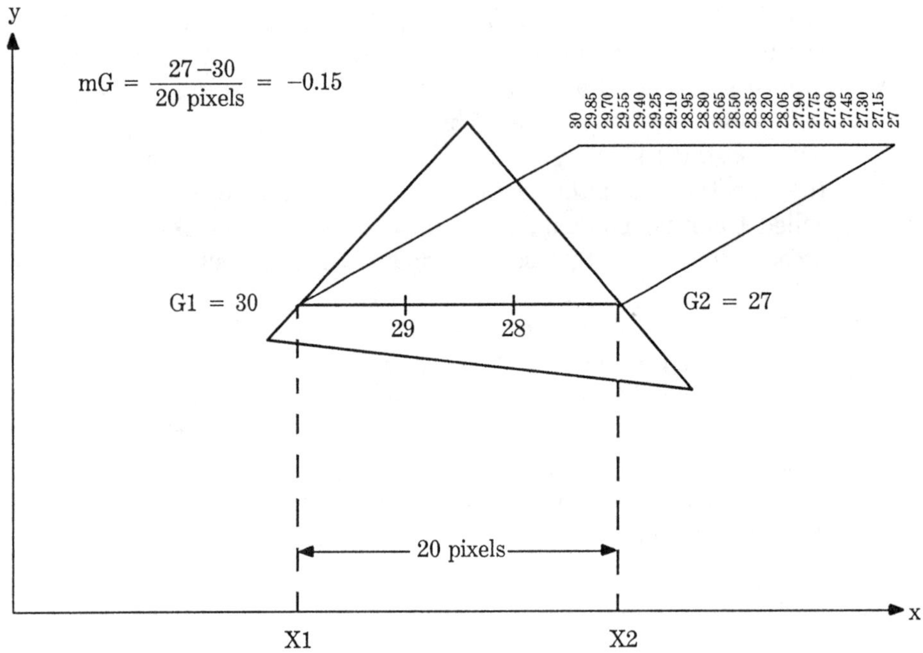

Figure 7-13. Pixel interpolation for Gouraud shading

line from 30 to 27. The green interpolant, mG, equals −0.15. Because the interpolant is a fraction less than the truncated portion of the pixel value, the pixel intensity changes do not occur at every pixel. However, the changes still occur linearly. That is why we interpolate with the fractional values and do not truncate dC/dX to zero when it is less than one. If we truncated to zero, the interpolation would be useless and all colors would be the same on the scan line until the right endpoint was reached. Note that this is only the color interpolation for the color green, and interpolation must be performed separately for each of the red, green, and blue colors.

The syntax and operation for the **faddp** and **pfaddp** instructions are shown in Figure 7-14. The instructions operate on 64 bits of pixel data at a time. For 8- and 16-bit pixel formats, four 16-bit intensity interpolations are performed in parallel, and for 32-bit pixels two are performed

```
Faddp     Add with Pixel Merge

Operation:     fdest  <-- fsrc1  + fsrc2
Shift, then load the MERGE register from fsrc1  + fsrc2 as defined in Table 7-3.

Syntax:   faddp      fsrc1,fsrc2,fdest


Pfaddp    Pipelined Add with Pixel Merge

Operation:     fdest  <-- last stage graphics result.
Last stage graphics pipeline <-- fsrc1  + fsrc2.
Shift, then load MERGE register from fsrc1  + fsrc2 as defined in Table 7-3.

Syntax:   pfaddp fsrc1,fsrc2,fdest
```

Figure 7-14. Operation and syntax for **faddp** *and* **pfaddp** *instructions*

in parallel. Beyond performing the addition operation, the **faddp** shifts the MERGE register as defined in Table 7-3.

Interpolations on 8-bit pixels use a 16-bit interpolant comprised of an 8-bit fraction in the lower bits, and the 8-bit integer in the upper 8 bits. Figure 7-15 illustrates the pixel value addition, MERGE register shifting, and the truncating load of the MERGE register. Shifting the four values of the MERGE register by 8 bits allows two **faddp** instructions to concatenate their results where the first is the interpolant for the even-numbered pixels, and the second is the interpolant for the odd-numbered pixels.

You will recall from Figure 7-3 that the 16-bit pixels contain two 6-bit fields and one 4-bit field where each field represents a color. The

Table 7-3. MERGE *Update for* faddp *Instruction*

Pixel Size (from PS*)*	*Fields Loaded From Result into* MERGE	*Right Shift Amount (Field Size)*
8	63..56, 47..40, 31..24, 15..8	8
16	63..58, 47..42, 31..26, 15..10	6
32	63..56, 31..24	8

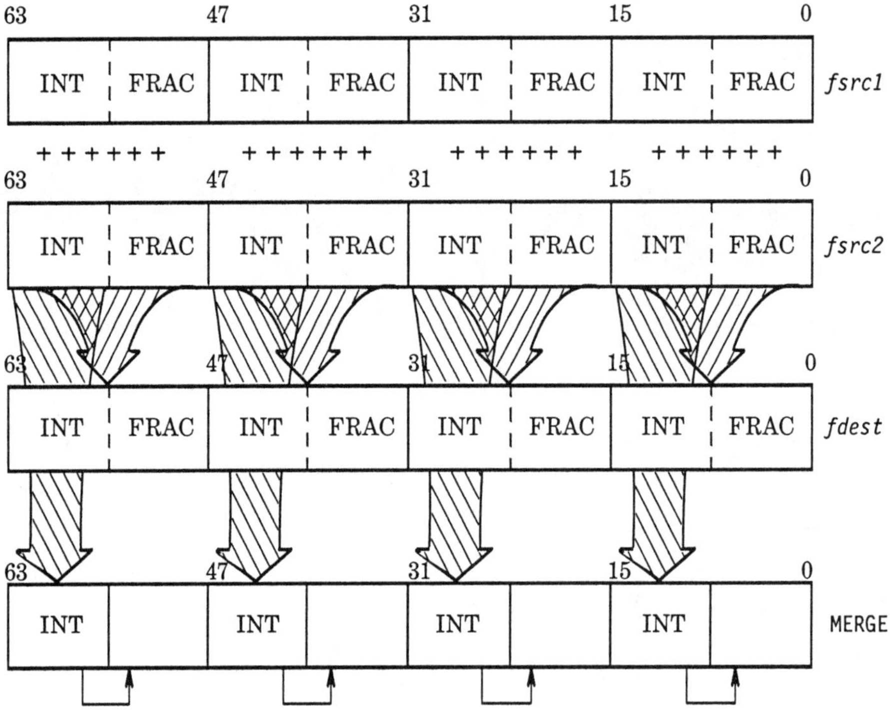

Figure 7-15. **faddp** *with 8-bit pixels*

faddp treats the 6 bits as the integer field to be transferred to the MERGE register, and uses a 10-bit fraction for the remaining bits. To concatenate the 16-bit pixel values comprising all three colors, three **faddp**s are required. Each **faddp** shifts the MERGE register by 6 as shown in Figure 7-16. Note that the first 6-bit pixel stored to the MERGE register is reduced to 4 bits with the shifting. Three consecutive **faddp** instructions will load each of the colors for four pixels into the MERGE register.

Using 32-bit pixels allows a 24-bit fraction as each color value is 8 bits. Figure 7-17 shows two 32-bit pixels operated on in parallel and the 8-bit shift that occurs in the MERGE register. Although the MERGE register allows for four color interpolations, normally, only the three corresponding to red, green, and blue are performed. The remaining 8 bits can be

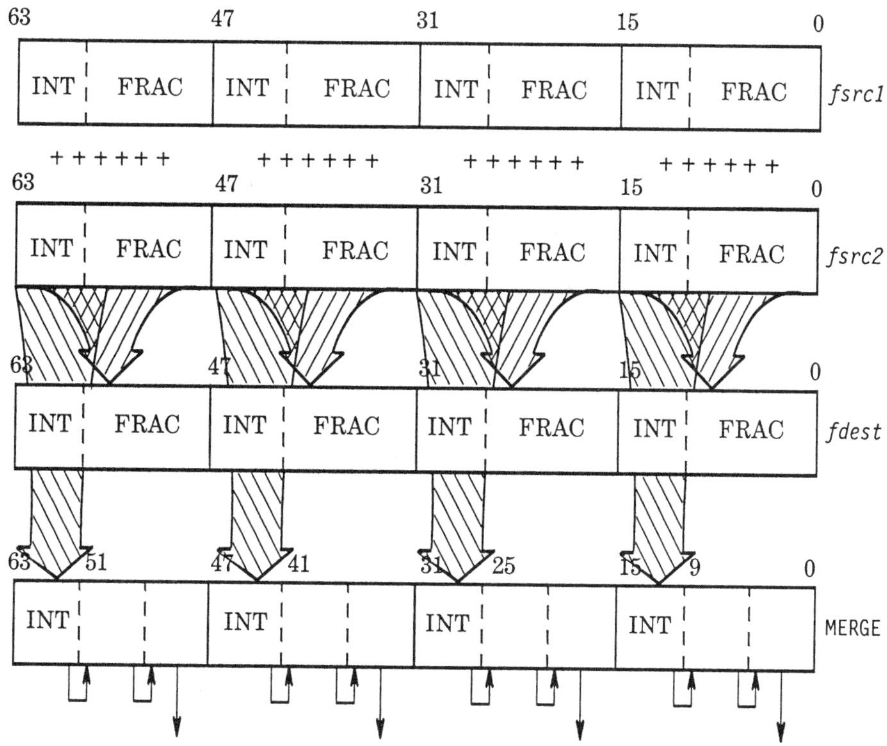

Figure 7-16. **faddp** *with 16-bit pixels*

used for some other characteristic such as texture, or a graphics system can implement a straight 24-bit color scheme. The 8 bits can be manipulated as part of the **form** instruction.

For each of the 8-, 16-, and 32-bit pixel examples described there are several things to consider. Although the fraction portion of the pixel value is truncated and not transferred to the MERGE register, it is a critical portion of the calculation. Successive interpolations will continue to sum the complete value, including the fraction, so that the integer color component will be properly incremented. Also note that for each color, the interpolant remains constant for the entire polygon. One final consideration is the transferring of the pixel data values from the MERGE

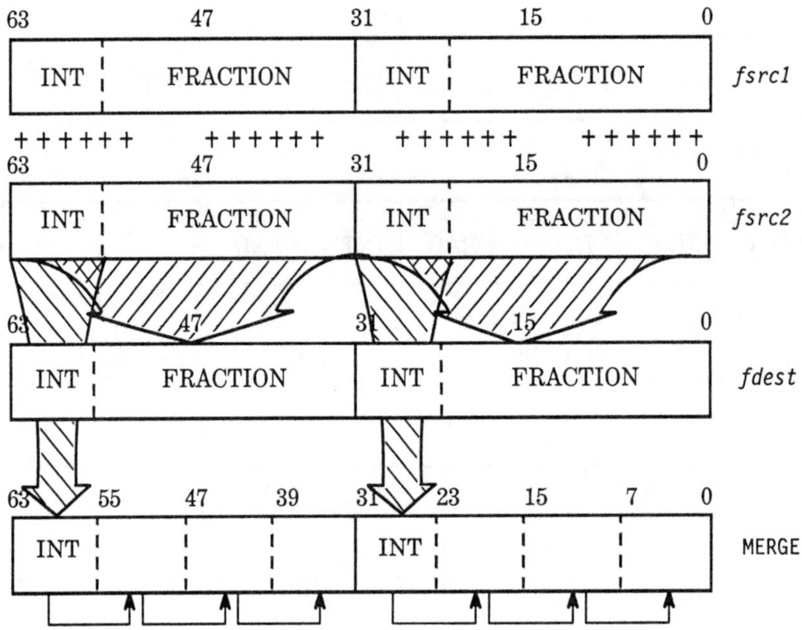

Figure 7-17. **faddp** *with 32-bit pixels*

register into a floating-point register with the **form** instruction. This is required so that the new pixel values can be stored with the pixel store instruction **pst**.

The OR with MERGE Register

The **form.dd** and **pform.dd** instructions shown in Figure 7-18 transfer data from the MERGE register to a floating-point register with an **OR** operation. The instruction also clears the contents of the MERGE register following the transfer. Transferring the MERGE contents is needed because the results for both distance interpolation and color interpolations are stored there. The **OR** operation can be used to set specific bits by placing a one in the corresponding bit position in *fsrc1*. If an **OR** operation is not desired, **f0** can be used for *fsrc1*.

```
Form Or with Merge Register

Operation:      fdest  <-- (fsrc1  OR MERGE).
MERGE <-- 0.

Syntax:  form fsrc1,fdest


Pform   Pipelined OR with Merge Register

Operation:      fdest  <-- last stage graphics result.
Last stage graphics pipeline <-- (fsrc1  OR MERGE).
MERGE <-- 0.

Syntax: pform   fsrc1,fdest
```

Figure 7-18. Operation and syntax for `form` ***and*** `pform` ***instructions***

Boundary Conditions and the Inner Loop

As you have seen with the instruction explanations, multiple pixels are operated on with each instruction. However, programs must function properly even if the number of pixels or the alignment of pixels is not in the proper boundary. The 64-bit operations of the i860 processor graphics instructions assume that the quantities are aligned on 8-byte boundaries. If they are not aligned, the odd pixels must be handled separately with respect to masking Z values near the end points, and with respect to initializing the accumulators. To better understand this, let's look at an example rendering procedure for 16-bit pixels. The register allocation of Figure 7-19 simplifies the examples as each register is used for only one purpose. The first step in the example is to set the pixel size in the `psr` as shown in Figure 7-20.

Z-Buffer Masking

For maximum performance, the example code operates on four 16-bit pixels in each loop. The program must avoid erroneously updating the

```
// REGISTER DEFINITIONS FOR RENDERING PROCEDURE
//      INTEGER LOCALS
    Ra       = r4   // Temporary
    Rb       = r5   // Temporary
    Rc       = r6   // Temporary
    Rd       = r7   // Temporary
//      INTEGER INPUTS
    X1       = r16  // X coordinate of starting point of line segment in pixels
    dX       = r17  // Width of scan line segment in number of pixels
    ZBP      = r18  // Z-buffer pointer to the current line segment
    Z1       = r19  // Initial Z value, fixed-point 16.16 format
    mZ       = r20  // Z slope, fixed-point 16.16 format
    FBP      = r21  // Graphics frame buffer pointer to the current line segment
    Red1     = r22  // Initial red intensity, fixed-point 6.10 format, plus .5
    Grn1     = r23  // Initial green intensity, fixed-point 6.10 format, plus .5
    Blu1     = r24  // Initial blue intensity, fixed-point 6.10 format, plus .5
    mR       = r25  // Red slope, fixed-point 6.10 format
    mG       = r26  // Green slope, fixed-point 6.10 format
    mB       = r27  // Blue slope, fixed-point 6.10 format
//      REAL LOCALS
    aZ       = f2   // Accumulated Z values
    aZh      = f3   //
    iZ1      = f4   // Z interpolant, coefficient 1.0
    iZ1h     = f5   //
    iZ3      = f6   // Z interpolant, coefficient 3.0
    iZ3h     = f7   //
    oldz     = f8   // Original values from the Z-buffer
    newz     = f10  // New Z-buffer values
    newzh    = f11  //
    newi     = f12  // New pixel values
    iR       = f14  // Red interpolant, coefficient 4.0
    iRh      = f15  //
    aR       = f16  // Accumulated red intensities
    aRh      = f17  //
    iG       = f18  // Green interpolant, coefficient 4.0
    iGh      = f19  //
    aG       = f20  // Accumulated green intensities
    aGh      = f21  //
    iB       = f22  // Blue interpolant, coefficient 4.0
    iBh      = f23  //
    aB       = f24  // Accumulated blue intensities
    aBh      = f25  //
    lZmask   = f26  // left-end Z mask
    lZmaskh  = f27  //
    rZmask   = f28  // right-end Z mask
    rZmaskh  = f29  //
```

Figure 7-19. Register assignments

```
// SET PIXEL SIZE TO 16
    ld.c        psr,    Ra          // Work on psr
    andnoth     0x00C0, Ra,     Ra  // Clear PS
    orh         0x0040, Ra,     Ra  // PS = 16-bit pixels
    st.c        Ra,     psr         //
```

Figure 7-20. Set pixel size to 16

Z-buffer when either the first or last pixel of a line segment is not at an 8-byte boundary. This is known as *Z masking*. The Z-buffer can be initialized with FFFEH with the value FFFFH used for masking. In this case, the **fzchks** instruction will always find the mask to be greater than any Z-buffer contents. A function that looks up and calculates the mask for right- or left-end aligned two-byte units is outlined in Figure 7-21.

Accumulator Initialization

The construction of Z and color interpolants can be performed in a concise manner when all of the pixels are in one 64-bit quantity. Continuing with the 16-bit pixel example, the code in Figure 7-22 constructs

```
.macro zmask l_align, r_align, Rx, Ry
//  l_align -- left-end alignment in two-byte units
//  r_align -- right-end alignment in two-byte units
//  Rx, Ry  -- scratch registers
//         Left-end OR masks                Right-end OR masks
//  Input          Output            Input        Output
// l_align         lZmask           r_align       rZmask
//    0      0000 0000 0000 0000       0     FFFF FFFF FFFF 0000
//    1      0000 0000 0000 FFFF       1     FFFF FFFF 0000 0000
//    2      0000 0000 FFFF FFFF       2     FFFF 0000 0000 0000
//    3      0000 FFFF FFFF FFFF       3     0000 0000 0000 0000
// If the first and last pixels are contained in the same 64-bit
// aligned set, then lZmask = lZmask OR rZmask.
.endm
```

Figure 7-21. Z mask procedure summary

```
// CONSTRUCT INTERPOLANTS iZ1 AND iZ3 GIVEN mZ
    ixfr        mZ,      iZ1
    shl         1,       mZ,      Ra  // Ra = 2*mZ
    adds        Ra,      mZ,      Ra  // Ra = 3*mZ
    ixfr        Ra,      iZ3
    fmov.ss     iZ1,     iZ1h         // Join each half in 64-bit register
    fmov.ss     iZ3,     iZ3h         // Join each half in 64-bit register
```

Figure 7-22. Construction of Z interpolants

the interpolants for a polygon. The interpolant, mZ, is transferred to a floating-point register, tripled, then transferred again, and finally assembled in the 64-bit floating-point register. The similar code for construction of the color interpolants is shown in Figure 7-23.

When the first pixel of a line segment is not at an 8-byte boundary, additional considerations are required. The initial accumulator values must consider the alignment of the first pixel. The desired accumulator initial values for both the Z and color components are given in Table 7-4. Note that each value is a composite of two terms: one that is a constant for each edge pair (n*mZ, n*mR, n*mG, n*mB) and one that can vary

```
// CONSTRUCT INTERPOLANTS iR, iG, iB GIVEN mR, mG, mB
    shl         18,     mR,     Ra  // Multiply each color slope by four, then
    shl         18,     mG,     Rb  //  shift by 16 to put the significant
    shl         18,     mB,     Rc  //  bits into the high-order half
    shr         16,     Ra,     mR  // Return significant 16 bits
    shr         16,     Rb,     mG  //  to low-order half.  Any sign bits
    shr         16,     Rc,     mB  //  in high-order half are gone.
    or          mR,     Ra,     Ra  // Join 16-bit quarters
    or          mG,     Rb,     Rb  //  in 32-bit register
    or          mB,     Rc,     Rc  //
    ixfr        Ra,     iR          // Join 32-bit halves
    ixfr        Rb,     iG          //  in 64-bit register
    ixfr        Rc,     iB          //
    fmov.ss     iR,     iRh         //
    fmov.ss     iG,     iGh         //
    fmov.ss     iB,     iBh         //
```

Figure 7-23. Construction of color interpolants

Table 7-4. Accumulator Initial Values

Alignment	*Initial Z Accumulator Values*	
0	Z1 – 1*mZ	Z1 – 3*mZ
2	Z1 – 2*mZ	Z1 – 4*mZ
4	Z1 – 3*mZ	Z1 – 5*mZ
6	Z1 – 4*mZ	Z1 – 6*mZ

Alignment	*Initial Color Accumulator Values (C = R, G, B)*			
0	C1 – 1*mC	C1 – 2*mC	C1 – 3*mC	C1 – 4*mC
2	C1 – 2*mC	C1 – 3*mC	C1 – 4*mC	C1 – 5*mC
4	C1 – 3*mC	C1 – 4*mC	C1 – 5*mC	C1 – 6*mC
6	C1 – 4*mC	C1 – 5*mC	C1 – 6*mC	C1 – 7*mC

with each scan line (*Z1, Red1, Grn1, Blu1*). The constant values can be precalculated. The code example in Figure 7-24 assumes this with the values given in Table 7-5. Depending on the alignment of each line segment, the proper value is retrieved from the table and added to the initial Z and color values.

Rendering Inner Loop

Now that you understand the instruction operations, the boundary conditions, and the accumulator initialization, it is time to examine a more complete example. The code example in Figure 7-25 operates on 16-bit pixels and uses a 16-bit Z-buffer. It handles one scanline segment of a polygon (constant y, varying x, z, and color). Calls are made to the accumulator initialization routine of Figure 7-23, and the Z mask procedure outline of Figure 7-21. After the calls, the program is executed entirely in dual-instruction mode. The left- end and right-ends of the line segment are handled by the code at the labels' "left-end" and "right-end." The inner-loop code handles all of the interior points.

```
// ACCUMULATOR INITIALIZATION TABLE
    .data; .align .double
acc_init_tab::  .double [16] 0
    .dsect
aBi:    .double     // Four initial 16-bit blue values
aGi:    .double     // Four initial 16-bit green values
aRi:    .double     // Four initial 16-bit red values
aZi:    .double     // Two initial 32-bit Z values
    .end
    .text
// INITIALIZE ACCUMULATORS
.macro acc_init  Lalign, Rtab, Rx, Ry, Fx, Fxh
//  Lalign -- left-end alignment (0..3) in two-byte units
//  Rtab   -- register to use for addressing the table
//  Rx, Ry, Fx, Fxh -- scratch registers
    mov         acc_init_tab,   Rtab    //
    shl         5,      Lalign, Lalign  // Multiply by row width
    adds        Lalign, Rtab,   Rtab    // Index row corresponding to alignment
    fld.d       aZi(Rtab),      aZ      // Z
    ixfr        Z1,     Fx              // Z
    fld.d       aRi(Rtab),      aR      // R--Load constant values
    shl         16,     Red1,   Rx      // R--Shift starting value to hi-order
    fmov.ss     Fx,     Fxh             // Z
    shr         16,     Rx,     Ry      // R--Red1 stripped of sign bits
    fiadd.dd    Fx,     aZ,     aZ      // Z
    or          Rx,     Ry,     Ry      // R--Form (Red1,Red1)
    ixfr        Ry,     Fx              // R--Put in 64-bit register
    fld.d       aGi(Rtab),      aG      // G
    shl         16,     Grn1,   Rx      // G
    fmov.ss     Fx,     Fxh             // R--Form (Red1,Red1,Red1,Red1)
    shr         16,     Rx,     Ry      // G
    fiadd.dd    Fx,     aR,     aR      // R--Add variables to constants
    or          Rx,     Ry,     Ry      // G
    ixfr        Ry,     Fx              // G
    fld.d       aBi(Rtab),      aB      // B
    shl         16,     Blu1,   Rx      // B
    fmov.ss     Fx,     Fxh             // G
    shr         16,     Rx,     Ry      // B
    fiadd.dd    Fx,     aG,     aG      // G
    or          Rx,     Ry,     Ry      // B
    ixfr        Ry,     Fx              // B
    fmov.ss     Fx,     Fxh             // B
    fiadd.dd    Fx,     aB,     aB      // B
.endm
```

Figure 7-24. Accumulator initialization

Table 7-5. Accumulator Initialization Table

Alignment	*Table Values*			
	*mZ	*mR	*mG	*mB
0	−1, −3	−1, −2, −3, −4	−1, −2, −3, −4	−1, −2, −3, −4
2	−2, −4	−2, −3, −4, −5	−2, −3, −4, −5	−2, −3, −4, −5
4	−3, −5	−3, −4, −5, −6	−3, −4, −5, −6	−3, −4, −5, −6
6	−4, −6	−4, −5, −6, −7	−4, −5, −6, −7	−4, −5, −6, −7

The inner loop consists of nine dual-instruction pairs. The loop performs and calculates everything required for four pixels. For the Z values, this includes four Z value interpolations, updating the Z-buffer from the prior loop iteration, constructing the Z values for storing in the next loop iteration, and fetching the Z values from the Z-buffer for the next loop iteration's pixels. For the color calculations, the loop execution includes interpolating four red pixel intensities, interpolating four green pixel intensities, interpolating four blue pixel intensities, and updating the display with the required pixel data. For the inner loop, four pixels are shaded in ten clock cycles. This gives a peak rate of 16 million pixels per second at 40 Mhz. Note that the nine instructions take ten clock cycles because the sequential **faddz** instructions at the beginning of the loop cause a one clock-cycle freeze.

In addition to the calculations performed, the loop also handles the loop control based on the right-end alignment. The pre-inner-loop code performs the calculations for the left-end pixels that are unaligned. Once in the inner loop, the right end must be checked to determine how to exit the loop. If the line segment is right aligned, the loop is exited to the aligned end label. If the right end is not aligned, the program falls through and executes the code at the right end label to handle the boundary case. The actual loop controlling variable is *dX* and is expressed as a number of pixels with the unaligned left pixels subtracted out. A value that is 3 MOD 4 indicates that the right end is aligned. This is why the inner loop compares the remaining pixel count to −5 (−5 MOD 4 = 3) to perform the aligned end detection.

```
//  RENDERING PROCEDURE
//      16-bit pixels, 16-bit Z-buffer
    and        3,      X1,      Ra  // Determine alignment of starting-point
    acc_init  Ra, Rb, Rc, Rd, Fa, Fah   // Initialize accumulators
    subs       4,      Ra,      Rb  // 4 - alignment
    subs       dX,     Rb,      dX  // Adjust dX by X1 alignment
    // If dX <= 0, then right end is in same set as left end
    and        3,      dX,      Rb  // Determine alignment of right end
    zmask      Ra, Rb, Rc, Rd       // Prepare both left- and right-end masks
left_end::  // Handle boundary conditions
    d.faddz    aZ,     iZ3,     aZ  // Interpolate 2 even Z values
      adds     -8,     FBP,     FBP // Anticipate autoincrement
    d.faddz    aZ,     iZ1,     aZ  // Interpolate 2 odd Z values
      adds     -8,     ZBP,     ZBP // Anticipate autoincrement
    d.form     lZmask, newz         // Mask 4 new values
      fld.d    8(ZBP), oldz         // Fetch 4 old Z values
    d.faddp    aB,     iB,      aB  // Interpolate 4 blue intensities
      mov      -4,     Ra           // Loop increment: 4 pixels
    d.faddp    aG,     iG,      aG  // Interpolate 4 green intensities
      adds     -4,     dX,      dX  // Prepare dX for bla at end of loop
    d.faddp    aR,     iR,      aR  // Interpolate 4 red intensities
      bla      Ra,     dX,      L1  // Initialize LCC
    d.form     f0,     newi         // Move 4 new pixels to 64-bit reg
      adds     5,      dX,      r0  // Are there any whole sets (dX < -5)?
L1: d.fzchks   oldz,   newz,   newz // Mark closer points in PM[7..4]
      bc       short_segment        // Get out now if no whole set
    d.fnop                          //
      fld.d    16(ZBP),oldz         // Fetch 4 old Z values
inner_loop:: // Handle all interior points
    d.faddz    aZ,     iZ3,     aZ  // Interpolate 2 even Z values
      nop                           //
    d.faddz    aZ,     iZ1,     aZ  // Interpolate 2 odd Z values
      fst.d    newz,   8(ZBP)++     // Update Z buf from prior loop
    d.form     f0,     newz         // Move 4 new Z values to 64-bit reg
      nop                           //
    d.fzchks   f0,     f0,      f0  // Shift PM[7..4] to PM[3..0]
      mov      -5,     Rb           // -5 mod 4 = 3, aligned right end
    d.faddp    aB,     iB,      aB  // Interpolate 4 blue intensities
      pst.d    newi,   8(FBP)++     // Store pixels indicated by PM[3..0]
    d.faddp    aG,     iG,      aG  // Interpolate 4 green intensities
      xor      Rb,     dX,      r0  // Are we at an aligned right end?
    d.faddp    aR,     iR,      aR  // Interpolate 4 red intensities
```

Figure 7-25. 3-D rendering procedure

```
        bc          aligned_end         // Taken if at an aligned right end -->
      d.form        f0,      newi       // Move 4 new pixels to 64-bit reg
        bla         Ra, dX, inner_loop  // Loop if not at end of line segment
      d.fzchks      ldz,    newz,  newz // Mark closer points in PM[7..4]
        fld.d       16(ZBP),       oldz // Fetch 4 old Z values for next loop
// End of inner_loop.  Right end not aligned

right_end:: // Handle boundary conditions
      d.faddz       aZ,      IZ3,    aZ  // Interpolate 2 even Z values
        nop                              //
      d.faddz       aZ,      iZ1,    aZ  // Interpolate 2 odd Z values
        fst.d       newz,    8(ZBP)++    // Update Z buf from prior loop
      d.form        rZmask, newz         // Mask 4 new Z values
        nop                              //
      d.fzchks      f0,      f0,     f0  // Shift PM[7..4] to PM[3..0]
        nop                              //
      d.faddp       aB,      iB,     aB  // Interpolate 4 blue intensities
        pst.d       newi,    8(FBP)++    // Store pixels indicated by PM[3..0]
      d.faddp       aG,      iG,     aG  // Interpolate 4 green intensities
        nop                              //
      d.faddp       aR,      iR,     aR  // Interpolate 4 red intensities
        nop                              //

aligned_end::   // No special boundary conditions
      d.form        f0,      newi        // Move 4 new pixels to 64-bit reg
        br          wrap_up              //
      d.fzchks      oldz,   newz, newz   // Mark closer points in PM[7..4]
        nop                              //

short_segment::
      d.fnop                             //
        adds        8,      dX,    r0    // Is right end in same set as left?
      d.fnop                             //
        bnc.t       right_end            // Branch taken if no.
      d.fnop                             //
        fld.d       16(ZBP),       oldz  // Fetch 4 old Z values

wrap_up:: // Store the unstored and leave dual mode.
      fzchks        f0,     f0,    f0    // Shift PM[7..4] to PM[3..0]
        fst.d       newz,   8(ZBP)++     // Update Z buf from prior loop
      fnop
        pst.d       newi,   8(FBP)++     // Store pixels indicated by PM[3..0]
```

Figure 7-25. 3-D rendering procedure **(continued)**

The inner loop example shows the efficiency that the i860 processor can achieve in displaying 3-D shaded objects with hidden surfaces removed. Using the dedicated graphics instructions, along with dual-instruction mode, is considerably faster for performing these final display operations than using only the RISC core instructions. A synergistic effect is created by these display speed-ups in that the i860 processor also performs calculations, such as the 3-D transform, very efficiently.

CHAPTER 8
PROGRAMMING FOR PARALLELISM

Several techniques can be used to exploit the parallelism available within the i860 microprocessor. The different techniques relate to the different types of parallelism available. The most basic form of parallelism on the i860 microprocessor is the instruction overlapping that results from the pipelined execution. The processor will automatically attempt to pipeline instruction execution, but its ability to do so can be enhanced by sequencing the instructions to avoid freeze conditions (see Appendix C for a summary of instruction timing and characteristics). Another type of parallelism is the dual-operation floating-point instructions that were explained at the end of Chapter 6, "Floating-Point Operations." The final type of parallelism within the i860 processor is a dual-instruction mode where the RISC core executes in parallel with the floating-point unit. This chapter introduces the dual-instruction mode followed by several examples that combine dual-instruction mode with dual-operation floating-point to illustrate some programming techniques for parallelism.

Issuing Multiple Instructions

The i860 processor can behave like traditional microprocessors and execute instructions in sequence as they appear in the instruction stream. This is called *SIM* (Single-Instruction Mode), and on each clock cycle the processor can execute either a RISC core operation or a floating-point operation. This single-instruction mode allows multiclock scalar floating-point operations to be overlapped with continued core execution. Although single-instruction mode does allow both a RISC instruction and a floating-point instruction to have overlapped execution, it does not allow simultaneous issue of instructions. Using single-instruction mode, the fastest execution rate achievable is one instruction per clock cycle.

To further increase the number of instructions per clock cycle, the i860 processor supports *DIM* (Dual-Instruction Mode) where both an integer and a floating-point instruction are issued simultaneously. In performing this, the RISC core fetches two 32-bit instructions per clock using the 64-bit wide instruction cache. Of the instructions fetched, one is executed by the RISC core and one by the floating-point unit. This parallelism is supported by the separate register files for integer and floating-point operations. The RISC core keeps the data flowing to the floating-point processing units by fetching and storing information to the floating-point registers, while the floating-point execution units are operating on the data already in the registers.

To take advantage of dual-instruction mode, the floating-point hardware can accept new instructions each clock by pipelining the floating-point execution units. The dual-operation instructions, introduced in Chapter 6, "Floating-Point Operations," initiate both an addition and a multiplication. Combining the dual-instruction mode with the dual-operation floating-point instructions allows the programmer to exploit the i860 processor's peak execution rate of one integer and two floating-point operations per clock cycle. Being able to control the hardware to this extent increases the programmer's ability to wring performance out of the i860 processor. This added performance does not come free, and writing optimum code sequences is often time-consuming and difficult.

Vector calculations involve repeating the same operation on a series of data values. Although there are no specific vector instructions on the i860 processor, the parallelism of the architecture can support traditional vector processing. Instead of one vector instruction, the inner loops of i860 processor's software vector routines operate up to the peak floating-point hardware rate of 80 MFlops (at 40 Mhz in single precision). The fine-grained software pipelining is more general than that found on traditional vector machines, and can also be used for many algorithms that cannot be vectorized. Graphics applications also benefit from dual-mode where the RISC core unit can execute pixel load and store instructions while the graphics unit performs pixel manipulations.

Dual-Instruction Mode

While in dual-instruction mode (dual-mode), the processor fetches, issues, executes, and produces results from two independent instructions at once. Dual-mode execution consists of aligned instruction pairs of a floating-point or graphics unit instruction in the lower slot and a core instruction in the upper slot. Referring to *dual-instruction execution* as a mode is a little misleading. It is a mode in the sense that the compiler, code generator, or assembly language programmer must indicate which portions of the program are to be executed in dual-instruction mode. It is not a mode in that explicit instructions to set and clear a mode bit are not required to make the transition in and out of dual-instruction mode.

The floating-point instructions include a Dual-mode bit (`D`-bit) in their encoding. If the i860 processor is executing in single-instruction mode, and encounters a floating-point instruction with the `D`-bit set, one more 32-bit instruction is executed before dual-mode begins. To continue executing in dual-mode, each floating-point instruction must have the `D`-bit set. If the i860 processor is executing in dual-mode and a floating-point instruction is encountered with a clear `D`-bit, then one more pair of instructions is executed before resuming single-instruction mode.

Dual-Instruction Mode Transitions

Assembly language programmers specify dual-mode by including in the mnemonic of a floating-point instruction a **`d.`** prefix or by using the assembler directive **.dual**. Both of the specifications cause the D-bit, bit 9, of the floating-point instruction to be set.

Dual-mode can be used for an extended sequence of dual-instruction pairs as Figure 8-1 illustrates. Here the **d.** prefix is used for a floating-point instruction to initiate the transition from single- to dual-mode. This first floating-point instruction must be aligned on a 64-bit boundary (the lowest three address bits being zero). The next instruction may be either a core instruction or a floating-point instruction with the D-bit set. The processor will then enter dual-mode and execute the following instructions as instruction pairs. When an instruction pair with the D-bit not set in the floating-point instruction is encountered, the i860 processor will execute one more instruction pair, then change to single-instruction mode.

Dual-mode can be used for a sequence as short as one instruction pair. As shown in Figure 8-2, the instruction following the **d.** floating-point instruction that initiates dual-mode is a floating-point instruction without the **d.** prefix (D-bit cleared). This causes one instruction pair (that is, the next two instructions) to be executed in dual-mode before execution changes back to single-mode. Due to the instruction alignment

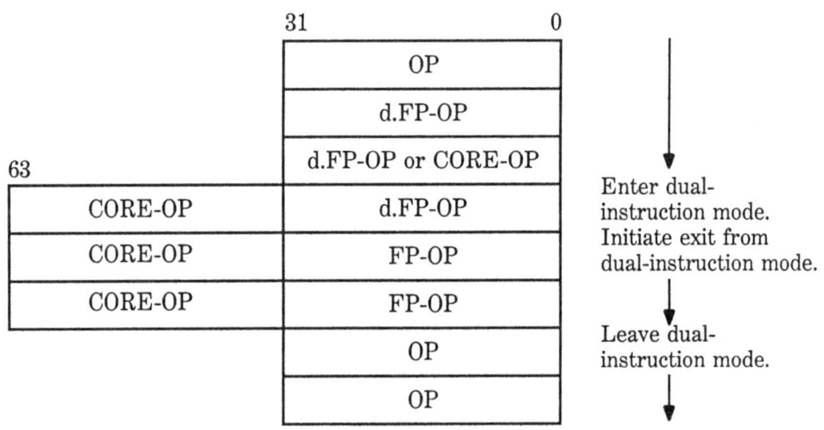

Figure 8-1. Extended dual-instruction mode transitions

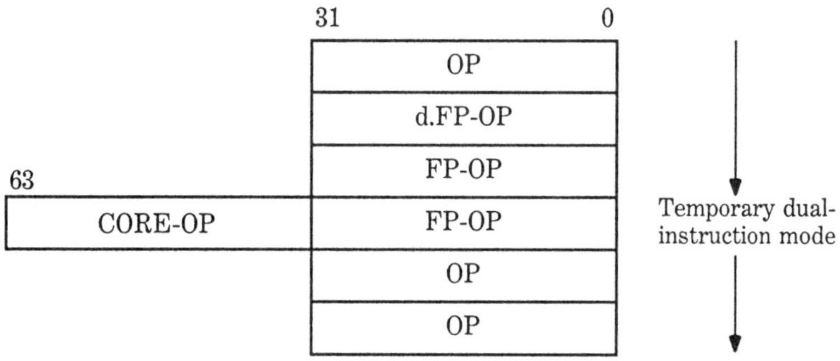

Figure 8-2. Minimum dual-instruction mode transitions

requirements, it is sometimes necessary to insert a no-operation instruction (**nop**) as padding for either the core or floating-point instruction. This padding can simplify program sequences by staying in dual-mode rather than by having multiple transitions in and out of dual-mode.

The floating-point **nop** used for dual-instruction mode has the encoding of **shrd r0, r0, r0**, because this instruction does not affect the states of the floating-point pipelines. Even though this is a core instruction, bit 9 is interpreted as the dual-instruction mode control bit. In assembly language, this instruction is specified as **fnop** or **d.fnop**. Note one quirk of the **fnop** is that because it is a core instruction, **d.fnop** cannot be used to initiate entry into dual-instruction mode.

When a dual-mode pair sequentially follows a delayed branch instruction in dual-instruction mode, both 32-bit instructions are executed as the delay slot operation. Dual-mode introduces some interaction combinations between the core and floating-point instructions that are not found when executing in single-mode. Following are some explanations for dual-mode interactions and a list of restrictions for dual-mode.

Core and Floating-Point Instruction Interaction

Because core and floating-point instructions will be executed at the same time, some unique interactions need to be considered. Five such conditions and how they behave follow.

1. If a branch-on-condition instruction (**bc** or **bnc**) is paired with a floating-point compare, the branch tests the value of the CC (Condition Code) before the compare. The compare will then update the value of the condition code. Note that the delayed conditional branches (**bc.t** and **bcn.t**) cannot be paired with floating-point compares.

2. If an **ixfr**, **fld**, or **pfld** loads the same register as a source operand in the floating-point instruction, the floating-point instruction references the register value before the load updates it. For example, if the register and memory values are

   f8 = 8.0 **f9** = 9.0 **f10** = 10.0 [mem(**r7**)] = 7.0

   The following instruction pair will load **r8** with the value 7.0 after the addition reads the 8.0 from **r8** to sum the result of 17.0 for **f10**:

   ```
   d.fadd.ss  f8, f9, f10;        fld.l r0(r7), f8
   ```

3. An **fst** or **pst** that stores a register that is the destination register of the companion pipelined floating-point operation will store the result of the companion operation. (See restriction 3 in the next section, "Dual-Instruction Mode Restrictions," for scalar floating-point instructions.) For example, if the register values are

   f8 = 8.0 **f9** = 9.0 **f10** = 10.0

   and the last stage of the floating-point adder contains 12.0, the following instruction pair will store the value 12.0 to memory location [**r7**]:

   ```
   d.fadd  f8, f9, f10;      fst.l  f10, r0(r7)
   ```

4. An **fxfr** instruction that transfers to a register referenced as a source by the companion core instruction will update the register after the core instruction accesses the register. The destination of the core instruction will not be updated if it is an integer register. Similarly, if the core instruction uses autoincrement indexing, the index register will not be updated. For example, if the register values are

f8 = 0.0 **r8** = 8

the following instruction pair will add the value 8, from the **r8**, to **r9**. The **fxfr** will transfer the floating-point zero to **r8** after the **add** has read the value 8.

```
d.fxfr  f8, r8;     addu  r8, r9, r10
```

5. When the core instruction would set or clear CC, for example, an addition instruction, and the floating-point instruction is **pfgt**, **pfle**, or **pfeq**, CC is set according to the result of the **pfgt**, **pfle**, or **pfeq**.

Dual-Instruction Mode Restrictions

To prevent collisions in register or condition-code hardware between the floating-point and the core units, the following restrictions must be followed. Fortunately, the programmer does not have to memorize them because the assembler will check for violations.

1. The result of placing a core instruction in the low-order 32 bits or a floating-point instruction in the high-order 32 bits is not defined (except for **shrd r0,r0,r0**, which is interpreted as **fnop**).
2. A floating-point instruction that has the D-bit set must be aligned on a 64-bit boundary (that is, the three least-significant bits of its address must be zero). This applies as well to the initial floating-point instruction that triggers the transition into dual-instruction mode, but it does not apply to the next sequential instruction.
3. When the floating-point operation is scalar and the core operation is **fst** or **pst**, the store should not use the result register of the floating-point operation. Also, when the core operation is **pst**, the floating-point instruction cannot be **(p)fzchks** or **(p)fzchkl**.
4. When the core instruction of a dual-mode pair is a control-transfer operation and the previous instruction had the D-bit set, the floating-point instruction must also have the D-bit set. In other words, an exit from dual-instruction mode cannot be initiated (first

instruction pair without the D-bit set) when the core instruction is a control-transfer instruction.

5. When the core operation is a **ld.c** or a **st.c** the floating-point operation must be **d.fnop**.
6. When the floating-point operation is **fxfr**, the core instruction cannot be **ld**, **st**, **call**, **calli**, **ixfr** or any instruction that updates an integer register (including autoincrement indexing). Furthermore, the core instruction cannot be a **fld**, **fst**, **pst**, or **pfld**, which uses an *isrc1* or *isrc2*, which are the same register as the *idest* of the **fxfr**.
7. A **bri** must not be executed in dual-instruction mode if any trap bits of the **psr** are set.
8. When the core operation is **bc.t** or **bnc.t**, the floating-point operation cannot be **pfeq**, **pfle**, or **pfgt**. The floating-point operation in the sequentially following instruction pair cannot be **pfeq**, **pfle**, or **pfgt** either.
9. A transition to or from dual-instruction mode cannot be initiated on the instruction following a **bri**.
10. An **ixfr**, **fld**, or **pfld** cannot update the same register as the companion floating-point instructions unless the destination is **f0** or **f1**. The destination registers are not permitted to overlap. For example, the following instructions must not be paired:

    ```
    d.fmul.ss  f5, f6, f9;    fld.q  0(r18), f8
    ```

11. In a locked sequence (created by the **lock** and **unlock** instructions), a transition to or from dual-instruction mode is not permitted.

Combining Dual-Instruction with Dual-Operation

The programming examples at the end of Chapter 6, "Floating-Point Operations," show how the i860 processor can deliver up to two floating-point results per clock cycle by using the pipelining and parallelism of the adder and multiplier units. Those examples make the unrealistic assumption that the data is already in the registers. The examples in this chapter go one step further and show how to maintain the throughput of the floating-point unit while simultaneously loading the data from main memory and controlling the data and program flow.

Vector Sum Example

Consider the simple problem to sum the single-precision elements of a long vector, where a vector is a list of numbers stored sequentially in memory. The problem can be solved by the C language function of Figure 8-3 where the entire operation is encapsulated in the statement

```
for (i=0,sum=0; i<n; i++) sum = sum + vec[i];
```

The function receives the address of the start of the vector in the variable *vec*, and the length of the vector in the variable *n*.

Figure 8-4 shows the assembly language that results from compiling the program using standard instruction scheduling optimizations. The address of the vector from variable *vec* is passed to the routine in register **r16**, then transferred to **r18**. The **r16** register is then used for the index i. The number of elements to be summed is in **r17**. The program compares **r17** to see if it is zero by the subtract (**sub 0,r17,r0**)

```
/*   Calculate vector sum of vector vec of length n */

float rvsumc(vec,n)
float vec[];
int n;
{
     register int i;
     register float sum;

     for  (i=0,sum=0; i<n; i++)
          sum = sum + vec[i];
     return (sum);
}
```

Figure 8-3. C language program for vector sum example

```
.file"rvsumc.c"
rvsumc:

// for (i=0,sum=0; i<n; i++)
     mov       r16,r18
     mov       r0,r16
     subs      0,r17,r0
     fmov.ss   f0,f16
     bnc       .L4
.L5:

// sum = sum + vec[i]
     fld.l     0(r18),f17
     adds      4,r18,r18
     adds      1,r16,r16
     subs      r16,r17,r0
     fadd.ss   f17,f16,f16
     bc        .L5
.L4:

// return (sum)
      bri r1
      fmov.sd  f16,f16

//_i      r16  local
//_sum    f16  local
//_vec    r18  local
//_n      r17  local
```

Figure 8-4. Compiler-generated code for vector sum example

and subsequent branch instruction (**bnc** .L4). If there are elements to be summed, the program enters the summation loop starting at label .L5. For each pass through the loop, the routine loads one single-precision value (**fld.l 0(r18), f17**) into the floating-point register **f17**; adjusts the memory pointer (**adds 4,r18,r18**); increments the loop counter (**adds 1,r16,r16**); via the condition code, CC, compares the loop counter to the number of elements (**subs r16, r17, r0**); adds the new floating-point value to the running sum (**fadd.ss f17,f16,f16**); and checking the condition code, CC (**bc** .L5), either exits the loop if the loop count has been reached, or makes another pass through the loop. Once the loop count has been reached, the processor returns to the program that called the vector sum routine (**bri r1**). The final instruction is an artifact of C program conventions where (**fmov.sd f16,f16**) serves to convert the single-precision result to double-precision, because C requires a double-precision result from functions.

Although dual-instruction mode is not used in the compiler output of the C routine, several steps were taken to avoid pipeline freezes. Within the summation loop, which is the bulk of the execution time for a long vector, the data from the load is not used in the next two instructions, thus avoiding a load data freeze. The next optimization is that the subtraction used to set the condition code is separated from the branch-on-condition code (**bc**) by one instruction. With this instruction scheduling, each pass through the loop adds approximately seven clocks of execution. (Remember **bc** is two clocks.) Although **fadd** is a three-clock instruction, here it takes only one clock, as the other two clocks of execution are overlapped with the core execution.

Figure 8-5 is an optimized routine that takes advantage of the pipelined floating-point adder unit and of dual-instruction mode. To better show the pairing of core and floating-point instruction in dual-instruction mode, the listing shows the core instruction of a dual-mode pair indented with respect to the corresponding floating-point instruction. To avoid showing excessive boundary conditions, the code here assumes that there are at least six elements to be summed. The program starts by loading the first two vector elements for the first pass of loop 1, initializing the counter variable and Loop-Condition-Code (LCC) while transitioning into dual-instruction mode, clearing the pipeline, and loading the third and fourth vector elements for the first pass of loop 2.

The summation loop is actually implemented as two loops designated with the starting labels L1 and L2. The loops are executed entirely in dual-instruction mode and are identical in function, but operate on different registers. The first loop, L1, adds **f20** and **f21** to the running totals in **f30** and **f31**, and loads new elements to the **f20** and **f21** registers with a single **fld.d** instruction. If there are additional elements, the program jumps to the second loop, L2. Loop 2 adds **f22** and **f23** to the running totals in **f30** and **f31**, and loads new elements into the **f22** and **f23** registers. Execution continues to alternate between loops 1 and 2 until there are no more elements to be loaded. Note that the instruction pair following the **bla** instruction is executed regardless of the branch decision.

```
// SINGLE-PRECISION VECTOR SUM
//    input:    r16  - vector address, r17 - vector size (must be > 5)
//    output:   f16  - sum of vector elements
       fld.d        r0(r16),  f20       // Load first two elements
       mov          -2,  r21            // Loop decrement for bla
                                        // Initiate entry into dual-instruction mode
       d.pfadd.ss   f0,       f0,  f0   // Clear adder pipe (1)
       adds         -6,  r17, r17  // Decrement size by 6
                                   // Enter into dual-instruction mode
     d.pfadd.ss     f0,  f0,  f0   // Clear adder pipe (2)
       bla          r21, r17, L1   // Initialize LCC
     d.pfadd.ss     f0,  f0,  f0   // Clear adder pipe (3)
       fld.d        8(r16)++, f22  // Load 3rd and 4th elements

L1::d.pfadd.ss f20, f30, f30       // Add f20 to pipeline
       bla          r21, r17, L2   // If more, go to L2 after
     d.pfadd.ss     f21, f31, f31  // adding f21 to pipeline and

       fld.d        8(r16)++, f20  // loading next f20:f21
     // If we reach this point, at least one element remains to be loaded.
     // r17 is either -4 or -3.
     // f20, f21, f22, and f23 still contain vector elements.
     // Add f20 and f22 to the pipeline, too.
     d.pfadd.ss     f20, f30, f30
       br      S              // Exit loop after adding
     d.pfadd.ss     f21, f31, f31  // f21 to the pipeline
       nop
L2::d.pfadd.ss f22, f30, f30       // Add f22 to pipeline
       bla          r21, r17, L1   // If more, go to L1 after
     d.pfadd.ss     f23, f31, f31  // adding f23 to pipeline and

       fld.d        8(r16)++, f22  // loading next f22:f23
     // If we reach this point, at least one element remains to be loaded.
     // r17 is either -4 or -3.
     // f20, f21, f22, and f23 still contain vector elements.
     // Add f20 and f21 to the pipeline, too.
     d.pfadd.ss     f20, f30, f30
       nop
     d.pfadd.ss     f21, f31, f31
       nop
S::                           // Initiate exit from dual mode
     pfadd.ss  f22, f30, f30  // Still in dual mode
       mov          -4,    r21
```

Figure 8-5. Optimized code for vector sum example

```
    pfadd.ss  f23, f31, f31  // Last dual-mode pair
      bte          r21, r17,   DONE    // If there is one more

      fld.l        8(r16)++, f20  // element, load it and
      pfadd.ss     f20, f30, f30  // add to pipeline
      // Intermediate results are sitting in the adder pipeline.

      // Let A1:A2:A3 represent the current pipeline contents
DONE::pfadd.ss f0,        f0,  f30  // 0:A1:A2       f30=A3
      pfadd.ss     f30, f31, f31  // A2+A3:0:A1    f31=A2
      pfadd.ss     f0,  f0,  f30  // 0:A2+A3:0     F30=A1
      pfadd.ss     f0,  f0,  f0   // 0:0:A2+A3
      pfadd.ss     f0,  f0,  f31  // 0:0:0         F31=A2+A3
      fadd.ss f30, f31, f16  // f16 = A1+A2+A3
      bri r1
      fmov.sd   f16, f16
```

Figure 8-5. Optimized code for vector sum example **(continued)**

When the loop count is reached, execution falls through the loops continuing to sum the elements already loaded into registers and loads the final elements. When the label S is reached, execution is returned to single-instruction mode and, if the number of elements is odd, one more load and addition is performed. The code denoted by the label DONE performs the final additions for any values still in the pipeline and combines the summation total into **f16**.

Several optimizations were used to reduce the execution time substantially for each vector element. First, instead of loading each vector element individually, they were loaded as pairs of values into adjacent floating-point registers. This halved the number of loads required. Second, instead of using scalar floating-point additions that require three clocks each if executed in immediate succession, pipelined floating-point additions were used at one clock each. Third, and the main point of this example, dual-instruction mode was used to combine the floating-point additions with the loop control instruction **bla**, and with the floating-point load instruction.

Because these three techniques were so successful in reducing the clocks for the summation loop, the routine had to be split into two separate loops. This allowed the two delay slots following the floating-point load instruction to be filled with operations that did not require the load data. The result of these optimizations is that a floating-point addition is performed in each clock of execution. For long vectors, the execution time for the setup code at the beginning, and the fixup code following the loops, will be negligible. The one clock per vector element is a seven times improvement over the scalar code shown in Figure 8-2. (Optimum scalar code could achieve four clocks per element.)

Matrix Product Example

The performance of applications such as the vector sum and matrix product is affected considerably by their cache hit rates. Since the computation portion of the code typically comprises a small loop, the code fits easily in the processor's instruction cache. However, for calculations that use (and reuse) massive amounts of data, any reasonably sized data cache will be insufficient to store the entire data set. For these calculations to achieve optimum performance, their memory access demands must be carefully considered. This section considers the computation involved in calculating the product of two matrices, and analyzes two memory access strategies as they apply to this calculation.

Calculating the product of two matrices involves extending the vector dot-product example of Chapter 6, "Floating-Point Operations," to encompass the additional dimension of each matrix. Where vector A will have one dimension (A_i), matrix A will have two dimensions ($A_{i,j}$). Consider the product of matrix $A = A_{i,j}$ of dimension L × M with matrix $B = B_{i,j}$ of dimension M × N, which will result in the matrix $C = C_{i,j}$ of dimension L × N, where

$$C_{i,j} = A_{i,1}B_{i,j} + A_{i,2}B_{2,j} + \ldots + A_{i,m}B_{m,j} \text{ (for } 1 \le i \le L,\ 1 \le j \le N)$$

This equation means that each element of matrix C is produced by adding all products obtained by multiplying each element of the A matrix row by the B matrix column. For example, element $C_{2,4}$ is the result of adding the products obtained by multiplying the second row of matrix A by the fourth column of matrix B.

The product of two two-dimensional matrices produces a two-dimensional matrix with the combined dimensions of the two source matrices. As indicated by the common dimension M above, the number of rows of B must be exactly the same as the number of columns in A. The resulting matrix dimensions are the row size of matrix A and the column size of matrix B.

The two-dimension matrix product operation is an extension of the one-dimension matrix product. The inner loop of performing a series of multiplications followed by additions is unchanged and each element of the result matrix is, in fact, formed in this manner. To extend the program to produce the entire matrix requires loading the first row of matrix *A* and performing the one-dimensional matrix product for the N columns of matrix *B*. This is repeated for the L rows of *A* to produce the L × N product matrix.

Now that the basic algorithm is understood, consider the total number of calculations required to perform the matrix product where

- M is the number of columns of *A* and the number of rows of *B*, which makes it the number of multiplications needed to obtain one value.
- M−1 is the number of additions needed to sum the products and obtain one value.
- L*N is the total number of elements in the resulting matrix *C*.

The number of operations required can be summarized as:

$$[M + (M-1)] * [L*N]$$

So, the matrix product of two [8 × 8] matrices requires 960 arithmetic operations, and two [100 × 100] matrices require 1,990,000 arithmetic operations. Because of the large number of arithmetic operations required, optimizations can have a tremendous performance benefit.

The examples in Figures 8-6 and 8-7 perform the calculations for a two-dimensional matrix product. Each example uses dual-instruction mode to perform the loading and loop control operations in parallel with dual-operation floating-point instructions. The examples differ in their approaches to memory access and cache usage. The example in Figure 8-6 depends solely on cached loads, while the example in Figure 8-7 depends on a mix of cached and noncached pipelined loads. To reduce complexity, these two examples require that the M dimension be a multiple of eight, and that the *A* matrix be stored in memory by row (successive memory addresses referring to the next element of the row), and that the *B* matrix be stored by column (successive memory addresses refer to the next element of the column). Data is fetched 32

```
// MATRIX MULTIPLY, C = A * B, CACHED LOADS ONLY
// Matrix A by row, matrix B by column
// Registers loaded by calling routine
A=r16     // pointer into A, stored in memory by rows
B=r17     // pointer into B, stored in memory by columns
C=r18     // pointer into C, stored in memory by rows
L=r19     // the number of rows in A
M=r20     // the number of columns in A and rows in B
N=r21     // the number of columns in B
// Registers used locally
RC=r28    // row/column counter decremented by bla for loop control
DEC=r27   // decrementor for row/column pointers
Ar=r26    // counter of rows in A
Bc=r25    // counter of columns in B
Bp=r24    // temporary pointer into B
SIZ=r23   // number of bytes in row of A or column of B
A1=f4; A2=f5; A3=f6; A4=f7; A5=f8; A6=f9; A7=f10; A8=f11
// matrix A row values
B1=f12;B2=f13;B3=f14;B4=f15;B5=f16;B6=f17;B7=f18;B8=f19
// matrix B column vals
T1=f20;T2=f21;T3=f22                 // temporary results
  shl              2, M, SIZ         // Number of bytes in M entries
  adds             -8, r0, DEC       // Set decrementor for bla
  adds             -8, M, RC         // Initialize row/column counter
  adds             -4, C, C          // Start C index one entry low

  d.fiadd.dd   f0, f0, f0            // Initiate dual-instruction mode
  adds             -1, L, Ar         // Make row counter zero relative
  d.fnop                             // First dual-mode pair
     bla       DEC, RC, start_row    // Initialize LCC
  d.fnop                             //
     subs        A, SIZ, A           // Start pointer to A one row low
start_row::                          // Executed once per row of A
  d.pfmul.ss   f0, f0, f0            //
     mov                B, Bp        // Point to first col of B
  d.pfmul.ss   f0, f0, f0            //
     adds        SIZ, A, A           // Point to next row of A
  d.pfmul.ss   f0, f0, f0            //
     fld.q              16(Bp), B5   // Load 4 entries of B
  d.pfadd.ss   f0, f0, f0            //
     fld.q              16(A), A5    // Load 4 entries of A
  d.pfadd.ss   f0, f0, f0            //
     adds        -1, N, Bc           // Initialize column counter
  d.pfadd.ss   f0, f0, f0            //
     fld.q              0(A), A1     // Load 4 entries of A
```

Figure 8-6. Matrix product example using cached loads only

```
inner_loop:: // Process eight entries of row of A with eight of col of B
  d.m12apm.ss  A5,  B5, T1          //
     fld.q           0(Bp), B1      // Load 4 entries of B
  d.m12apm.ss  A6, B6, T1           //
     adds       32, A, A            // Bump pointer to A by 8 entries
  d.m12apm.ss  A7, B7, T1           //
     adds       32, Bp, Bp          // Bump pointer to B by 8 entries
  d.m12apm.ss  A8, B8, T1           //
     fld.q           16(Bp), B5     // Load 4 entries of B
  d.m12apm.ss  A1, B1, T1           //
     fld.q           16(A), A5      // Load 4 entries of A
  d.m12apm.ss  A2, B2, T1           //
     nop                            //
  d.m12apm.ss  A3, B3, T1           //
     bla    DEC, RC, inner_loop     // Loop until end of row/column
  d.m12apm.ss  A4, B4, T2           //
     fld.q           0(A), A1       // Load 4 entries of A
// End Inner Loop.  End of row/column
  d.m12apm.ss  f0, f0, T3           //
     subs        A, SIZ, A          // Set A pointer back to beginning of row
  d.m12apm.ss  f0, f0, T1           //
     adds        -8, M, RC          // Reinitialize row/column counter
  d.m12apm.ss  f0,  f0, T2          //
     nop                            //
  d.pfadd.ss   f0, f0, T3           //
     bla       DEC, RC, inner_loop  // Won't branch; initializes LCC
  d.pfadd.ss   f0, f0,   T1         //
     fld.q           16(A), A5      // Load 4 entries of A
  d.pfadd.ss   f0, f0,   T2         //
     fld.q           16(Bp), B5     // Load 4 entries of B
  d.fadd.ss        T1, T3, T3       //
     fld.q           0(A), A1       // Load 4 entries of A
  d.fadd.ss        T2, T3, T3       //
     adds       -1, Bc, Bc          // Decrement column counter
  d.pfadd.ss   f0, f0, f0           //
     fst.l           T3, 4(C)++     // Store row/column product in C
// Continue with next column of B?
  d.pfadd.ss   f0, f0, f0           //
     bnc.t           inner_loop     // CC controlled by prior adds
  d.pfadd.ss   f0, f0, f0           //
     nop                            //
// Continue with next row of A?
  d.fnop                            //
```

Figure 8-6. Matrix product example using cached loads only **(continued)**

```
   xor          Ar, r0, r0   // Is row counter zero?
d.fnop                       //
   bnc.t        start_row    // Taken if row counter not zero
d.fnop                       //
   adds     -1, Ar, Ar       // Decrement row counter
fnop                         // Initiate exit from dual mode
   nop                       //
fnop                         // Last dual-mode pair
   nop                       // End
```

Figure 8-6. Matrix product example using cached loads only (continued)

bytes beyond the higher-address end of both matrices, and programmers should ensure that page protection faults do not occur due to these accesses.

The example in Figure 8-6 uses the **fld** instruction for all floating-point loads, which places the elements of both matrices *A* and *B* in the cache. This is the ideal approach for small matrices where the total matrix data will fit in the data cache. Here, the first access to an element will load the cache from memory and subsequent accesses to the same memory address will find the elements in the cache and retrieve them at a rate of four per clock. Using the **fld.q** instruction, four single-precision elements can be retrieved from the cache with each load instruction. This allows fully overlapping the data accesses as well as loop control with **m12apm** dual-operation floating-point instructions in the inner loop.

If the matrices are large, all of the data will not fit in the cache, and performance will degrade due to cache misses. This is called *cache thrashing.* The larger the matrices, the more thrashing will occur. The problem is exacerbated by the pattern of access for the columns of matrix *B*. Each column of matrix *B* is used once, then not used again until all of the other columns have been used.

The example in Figure 8-7 uses the **fld** instruction for all elements of each row of *A*, and uses the **pfld** instruction to pass all columns of *B* against each row of *A*. This method makes better use of the data cache by placing only the rows of *A* in the cache. More load instructions are required, because a **pfld** can load at most two single-precision operands. Still, with pipelined memory cycles, it remains possible to

```
// MATRIX MULTIPLY, C = A * B, CACHED AND PIPELINED LOADS MIXED

// Matrix A by row, matrix B by column
// Registers loaded by calling routine
A=r16     // pointer into A, stored in memory by rows
B=r17     // pointer into B, stored in memory by columns
C=r18     // pointer into C, stored in memory by rows
L=r19     // the number of rows in A
M=r20     // the number of columns in A and rows in B
N=r21     // the number of columns in B
// Registers used locally
Ap=r29    // temporary pointer into A
RC=r28    // row/column counter decremented by bla for loop control
DEC=r27   // decrementor for row/column pointers
Ar=r26    // counter of rows in A
Bc=r25    // counter of columns in B
Bp=r24    // temporary pointer into B
SIZ=r23   // number of bytes in row of A or column of B
A1=f4; A2=f5; A3=f6; A4=f7; A5=f8; A6=f9; A7=f10;A8=f11 // matrix A row values
B1=f12;B2=f13;B3=f14;B4=f15;B5=f16;B6=f17;B7=f18;B8=f19 // matrix B column vals
T1=f20;T2=f21;T3=f22
// temporary results
  mov             B, Bp         // Pointer to B
  shl             2, M, SIZ     // Number of bytes in M entries
  adds            -8, r0, DEC   // Set decrementor for bla
  adds            -8, M, RC     // Initialize row/column counter
  d.fiadd.dd  f0, f0, f0        // Initiate dual-instruction mode
  adds            -4, C, C      // Start C index one entry low

  d.fnop                        // First dual-mode pair
     adds      -1, L, Ar        // Make row counter zero relative
  d.fnop                        //
     bla      DEC, RC, start_row // Initialize LCC
  d.fnop                        //
     mov            A, Ap       // Pointer to A
start_row::                     // Executed once per row of A
  d.pfmul.ss  f0, f0, f0        //
     pfld.d         0(Bp), f0   // Load 2 entries of B into load pipe
  d.pfmul.ss  f0, f0, f0        //
     pfld.d         8(Bp)++, f0 // Load the second 2 entries of B into load pipe
  d.pfmul.ss  f0, f0, f0        //
```

Figure 8-7. Matrix product example using cached and noncached pipeline loads

```
   pfld.d          8(Bp)++, f0  // Load  2 entries of B into load pipe
 d.pfadd.ss   f0, f0, f0        //
   fld.q           0(Ap), A1    // Load 5th and 6th entries of A
 d.pfadd.ss   f0, f0, f0        //
   pfld.d          8(Bp)++, B1  // Load 2 entries of B
 d.pfadd.ss   f0, f0, f0        //
   adds         -1, N, Bc       // Initialize column counter

 d.fnop                         //
   pfld.d          8(Bp)++, B3  // Load 2 entries of B
inner_loop:: // Process eight entries from row of A with eight from col of B
 d.m12apm.ss  A1, B1, f0        //
   fld.q           16(Ap)++, A5 // Load 4 entries of A
 d.m12apm.ss  A2, B2, f0        //
   pfld.d          8(Bp)++, B5  // Load 2 entries of B
 d.m12apm.ss  A3, B3, f0        //
   pfld.d          8(Bp)++, B7  // Load 2 entries of B
 d.m12apm.ss  A4, B4, f0        //
   fld.q           16(Ap)++, A1 // Load 4 entries of A
 d.m12apm.ss  A5, B5, f0        //
   nop                          //
 d.m12apm.ss  A6, B6, f0        //
   pfld.d          8(Bp)++, B1  // Load 2 entries of B
 d.m12apm.ss  A7, B7, f0        //
   bla        DEC, RC, inner_loop // Loop until end of row/column
 d.m12apm.ss  A8, B8, f0        //
   pfld.d          8(Bp)++, B3  // Load 2 entries of B
// End Inner Loop.  End of row/column
 d.m12apm.ss  f0, f0, f0        //
   nop                          //
 d.m12apm.ss  f0, f0, f0        //
   adds         -8, M, RC       // Reinitialize row/column counter
 d.m12apm.ss  f0, f0, f0        //
   mov             A, Ap        // Set A pointer back to beginning of row
 d.pfadd.ss   f0, f0, T3        //
   fld.q           0(Ap), A1    // Load first 4 entries of row of A
 d.pfadd.ss   f0, f0,   T1      //
   bla        DEC, RC, inner_loop // Won't branch; initializes LCC
 d.pfadd.ss   f0, f0,   T2      //
   nop                          //
 d.fadd.ss         T1, T3, T3   //
   nop                          //
```

***Figure 8-7. Matrix product example using cached and noncached pipeline loads* (continued)**

```
  d.fadd.ss         T2, T3, T3      //
     adds        -1, Bc, Bc         // Decrement column counter
  d.pfadd.ss   f0, f0, f0           //
     fst.l             T3, 4(C)++   // Store row/column product in C
// Continue with next column of B?
  d.pfadd.ss   f0, f0, f0           //
     bnc.t             inner_loop   // CC controlled by prior adds

  d.pfadd.ss   f0, f0, f0           //
     nop                            //
// End of all columns of B
  d.fnop                            //
     mov               B, Bp        // Point to first col of B
  d.fnop                            //
     adds        A, SIZ, A          // Bump pointer to A by one row
  d.fnop                            //
     mov               A, Ap        // Set A index to beginning of next row
// Continue with next row of A?
  d.fnop                            //
     xor               Ar, r0, r0   // Is row counter zero?
  d.fnop                            //
     bnc.t             start_row    // Taken if row counter not zero
  d.fnop                            //
     adds        -1, Ar, Ar         // Decrement row counter
  fnop                              // Initiate exit from dual mode
     nop                            //
  fnop                              // Last dual-mode pair
     nop                            // End
```

Figure 8-7. ***Matrix product example using cached and noncached pipeline loads*** **(continued)**

overlap the loading of the eight items from matrix *A*, the eight items from matrix *B*, and the loop control with the eight **m12apm** instructions in the inner loop.

The strategy of Figure 8-7 is more suitable for larger matrices than the strategy in Figure 8-6 because, even in the extreme case where only one row of *A* fits in the cache, cache misses occur only the first time each row is processed. However, if dimension M is so great that not even one row of *A* fits entirely in the cache, cache thrashing will still occur. For such matrices it may be prudent to subsector the matrices, perform the calculations on each sector, then combine the sector results for the total solution. On the other hand, for small matrices, the example in Figure 8-7 may not perform as well as that in Figure 8-6 because, even if there is sufficient space in the cache, the algorithm will not use it. Instead, it will generate external bus traffic for all elements of *B* repeatedly.

Aside from the caching issues, the programs of both examples in Figures 8-6 and 8-7 perform one dual-operation floating-point instruction for each of the eight instruction pairs of the inner loop. Therefore, the algorithm used for these programs has a peak execution rate equal to the maximum rate of the processor (80 MFlops at 40 Mhz). Let's see what taking away one of the simplifying assumptions will do to our coding algorithm. The programs in Figures 8-8 and 8-9 are similar to those of Figures 8-6 and 8-7, but they are more realistic in assuming both matrices *A* and *B* are stored by column (as in the Fortran programming language). This causes a complication in accessing the rows of matrix *A* during the inner loop.

The inner loop of each of the four programs processes eight entries of a row of *A* with eight entries of a column of *B*. For the examples in Figures 8-6 and 8-7, four elements of matrix *A* row could be accessed with a single quad floating-point load. However, for the examples in Figures 8-8 and 8-9, the row elements are not adjacent in memory and therefore must be accessed individually. For the example in Figure 8-8, which uses all cached loads, the row elements of matrix *A* are loaded with separate **fld.l** instructions. To set the pointer to the next row element, autoincrement addressing with the stride length for vector *A* is used. Unfortunately, this increases the number of core operations in the inner loop to 11. Because the number of floating-point operations remains constant at 16, there are unused floating-point halves of the instruction pairs. This reduces the maximum execution rate of the inner loop to 58 MFlops at 40 Mhz.

Having excess core load instructions also extends the number of instructions for the inner loop of the program in Figure 8-9. Here the problem is made worse due to the pipelined loads for the columns of matrix *B*. Quad-word (16-byte) pipelined floating-point loads do not exist in the i860 processor, so the loads for *B* are performed as multiple double-word pipelined floating-point loads. This extends the inner loop to 13 instruction pairs for the same 16 floating-point operations, thus reducing the maximum performance rate of the loop to 49 MFlops at 40

```
// MATRIX MULTIPLY, C = A * B, CACHED LOADS
// ASSUMES all matrices stored by columns.
A=r16     // pointer into A, stored in memory by columns
B=r17     // pointer into B, stored in memory by columns
C=r18     // pointer into C, stored in memory by columns
L=r19     // the number of rows in A
M=r20     // the number of columns in A and rows in B
N=r21     // the number of columns in B
// Registers used locally
Cp=r30    // pointer for storing results to each entry of Ap=r29
// temporary pointer into A
RC=r28    // row/column counter decremented by bla for loop control
DEC=r27   // decrementor for row/column pointers
Ar=r26    // counter of rows in A
Bc=r25    // counter of columns in B
Ars=r24   // temporary pointer into A. Points to start of each row
Bs=r23    // number of bytes in column of B
As=r22    // number of bytes in column of A (A stride)
A1=f4; A2=f5; A3=f6; A4=f7; A5=f8; A6=f9; A7=f10; A8=f11 // matrix A row values
B1=f12;B2=f13;B3=f14;B4=f15;B5=f16;B6=f17;B7=f18;B8=f19 // matrix B column vals
T1=f20;T2=f21;T3=f22              // temporary results
    shl             2,M,Bs        // Bs <-- bytes in column B
    shl             2,L,As        //As=bytes in column of A
    adds            -8,M,RC       // Initialize row/col counter
    adds            -8,r0,DEC     // Set decrementor for bla

    adds            -1,N,Bc       // Make row counter zero relative

    bla             DEC,RC,start_colB // Initialize LCC
    addu            -4,C,Cp

    nop         // for alignment

start_colB::    // Executed once per col of B
    d.pfmul.ss      f0,f0,f0            // Flush Multiplier stages (first)
      fld.q           0(B),f12
    d.pfmul.ss      f0,f0,f0
      mov             A,Ap
    d.pfmul.ss      f0,f0,f0            // Flush Multiplier stages (third)
      nop
    d.pfadd.ss      f0,f0,f0            // clear Adder stages (first)
      fld.l           0(Ap),f4
    d.pfadd.ss      f0,f0,f0            //
      mov             A,Ars
    d.pfadd.ss      f0,f0,f0            //
      adds            -1,L,Ar
```

Figure 8-8. Matrix product example using cached loads only

```
inner_loop::     // Process 8 entries of row of A with 8 of col of B
// here f12:f15 have 4 entries of B.  f4 has 1 entry of A.
    d.fnop
      fld.q           16(B)++,f16     // Load 4 entries of B
    d.fnop
      fld.l          As (Ap)++,f5     // Load 2nd entry of A
    d.fnop
      fld.l          As (Ap)++,f6
    d.ml2apm.ss     f4,f12,f0         //
      fld.l          As (Ap)++,f7
    d.ml2apm.ss     f5,f13,f0
      fld.l          As (Ap)++,f8
    d.ml2apm.ss     f6,f14,f0
      fld.l          As (Ap)++,f9
    d.ml2apm.ss     f7,f15,f0
      fld.l          As (Ap)++,f10
    d.ml2apm.ss     f8,f16,f0
      fld.l          As (Ap)++,f11
    d.ml2apm.ss     f9,f17,f0           //
      fld.q           16(B)++,f12       // Load 4 entries of B
          // for next pass thru inner_loop
    d.ml2apm.ss     f10,f18,f0          //
      bla             DEC,RC,inner_loop // Loop until end of row/column
    d.ml2apm.ss     f11,f19,f0          //
      fld.l          As (Ap)++,f4  // Load 1 entry of A for next pass
// End inner loop.  End of row/column
// Inner_loop performance:
//   (16 flops / 11_instr_pairs)
end_rowA::
    d.ml2apm.ss     f0,f0,f0          // Advance Mul/Adder stages (1)
      addu            4,Ars,Ars       //point to next rowA
    d.ml2apm.ss     f0,f0,f0
      subu            B,Bs,B          // back to start of Bcol
    d.ml2apm.ss     f0,f0,f0          // Advance Mul/Adder stages (3)
      adds            -8,M,RC
    d.pfadd.ss      f0,f0,f20         // f20 <-- partial sum
      fld.q           0(B),f12
    d.pfadd.ss      f20,f21,f21       // f21 <-- partial sum
      mov             Ars,Ap //next row A for this 1 col B
    d.pfadd.ss      f0,f0,f22         // f22 <-- partial sum
      nop
    d.pfadd.ss      f0,f0,f0          // Advance to get result (2)
      nop
    d.pfadd.ss      f22,f21,f21       // Advance to get result (3)
      fld.l          0(Ap),f4         //prefetch for next inner_loop
    d.pfadd.ss      f0,f0,f0          // Advance and clear stages  (1)
      bla             DEC,RC,next_rowA // Re-init LCC
```

Figure 8-8. Matrix product example using cached loads only **(continued)**

```
    d.pfadd.ss      f0,f0,f0          // Advance and clear stages (2)
      adds            -1,Ar,Ar  // Decrement row counter
next_rowA::
store_it::
// Check whether to continue with next row of A
    d.pfadd.ss      f0,f0,f22         // Get a row/col product in C
      bnc.t           inner_loop      // CC controlled by Ar adds

    d.fnop                            //
      fst.l           f22,4(Cp)++     // Store the row/col product in C
end_colB_allA::
// Check whether to continue with next col of B
    d.fnop                            //
      fst.l           f22,4(Cp)++     // Store the row/col product in C
     //fst.l duplicated here, because of bnc.t skipping next instruction
    d.fnop
      adds            -1,Bc,Bc
    d.fnop                            //
      bnc.t           start_colB      // Taken if Bc nonneg
    d.fnop                            //
      addu            B,Bs,B
all_done::
    fnop                              // Initiate exit from dual-inst mode
     nop
    fnop                              // Last dual-inst mode pair

      nop
```

Figure 8-8. Matrix product example using cached loads only **(continued)**

Mhz. To prevent the degradation for this case, the algorithm should be changed to cache the *B* matrix columns and pipeline load the *A* matrix rows.

Using the **pfld** instruction has an additional characteristic that should be noted. When **fld** instructions are first executed, and load data from memory into the register, the adjacent 32-byte cache line is loaded into the cache. Conversely, **pfld** instructions load only the requested value into the register, and do not cause a cache line fill. If an application operates on data that is not stored in memory sequentially, **fld** instructions may cause an application to load data that is not needed. Thus the application may become cache-bound even though the actual data requested could have fit in the cache.

```
//MATRIX MULTIPLY, C = A * B, CACHED AND PIPELINED LOADS
//            (Matrix A is cached, B is not)
// ASSUMES all matrices stored by columns.
//-----------------------------------------------------//
// Registers loaded by calling routine
A=r16     // pointer into A, stored in memory by columns
B=r17     // pointer into B, stored in memory by columns
C=r18     // pointer into C, stored in memory by columns
L=r19     // the number of rows in A
M=r20     // the number of columns in A and rows in B
N=r21     // the number of columns in B
// Registers used locally
Cp=r30    // pointer for storing results to each entry of C
Ap=r29    // temporary pointer into A
RC=r28    // row/column counter decremented by bla for loop control
DEC=r27   // decrementor for row/column pointers
Ar=r26    // counter of rows in A
Bc=r25    // counter of columns in B
Bp=r24    // temporary pointer into B
As=r22    // number of bytes in column of A
A1=f4; A2=f5; A3=f6; A4=f7; A5=f8; A6=f9; A7=f10; A8=f11 // matrix A row values
B1=f12;B2=f13;B3=f14;B4=f15;B5=f16;B6=f17;B7=f18;B8=f19 // matrix B column vals
T1=f20;T2=f21;T3=f22
// temporary results

  mov            B,Bp              // Pointer to B
  shl            2,L,As            // # bytes in a col of A
  adds           -8,r0,DEC         // Set decrementor for bla
  adds           -8,M,RC           // Initialize column counter
  adds         -1,L,Ar             // Make row counter zero relative
  nop                              // for alignment
  d.fiadd.dd     f0,f0,f0          // Initiate dual-instruction mode

  subs           C,As,Cp           // Start C index one row low

  d.fnop                           // First dual-mode pair
   bla       DEC,RC,start_row      // Initialize LCC
  d.fnop                           //

   mov           A,Ap              // Pointer to A

start_row::                        // Executed once per row of A
  d.pfmul.ss     f0,f0,f0          //
   pfld.d           0(Bp),f0       // Load 2 entries of B into load pipe
  d.fnop
   fld.l  0(Ap),f4                 // Fetch 1 entry A
  d.pfmul.ss     f0,f0,f0          //
   pfld.d           8(Bp)++,f0     // Load 2 entries of B into load pipe
  d.fnop
   fld.l  As (Ap)++,f5             // Fetch 1 entry A
  d.pfmul.ss     f0,f0,f0          //
   pfld.d           8(Bp)++,f0     // Load 2 entries of B into load pipe
  d.pfadd.ss     f0,f0,f0          //
   fld.l       As (Ap)++,f6
```

Figure 8-9. Matrix product example using cached and noncached pipeline loads

```
   d.pfadd.ss      f0,f0,f0           //
    pfld.d            8(Bp)++,f12     // Load 2 entries of B
   d.fnop
    fld.l  As (Ap)++,f7               // Fetch 4th entry A
   d.pfadd.ss      f0,f0,f0           //
    adds         -1,N,Bc              // Initialize column counter
   d.fnop
    pfld.d            8(Bp)++,f14     // Load 2 entries of B

inner_loop:: // Process 8 entries from row of A with 8 from col of B
  // Here, already f4:f7   = 4 entries of A
  //                f12:f15 = 4 entries of B
  //  Pfld pipeline is full with 6 more B entries
  d.m12apm.ss    f4, f12,f0           //
   fld.l      As (Ap)++,f8
  d.m12apm.ss    f5, f13,f0           //
   pfld.d            8(Bp)++,f16 // Load 2 entries of B
  d.m12apm.ss    f6, f14,f0           //
   fld.l      As (Ap)++,f9
  d.fnop
   pfld.d            8(Bp)++,f18 // Load 2 entries of B

 d.m12apm.ss     f7, f15,f0           //
  fld.l      As (Ap)++,f10
 d.fnop
  fld.l      As (Ap)++,f11
 d.fnop
  fld.l      As (Ap)++,f4
 d.m12apm.ss     f8,f16,f0           //
  fld.l      As (Ap)++,f5
 d.m12apm.ss     f9,f17,f0           //
  pfld.d            8(Bp)++,f12 // Load 2 entries of B
 d.fnop
  fld.l      As (Ap)++,f6
 d.fnop
  fld.l      As (Ap)++,f7

end_inner::
 d.m12apm.ss     f10,f18,f0           //
  bla       DEC,RC,inner_loop         // Loop until end of row/column
 d.m12apm.ss     f11,f19,f0           //
  pfld.d            8(Bp)++,f14       // Load 2 entries of B
// End Inner Loop.  End of row/column
// Inner loop performance:
//   16 flops/(13-inst-pairs)

_1rowAcolB_done::
 d.m12apm.ss     f0, f0, f0           //
  nop                                 //
 d.m12apm.ss     f0, f0, f0           //
  adds        -8,M,RC                 // Reinitialize BLA row/column counter
 d.m12apm.ss     f0, f0, f0           //
  mov               A,Ap              // Set A pointer back to beginning of row
```

***Figure 8-9. Matrix product example using cached and noncached pipeline loads* (continued)**

```
 d.pfadd.ss f0, f0, f22            //
  fld.l     0(Ap), f4              // Load first entry of row of A
 d.pfadd.ss f0, f0,   f20          //
  bla       DEC,RC,nowhere         // Won't branch; initializes LCC
 d.pfadd.ss f0, f0,   f21          //
  fld.l     As (Ap)++,f5
nowhere::
 d.fadd.ss       f20,f22,f22
  fld.l     As (Ap)++,f6
 d.fadd.ss       f21,f22,f22       //
  adds      -1,Bc,Bc               // Decrement column counter

store_it:
 d.pfadd.ss f0, f0, f0             //
  fst.l     f22,As (Cp)++          //Store rowA*colB product in C (by Rows)
// Continue with next column of B?
 d.pfadd.ss f0, f0, f0             //
  bnc.t     inner_loop             // CC controlled by prior adds
 d.pfadd.ss f0, f0, f0
  fld.l     As (Ap)++,f7
// End of all columns of B
end_1rowA_allB::
 d.fnop
  mov       B,Bp                   // Point to first col of B
 d.fnop
  adds      4,A,A                  // Bump pointer to A by one row
 d.fnop
  adds      4,C,C                  // Point permanently to next row of C
 d.fnop
  mov       A,Ap                   // Set A index to beginning of next row
// Continue with next row of A?
d.fnop
 adds       -1,Ar,Ar               // Decrement row counter
d.fnop
 bnc.t      start_row              // Taken if Ar (row counter) not neg

d.fnop
 subs       C,As,Cp                // point 1 stride below next result row
// end of all loops
end_all::
 fnop                              // Initiate exit from dual mode
  nop
 fnop                              // Last dual-mode pair
  nop                              // End
```

***Figure 8-9. Matrix product example using cached and noncached pipeline loads* (continued)**

Vector Computation Model

The computation model of the i860 processor, as shown in these last four programs, can perform similarly to supercomputers such as the Cray 1. Figure 8-10 is intentionally drawn to highlight the i860 processor in this manner. The basic model for the i860 processor is that data can be accessed from external memory and stored in the data cache where it is available at a higher bandwidth. This corresponds to the scalar and vector registers of the Cray 1. The scalar registers of the Cray 1 have two levels of storage, like the cache and registers of the i860 processor, while the vector registers arranged as 64-element segments can directly feed the functional units. For both the Cray 1 and the i860 processor, the memory hierarchy for data storage is visible to the programmer. This differs from most processors where the data cached is a function of a program's locality.

The floating-point units of the Cray 1 are a multiplier, an adder, and a reciprocal approximator. The multiplier and adder support chaining. *Chaining* occurs when the results from one functional unit are fed into another functional unit. The analogous method for doing this on the i860 processor is dual-operation instructions. Both methods can produce results at a rate of one per clock cycle, and intermediate data does not have to be stored to memory nor to registers before it is used. The Cray 1 uses the reciprocal approximator for performing division as does the i860 processor.

In this chapter you have seen how to use the advanced features of the i860 processor in order to greatly increase the efficiency of programs. Dual-instruction mode is an effective way to sustain the performance of floating-point computations by executing load, store, and loop control operations in parallel. Even when the data sets of a problem are very large, programs can use the different caching and noncaching loads to limit performance degradation. Although these programming techniques are new for microprocessors, they are not new for computers because the i860 processor has borrowed some of the techniques used in supercomputers like the Cray 1.

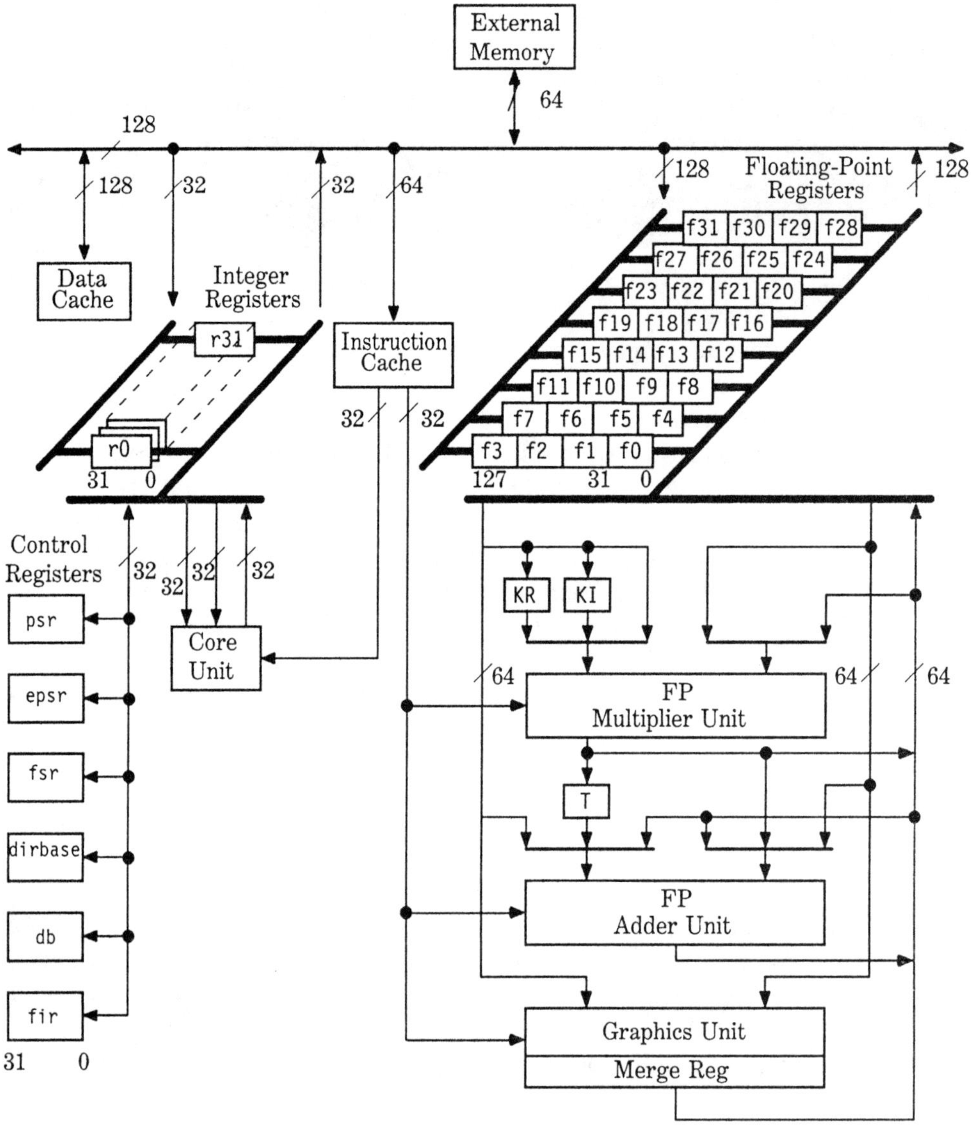

Figure 8-10. i860 processor as a vector machine

CHAPTER 9
OPERATING SYSTEM SUPPORT

Operating system programming is one of the most challenging aspects of programming. The operating system must manage a computer's resources, such as memory, and provide support for traps and interrupts. Multitasking operating systems have additional requirements for task management. Microprocessors vary considerably in operating system support provided. The i860 processor has the instructions and required hardware to support many types of operating systems, including demand-paged multitasking systems.

First, this chapter explains the support the i860 processor provides for multitasking virtual memory operating systems and how to use the processor's paging hardware to implement virtual memory management and protection. How to handle system issues and the complications that result from the processor's on-chip caches are included in this section. Second, this chapter explains how to use the lock features for supporting multitasking and multiprocessing. Third, a strategy for trap handling for the i860 processor is explained. For the system programmer these details are extremely important, but much of the detailed information in this chapter is not necessary for application programmers.

Virtual Memory

Virtual memory allows very large programs, or multiple programs, to be executed as if the entire program were in main memory, even though portions are still in secondary memory (on disk). For example, if there is a large program that has 20 MB of data, and the computer has only 8 MB of memory, the operating system can still load and run the program. In effect, the memory of a computer is increased by using virtual memory.

Virtual memory was developed to relieve application programmers from having to program the memory management into their applications. For example, application programs that use overlays require the programmer to indicate explicitly which parts of the program must be in memory simultaneously, and which parts need not coexist. Each time the program is revised, the overlays must also be revised. Virtual memory manages physical memory with the operating system, not the application program. This has advantages beyond overlays for multitasking systems that must protect and isolate multiple applications.

To use virtual memory, a program must be divisible into pieces, where individual pieces of the program can be either in memory or swapped to disk. A method where the pieces are variable in size, and relate in some way to the organization of the program, is called *segmentation.* Using segmentation has advantages beyond overlays for multitasking and protection. Segmentation has, however, several shortcomings. If a computer uses segments that vary in size, allocating and deallocating memory segments becomes more difficult and results in memory fragmentation. Forcing a fixed size segment has problems of its own. If the segment size is too small, such as a 64K segment, it is visible to the application program and is very cumbersome. If the segment size is too large, it is too difficult for a computer to keep the segmentation processing invisible to the user.

Virtual Addressing

Page-based memory management is an alternative to using segment-based memory management. Paging is transparent to the application program and uses a uniform page size for memory allocation. The paging hardware translates the virtual address (sometimes called the *logical address*) seen by application programs into a physical address that is used to access the physical memory. This allows applications to use areas (pages) of memory in some sequential structure, although the physical location of these areas (pages) may be scattered throughout physical memory. The information to translate a virtual address to a physical address is set up and managed by the operating system by the use of page tables. *Virtual addresses* are seen by the program, while *physical addresses* are those on the processor pins (assuming, as in the case of the i860 processor, the memory management unit is on-chip).

Like mainframe computers, the page tables that the i860 processor supports are arranged in a two-level hierarchy. The start of the page directory is pointed to by the directory table base pointer located in the **dirbase** register. As shown in the translation diagram of Figure 9-1, the

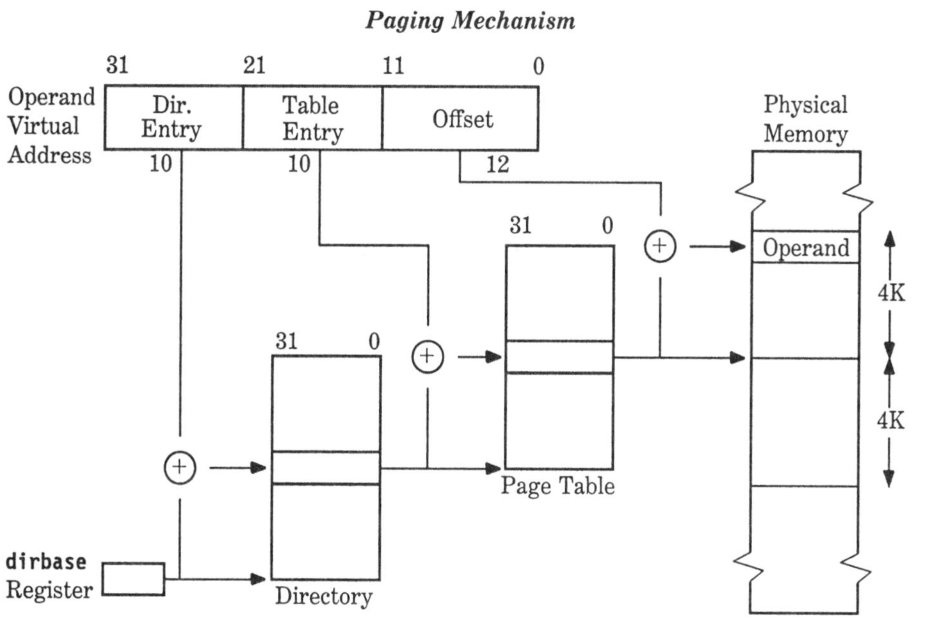

Figure 9-1. Virtual address parsing and two-level paging scheme

processor uses the upper 10 bits of the virtual address as an index into the page directory. Each directory entry is 32-bits long, of which 20 bits are of addressing information (A31 through A12). These 20 bits contain the base address of a page table. The processor uses these 20 bits and the middle 10 bits of the linear address to access the particular entry from the page table. The page table entries are also 32-bits long and contain 20 bits of address mapping information. When these 20 bits are combined with the lower 12 bits of the virtual address, they form the 32-bit physical address.

The page directory is one-page long and contains addresses for 1024 (2^{10}) page tables. Page tables are also one-page long and have 1024 (2^{10}) entries, each describing a page. Each page is 4K (2^{12}) in size. A simple calculation, $2^{10} * 2^{10} * 2^{12}$, shows that the page tables map the entire 4-gigabyte (2^{32}) address space of the processor.

The Translation Look-a-Side Buffer (TLB)

While paging is enabled, translation information is required for all memory accesses. If the processor had to access the translation information from the page tables in memory each time that a reference was made, performance would suffer greatly. To save the overhead of the page table look-ups, the processor automatically caches mapping information for 64 recently used pages in an on-chip TLB (Translation Look-a-Side Buffer). The TLB's 64 entries cover 4K each, providing a total cover of 256K of memory addresses.

As indicated in Figure 9-2, only when the processor does not find the mapping information for a page in the TLB does it perform a page table look-up from information stored in memory. To improve hit rates, the TLB is *four-way set-associative* as illustrated in Figure 9-3. This means each translation can be stored in any of four locations in the TLB.

When a memory access results in a TLB miss, the processor will replace an older TLB entry with the new entry that is likely to be used again. With the i860 processor, the TLB miss processing, sometimes called a *table walk*, is performed entirely in hardware. The table walk searches through the page directory and the page table to retrieve the translation information to perform the memory access, and the processor caches this information in the TLB. The instruction that caused the TLB miss is restarted and uses the new TLB entry for determining the physical address.

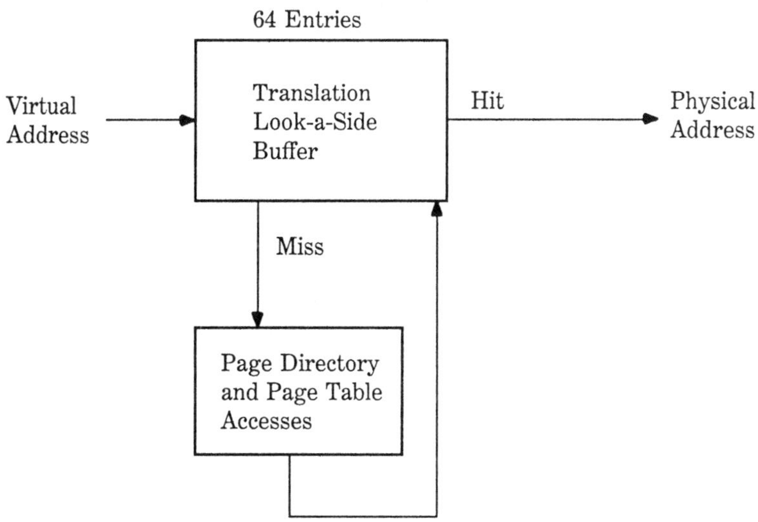

Figure 9-2. Address translations check the TLB before accessing the page tables

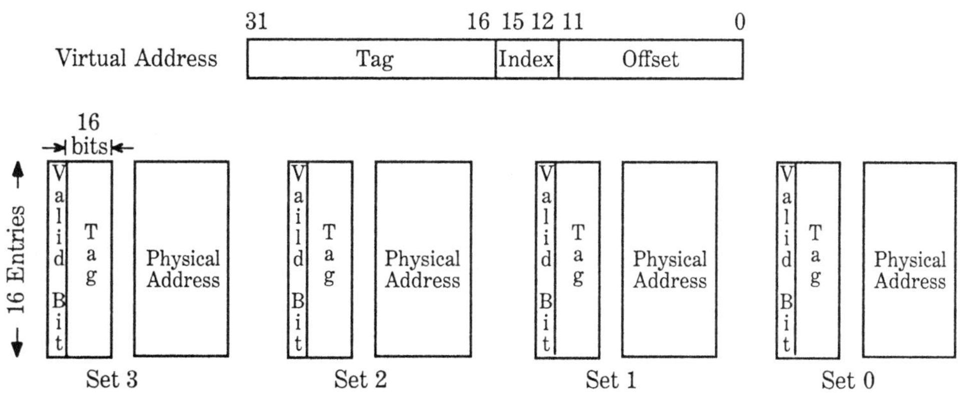

Figure 9-3. Four-way set-associative TLB organization

During hardware TLB miss processing, the i860 processor looks only in external memory for page directories and tables, *not in the internal data cache.* Therefore, any code that modifies the page directories or tables must make sure the changes are reflected in external memory. This can be done by flushing the data cache after the modification, or avoiding caching the tables. Both of these methods are discussed later in this chapter. Also, the system software must flush the TLB after making changes to the page tables to ensure that stale page table entries are not used. Because the TLB is four-way set-associative, a new entry can be placed in any of four TLB locations. The set-associative TLB uses a random replacement algorithm.

Page-Based Memory Management

The information for efficient memory management lies within the page directory entries and page table entries. In Figure 9-4, the lower 12 bits in each page entry contain several control bits. These control bits are used by the operating system to keep track of which pages are in main memory, which pages should be swapped-out in favor of a new page, and which pages must be written back to disk when discarded.

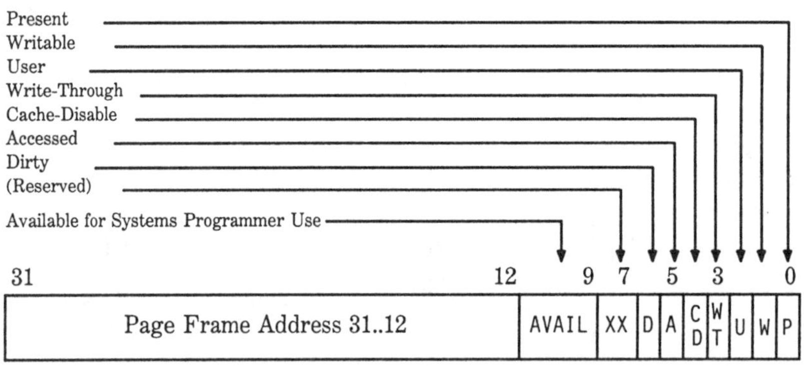

Note: X indicates Intel Reserved. Do Not Use.

Figure 9-4. Page entry format for page directory and page table entries

When the P (present) bit is set to one in the page table, that indicates the page entry is valid and can be used in address translation. When the P bit is a zero, the page information is not valid. An invalid page entry will never be loaded into the processor's TLB, because an access to an invalid page will cause a trap to be processed by the page fault handler. The page fault handler must copy the needed page into memory from disk and return execution to the program.

What happens if there is no more room in physical memory to load in another page? This is sometimes referred to as *memory overcommit* and requires the handler to decide which presently loaded page should be removed from active memory. Although the handler cannot be sure which pages will not be needed in the future, it can make a good guess based on the least recently used pages. The A (accessed) bit and the bits marked AVAILable are managed to determine which pages have not been recently used. The A bit is automatically set to one in memory and the TLB by the processor's hardware whenever it accesses a page directory entry or page table entry where the A bit is zero. The bit can be cleared only by software.

The A bit, combined with managing the AVAILable for operating system bits, allows an approximation of a LRU (least recently used) algorithm to be implemented for page management. By periodically clearing the A bits, and keeping a frequency counter in the AVAILable field, the operating system can keep track of those pages that are not frequently used. The A bits are periodically scanned, and the algorithm increments the frequency count if the page is accessed and decrements it if the page is not accessed. This causes pages to become more vulnerable to replacement as they are no longer used. To prevent new pages from being quickly replaced, they are given a frequency count in the middle of the range when they are brought into memory. Many other algorithms and variations of LRU can be implemented for managing page replacement.

Once the operating system determines the page to be removed from main memory, the operating system must then decide if the page needs to be written back to disk. The D (dirty) bit indicates if the page has been written to. If the D bit is set, then the operating system knows that it must be written back to disk. If the D bit is not set, the copy of the page that is currently on the disk is the most recent version and the page in memory can simply be overwritten instead of written back to disk.

This method of swapping pages in and out of memory is called *demand paging.* It is critical for operating systems that use virtual memory management.

Multitasking

In order to meet the goal of being transparent to application programs, virtual memory management must hide the complications introduced by multitasking operating systems. Effective multitasking requires a timing source to indicate when a task switch is required, and a method to manage the different tasks. The timing source is provided easily by the system hardware, but the task management requires both hardware and software.

Multitasking operating systems were developed in the 1960s to allow multiple users to *time share* a central computer. Time sharing permits users to connect from terminals to the central computer where the computer's operating system gives each user the sense that he or she has an entire machine, although with less performance. The central computer accomplishes this illusion by a time-slicing technique where the processor's time is divided between the connected users. It is with a time-slicing multitasking operating system, that the central computer can support multiple users simultaneously with what appears to be individual machines of their own. The user's perception of having an entire machine is often referred to as a *virtual machine.*

Multitasking has become increasingly important and is not just for time-shared multiuser systems. With the increased power of microprocessors, single-user systems can process background applications while providing an acceptable level of performance for foreground applications. Although switching between tasks involves some overhead, if switching is infrequent, the cost is minimal when compared to overall processing.

Protection For multitasking, a protection mechanism is needed to prevent application programs from destroying each other and from causing the entire system to crash. The operating system must prevent user programming errors that attempt to write over other tasks or the operating system in memory or, worse yet, on disk. Fortunately, user programs can be restricted from accessing operating system memory, and user programs are restricted from directly accessing the computer's hardware devices.

To enforce this security, paging includes a protection mechanism that allows user/supervisor and read/write protection. Each page has `U/S` (User/Supervisor) and `W/R` (Write/Read) bits. By managing these bits, the operating system can allow user programs to have read and write, read only, or no access rights to a given page or page group. If a memory access violates any of the page protection attributes, such as user-level code writing a read-only page, a trap will be generated. When the processor is executing at user level, only pages that are marked *user-level* are accessible. This protects supervisor code and data from being accessed by user-level programs. While executing at supervisor level, all pages are readable. In most operating system implementations, supervisor-level programs can write to any page, regardless of the `W` (Write) bit. However, the operating system can choose to implement supervisor-level write protection by setting the `WP` (Write Protect) bit of the **epsr** register. When `WP` is set, supervisor-level writes will cause a trap if the `W` bit equals zero for the page being written.

Supervisor-level write protection can be used to implement a memory management feature called *copy-on-write.* This allows more than one process to share data pages without each program having its own copy. For example, a UNIX system call to create a child process does not have to make a physical copy of all of the memory pages. Instead, the page tables for the new process are modified so that each process may access the same physical region of memory, without write authority. The operating system has to make an additional copy of the page only when one of the processes performs a write. Thus, the copying of the page is deferred until a time it is really needed, and avoided if never needed.

The protection attributes of page directory entry are combined with those of the page table entry to determine the actual attributes for the page. Table 9-1 resolves the combined protection rights for pages depending on the two levels of entry attributes, and the setting of the `WP` (Write Protect) bit. When a write does occur to a writable page, the `D` (dirty) bit must already be 1 in the page table entry, or a trap will occur. For such a trap, the trap handler must ensure that no obsolete copy of the page table entry (with the `D` bit cleared) exists in the TLB. To ensure this, the trap handler must set the `D` bit in the page table entry in memory, and then invalidate the TLB. When the write instruction is reissued, TLB miss processing hardware will load the new TLB entry that has the D bit set, and the write operation can be completed.

The two remaining bits in the page table entries, the WT (write-through) and the CD (cache-disable) bits, are used for software control of the caching. If either of these bits is set, the processor will not cache data for memory reads of those pages. Once data is in the cache, however, modifying the WT or CD bits will not affect the accesses.

Table 9-1. Combined Protection Rights

Page Directory Entry		*Page Table Entry*		*Combined Protection*		
				User Access	*Supervisor Access*	
U bit	W bit	U bit	W bit	WP=X	WP=0	WP=1
0	0	0	0	N	R/W	R
0	0	0	1	N	R/W	R
0	0	1	0	N	R/W	R
0	0	1	1	N	R/W	R
0	1	0	0	N	R/W	R
0	1	0	1	N	R/W	R/W
0	1	1	0	N	R/W	R
0	1	1	1	N	R/W	R/W
1	0	0	0	N	R/W	R
1	0	0	1	N	R/W	R
1	0	1	0	R	R/W	R
1	0	1	1	R	R/W	R
1	1	0	0	N	R/W	R
1	1	0	1	N	R/W	R/W
1	1	1	0	R	R/W	R
1	1	1	1	R/W	R/W	R/W

Notes:

N = no access allowed

R = read access only

R/W = both reads and writes allowed

X = don't care

The WT bit is a little misleading as the processor's on-chip data cache has no way of implementing a write-through policy (where memory, in addition to the cache contents, is updated on write hits). This bit is for future versions of the i860 processor that will have write-through capability. For the current i860 processor, the WT and CD bits disable the data caching of the associated page, but only the CD bit disables the instruction caching. Systems can make use of having two separate bits. Depending on the setting of the PBM (page bit mode) in the **epsr** register, one of the two bits is driven on the processor's external pin named PTB. A system with an external second-level cache can make use of this pin to control which pages are cached in the second-level cache.

Address Translation Algorithm

The algorithm below defines how the on-chip MMU translates each virtual address to a physical address. Let DIR, PAGE, and OFFSET be the fields of the virtual address; let PFA1 and PFA2 be the page frame address fields of the first- and second-level page tables, respectively; DTB is the page directory table base address stored in the **dirbase** register.

1. Read the PDE (Page Directory Entry) at the physical address formed by DTB:DIR:00. Note that the data cache is not accessed during PDE and PTE (Page Table Entry) fetches; therefore, the operating system must ensure that main memory contains up-to-date copies of the page entries.
2. If P in the PDE is zero, generate a data or instruction-access fault.
3. If W in the PDE is zero, the operation is a write, and either the U bit of the **psr** is set or WP=1, generate a data-access fault.
4. If the U bit in the PDE is zero and the U bit in the **psr** is set, generate a data- or instruction-access fault.
5. If A in the PDE is zero and if the TLB miss occurred while the bus was locked, generate a data- or instruction-access fault. As explained later, the trap allows software to set the A to one and restart the sequence. This avoids ambiguity in determining what

address corresponds to a locked semaphore for external bus hardware use. That is, the trap prevents *nested locks.*

6. If the A in the PDE is zero and if the TLB miss occurred while the bus was not locked, assert LOCK#, refetch the PDE, set A, and store the PDE, deasserting LOCK# during the store.
7. Locate the PTE at the physical address formed by PFA1:PAGE:00.
8. Perform the P, A, W, and U checks as in steps 3 through 6 with the second-level PTE.
9. If D in the PTE is clear and the operation is a write, generate a data-access fault.
10. Form the physical address as PFA2:OFFSET.

Virtual Cache Complications

To fully understand how to implement a demand paging system for a multitasking operating system on the i860 processor, it is necessary to understand the details of how the on-chip caches work. Although the organization of the caches and the TLB have already been described, this section goes to much greater detail and requires more than a casual reading to understand the subtle points. The implementation of the i860 processor caches should not be considered an architectural feature; it is likely to change in subsequent generations. This description is specific to the first generation i860 processor only.

Both the data and instruction caches are *virtually mapped.* This means that the tags used for cache accesses are from the virtual address, not the translated physical address. (Recall from Figure 3-13 that the cache index is the same for the physical and virtual addresses.) In designing the i860 processor, the cache-access time was one of the limiting factors in the CPU clock frequency and thus directly affects overall processor performance. Using virtually addressed caches allows the cache access to occur in parallel with the TLB look-up resulting in higher operating frequency and higher overall performance. However, virtual caches put additional requirements on the operating system. There are two types of aliasing that the operating system must avoid.

Aliasing In general, each task in a multitasking system has its own virtual address space, sometimes called a *context*. This is necessary so that multiple tasks can be resident in memory, and not be cognizant of the paging operation. The first type of aliasing to avoid is where two tasks have data or code at the same virtual address that corresponds to different physical locations. To prevent this, the paging tables must be different for each task. To implement this, the operating system changes the pointer to the page directory base (an alternate method would be to overwrite the page directory entries), and flushes the TLB whenever contexts are changed. The TLB is flushed by writing a zero to the ITI bit in the **dirbase** register, which also serves to invalidate the instruction cache.

The second type of data aliasing to avoid is when two different tasks use the same physical memory while accessing it through different virtual addresses. As just described, the operating system updates the paging tables used and invalidates the TLB and instruction cache during the task switch. If the data cache is not flushed, the same physical memory could reside at two virtual addresses in the cache. This would cause a problem where writes would update only one of the two copies of the data. To avoid this malady, the data cache must be flushed immediately prior to changing the address mapping information.

Data Cache Protection You will recall that with the i860 processor's pipelined instruction execution, an instruction fetch can occur at the same time as a previous instruction's data access. In order to allow these two operations to occur in parallel the i860 processor has a Harvard architecture. This simply means that separate data and instruction caches are used, as opposed to a unified cache which contains both instructions and data.

With virtually tagged caches, the translation information is not needed to determine if the access is a cache hit. However, data cache accesses must check the protection bits of the TLB. The i860 processor uses only one TLB for both caches and gives data accesses priority at the TLB so that the protection checks can be performed. Instruction cache accesses need only the TLB when performing cache miss processing (where the TLB will provide the physical address of the memory being fetched).

If no data cache access is using the TLB, the instruction cache access will perform the TLB look-up in parallel with its cache look-up. By doing this, the physical address for the memory fetch is available immediately if the instruction cache look-up was a miss. The processor only checks the protection bits for instruction accesses at the time the instruction is brought into the cache. Although this may allow a user task to execute supervisor code, the task remains a user task and cannot access supervisor data due to the 100% data-access protection checking.

Writeback Caching The data cache uses a writeback memory update policy. *Writeback* means that when data is read into the cache, then modified (by a write instruction), the only copy of the modified data (also called dirty data) is in the cache. Thus, the data cache cannot simply be invalidated, or the only valid copy of the data would be lost. Instead, the cache data must update main memory with the modified data before the cache can be invalidated. The modified data will update the main memory in one of two ways.

First, if some other data item is read into the cache at the same entry number (of the 128 entries), it may replace the modified cache contents. In this case, the modified data will automatically be written back to memory. Because the data cache is two-way set-associative with a random replacement algorithm, there is no certainty in which set is updated or written back due to replacement reads. The second method explicitly writes the modified data to memory with the **flush** instruction.

Data Cache Flush The **flush** instruction, shown in Figure 9-5, is a supervisor mode instruction used to force modified data in the data cache to external memory. The **flush** instruction specifies the 32-bit

```
flush          #const(isrc2)          (Normal)
flush          #const(isrc2)++        (Autoincrement)

Replace the block in data cache that has address (#const + isrc2).
Write the block to memory if it was modified.
Contents of block undefined after the writeback.
IF autoincrement
THEN isrc2 <— #const + isrc2
FI
```

Figure 9-5. Format and operation of the* flush *instruction

address *#const* + *isrc2* that must be aligned on a 16-byte boundary. The low-order 12 bits of the address used for the **flush** instruction choose one of 128 32-byte cache blocks of the two-way set-associative data cache. The upper 20 bits of (*#const* + *isrc2*) get placed into the tag array entry by the **flush** instruction. The particular block that is flushed is controlled by the RB (replacement block) field of the **dirbase** register. The **flush** instruction will force any modified data from the cache. The **flush** instruction leaves the data portion of the block undefined. Also, the register in the *idest* field of the instruction will be left undefined and is encoded to **r0** by the assembler.

Figure 9-6 shows the flush routine that writes all of the modified cache contents back to memory. This is performed by stepping through the 128 cache entries sequentially and performing the **flush** instruction. Note that the data cache entries have no validity bits. To invalidate the entry, the **flush** instruction updates the tag of the entry with the address that is reserved for use with the **flush** routine and should not be accessed during normal program execution. This ensures that, when flushing the cache before a task switch, cached data items from the old task are not transferred to the new task. In this program example, the 4K flush address space is used for replacing the address of both sets of the 8K data cache.

The routine makes one pass through the 128 entries for each set of the cache where the set is distinguished by the RB field in the **dirbase** register. Before the first pass, the RC (replacement control) field in the **dirbase** register is set to two (10b) and the RB (replacement block) is set to zero. Each **flush** instruction references the 32nd byte of the reserved memory area. This causes the 128 entries of the "zeroth" set of the data cache tags to be replaced by the **flush** instruction addresses. The RB bits are then changed to one and the sequence of 128 **flush** instructions is repeated, this time updating the "other" set of the cache's tags.

Not all of the entries in the cache will have modified data in them. The **flush** instruction will always update the tags of the cache line it replaces, but will only write the data from the cache back to memory if the data has been modified by the processor.

There are two bits per 32-byte cache line to indicate if that half of the cache line has been modified. Therefore, writebacks may be of 16 or 32 bytes. A routine using **ld.l** instructions instead of the **flush** instruction would also work in causing the writeback cycles. The routine would take considerably longer, however, as the **flush** instruction does not waste time fetching new data on the bus to put into the cache.

```
// CACHE FLUSH PROCEDURE
// Rw, Rx, Ry, Rz represent integer registers
// FLUSH_P_H is the high-order 16 bits of a pointer to reserved area
// FLUSH_P_L is the low-order 16 bits of the pointer, minus 32

      ld.c  dirbase,Rz
      or    0x800,  Rz, Rz    // RC <-- 0b10 assuming was 00)
      adds  -1,    r0,   Rx   // Rx <-- -1 loop increment)
      call  D_FLUSH
      st.c  Rz,    dirbase    // Replace in block 0
      or    0x900,  Rz, Rz    // RB <-- 0b01
      call  D_FLUSH
      st.c  Rz,    dirbase    // Replace in block 1
      xor   0x900,  Rz, Rz    // Clear RC and RB
// Change DTB, ATE, or ITI fields here, if necessary
      st.c  Rz,    dirbase
D_FLUSH:
      orh   FLUSH_P_H,  r0,  Rw      // Rw <-- address minus 32
      or    FLUSH_P_L,  Rw,  Rw      //  of flush area
      or    127,  r0,   Ry    // Ry <-- loop count
      ld.l  32(Rw), r31       // Clear any pending bus writes
      shl   0,     r31,  r31  // Wait until load finishes
      bla   Rx,    Ry, D_FLUSH_LOOP // One time to initialize LCC
      nop
D_FLUSH_LOOP:
      bla   Rx,    Ry, D_FLUSH_LOOP // Loop; execute next instruction
                                    //   for 128 lines in cache block
      flush 32(Rw)++          // Flush and autoincrement to next line
      bri          r1         // Return after next instruction
      ld.l  -512(Rw),    r0   // Load from flush area to clear pending
                              //  writes. A hit is guaranteed.
```

Figure 9-6. Data cache flush routine

One caveat of the **flush** instruction is that, although it writes the cache data back to memory and replaces the data with undefined values, it does not always clear the modified bits. Therefore, when the lines which had modified data are later replaced, writebacks may occur to the addresses used by the **flush** instruction. This will not cause any problems because that area should not be used to store valid data. The operating system needs to ensure that the reserved memory area is valid with the proper page translation information available for any task that may be executing with the **flush** addresses still in the data cache.

Also, the reserved memory area must accept processor write cycles (by returning READY#). This requirement is a result of how writebacks are handled.

Writeback Address Translation Although the automatic data write back of modified data is handled by the hardware following read miss processing, because the cache is virtually addressed, the cache line will use the current task's page tables to determine the physical address for the write back. Therefore, the writeback cycle must access the TLB to determine the proper address to store the write data. To ensure that writebacks occur only to virtual addresses that have valid page mapping and are translated to the proper physical addresses, the data cache needs to be flushed when changing contexts or invalidating a page table entry. Note also that during writeback look-ups, the TLB does not perform any of the protection checks. (This allows an operating system to mark page table entries as not present before flushing the cache, a useful feature for shared memory multiprocessing systems.)

You will recall that the TLB must be invalidated whenever a page directory or table entry is changed in memory. This assures that the new paging information will be used for subsequent accesses. Table 9-2 indicates which modifications to page table entries can occur without needing to flush the data cache.

Breakpoints

Debugging programs on the i860 processor is made easier by the processor's support for code and data breakpoints. Code breakpoints are implemented with the **trap** instruction while data breakpoints are facilitated with the data breakpoint control register (**db**). The following section describes how to implement code breakpoints. The data breakpoint register was described earlier in Chapter 4, "Machine Organization," and accessing the control registers is described following the code breakpoints.

The Trap Instruction The **trap** instruction is used to implement supervisor calls and code breakpoints. When the **trap** instruction is encountered, a trap will be generated with the IT bit in the **psr** set. The

Table 9-2. Cache Flush Requirements for Page Table Modifications

Action	*Flush Data Cache*	*Invalidate Instruction Cache/TLB* (ITI=1)
Changing to A=1	No	No
Changing to P=1	No	No
Changing to P=0	Yes*	Yes
Changing to D=1	No	Yes
Changing protection (U,W,CD,WT)	No	Yes
Changing PFA in a used** PTE	Yes	Yes
Changing **dirbase** DTB	Yes	Yes
Changing **dirbase** ATE	Yes	Yes
Self-modifying code	Yes***	Yes

* When marking a page no-longer-present, a flush must be done before the PFA in the PTE is changed. But the flush can be done after the P=0 change.

** "Used" means a PTE that at sometime past had P=1. Flush the data cache *before* making the PTE change; ITI after the change).

*** The entire data cache need not be flushed, only the lines that might contain modified code.

trap instruction leaves the contents of *rdest* undefined after the operation, and therefore *rdest* should be encoded as **r0**. The *src1* and *src2* fields can be used to encode the type of trap. User-level programs typically execute the **trap** instruction to request operating system functions where each function has a predetermined encoding for *src1* and *src2*. Implementing code breakpoints with the **trap** instruction requires writing to code space.

Writing to Code Space Because of the i860 processor's separate data and instruction caches, special care is required for data writes to code space, also known as *self-modifying code,* to ensure that data writes are reflected in the instruction cache. Although the use of self-modifying code is infrequent, it may be required in a limited number of cases. One example is a debugger that sets a code breakpoint by replacing the breakpoint location with the **trap** instruction. A simple store to the location of the instruction will not update the instruction if it is already in the processor's on-chip instruction cache. Also, if the store location is in the data cache, the **trap** instruction will be modified only in the data cache, and even an instruction cache miss access will not retrieve it from the data cache.

The solution is simple; after the store operation, flush the modified information out of the data cache, and invalidate the instruction cache. It is not actually necessary to flush the entire data cache, only the possible locations of the modified data. This is one of the rare cases where you know the virtual address of the location you want copied to main memory, and can flush the two possible locations in the cache (one in each set), without flushing the entire cache. The address used for the flush operation must consist of the 20 most significant bits of the memory reserved for data cache flushing, along with the low-order 12-bit index of the modified location address. Both sets of the two-way set-associative data cache must be flushed to ensure that the **trap** instruction is now in the external main memory. If the page of code that has been modified was a write-through page, then the code would never have been fetched into the data cache and the data cache does not need to be flushed at all.

Once the **trap** instruction is in main memory, the instruction cache must be invalidated so that the instruction fetches will occur to main memory, and not be supplied by instructions already in the instruction cache. Invalidating the instruction cache is quickly done by setting the ITI bit in the **dirbase** register.

Control Register Access

The two instructions, **ld.c** (load from control register) and **st.c** (store to control register), shown in Figure 9-7, transfer data from *ctrlreg* to or from a general-purpose register. The function of each control register is defined in Chapter 4, "Machine Organization." *Ctrlreg* is specified by a code in the *src2* field of the instruction, as defined in Table 9-3.

User-level programs may read the complete contents of the control registers. User programs may wish to read the pixel size and shift count values from the **psr**; and the big endian bit, data cache size, processor

Instruction	*Operation*
`ld.c` *csrc2. idest* *idest <-- csrc2*	(Load from control register)
`st.c` *isrc1ni, csrc2* *csrc2 <-- isrc1ni*	(Store to control register)

Figure 9-7. Control register access instructions

type, and processor stepping number from the **epsr**. As indicated in Table 9-3, some registers, or parts of registers, are write-protected when the U bit in the **psr** is set (indicating user-level execution). A store

Table 9-3. Control Register Encoding

	Register	*src2 Code*	*User Mode Write Protected?*
fir	(Fault instruction)	0	N/A ***
psr	(Processor status)	1	Yes *
dirbase	(Directory base)	2	Yes
db	(Data breakpoint)	3	Yes
fsr	(Floating-point status)	4	No
epsr	(Extended process status)	5	Yes **

* Only the **psr** bits BR, BW, PIM, IM, PU, U, IT, IN, IAT, DAT, FT, DS, DIM, and KNF are write-protected.

** The processor type, stepping number, and cache size cannot be changed from either user or supervisor level.

*** The **fir** register cannot be written by the **st.c** instruction.

to those registers or bits is ignored when the i860 processor is at user level. User-level stores to the **psr** may be used to alter the pixel size and shift count.

The trap handler makes extensive use of the various control register bits in **psr**, **fsr**, and **epsr**. Only the trap handler can use the **st.c** to set the trap bits (IT, IN, IAT, DAT, FT) of the **psr**. When a trap occurs, the **fir** contains the address of the instruction that caused the trap. To retrieve the **fir** contents, the trap handler executes a **ld.c fir**, **r***X* where *X* denotes any of the integer registers. The **ld.c fir**, **r***X* anytime, except the first time after a trap occurs, will place the address of the **ld.c** instruction into **r***X*.

Locks and Resource Sharing

Multitasking and multiprocessor systems require a mechanism to manage sharing a common resource. For example, consider a banking system with a common database in shared memory. Without proper synchronization between tasks and processors, the database could become corrupted.

Suppose several processes are running on a bank's computer system. One process subtracts money for checks drawn against your account. The process will search through the database until it finds your account. It will then read your current balance, subtract the amount of the check drawn, and write back the new balance. But, what if before the checks balancer writes back the new balance, the automatic teller machine attempts to credit your account with a deposit you just made? The automatic teller process will read the unmodified account balance, add the amount of the deposit, and then write back the new balance. Whichever process writes the new balance back first will be overwritten by the second process. In either case the balance will be wrong.

Semaphores

This problem can be avoided by using a *semaphore.* A semaphore is a memory location that tells one process that another process is currently using a shared resource, and therefore it should wait. For the example above, you would have a semaphore associated with your checking account. When the check balancer process finds your account in the database it will check the semaphore and find its value to be zero, indicating it is not in use. It would then set the semaphore to a one, and perform the account modification. While the modification is taking place, the automatic teller process would examine the semaphore for your account and find its value is a one. The automatic teller machine would not attempt to access the account until the semaphore becomes a zero. When the check balancer process completes updating the account balance, it clears the semaphore to a zero. The second process is now free to set the semaphore to one, read in the new balance, and perform its modifications.

Although this solves the problem of accesses to the database entries, it introduces the problem of ordering accesses to the semaphore. For example, if the events occur in the following sequence:

1. The first process reads the semaphore and finds a zero.
2. The second process reads the semaphore and also finds a zero.
3. The first process writes a one to the semaphore and assumes ownership.
4. The second process writes a one to the semaphore and also assumes ownership.

You see that this leaves us in the same predicament as not having a semaphore at all. The solution lies in ensuring a process can read the semaphore, modify the semaphore, and write the semaphore back to memory without fear of another process accessing the semaphore during the sequence. The sequence is known as a *read-modify-write sequence.* During a read-modify-write sequence, a single-processor multitasking system must be able to block out external timer interrupts that cause a task switch to occur. Multiprocessor systems additionally must guarantee that the read-modify-write sequence for each processor will not allow other processors access to the semaphores during the read, modify, or write.

The Lock Mechanism

On the i860 processor a locking mechanism is used to guarantee that a process can perform steps 1 and 3, without another process or processor performing a step 2. The lock mechanism consists of a `LOCK#` pin on the processor's bus, and the general **`lock`** and **`unlock`** instructions shown in Figure 9-8. The lock mechanism allows programs running in either user or supervisor level to perform indivisible read-modify-write sequences in multiprocessor and multitasking systems. A sequence of up to 30 general instructions can be used in conjunction with the **`lock`** and **`unlock`** instructions to implement either simple semaphores, or more complex interlocked operations. The 30-instruction limit is sufficient to allow any reasonable lock protocol and prevents user-level instructions from blocking out interrupts for extended periods of time.

If locked sequences are interrupted due to a trap or fault, they must be restarted from the beginning, in order to re-establish the locked status. To make this possible several restrictions are introduced to the lock sequence. The interlocked sequence must not branch outside of the 30 sequential instructions following the **`lock`** instruction. If the lock sequence has more than one store instruction, the software must ensure that no traps occur after the first non-reexecutable store. To ensure that the other store instructions will not cause data-access faults, the sequence must first store unmodified values in the other store locations. To ensure that no instruction-access fault occurs, any code that is not restartable should not span a page boundary. Also, the **`intovr`** and **`trap`** instructions should not be used within a locked sequence.

`lock` (Begin interlocked sequence)

Set `BL` in **`dirbase`**. The next load or store that misses the cache locks that location, preventing locked access to it by other processors. External interrupts are disabled from the first instruction after the **`lock`** until the location is unlocked.

`unlock` (End interlocked sequence)

Clear `BL` in **`dirbase`**. The next load or store unlocks the location (regardless of whether it hits in the cache). Interrupts are enabled.

Figure 9-8. Format and operation of the lock and unlock instructions

The trap handler must recognize if a lock sequence was in progress during the trap. This is done by examining several bits of the control registers. If a trap occurs after a **lock** instruction but before the load or store that follows the corresponding **unlock**, the processor clears the BL bit of **dirbase** and sets the IL (interlock) bit of **epsr**. If, following a **lock** instruction, the processor does not encounter a load or a store following an **unlock** instruction by the time it has executed 30 instructions, it triggers an instruction **trap**. In such a case, the trap handler will find both IL and IT set. The instruction pointed to by **fir** may or may not have been executed. If while executing a locked sequence, the processor encounters another **lock** instruction before unlocking the bus, the instruction is ignored. Also, if the processor encounters an **unlock** instruction with no preceding **lock**, the instruction is ignored.

The **lock** instruction alone will disable interrupts until the **unlock** instruction. Although this is sufficient to implement semaphores for single-processor multitasking systems, for multiprocessor systems, it is important to consider the instructions' effect on the LOCK# pin. The LOCK# pin is not active until the first data access that misses the data cache. Multiprocessor systems should make sure that the load instruction references noncacheable memory. The **unlock** instruction will enable interrupts and unlock the memory location with the next load or store instruction regardless of whether it hits in the cache. The behavior of the **unlock** instruction guarantees at least one clock cycle of LOCK# pin deactivation between locked sequences.

When multiple locations are accessed during a locked sequence, only the first location with a cache miss is guaranteed to be locked against access by other processors. For high-performance multiprocessor systems, this allows a read-for-ownership locking policy (also called *nonblocking*), instead of locking the system bus. Read-for-ownership allows one location per processor to be locked, with the other processors still able to access *nonlocked* locations in memory. Other processors attempting to access the locked locations will have their access delayed by hardware until the locations are unlocked.

Lock Examples

Figure 9-9 illustrates using the **lock** and **unlock** for some common examples. The first example is the locked test and set semaphore operation described earlier. The processor performs the **lock** operation, and

```
// LOCKED TEST AND SET
//     Value to put in semaphore is in r23

       lock                    //
       ld.b   semaphore, r22   // Put current value of semaphore in r22
       unlock                  //
       st.b   r23, semaphore   //

// LOCKED LOAD-ALU-STORE

       lock                    //
       ld.l   word,       r22  //
       addu   1,    r22,  r22  // Can be any ALU operation
       unlock                  //
       st.l   r22,     word    //

// LOCKED COMPARE AND SWAP
//     Swaps r23 with word in memory, if word = r21

       lock                    //
       ld.l   word,       r22  //
       bte    r22,  r21,  L1   //
       mov    r22,        r23  // Executed only if not equal
L1:    unlock                  //
       st.l   r23,    word     //
```

Figure 9-9. Example usage of* `lock` *and* `unlock` *instructions

then loads from the memory location semaphore into **r22**. The processor then stores the value it had in **r23** back to memory and unlocks the bus. The program then tests the value of **r22** to see if it was the owner of the semaphore and the corresponding resource. The second example is the locked load-ALU-store sequence. Here an ALU operation is performed on a data word before it is returned to memory. This type of sequence is useful for implementing a counting semaphore. The third example is a locked compare and swap. Here, the program compares a word in memory to the contents of **r21** and writes back the contents of **r23** if the memory value is equal to **r21**, or writes back the unmodified value read if **r21** does not equal the value in memory. A sequence such as this could be used for writing a process identification number to a semaphore when gaining ownership.

	Indication		Caused by	
Type	psr, epsr	fsr	Condition	Instruction
Instruction Fault	IT OF IL		Software traps Missing unlock	**trap**, **intovr** Any
Floating-Point Fault	FT	SE AO, MO AU, MU AI, MI	Floating-point source exception Floating-point result exception overflow underflow inexact results	Any M or A unit except **fmlow** Any M or A unit except **fmlow**, **pfgt**, **pfle**, and **pfeq**. Reported on any F-P instruction plus **pst**, **fst**, and sometimes **fld**, **pfld**, **ixfr**
Instruction-Access Fault	IAT		Address translation exception during instruction fetch	Any
Data Access-Fault	DAT*		Load/store address translation Misaligned operand address Operand address matches **db** register	Any load/store Any load/store Any load/store
Interrupt	IN		External interrupt	
Reset	No trap bits set		Hardware RESET signal	

* These cases can be distinguished by examining the operand addresses

Table 9-4. Trap Types

In addition to being activated through software, the LOCK# pin is automatically asserted during read-modify-write sequences associated with TLB miss processing. For example, if a load instruction causes a TLB miss, the page directory entry is read from memory. If the A (accessed) bit of the page directory entry is not set, the processor will reread the page directory entry with LOCK# asserted, set the A bit, and write the modified entry to memory. If, during a programmer-invoked lock sequence, a TLB miss that requires setting the A bit in a page entry occurs, a trap will occur. This allows the trap handler to set the A bit in memory and restart the sequence. This avoids ambiguity in determining what address corresponds to a locked semaphore for external bus hardware use.

Traps and Interrupts

Traps are caused by exceptional conditions detected in programs or by external interrupts. Traps suspend normal program flow and execute instead a special program known as a *trap handler.*

Types of Traps

Traps are divided into the types shown in Table 9-4.

Trap-Handler Invocation

This section applies to traps other than reset. When a trap occurs, execution of the current instruction is aborted. The instruction is usually restartable as will be described later in this section. The processor takes the following steps to update the **psr** status bits while transferring control to the trap handler:

1. Copies U (user mode) of the **psr** into PU (previous U).
2. Copies IM (interrupt mode) into PIM (previous IM).
3. Sets U to zero (supervisor mode).

4. Sets IM to zero (interrupts disabled). This guards against further interrupts until the trap information can be saved.
5. If the processor is in dual-instruction mode, it sets DIM; otherwise DIM is cleared.
6. If the processor is in single-instruction mode and the next instruction will be executed in dual-instruction mode, or if the processor is in dual-instruction mode and the next instruction will be executed in single-instruction mode, DS is set; otherwise, it is cleared.
7. The appropriate trap type bits in **psr** and **epsr** are set (IT, IN, IAT, DAT, FT, IL). Several bits may be set if the corresponding trap conditions occur simultaneously.
8. An address is placed in the fault instruction register (**fir**) to help locate the trapped instruction. In single-instruction mode, the address in **fir** is the address of the trapped instruction itself. In dual-instruction mode, the address in **fir** is that of the floating-point half of the dual instruction. If an instruction- or data-access fault occurred, the associated core instruction is the high-order half of the dual instruction (**fir** + 4). In dual-instruction mode, when a data-access fault occurs in the absence of other trap conditions, the floating-point half of the dual instruction will already have been executed.
9. Clears the BL bit of **dirbase** and deasserts LOCK#.

The processor begins executing the trap handler by transferring execution to virtual address 0xFFFFFF00. The trap handler begins execution in single-instruction mode. The trap handler must examine the trap-type bits in **psr** (IT, IN, IAT, DAT, FT) and **epsr** (IL, OF) to determine the cause or causes of the trap.

Saving State To support nesting of traps, the trap handler must save the current state before another trap occurs. An interrupt stack must be implemented in software. Interrupts can then be reenabled by clearing the trap-type bits and setting IM to the value of PIM. The branch-indirect instruction is sensitive to the trap-type bits; therefore, clearing the trap-type bits is a prerequisite to using the **bri** instruction subsequently in the trap handler.

The items that make up the current state may include any of the following:

- The **fir**
- The **psr**
- The **epsr**
- The **fsr**
- The **dirbase** register
- The MERGE register
- The KR, KI, and T registers
- Any of the four pipelines
- The floating-point and integer register files

Inside the Trap Handler Although most activities of trap handlers are application and system dependent, programmers should be aware of the following requirements that are imposed by the i860 microprocessor architecture:

1. For all types of traps, the trap handler must check the IL bit of **epsr** to determine if a locked sequence is being interrupted.
2. The trap handler must execute **ld.c, fir**, *idest* once for each trap. Failure to do so prevents **fir** from receiving the address of the next trap.
3. The trap handler must parse the instruction at **fir** − 4, to determine if the trapped instruction was in the delay slot of a delayed branch.

Returning from the Trap Handler Returning from a trap handler requires the following steps:

1. Restoring the pipeline states, including the **fsr**, KR, KI, T, and MERGE registers, where necessary.

2. Subtracting *src1* from *src2*, when a data-access fault occurred on an autoincrementing load/store instruction and a floating-point trap did not also occur.
3. Determining where to resume execution by inspecting the instruction at **fir** – 4. The details for this determination are given in the following section.
4. Updating **psr** with the value to be used after return. It may be necessary to set the KNF bit in **psr**. The requirements for KNF are given in a following section.
5. Restoring the integer and floating-point register files, except for the register that holds the resumption address.
6. Executing an indirect branch to the resumption address, making sure that at least one of the trap bits is set in the **psr**. Neither the indirect branch nor the following instruction may be executed in dual-instruction mode.
7. Restoring the register that holds the resumption address. This is executed in the delay slot of the **bri** instruction.

Determining Where to Resume To determine where to resume execution upon leaving the trap handler, examine the instruction at address **fir** – 4. If this instruction is not a delayed control instruction, then execution resumes at the address in **fir**.

If, on the other hand, the instruction at **fir** – 4 is a delayed control instruction, that is, one that executes the next sequential instruction on branch taken, the normal action is to resume at **fir** – 4 so that the control instruction that did not finish because of the trap is also reexecuted. If the instruction at **fir** – 4 is a **bla** instruction, then *src1* should be subtracted from *src2* before reexecuting.

The one variance from this strategy occurs when the instruction at **fir** – 4 is a conditional delayed branch, **bc.t** or **bnc.t**, the instruction at **fir** is a **pfgt**, **pfle**, or **pfeq**, and a source exception has occurred. To implement the IEEE standard for unordered compares, the trap handler may need to change the value of CC. In this case it cannot resume at **fir** – 4, because the new value of CC might cause an incorrect branch. Instead, the trap handler must interpret the conditional branch instruction and resume at its target.

When examining **fir** − 4, take care not to cause a page fault. If the location in **fir** is at the beginning of a page, then **fir** − 4 is in the prior page. If the prior page is not present, then examining **fir** − 4 will cause a page fault. In this case, however, the instruction at **fir** − 4 could not have been a delayed control instruction; therefore it is not necessary to examine **fir** − 4. Note that, when determining whether the prior page is not present, it is necessary to inspect both the page table and its page directory entry.

If the i860 microprocessor was in dual-instruction mode and execution is to resume at **fir** − 4, DS should be set and DIM cleared in the **psr**. Clearing DIM prevents the floating-point instruction associated with the control instruction from being reexecuted. Setting DS forces the processor back to dual-instruction mode after executing the control instruction.

Every code section should begin with a **nop** instruction so that **fir** − 4 is defined even in case a trap occurs on the first real instruction of the code section. Furthermore, this **nop** should not be the target of any branch or call.

Setting KNF The KNF bit of **psr** should be set if the trapped instruction is a floating-point instruction that should not be reexecuted; otherwise, KNF is left unchanged. Floating-point instructions should not be reexecuted under the following conditions:

- The trap was caused in dual-instruction mode by a data-access fault or an **intovr** instruction and there are no other trap conditions. In this case, the floating-point instruction has already been executed.
- The trap was caused by a source exception on any floating-point instruction except when a **pfgt**, **pfle**, or **pfeq** follows a conditional branch, as already explained. The trap handler determines the result that corresponds to the exceptional inputs; therefore, the instruction should not be reexecuted.

Instruction Fault

To indicate an instruction fault, the processor sets the IT bit before entering the trap handler. This fault is caused by any of the following conditions:

- By the **trap** instruction. Refer to the trap instruction description earlier.
- By the **intovr** instruction. The trap occurs only if OF in **epsr** is set when **intovr** is executed. The trap handler should clear OF before returning. Refer to the **intovr** instruction in Chapter 5, "RISC Core Operations."
- By the lack of an **unlock** instruction (and subsequent load or store) within 30 instructions of a lock. In this case IL is also set. When the trap handler finds IL set, it should scan backwards for the **lock** instruction and restart at that point. The absence of a **lock** instruction within 30 instructions of the trap indicates a programming error. Refer to the **lock** instruction earlier in this chapter.

Note that **trap** and **intovr** should not be used within a locked sequence; otherwise, it would not be possible to distinguish among the above cases.

Floating-Point Fault

The floating-point faults of the i860 microprocessor support the floating-point exceptions defined by the IEEE standard as well as some other useful classes of exceptions. The i860 microprocessor divides these into two classes:

- **Source exceptions** This class includes the following:

  All the invalid operations defined by the IEEE standard, including operations on signaling NaNs
  Division by zero
  Operations on quiet NaNs, denormals and infinities (operations on these data types are implemented by software)

- **Result exceptions** This class includes the overflow, underflow, and inexact exceptions defined by the IEEE standard

The floating-point fault occurs only on floating-point instructions, and on **pst**, **fst**, **fld**, **pfld**, and **ixfr**. No floating-point fault occurs when **pst**, **fst**, **fld**, **pfld**, or **ixfr** transfers an operand that is not a valid floating-point value. That is, any data can safely be moved between floating-point registers, integer registers, and memory without the requirement of a valid floating-point format for the data. So pixel values and integers moved to and from floating registers are "safe."

Source Exception Faults When used as inputs to the floating-point adder or multiplier, all exceptional operands including infinities, denormalized numbers and NaNs, cause a floating-point fault and set the SE (Source Exception) bit in the **fsr**. Source exceptions are reported on the instruction that initiates the operation. For pipelined operations, the pipeline is not advanced. The trap handler can reference both source operands and the operation by decoding the instruction specified by **fir**.

In the case of dual operations, the trap handler has to determine which special registers the source operands are stored in and inspect all four source operands to see if one or both operations must be revised to conform. It can then compute the appropriate result and store the result in *fdest,* in the case of a scalar operation, or replace the appropriate first-stage result, in the case of a pipelined operation.

Note that, in the following sequence, inappropriate use of the FTE bit of the **fsr** can produce an invalid operand that does not cause a source exception:

1. Floating-point traps are masked by clearing the FTE bit.
2. A dual-operation instruction causes underflow or overflow leaving an invalid result in the T register.
3. Floating-point traps are enabled by setting the FTE bit.
4. The invalid result in the T register is used as an operand of a subsequent instruction.

When the result of an operation would normally cause a source exception, it can be inserted into the pipeline without an exception as follows:

1. Disable traps by clearing FTE.
2. Perform a pipelined add of the value with zero or a multiply by one.

3. Set the result-status bits of **fsr** to "normal" by **st.c** to **fsr** with the U bit set and zeros in the appropriate unit's result-status bits. The other unit's status must be set to the saved status for the first pipeline stage.
4. Reenable traps by setting FTE.
5. Set KNF in the **psr** to avoid reexecuting the instruction.

The trap handler should ignore the SE bit for faults on **fld**, **pfld**, **fst**, **pst**, and **ixfr** instructions when in single-instruction mode, or when in dual-instruction mode and the companion instruction is not a multiplier or adder operation. The SE value is undefined in this case.

The trap handler should process result exceptions as in the following descriptions and then reexecute the instruction before processing source exceptions.

Result Exception Faults The class of result exceptions includes any of the following conditions:

- **Overflow** The absolute value of the rounded true result would exceed the largest finite number in the destination format.
- **Underflow when FZ is clear** The absolute value of the rounded true result would be smaller than the smallest finite number in the destination format.
- **Inexact result when TI is set** The result is not exactly representable in the destination format. For example, the fraction 1/7 cannot be precisely represented in binary form. This exception occurs frequently and indicates that some generally acceptable accuracy has been lost.

The point at which a result exception is reported depends on whether pipelined operations are being used.

- **Scalar nonpipelined operations** Result exceptions are reported on the *next* floating-point (**fst.x** or **pst.x** and sometimes **fld**, **pfld**, **ixfr**) instruction *after* the scalar operation. The instructions **fld**, **pfld**, and **ixfr** report results exceptions when the *fdest* of these instructions overlap the *fdest* of the instruction that caused the exception.

When a trap occurs, the last stage of the affected unit contains the result of the scalar operation. The result is also written to the register indicated by the RR field of the **psr**.

- **Pipelined operations** Result exceptions are reported when the result is in the last stage and the *next* floating-point (**fst.x** or **pst.x** and sometimes **fld**, **pfld**, **ixfr**) instruction is executed. The instructions **fld**, **pfld**, and **ixfr** report result exceptions when the *fdest* of these instructions overlap the *fdest* of the instruction that caused the exception. When a trap occurs, the pipeline is not advanced, and the last-stage results that caused the trap remain unchanged.

When no trap occurs either because FTE is clear or because no exception occurred, the pipeline is advanced normally by the new floating-point operation. The result-status bits of the affected unit are undefined until the point that result exceptions are reported. At this point, the last-stage result-status bits (bits 29. . .22 and 16. . .9 of the **fsr**) reflect the values in the last stages of both the adder and multiplier. For example, if the last-stage result in the multiplier has overflowed and a **pfadd** is started, a trap occurs and MO is set.

For scalar operations, the RR bits of **fsr** specify the register in which the result was stored. RR is updated when the scalar instruction is initiated. The trap, however, occurs on a subsequent instruction. Programmers must prevent intervening stores to **fsr** from modifying the RR bits. Prevention may take one of the following forms:

- Before any store to **fsr** when a result exception may be pending, execute a dummy floating-point operation to trigger the result-exception trap.
- Always read from **fsr** before storing to it, and mask updates so that the RR, RM, and FZ bits are not changed.

For pipelined operations, RR is cleared; the result is in the pipeline of the appropriate unit.

In either case, the result has the same mantissa as the true result and has an exponent which is the low-order bits of the true result. The trap handler can inspect the result, compute the result appropriate for that instruction (a NaN or an infinity, for example) and store the correct result. The result is either stored in the register specified by RR if non-zero, or in the last stage of the pipeline if RR = zero. The trap handler must clear the result status for the last stage, then reexecute the trapping instruction.

Result exceptions may be reported for both the adder and multiplier units at the same time. In this case, the trap handler should fix up the last stage of both pipelines. Note that floating-point result exceptions may occur many instructions after the erring instructions. Thus the trap handler's general strategy is to derive an acceptable result for that instruction, and resume program execution at the later instruction that caused the trap report.

Instruction-Access Fault

This trap results from a page-not-present exception during instruction fetch. If a supervisor-level page is fetched while at user level, an exception may or may not occur. The exception occurs then only if an instruction cache miss also occurred.

Data-Access Fault

This trap results from an abnormal condition detected during data operand fetch or store. Such an exception can be due to only one of the following causes:

- An attempt is being made to write to a page whose D bit is clear.
- A memory operand is misaligned and is not located at an address that is a multiple of the length of the data.
- The address stored in the **db** (data breakpoint) register is equal to one of the addresses spanned by the operand.
- The operand is in a not-present page.
- An access is being attempted in violation of the memory protection scheme described earlier in this chapter.
- The A bit is zero during address translation within a locked sequence.

Interrupt Trap

An interrupt is an event that is signaled from an external source via the INT pin. If the processor is executing with interrupts enabled (IM set in the **psr**) the processor sets the interrupt bit IN in the **psr**, and generates an interrupt trap. Vectored interrupts are implemented by interrupt controllers and software. Note that the INT bit of the **epsr** will reflect the state of the external interrupt pin. Thus software can know an interrupt is pending, even when the trap is prevented due to masked interrupts (IM equal to zero).

Reset Trap

When the i860 microprocessor is reset, execution begins in single-instruction mode at address 0xFFFFFF00. This is the same address as for other traps. The reset trap can be distinguished from other traps by the fact that no trap bits are set, with the state as follows. The instruction cache is invalidated. The modified status bits of the data cache tags are cleared, but the tags may have any value. The bits DPS, BL, and ATE in **dirbase** are cleared. CS8 is initialized by the value at the INT pin just before the end of the processor reset (RESET transition from high to low). The read-only fields of the **epsr** are set to identify the processor, while the IL, WP, PBM, and BE bits are cleared. The bits U, IM, BR, and BW in **psr** are cleared. All other bits of **psr** and all other register contents are undefined. Refer to Table 9-5 for a summary of these initial settings.

The software must ensure that the data cache is flushed and that control registers are properly initialized before performing operations that depend on the values of the cache or registers. The **fir** must be initialized with a **ld.c fir, r0** instruction. Otherwise **fir** may retain the value it had before the reset pin was asserted. Any trap locks a value into **fir** until the first **ld.c** from **fir**.

Reset code must initialize the floating-point pipeline states to zero, using dummy **pfadd**, **pfmul**, **pfiadd** instructions. Floating-point traps must be disabled to ensure that no spurious floating-point traps are generated.

After a reset the i860 microprocessor starts execution at supervisor level, U=0. Before branching to the first user-level instruction, the

Table 9-5. Initial Settings

Registers	*Initial Value*
Integer Registers	*Undefined*
Floating-Point Registers	*Undefined*
psr	U, IM, BR, BW = 0; others = *undefined*
epsr	IL, WP, PBM, BE = 0; Processor Type, Stepping number, DCS are read-only; others are *undefined*
db	*Undefined*
dirbase	DPS, BL, ATE = 0
fir	*Undefined*
fsr	*Undefined*
KR, KI, MERGE, T	*Undefined*

Caches	*Initial Value*
Instruction Cache	Flushed
Data Cache	*Undefined.* All modified bits = 0
TLB	Flushed

reset trap handler or subsequent initialization code has to set PU and a trap bit so that an indirect branch instruction will copy PU to U, thereby changing to user level.

Pipeline Preemption

Each of the four pipelines (adder, multiplier, load, graphics) contains state information. The pipeline state must be saved when a process is preempted or when a trap handler performs pipelined operations using the same pipeline. The state must be restored before resuming the interrupted code.

Floating-Point Pipelines The floating-point pipeline state consists of the following items:

1. The floating-point status register **fsr** including the third-stage result status

2. Unstored results from the first, second, and third stages. The number of stages that exist in the multiplier pipeline depends on the sizes of the operands that occupy the pipeline. The MRP bit of **fsr** helps determine how many stages are in the multiplier pipeline
3. The result-status bits for the first two stages
4. The contents of the KR, KI, and T registers

Load Pipeline The pipeline state for **pfld** instructions can be saved by performing three **pfld** instructions to a dummy address. Thus, the pipeline is advanced three stages, causing the last three data items to be moved from the pipeline into registers, which the program must save in some memory area. The size of each saved value is indicated by the value of the LRP bit of the **fsr**. Note that the load pipeline must be saved before changing the BE bit of **epsr** if endian changes are needed.

The load pipeline can be restored performing three **pfld** instructions using the memory addresses of the saved values. The pipeline will then contain the same three values it held before the preemption.

Graphics Pipeline The graphics pipeline has only one stage. To flush the pipeline, execute a **pfiadd f0**, **f0**, *fdest*. The only other state information for the graphics unit resides in the PM and PS bits of **psr**, the IRP bit of the **fsr**, and in the MERGE register. Store the MERGE register with a form instruction. Restore the MERGE register by using **faddz** instructions.

Pipeline Preemption Figure 9-10 shows how to save the pipeline state, and Figure 9-11 shows how to restore the pipeline state. Trap handlers manipulate the result-status bits in the floating-point pipelines while preparing for pipeline resumption. By storing to **fsr** with the U bit set, the result-status bits are loaded into the first stage of the pipelines of the floating-point adder and multiplier. The updated result-status bits of the multiplier or adder are propagated one stage for each pipelined floating-point operation for that unit. When they reach the last stage, they override the normal result-status bits computed from the last-stage result. The result-status bits in the **fsr** always reflect the last-stage result status and cannot be directly set by software.

Note that the programs in Figures 9-10 and 9-11 are not optimized for speed. Some rearrangement of instruction ordering could avoid freeze locks.

```
// The symbols Mres3, Ares3, Mres2, Ares2, Mres1, Ares1,
//  Ires1, Lres, KR, KI, and T refer to 64-bit FP registers.
// The symbols Fsr3, Fsr2, Fsr1, Mergelo32, Mergehi32, and Temp
//  refer to integer registers.
// The symbols Lres3m, Lres2m, and Lres1m refer to memory locations.
// The symbol Dummy represents some readable location that is always present, (e.g. 0(r0)).

// Save third, second, and first stage results
    fld.d      DoubOne,        f4 // get double-precision 1.0
    ld.c       fsr,     Fsr3      // save third stage result status
    andnot     0x20,    Fsr3, Temp // clear FTE bit
    st.c       Temp,    fsr       // disable FP traps
    pfmul.ss   f0,      f0,   Mres3 // save third stage M result
    pfadd.ss   f0,      f0,   Ares3 // save third stage A result
    pfld.d     Dummy,   Lres      // save third stage pfld result
    fst.d      Lres,    Lres3m    //  ... in memory
    ld.c       fsr,     Fsr2      // save second stage result status
    pfmul.ss   f0,      f0,   Mres2 // save second stage M result
    pfadd.ss   f0,      f0,   Ares2 // save second stage A result
    pfld.d     Dummy,   Lres      // save second stage pfld result
    fst.d      Lres,    Lres2m    //  ... in memory
    ld.c       fsr,     Fsr1      // save first stage result status
    pfmul.ss   f0,      f0,   Mres1 // save first stage M result
    pfadd.ss   f0,      f0,   Ares1 // save first stage A result
    pfld.d     Dummy,   Lres      // save first stage pfld result
    fst.d      Lres,    Lres1m    //  ... in memory
    pfiadd.dd  f0,      f0,   Ires1 // save vector-integer result
// Save KR, KI, T, and MERGE
    andnot     0x2C,    Fsr1, Temp // clear RM, clear FTE
    or         4,       Temp, Temp // set RM=01, round down, so -0
    st.c       Temp,    fsr        //  is preserved when added to f0
    r2apt.dd   f0,      f4,     f0 // M first stage contains KR
                                   // A first stage contains T
    i2p1.dd    f0,      f4,     f0 // M first stage contains KI
    pfmul.dd   f0,      f0,     KR // save KR register
    pfmul.dd   f0,      f0,     KI // save KI register
    pfadd.dd   f0,      f0,     f0 // adder third stage gets T
    pfadd.dd   f0,      f0,     T  // save T-register
    form       f0,              f2 // save MERGE register
    fxfr       f2,      Mergelo32
    fxfr       f3,      Mergehi32
```

Figure 9-10. Saving pipeline states

```
// The symbols Mres3, Ares3, Mres2, Ares2, Mres1, Ares1,
//  Ires1, KR, KI, and T refer to 64-bit FP registers.
// The symbols Fsr3, Fsr2, Fsr1, Mergelo32, Mergehi32, and Temp
//  refer to integer registers.
// The symbols Lres3m, Lres2m, and Lres1m refer to memory locations.

    st.c       r0,     fsr          // clear FTE
// Restore MERGE
    shl        16, Mergelo32,  r1   // move low 16 bits to high 16
    ixfr       r1,     f2
    shl        16, Mergehi32,  r1   // move low 16 bits to high 16
    ixfr       r1,     f3
    ixfr       Mergelo32,      f4
    ixfr       Mergehi32,      f5
    faddz      f0,     f2,     f0   // merge low 16s
    faddz      f0,     f4,     f0   // merge high 16s
// Restore KR, KI, and T
    fld.l      SingOne,        f2   // get single-precision 1.0
    fld.d      DoubOne,        f4   // get double-precision 1.0
    pfmul.dd   f4,     T,      f0   // put value of T in M 1st stage
    r2pt.dd    KR,     f0,     f0   // load KR, advance T
    i2apt.dd   KI,     f0,     f0   // load KI and T
// Restore 3rd stage
    andh       0x2000, Fsr3,   r0   // test adder result precision ARP
    bc.t       L0                   // taken if it was single
    pfamov.ss  Ares3,  f0,     f0   // insert single result
    pfamov.dd  Ares3,  f0,     f0   // insert double result
L0: orh        ha%Lres3m, r0,  r31
    andh       0x400,  Fsr3,   r0   // test load result precision LRP
    bc.t       L1                   // taken if it was single
    pfld.l     l%Lres3m(r31),  f0   // insert single result
    pfld.d     l%Lres3m(r31),  f0   // insert double result
L1: andh       0x1000, Fsr3,   r0   // test multiplier result precision MRP
    bc.t       L2                   // taken if it was single
    pfmul.ss   Mres3,  f2,     f0   // insert single result
    pfmul3.dd  Mres3,  f4,     f0   // insert double result
L2: or         0x10,   Fsr3,   Temp // set U (update) bit so that st.c
                                    //   will update status bits in pipeline
    andnot     0x20,   Temp,   Temp // clear FTE bit so as not to cause traps
    st.c       Temp ,  fsr          // update stage 3 result status
// Restore  2nd stage
    andh       0x2000, Fsr2,   r0   // test adder result precision ARP
    bc.t       L3                   // taken if it was single
    pfamov.ss  Ares2,  f0,     f0   // insert single result
    pfamov.dd  Ares2,  f0,     f0   // insert double result
```

Figure 9-11. Restoring pipeline states

```
L3: orh         ha%Lres2m, r0,  r31
    andh        0x400,  Fsr2,   r0  // test load result precision LRP
    bc.t        L4                  // taken if it was single
    pfld.l      l%Lres2m(r31),  f0  // insert single result
    pfld.d      l%Lres2m(r31),  f0  // insert double result
L4: or          0x10,   Fsr2,  Temp // set update bit
    andnot      0x20,   Temp,  Temp // clear FTE
    andh        0x1000, Fsr2,   r0  // test multiplier result precision MRP
    bc.t        L5                  // taken if it was single
    pfmul.ss    Mres2,  f2,     f0  // insert single result
    pfmul3.dd   Mres2,  f4,     f0  // insert double result
L5: st.c        Temp,   fsr         // update stage 2 result status
// Restore 1st stage
    andh        0x1000, Fsr1,   r0  // test multiplier result precision MRP
    bc.t        L6                  // skip next if double
    pfmul.ss    Mres1,  f2,     f0  // insert single result
    pfmul3.dd   Mres1,  f4,     f0  // insert double result
L6: andh        0x2000, Fsr1,   r0  // test adder result precision ARP
    bc.t        L7                  // taken if it was single
    pfamov.ss   Ares1,  f0,     f0  // insert single result
    pfamov.dd   Ares1,  f0,     f0  // insert double result
L7: orh         ha%Lres1m, r0,  r31
    andh        0x400,  Fsr1,   r0  // test load result precision LRP
    bc.t        L8                  // taken if it was single
    pfld.l      l%Lres1m(r31),  f0  // insert single result
    pfld.d      l%Lres1m(r31),  f0  // insert double result
L8: andh        0x800,  Fsr1,   r0  // test vector-integer result precision IRP
    bc.t        L9                  // taken if it was single
    pfiadd.ss   f0, Ires1,  f0      // insert single result
    pfiadd.dd   f0, Ires1,  f0      // insert double result
L9: or          0x10,   Fsr1,  Fsr1 // set U (update) bit
    st.c        Fsr1,   fsr         // update stage 1 result status
    st.c        Fsr3,   fsr         // restore nonpipelined FSR status
```

Figure 9-11. Restoring pipeline states (continued)

CHAPTER 10
APPLICATION EXAMPLE: THE FAST FOURIER TRANSFORM

In this chapter we will look at applying the i860 microprocessor to a real-world application, the FFT (Fast Fourier Transform). The FFT algorithm is used universally in DSP (digital signal processing) applications. This chapter begins with a very brief overview of basic DSP theory. Then, after a discussion of the operation and mathematical function of the FFT, you will look at coding the FFT inner loop—called the butterfly. Finally, the performance will be discussed as you code the butterfly for the i860 processor, starting with a simple implementation, and finishing with a highly optimized one.

Digital Signal Processing Basics

Digital signal processing (DSP) is increasingly prevalent in computing. The first step in applying DSP to real-world applications requires converting a continuously varying (analog) signal to digital form. Next, the digital form must be mathematically manipulated. Finally, some applications require results to be returned in analog form. The instruments for converting between analog and digital signals continue to improve. Although the performance capabilities of microprocessors has increased, most general purpose processors lack the computational capabilities to perform the required manipulations.

Analog signals include voice, images, and electrical representations of measured phenomena (for example, light intensity, temperature, pressure, and position). Today, inexpensive components are available to convert voiceband analog signals to and from their digital representations. Also, instruments such as fax machines, optical scanners, and frame grabbers can convert analog signals into digital data. Output devices such as high-resolution graphics monitors and laser printers can represent the processed data.

The need for more sophisticated computational capabilities for general purposes has increased along with the increased data available digitally. Applications such as speech recognition, image processing, and character recognition require heavy mathematical computations. Instead of providing a dedicated processor for each, systems can offer a wider range of functions at a reduced cost by including a programmable centralized processor. Using a general purpose microprocessor that includes DSP capabilities as the central processor lowers the incremental costs of supporting these applications.

Digitizing Signals

The first challenge of a digital system is to convert an analog signal into numerical representation. Analog signals exist as a continuous-time signal. The magnitude of an analog signal can be represented by varied voltage or current amplitudes. To convert from a continuous-time signal to a discrete-time representation, the signal must be sampled at regular intervals.

Figure 10-1 shows an analog signal being sampled and converted to a digital representation. The samples are taken at regular intervals called the sampling frequency. The sampling frequency must be high enough so that no essential data is lost in the conversion. The Nyquist Sampling Theorem states that the sampling frequency must be at least twice the highest frequency contained in the data. For example, the upper frequency limit of human hearing is 20 kHz, so the digital audio sampling rate must be above 40 kHz and, in fact, the audio compact disk (CD) rate is 44.1 kHz.

If the sampling frequency is not high enough, information can be lost in the conversion from analog to digital. Undersampled data can result in aliasing, where high frequency data is misinterpreted. Although not technically exact, a familiar example of this occurs when you observe the spokes of a turning wheel. At low speed the direction of the spokes is visible. At higher speeds, however, the spokes may appear to be still, or moving very slowly; they can even appear to be moving backwards. These misinterpretations occur because information is being lost during visual interpretation. This visual behavior does have some advantages; for example, motion picture films appear to your eye as smooth motion although the frames are changing 24 times per second.

Processing signals digitally has many advantages over the analog

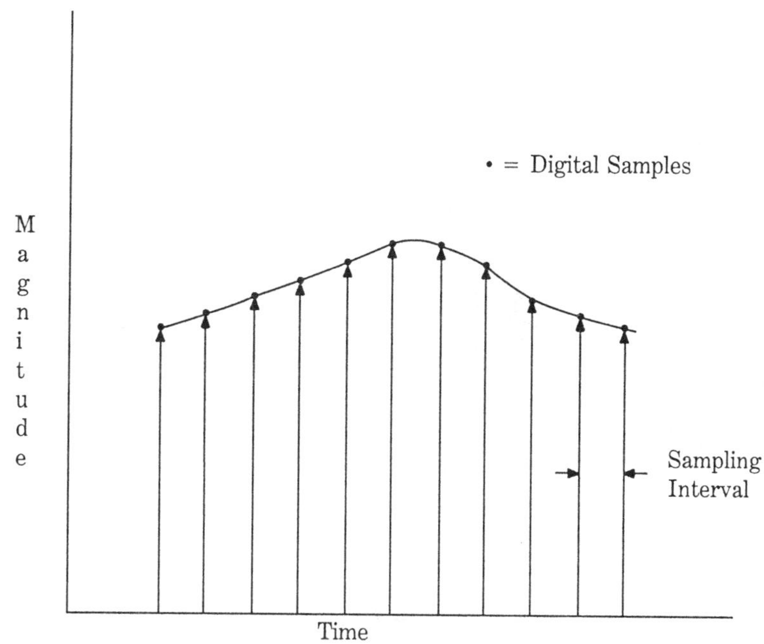

Figure 10-1.* *Sampling an analog waveform

counterpart. Digital signals can be stored and processed without loss of fidelity, and because they are programmable they are more flexible. Therefore, the same system can be used for filtering, encoding, compressing, and decompressing signals as well as for higher-level functions, such as recognition.

Signal Representation

The model for processing sampled signal data involves converting from time-relative (time-domain) representation to frequency-relative (frequency-domain) representation. This is because it is more convenient, for both analog and digital systems, to process signals in the frequency domain. For example, a graphic equalizer for a stereo system separates the signal into frequency ranges, and includes gain control for each of the ranges. Unfortunately, signals usually exist in the time domain and must be converted to the frequency domain.

To understand the conversion from time domain to frequency domain you must first understand *signal composition*. Any waveform can be decomposed into a combination of sine waves superimposed on each other. Why are sine waves chosen as the building blocks for frequency analysis? For several reasons:

1. Sines (or cosines) are easy to manipulate mathematically. That is, differentiation and integration thereof are trivial, and many equations representing physical phenomena often have sinusoidal solutions.
2. Real-world systems tend to exhibit sinusoidal behavior. For example, the vertical position of a point on a rolling wheel as a function of time is a sinusoid. Also, many useful electronic circuits oscillate with sine voltages, and structures like bridges and buildings vibrate sinusoidally.
3. The smooth edges of the sine curve are easily produced, while the abrupt transitions of square waves require more energy to create.

For ease of mathematical representation and computation, complex arithmetic is often employed to represent signals for DSP. Complex numbers take the form $A + jB$, where A is called the "real" component,

B is called the "imaginary" component, and j equals the square root of negative one. The complex form allows handy interchange between sine and exponential representation because:

$$e^{-jt} = \cos(t) - j\sin(t)$$

Complex values conveniently represent the behavior of real-life objects such as mechanical systems and electrical systems. For example, the behavior of circuit elements such as capacitors and inductors cannot be represented with simple real numbers (numbers without the imaginary component). This is because real numbers lack the ability to describe the time-dependent energy storage of capacitors and inductors. When such a circuit is stimulated by a sine wave, complex numbers make the representation and computation much simpler. This is because a complex number can represent not only the magnitude (that is, voltage) of a sine wave, but also its phase (the time at which the wave crosses zero)—both of which are required to characterize the wave.

The *Discrete Fourier Transform* (DFT) converts samples of a time-domain signal to samples of the different signal frequencies and their amplitudes. To perform the conversion, the DFT calculation requires n^2 complex multiplications and additions; where n equals the number of samples and is usually a power of two. The *Fast Fourier Transform* (FFT) is an elegant implementation of the DFT, which reduces the number of complex multiplications and additions required to $n\log_2 n$. That is more than 100 times fewer for a 1024-point FFT. The FFT algorithm also has the advantage of not requiring data storage beyond the original data samples.

The Fast Fourier Transform

Discrete Fourier Transforms (DFTs) change time-domain data samples into a frequency-domain profile of the sampled signal. To accomplish the transform, a DFT adds combinations of the input data samples after multiplying those inputs with weighing factors. Each result in the frequency domain comes from a weighted sum of all data samples. The weighing (W) factors are called *twiddles*, and are complex cosine/sine values for each particular frequency.

The DFT $X(k)$ of a time-domain signal $x(t)$ is defined by:

$x(n)$ = time-domain samples of the signal, $n = 0,1,\ldots N-1$
$X(k)$ = the Discrete Fourier Transform of $x(n)$, $k=0,1,\ldots N-1$
= a frequency domain equivalent of $x(n)$
$= \Sigma\, x(n)*W^{nk}$, $n=0$ to $N-1$, and $W^{nk} = e^{-j2\pi nk/N}$, where $j = \sqrt{-1}$
$= \Sigma\, x(n)*(\cos(2\pi nk/N) - j*\sin(2\pi nk/N))$

The $(N-1)$ complex additions and $(N-1)$ complex multiplications required for each $X(k)$ make the DFT into an order(N^2) computation.

Fortunately, the FFT decomposes this to an order($N*\log_2 N$) algorithm by splitting the N-sum into units of 2-sums. Thus, a DFT of 1024 input points requiring about two million operations reduces to an FFT requiring about fifteen thousand operations. The 2-sum units are called *butterflies* because they produce two output values from two inputs, with the butterfly-shaped data flow shown in Figure 10-2. (Some FFT algorithms, called Radix-4, use 4-input, 4-output butterflies). The butterfly calculations are executed in stages, with $\log_2 N$ stages and N/2 butterflies per stage.

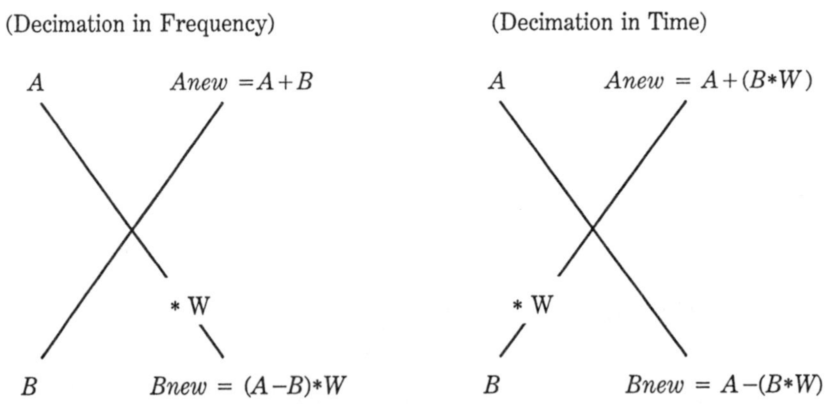

Figure 10-2. FFT butterfly data flow (A and B each are complex numbers)

As indicated in Figure 10-2, the subdivision, or decimation, of the N-sum into butterflies can be done via two different methods: DIF (*Decimation in Frequency*) or DIT (*Decimation in Time*). The methods differ in the ordering of twiddles and the form of the butterfly arithmetic, but they yield the same answer. They are based on different mathematical derivations of the FFT: DIT results from recursively splitting the input time-domain samples into an even-indexed group and an odd-indexed group, while DIF comes from splitting the DFT output frequency-domain points into odd/even groups.

The Butterfly Defined

Let *A* = the first input to the butterfly (complex number, composed of real part *AR* and imaginary part *AI*)
B = the second input to the butterfly (complex, *BR* and *BI*)
W = twiddle factor (also complex, *WR* and *WI*)
Anew = complex result No. 1, which overwrites *A*
Bnew = result No. 2, which overwrites *B*

For a Decimation in Time (DIT) butterfly,

$$Anew = A + (B*W)$$
$$Bnew = A - (B*W)$$

The complex addition, subtraction, and multiplication of a butterfly decompose into four real multiplications, three real additions, and three real subtractions:

$$tempR = (WR*BR) - (WI*BI)$$
$$tempI = (WR*BI) + (WI*BR)$$
$$AnewR = AR + tempR \qquad BnewR = AR - tempR$$
$$AnewI = AI + tempI \qquad BnewI = AI - tempI$$

For a Decimation in Frequency (DIF) butterfly,

$$Anew = A + B$$
$$Bnew = (A - B)*W$$

The real operations (four multiplications and six additions/subtractions) remain, but the equations differ and two subtractions must precede the four multiplications:

$$AnewR = AR+BR \quad tempR = AR-BR$$
$$AnewI = AI+BI \quad tempI = AI-BI$$

$$BnewR = (tempR*WR) - (tempI*WI)$$
$$BnewI = (tempR*WI) + (tempI*WR)$$

The stages, twiddles, and butterflies for 8-point FFTs are shown in Figures 10-3 and 10-4. For larger values of N, the data flow patterns are very similar, with N/2 butterflies executed at each stage and a greater number of stages. Refer to a DSP textbook for a complete discussion of FFT algorithms.

Several features of the i860 processor's CPU can be exploited in an FFT. The floating-point multiplier and adder can produce one product and one sum per cycle simultaneously using *dual-operation* instructions. To fetch the inputs and store outputs of the butterfly, *dual-instruction mode* allows a memory fetch or store simultaneous with the multiply and add. Four floating-point numbers can be stored with one instruction,

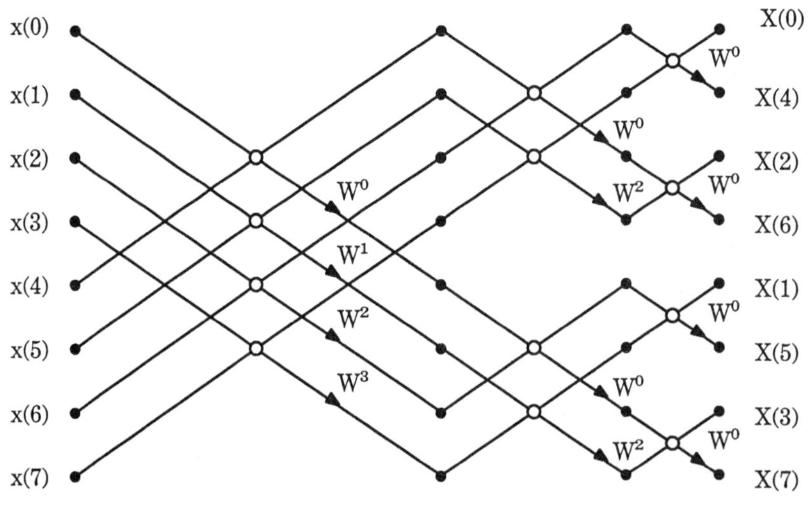

Figure 10-3. Eight-point decimation in frequency data flow

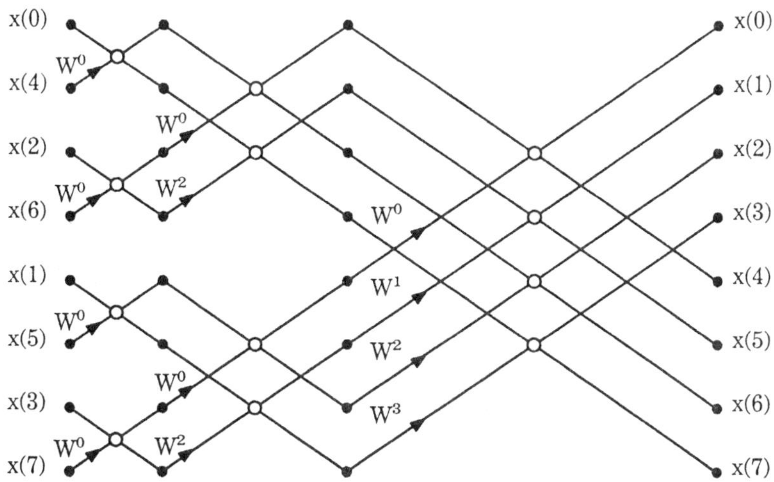

Figure 10-4. Eight-point decimation in time data flow

using the quad-word store instruction **fst.q**. Likewise, 16 bytes can be fetched with one **fld.q** instruction.

However, the use of pipelining, dual-instruction mode, and dual-operation instructions makes the coding somewhat tricky. Therefore, let us gradually evolve a butterfly implementation—from the simplest scalar code to a top-performance parallel version. The evolution will produce a speed-up of over four times.

FFT Performance

The performance for an FFT calculation can be extrapolated from the time required to perform the inner loop butterfly. The butterfly performance can be quoted in MFlops where each butterfly includes ten floating-point operations. A formula for the MFlop performance of the code comes from:

$$\text{MFlops} = \frac{\text{(Millions of Flops)}}{\text{Seconds}}$$

$$= \frac{\text{(10 Flops)}}{\text{butterfly}} * \frac{\text{(1 butterfly)}}{N \text{ clocks}} * \frac{\text{(clock frequency in Mhz)}}{\text{1 second}}$$

$$\text{MFlops} = \frac{10 \quad * \quad \text{clock frequency}}{N}$$

We assume ten floating-point operations per butterfly and N is the number of clock cycles required by the butterfly.

Now it is time to begin looking at coding the FFT for the i860 processor. To make it easier for you to understand what is going on in the programs, the code uses symbolic variable names for data registers in the operations. For the i860 processor, the data operations occur on the operands in the registers. The variable names and their register assignments are shown in Figure 10-5; these definitions match the syntax of the UNIX M4 macro preprocessor.

Scalar FFT Butterfly

The code in Figure 10-6 consists of the algebraic equations of the DIT butterfly translated into floating-point addition, subtraction, and multiplication instructions. Each pass through the butterfly loop performs ten floating-point operations.

The floating-point operations correspond to the **fadd**, **fsub**, and **fmul** scalar instructions. Each of these operations requires 3 clock cycles, for a total of 30 cycles per butterfly.

Also included in the example are the loads from memory of butterfly inputs, and stores of outputs. In the simplest case, the B and W values could be loaded immediately before they are operated on by placing the load instruction at label "bfly" for each iteration. However, the

```
//AR is real part of first butterfly input
//AI is imaginary "  "
//BR and BI are the second input

define(AR,f12)      define(AI,f13)
define(AR_AI,f12)
define(BR,f14)      define(BI,f15)
define(BR_BI,f14)

define(WR,f30)      // twiddle factors
define(WI,f31)      define(WR_WI,f30)
define(PR,f28)      // Product of B*W, Real Part
define(PI,f29)

define(temp1,f20)   define(temp2,f21)
define(temp3,f22)   define(temp4,f23)

define(AnewR,f16)   // results (replaces original input)
define(AnewI,f17)   define(AnewI_AnewR,f16)
define(BnewR,f18)
define(BnewI,f19)   define(BnewI_BnewR,f18)

define(Aptr,r18)    //address of first input to butterfly
define(Bptr,r19)    // "      "  second  "      "
define(Wptr,r20)    //address into twiddle array
define(Wincr,r21)   // stride of twiddle accesses (W_increment)

define(neg1,r24)    // constant negative 1
define(count,r25)   // counter for loop iterations
define(STore,r26)   // another pointer
define(offset,r27)  // distance (in bytes) between A & B
//-------------------------------------------------------------
```

Figure 10-5. Variable names and register assignments for coding examples

programmer can hide the latency of loaded data by inserting other useful instructions directly following the load. Here the **fld** (floating register load) fetches the B and W values in the middle of the loop, allowing several clocks between the request and the use of the data. The alternative of load-immediately-before-use would cost two clocks per loop iteration (7% of performance here, and a greater percentage in

```
//------------------------------------------------------------------
//scalar DIT butterfly:  30 Clocks, 13.3 MFlops at 40 MHZ.

inits::
// access first B & W before loop begins
fld.d    8(Bptr)++,BR_BI        // BR_BI <-- mem[Bptr+8],
                                // Bptr <-- Bptr+8
fld.d    Wincr (Wptr)++,WR_WI   // WR_WI <-- mem[Wptr+Wincr],
                                // Wptr <-- Wptr + Wincr

bfly::                          // the loop begins here.
fmul.ss      BR,WR,temp3        // temp3 <--  BR * WR
fmul.ss      BI,WI,temp1        // temp1 <--  BI * WI

fld.d    8(Aptr)++,AR_AI        // AR_AI <-- mem[Aptr+8],
                                // Aptr <-- Aptr+8

fsub.ss      temp3,temp1,PR     // PR <-- temp3 - temp1
fmul.ss      BR,WI,temp4        // temp4 <--  BR * WI
fmul.ss      BI,WR,temp2        // temp2 <--  BI * WR

fld.d    8(Bptr)++,BR_BI        // BR_BI <-- mem[Bptr+8],
                                // Bptr <-- Bptr+8
                                //for next loop
fld.d    Wincr (Wptr)++,WR_WI   // WR_WI <-- mem[Wptr+Wincr],
                                // Wptr <-- Wptr + Wincr

fadd.ss      temp2,temp4,PI     // PI <-- temp2 + temp4
fsub.ss      AR,PR,BnewR        // BnewR <--  AR-PR
fsub.ss      AI,PI,BnewI        // BnewI <--  AI-PI

fadd.ss      AR,PR,AnewR        // AnewR <--  AR+PR
fst.d    BnewR_BnewI,-8(Bptr)   // mem[Bptr-8] <-- BnewR_BnewI
                                // use -8 because Bptr already at next element

fadd.ss      AI,PI,AnewI        // AnewI <--  AI+PI
bla neg  1,count,bfly           // delayed conditional branch to bfly
fst.d    AnewR_AnewI,0(Aptr)    // mem[Aptr] <-- AnewR_AnewI


//------------------------------------------------------------------
```

Figure 10-6. Butterfly code: scalar instructions

the successively faster versions we will develop). Note that the first loads are performed outside of the loop and the loads for the next loop iteration are performed inside the loop.

Here are some facts that may help you to understand the programming optimizations better. While **fld** incurs a two-cycle delay if the destination register is used by the next instruction, **ld** (integer load) incurs only a one-cycle delay. If the instruction immediately after **ld**, or the two instructions after the **fld**, do not use the destination register, *no* delay occurs. The one-cycle delay comes from the time required to access the data cache, assuming no cache miss. The extra cycle of **fld** occurs because the integer register file has an extra bypass path to the arithmetic unit. Such a bypass would have been much harder to implement in the design of the i860 microprocessor for **fld**, because **fld** may update four floating-point registers and feed three separate units—adder, multiplier, and graphics.

In the code example, 8-byte loads and stores are employed, manipulating both the real and imaginary components of a complex value in a single instruction and single clock. For example,

```
fld.d  8(Bptr)++, BR_BI
```

puts four bytes into *BR* and four bytes into *BI*, where *BR* and *BI* are successive floating registers such as **f14** and **f15**. The + + in the **fld** instruction specifies autoincrement addressing mode where the constant, 8 in this case, is added to the memory pointer automatically. This avoids a separate addition instruction for incrementing the memory pointer.

The final store,

```
fst.d   AnewR_AnewI,0(Aptr)
```

is performed in the delay slot of the conditional branch instruction **bla**. The actual branching due to the **bla** instruction is delayed by one instruction, and the processor executes the **fst** instruction while fetching the target of the branch.

Pipelined Butterfly

Figure 10-7 shows a butterfly in which the scalar (3 clock cycles each) operations have been replaced by their pipelined (1 clock cycle each)

```
//-------------------------------------------------------------------
//pipelined DIT FFT butterfly:  23 clocks (17.4 MFlops)

fld.d       8(Bptr)++,BR_BI //access first B & W before loop begins
fld.d       Wincr (Wptr)++, WR_WI

bfly::
pfmul.ss    BR,WR,f0         //dest will be temp3
pfmul.ss    BI,WI,f0         //dest=templ
pfmul.ss    BR,WI,f0         //dest=temp4

fld.d       8(Aptr)++,AR_AI
pfmul.ss    BI,WR,temp3      //dest=temp2.  temp3 <-- BR*WR

pfmul.ss    f0,f0,templ      // BI*WI
pfmul.ss    f0,f0,temp4      // BR*WI
pfmul.ss    f0,f0,temp2      // BI*WR

fld.d       8(Bptr)++,BR_BI
fld.d       Wincr (Wptr)++, WR_WI

pfsub.ss    temp3,templ,f0   //dest= PR = (BR*WR) - (BI*WI)
pfadd.ss    temp2,temp4,f0   //dest= PI
pfadd.ss    f0,f0,f0

pfsub.ss    AR,PR,PR         //start AR-PR.  Dest will be BnewR.
pfsub.ss    AI,PI,PI
pfadd.ss    AR,PR,f0

pfadd.ss    AI,PI,BnewR
pfadd.ss    f0,f0,BnewI
pfadd.ss    f0,f0,AnewR
pfadd.ss    f0,f0,AnewI

fst.d       BnewR_BnewI,-8(Bptr)
bla         negl,count,bfly
 fst.d      AnewR_AnewI,r0(Aptr)
//-------------------------------------------------------------------
```

Figure 10-7. Butterfly code: pipelined instructions

counterparts. This results in a 40% speed-up even though more instructions are executed—extra **pfmul** and **pfadd** instructions are required to explicitly flush results from each pipeline. That is, the pipelines do not advance with each clock, but only with each instruction that manipulates that pipe. In an example later in this chapter, techniques to avoid the extra instructions will be clarified. Note that the replacement of scalar with pipelined instructions is fairly simple; the only "trick" is moving the destination register into the third successive instruction. For example, the first instruction:

```
fmul.ss  BR,WR, temp3
```

becomes

```
pfmul.ss BR,WR, f0
```

and the *temp3* destination register moves to the fourth **pfmul**:

```
pfmul.ss BI,WR, temp3
```

The performance for the pipelined butterfly code is 17.4 MFlops.

DIM Pipelined Butterfly

The pipelined butterfly is converted to dual-instruction mode (DIM) in Figure 10-8. The RISC core operations—load, store, and branch—become free, executed simultaneously with floating-point instructions. Performance improves 35%, from 17.4 MFlops to 23.5 MFlops. Conversion to DIM consists of:

1. Prefixing all the floating-point instructions with **d.** (forcing the assembler to set the dual-mode bit in the instruction format).
2. Moving the **bla** (Branch-Loop-and-Add) from the bottom of the loop, so that it is followed by a DIM pair of instructions, rather than the single **fst.d**.

3. Inserting enough core **nop** (no operation) instructions to equalize the count of floating-point and core operations.

The additional **nop**s may seem wasteful, but they cost very little extra memory space (44 bytes in this case) and no extra execution time. A more advanced implementation of the butterfly would replace some of the **nop**s with **and** and **addu** instructions, to implement modulo addressing on the *W*-values. Note that the remaining **nop**s could be avoided by removing some of the **d.** prefixes from the floating-point instructions and thus switching between single- and dual-instruction modes. No

```
//-----------------------------------------------------------------
//DIM (Dual-Instruction-Mode) FFT butterfly:  17 clocks (23.5 MFlops)

fld.d    8(Bptr)++,BR_BI      //loading BR,BI,WR,WI for first loop
fld.d    Wincr (Wptr)++,WR_WI

//  Floating-Point Op         ;    Core Op
bfly::
d.pfmul.ss     BR,WR,f0       ;    nop
d.pfmul.ss     BI,WI,f0       ;    nop
d.pfmul.ss     BR,WI,f0       ;    fld.d        8(Aptr)++,AR_AI

d.pfmul.ss     BI,WR,temp3    ;    nop
d.pfmul.ss     f0,f0,temp1    ;    fld.d        8(Bptr)++,BR_BI
d.pfmul.ss     f0,f0,temp4    ;    fld.d        Wincr (Wptr)++,WR_WI
d.pfmul.ss     f0,f0,temp2    ;    nop

d.pfsub.ss     temp3,temp1,f0  ;   nop  //dest=PR
d.pfadd.ss     temp2,temp4,f0  ;   nop  //dest=PI
d.pfadd.ss     f0,f0,f0        ;   nop

d.pfsub.ss     AR,PR,PR       ;    nop   //start AR-PR
d.pfsub.ss     AI,PI,PI       ;    nop
d.pfadd.ss     AR,PR,f0       ;    nop
d.pfadd.ss     AI,PI,BnewR    ;    nop

d.pfadd.ss     f0,f0,BnewI    ;    fst.d      BnewR_BnewI,-8(Bptr)
d.pfadd.ss     f0,f0,AnewR    ;    bla        negl,count,bfly
d.pfadd.ss     f0,f0,AnewI    ;    fst.d    AnewR_AnewI,r0(Aptr)
//-----------------------------------------------------------------
```

Figure 10-8. Butterfly code: pipelined instructions with dual-instruction mode

additional delays would be incurred by switching from DIM to SIM (single-instruction mode) and back to DIM; however, it would make the coding more complicated. Rather than removing the **nop**s here, we will eliminate them later by attrition as we shorten the sequence of floating-point instructions.

For clarity, the instructions are shown paired on the same line, but that is not required by the assembler syntax. The core instruction can appear on the next line after the concomitant floating-point instruction. The semicolons (;) do not indicate comments, but serve to separate statements, as in C-programs.

When a pipelined floating-point instruction updates a register used in the **fst** paired with it, as in

```
d.pfadd.ss  f0,f0, AnewI;       fst.d  AnewR_AnewI, r0(Aptr)
```

the updated value is used by the store.

Note that the original scalar loop in Figure 10-6 could be converted to DIM, but the payoff would be negligible. With scalar floating-point instructions, a core instruction such as **fld** or **bla** can begin in the next clock cycle, and is totally overlapped with the execution of the scalar floating-point operation.

DIM and Dual-Operation Butterfly

Figure 10-9 introduces some dual-operation floating-point instructions. The dual-operations advance both the multiplier and adder pipelines, producing a result from each. The two instructions

```
pfmul.ss  f0,f0, temp4
pfsub.ss  temp3,templ, f0
```

were replaced by a single

```
mrmls2.ss temp3,templ, temp4
```

Similarly,

```
pfmul.ss  f0,f0, temp2
pfadd.ss  temp2,temp4, f0
```

were replaced by

```
r2pl.ss  temp4,f0, f0
```

The mergers of add-multiply to a single dual-operation were fairly easy, because the multiplier needed no new input in either case. The removal of two clocks per loop improved performance another 13%.

```
//-----------------------------------------------------------------
//DIM and Dualop FFT butterfly: 15 clocks (26.7 MFlops)

fld.d   8(Bptr)++,BR_BI
fld.d   Wincr (Wptr)++,WR_WI

//  Floating-Point Op       ;   Core Op
bfly::
d.pfmul.ss    BR,WR,f0        ;   nop
d.pfmul.ss    BI,WI,f0        ;   nop
d.pfmul.ss    BR,WI,f0        ;   fld.d       8(Aptr)++,AR_AI

d.pfmul.ss    BI,WR,temp3     ;   nop
d.pfmul.ss    f0,f0,templ     ;   fld.d       8(Bptr)++,BR_BI

//replaced by mrmls2: pfmul.ss f0,f0,temp4  and pfsub.ss temp3,templ,f0
//replaced by r2pl:   pfmul.ss f0,f0,temp2  and pfadd.ss temp2,temp4,f0

d.mrmls2.ss   temp3,templ,temp4; fld.d  Wincr (Wptr)++,WR_WI
d.r2pl.ss     temp4,f0,f0     ;   nop

d.pfadd.ss    f0,f0,f0        ;   nop

d.pfsub.ss    AR,PR,PR        ;   nop    //start AR-PR
d.pfsub.ss    AI,PI,PI        ;   nop
d.pfadd.ss    AR,PR,f0        ;   nop
d.pfadd.ss    AI,PI,BnewR     ;   nop

d.pfadd.ss    f0,f0,BnewI     ;   fst.d      BnewR_BnewI,-8(Bptr)
d.pfadd.ss    f0,f0,AnewR     ;   bla        negl,count,bfly
d.pfadd.ss    f0,f0,AnewI     ;   fst.d    AnewR_AnewI,r0(Aptr)

//Of course, more pfmul and pfadd ops could be combined into dual-operations
//-----------------------------------------------------------------
```

Figure 10-9. Butterfly code: Dual-instruction mode with dual-operation instructions

Butterfly with pfld

Figure 10-10 includes the **pfld** instruction to fetch *W* values, rather than the standard **fld**. Thus the *W* values are not fetched into the data

```
//--------------------------------------------------------------
//DIM and Dualop FFT butterfly with pfld:  15 clocks

fld.d    8(Bptr)++,BR_BI

pfld.d    Wincr (Wptr)++,f0      // Start first W load into 3-stage pipeline
pfld.d    Wincr (Wptr)++,f0
pfld.d    Wincr (Wptr)++,f0

pfld.d    Wincr (Wptr)++,WR_WI

//   Floating-Point Op          ;     Core Op
bfly::
d.pfmul.ss    BR,WR,f0          ;     nop
d.pfmul.ss    BI,WI,f0          ;     nop
d.pfmul.ss    BR,WI,f0          ;     fld.d      8(Aptr)++,AR_AI

d.pfmul.ss    BI,WR,temp3       ;     nop
d.pfmul.ss    f0,f0,temp1       ;     fld.d      8(Bptr)++,BR_BI

d.mrmls2.ss   temp3,temp1,temp4 ;     pfld.d     Wincr (Wptr)++,WR_WI
d.r2p1.ss     temp4,f0,f0       ;     nop

d.pfadd.ss    f0,f0,f0          ;     nop

d.pfsub.ss    AR,PR,PR          ;     nop   //start AR-PR
d.pfsub.ss    AI,PI,PI          ;     nop
d.pfadd.ss    AR,PR,f0          ;     nop
d.pfadd.ss    AI,PI,BnewR       ;     nop

d.pfadd.ss    f0,f0,BnewI       ;     fst.d      BnewR_BnewI,-8(Bptr)
d.pfadd.ss    f0,f0,AnewR       ;     bla        negl,count,bfly
d.pfadd.ss    f0,f0,AnewI       ;     fst.d     AnewR_AnewI,r0(Aptr)

//--------------------------------------------------------------
```

Figure 10-10.* *Butterfly code: dual-instruction mode with dual-operation instructions and pipelined floating-point loads

cache, but rather directly to the floating-point registers from memory. Therefore, the data cache will contain only *A* and *B* values. This control of caching becomes important for 1024-point (and larger) FFTs, where *A* and *B* occupy the full 8K of data cache space. If *W* also required cache space, *thrashing* would result. Thrashing occurs when a program's data accesses do not exhibit locality and caching does not improve their performance. Although an FFT re-uses the *A* and *B* values many times, the *W* values are not used as often, further motivating the exclusion of *W* from the cache. Only in the first stage of the FFT are all the *W* elements used; successive stages use fewer and fewer elements, which are separated by larger and larger strides.

Note that the only change required for the conversion to the pipelined **pfld** was priming the load pipeline with three initial **pfld** instructions, *outside* of the loop. Like the pipelined addition instructions, **pfld** updates *fdest* with the value from the third previous **pfld** instruction.

Full Optimization DIM Dual-Operation Butterfly

To convert to an *optimal butterfly,* more tricks are required, as shown in Figure 10-11. Note that the adder executes six operations and the multiplier four to accomplish the butterfly. Thus the butterfly is adder-bandwidth-limited to six clocks, best case. To maintain adder activity, the loop must be "unrolled" to do two butterflies per iteration. That allows the adder to work on a previous butterfly's *Anew* and *Bnew*, while the current butterfly's products propagate through the multiplier. Unrolling also aids overlapping of cache accesses with arithmetic, as the next butterfly's inputs can be fetched during calculations for the current one. Sixteen-byte **fst.q** instructions are used to update results, with all four result values from both butterflies stored in a single clock cycle. (Use of **fst.q** is not feasible without the unrolling.) To achieve better adder utilization, the order of intermediate result creation was revised. The revision allows multiplier outputs to feed directly to the adder, removing the need for the temporary registers *temp1* through *temp4.* It also allows smooth interleaving of the two butterflies' additions.

When both the adder and multiplier must get useful inputs in a single cycle, the KR and KI registers can be used to hold *WR* and *WI*. Thus some of the multiplies don't require both the *src1* and *src2* fields of the instruction. Likewise, the adder can be fed from the T-register

```
//---------------------------------------------------------------
//Optimal DIT FFT butterfly:  7 Clocks (57.1 MFlops)
//      (2 butterflies per loop:  20 Flops in 14 clocks)
//
// ARe is the Real Part of the "even" butterfly A-input (0th, 2nd, 4th...)
// ARo is the Real Part of the "odd" butterfly (1st, 3rd, 5th...)
//
// Floating-Point Op          ;    Core Op
bfly::
d.r2apl.ss   AIe,BRe,PI         ; pfld.d Wincr (Wptr)++,WRo_WIo
d.pfsub.ss   AIe,PI ,Bnew_Re    ; fld.d  8(Aptr)++,ARe_AIe
d.pfadd.ss   ARo,PR ,PR         ; fld.d  8(Bptr)++,BRo_BIo
d.pfmul.ss   WIe,BIe,f0         ; nop
d.r2pt.ss    WRo,BIe,Anew_Ie    ; pfld.d Wincr (Wptr)++,WRe_WIe
d.ratls2.ss  ARo,PR ,Bnew_Ie    ; nop
d.i2st.ss    WIo,BRe,Anew_Ro    ; nop
//...................................................................
d.r2apl.ss   AIo,BRo,PI         ; nop
d.pfsub.ss   AIo,PI ,Bnew_Ro    ; fld.d  8(Aptr)++,ARo_AIo
d.pfadd.ss   ARe,PR ,PR         ; fld.d  8(Bptr)++,BRe_BIe
d.pfmul.ss   WIo,BIo,f0         ; nop
d.r2pt.ss    WRe,BIo,Anew_Io    ; fst.q  Anew_Re,16(STore)++
d.ratls2.ss  ARe,PR,Bnew_Io     ; bla    neg2,count,bfly
d.i2st.ss    WIe,BRo,Anew_Re    ; fst.q  Bnew_Re,offset(STore)

// Anew_Re, Anew_Ie, Anew_Ro, Anew_Io are stored to 4 contiguous
// memory words
//---------------------------------------------------------------
```

Figure 10-11. Butterfly code: Optimized Decimation in Time (DIT)

and multiplier output, as in the **d.i2st.ss** instruction. Then both inputs can feed the multiplier or KI register.

A diagram of the i860 processor pipelines for the two-butterfly loop appears in Figure 10-12. The value in each column represents the result of the execution of the instruction at left. M1, M2, and M3 are the three stages of the multiplier, and A1, A2, and A3 are the adder pipeline. The column labeled "Write" shows which floating-point register is updated. To simplify the diagram, the four products are renamed as follows:

$$BR*WR = K \qquad BI*WI = L$$
$$BI*WR = M \qquad BR*WI = N$$

Registers and Pipeline Stages

Instruction			Multiplier stages				Adder stages			
bfly::	// KR ..	KI	M1	M2	M3	T	A1	A2	A3	Write.
d.r2apl.ss	//		K2	N1	–	M1	AnewI0	PR1	BnewR0	PI0
d.pfsub.ss	//		K2	N1	–	M1	BnewI0	AnewI0	PR1	BnewR0
d.pfadd.ss	//		K2	N1	–	M1	AnewR1	BnewI0	AnewI0	PR1
d.pfmul.ss	//		L2	K2	N1	M1	AnewR1	BnewI0	AnewI0	–
d.r2pt.ss	// WRo		M2	L2	K2	–	M1+N1	AnewR1	BnewI0	AnewI0
d.ratls2.ss	//		–	M2	L2	K2	BnewR1	PI1	AnewR1	BnewI0
d.i2st.ss	//	WIo	N2	–	M2	K2	K2-L2	BnewR1	PI1	AnewR1
	//	....	....	....	....	....	....	....	....	....
	// KR ..	KI	M1	M2	M3	T	A1	A2	A3	Write.
d.r2apl.ss	//		K3	N2	–	M2	AnewI1	PR2	BnewR1	PI1
d.pfsub.ss	//		K3	N2	–	M2	BnewI1	AnewI1	PR2	BnewR1
d.pfadd.ss	//		K3	N2	–	M2	AnewR2	BnewI1	AnewI1	PR2
d.pfmul.ss	//		L3	K3	N2	M2	AnewR2	BnewI1	AnewI1	–
d.r2pt.ss	// WRe		M3	L3	K3	–	M2+N2	AnewR2	BnewI1	AnewI1
d.ratls2.ss	//		–	M3	L3	K3	BnewR2	PI2	AnewR2	BnewI1
d.i2st.ss	//	WIe	N3	–	M3	K3	K3-L3	BnewR2	PI2	AnewR2
	//	....	....	....	....	....	....	....	....	....
	// KR ..	KI	M1	M2	M3	T	A1	A2	A3	Write.

Figure 10-12. Pipeline stages for optimal Decimation in Frequency (DIF) FFT code

Scheduling of instructions was done with the pipeline diagram introduced in Chapter 6, "Floating-Point Operations." Begin by placing the desired results in the right-most column, then tracing progress backwards through the adder. When adder inputs are products (of the multiplier), one product is saved in the T-register for one cycle while the other product propagates through the multiplier's final stage. Those products can be traced back on the multiplier pipeline, to determine at which instruction the multiplier inputs must be provided.

Some trial and error ordering of the desired outputs is needed to devise a sequence that keeps the adder pipeline full. An opcode is chosen for each slot for its ability to load the KR or KI register, or to initiate an adder operation simultaneous with the multiplications required to calculate PR and PI.

Handy hints to assist dual-operation scheduling include:

1. *Feedback* the adder result to the adder or multiplier, whenever possible. Thus the *src1* and/or *src2* fields of the instruction are available to feed the other unit, and a useful simultaneous add and multiply is initiated.

2. *Freeze* one of the pipes, by using a **pfadd** or **pfmul**, when appropriate. In the butterfly, where six adds are done for every four multiplies, freezing of the multiplier (during **pfadd**) does not degrade performance. The freeze allows multiplier results to be held until needed in the adder.

3. The T-*register* can hold a multiplier result for several cycles until needed in the adder.

4. *Unroll* a loop to do two iterations. That provides time to fetch inputs for iteration Number 2 while calculating iteration Number 1, and store results of iteration Number 1 (and fetch more inputs) while calculating iteration Number 2. Some loops may benefit from greater unrolling, to three or more values per loop.

DIT versus DIF

As previously mentioned, FFT algorithms can employ Decimation in Frequency (DIF) instead of Decimation in Time. A DIF butterfly allows a more convenient sequence of arithmetic:

1. Subtract (DR <-- $AR-BR$, DI <-- $AI-BI$)
2. Multiply ($WR*DR, WI*DI, WR*DI, WI*DR$)
3. Add partial products to produce *Bnew*
4. Add ($AR+BR$, $AI+BI$) to produce *Anew*

The additions of ($AR+BR$) and ($AI+BI$) can be done anywhere in the calculation sequence, moving easily to fill gaps in the coding pipeline. In fact, DIF allows a 15% faster version of the FFT butterfly; the DIF butterfly can be done in six clock cycles, while the DIT takes seven clock cycles, as shown in Figure 10-13.

DIF affords a convenience for FFTs used for signal convolution, because a data-movement operation called "bit-reversal" can be avoided

```
// Each butterfly = 1 complx multiply, 1 complx add, 1 complx subtract
// =     4 multiply, 3 add,3 subtract
//       3 8-byte fetches (A, B, W)
//       2 8-byte stores (A, B)
// 6 cycles per butterfly
// inner_loop: iterates "offset/2" times (eg, N/4 for stage 1, N/8 for
// stage2), for each group. It does 2 butterflies per iteration
// See listing difstep.ss for variable name definitions

inner_loop::
d.r2pt.ss WR,DI,FR      ;  pfld.d  wind (wstart),WRo
d.pfsub.ss AR,BR,ERo    ;  fld.d   8 (FEtch)++,ARo
d.ratls2.ss AI,BI,EIo   ;  fld.d   offset (FEtch),BRo
d.i2st.ss  WI,DR,FI     ;  fst.q   ER,16(STore)++
//update ER/EI/ERo/EIo
d.ratlp2.ss AR,BR,DR    ;  adds  wincr,wind,wind
d.ialp2.ss AI,BI,DI     ;  pfld.d  wind (wstart),WR
//no need for modulo-check ("and") here,
// as odd num of W's have been fetched.

d.r2pt.ss WRo,DI,FRo    ;  adds wincr,wind,wind
d.pfsub.ss ARo,BRo,ER   ;  fld.d   8 (FEtch)++,AR
d.ratls2.ss AIo,BIo,EI  ;  fld.d   offset (FEtch),BR
d.i2st.ss  WIo,DR,FIo   ;  fst.q   FR, offset (STore)
 //update FR/FI/FRo/FIo
d.ratlp2.ss ARo,BRo,DR  ;  bla decrem,somecount, inner_loop
d.ialp2.ss AIo,BIo,DI   ;  and wlimit,wind,wind //modulo.
```

Figure 10-13. Butterfly code: optimized decimation in Frequency

in DIF. (Bit-reversal will be clarified later.) Convolution is a common motivation for FFTs, useful for determining the output of a system. The convolution operation consists of integrating the product of the input waveform and the *system response function.* That convolution is fairly costly in the time domain, but in the frequency domain, the FFTs of the two signals can simply be multiplied to produce the frequency-domain equivalent of their convolution.

The Complete FFT Program

The complete DIF FFT subroutine is listed at the end of this chapter. Prior to the inner loop of two butterflies, start-up code primes the pipelines and initializes pointers. After the loop completes iterations, some rollout code (labeled **`last_bfly`**) resets pointers and saves final results.

The program includes both assembly and Fortran components. Input data can number any power of 2 from 16 to 1024 points.

The listing labeled *fft.f* is a Fortran Decimation In Time algorithm, while *diff.f* is the high-speed routine callable by C or Fortran applications. It in turn calls `difstep`, which is implemented in assembly code (*difstep.ss*). *difstep* is called once per stage of the FFT. A Fortran version, *difstepf.f* is included for clarity.

The mixture of Fortran and assembly code is accomplished by passing function inputs and outputs in registers. Only pointers and integer values were used in these code examples, but floating-point parameters can also be exchanged. A calling program feeds arguments to a function in **r16**, **r17**, and higher-numbered integer registers (for integer and pointer arguments). The callee is permitted to destroy the contents of those registers, but **r1**:**r15** must be preserved.

Fortran passes values to subroutines indirectly, as pointers. Thus, **r16** will not be the first input parameter, but rather the *address* of the first parameter in memory.

Programs similar to these can be written for performing Decimation in Time. The algorithms can also be extended for real data where N real data points are treated as N/2 complex points. The output must then be post-processed to compensate for the treatment of the real points as complex.

Bit Reversal

Due to their structure, FFT algorithms have the side effect of scrambling the ordering of output data. For Radix-2 FFTs, the output is in bit-reversed order—for example, the value for frequency one is *not* at location one in the output array, but at location N/2. Time to unscramble the output is often *not* included in FFT benchmarking, because scrambled output is fine for some signal-processing uses such as convolution. In any event, unscrambling consists of swapping the locations of pairs of output values. Alternatively, input values can be shuffled, as Decimation in Time usually does before the first stage, as shown in Figure 10-4. (To avoid the shuffling of input in DIT, the twiddles must be accessed in bit-reversed order.) As an example of bit-reversal, for 256 points the reordering involves:

SWAP X(i) and X(j), where i = 'klmnopqr'b and j = 'rqponmlk'b.

The second index (j) contains the same bits as (i), but in opposite order.

The assembly code for bit-reversal (*bitrev.ss*) fetches the indices of two elements to be swapped from a pre-allocated array of indices, and swaps the data elements. Again, **pfld.d** keeps the indices out of the cache. That assembly version of bit-reversal is approximately seven times faster than the standard Fortran routine, which is included in the *fft.f*. The array of indices can be generated by printing out the values generated during operation of the standard Fortran FFT program version; similarly, the twiddle W values can be preallocated and generated using program *fft.f*.

The FFT Program Listings

Here is the complete FFT subroutine.

diff.f

Fortran module for a fast Decimation In Frequency (DIF) Radix-2 FFT.

```
C-------------------------------------------
C File: diff.f
C  FFT -- Decimation in Freq, radix-2, inplace, 1-dimen

C Inputs:
C   A= complex array of input, up to 1024 pts, single-prec float
C   M= log of number of pts
C     = (Number of stages of FFT)
C   N = number of points
C       ie, N= 2**M = number of pts
C   W= complex array of twiddle factors, length N/2.
C   REV= 0 if bitreversed output ok.  1=must re-order output
C
C Outputs:
C       A = complex fft of input A
C
        subroutine diff(a,m,N,W,REV)
        integer m,N, i, j,k, REV,wlimit
        integer offset, stage, groups, wincr,powers2(0:10)
        complex a(n),w(N/2),temp

        data powers2 /1,2,4,8,16,32,64,128,256,512,1024/

C Twiddle factor array w(k) has (cos,-sin) of 2pi*k/N
CC Assume the caller provides w(k) constants ALREADY initialized
C----------------------------------
C Pre-touch data into cache, for 8kByte fft:
        IF (N .gt. 513) THEN
                call fetch(a,%VAL(n))
        ENDIF
        wlimit = 8*((N/2) - 1)

C----------------------------------
        DO 20 stage = 1,m
                groups = powers2(stage-1)
C groups=number of times the twiddle factors are used, ie, the number of
C  smaller DFTs the stage is split into.
C       offset gets N/2,N/4,N/8,N/16,...
                offset = powers2(m-stage)
                wincr = groups
                call difstep(a,w,groups,offset,wincr,wlimit)
20      CONTINUE
C----------------------------------
        IF (REV .ne. 0) THEN
cc REV .ne. 0  means must do bit-reversal reordering of output
        call bitrev(a,%VAL(M),n)
        ENDIF

        RETURN
        END
C---------------------------------------------
```

difstep.ss

Assembly code which does all FFT butterflies; called by *diff.f*

```
//-----------------------------------------
// difstep.ss: do one stage of fft butterflies
// DIF = Decimation in Frequency, radix-2, inplace, 1-dimension
//---------------------------------
// Do one entire stage (n/2 butterflies).  Sample invocation:
//  call difstep(a,w,groups,offset,wincr,wlimit)
//===================================================
// Inputs:
//   A= complex array of input, single-prec float
//       (complex stored as 4byte real, 4byte imag contiguously)
//   W=  pointer to array of twiddle factors.  Assuming W(k) is
//      CMPLX(cos(2pi*k/N)),-sin(2pi*k/N))  for k=0 to (N/2)-1.
//   offset = distance (in units of "elements") between
//      the 2 input values for each butterfly.
//      Offset also is the number of butterflies done per "group".
//   groups = N/(2*offset). The number of sub-DFTs this stage is split.
//   wincr = distance (except for scale-by-8byte sizeof(complex)) between
//      successive W values for successive butterflies
//   wlimit =max index, in bytes, of W table.
//
// Outputs:
//   A= complex radix-2 butterflied version of input.
//-------------------------------------------------------
define(astart, r16)  //input data base address
define(wstart,r17)   //twiddle array ptr. Because W-contents depend on N,
                     //we will assume the caller has initialized W() array.
define(groups,r18)   //groups=number of sub-DFTs this stage is split into.
define(offset,r19)   //offset (initially elements, mult by 8 to get bytes)
// between node and its dual (the 2 numbers to butterfly, ie. A and B)
define(wincr,r20)    //increment between successive W values. Remains
                     //constant within a given stage. For Decimation in
                     //Freq, wincr addressing is:
                     //  +8 for offset=N/2 (W0,W1,W2,W3,...W(n-1))
                     //  +16    offset=N/4 (W0,   W2,   W4, ...  ) etc...
define(wlimit,r21)   //max index, in bytes, of W table.
define(wind,r22)     //current index, in bytes, of W table.
define(offset2,r23)  //offset*2
define(decrem,r24)   //bla decrement
define(somecount,r25)//bla counter
define(FEtch, r26)   //pointer to 1st component of butterfly (load)
define(STore,r27)    // " " 1st component of butterfly (store)

//f4:f7 spare
define(AR, f12)      //element A, real component
define(AI, f13)      //" ", imag
define(ARo,f14)      //extra A value, for prefetch (o="odd")
```

```
define(AIo,f15)
define(BR, f16)  //element B, real component
define(BI, f17)
define(BRo,f18)  //extra B value, for prefetch
define(BIo,f19)

define(ER, f20)  //A+B, real (ER = AR + BR)
define(EI, f21)  //"   imag "
define(ERo,f22)  //A+B, real, previous loop's value
define(EIo,f23)  //"   imag "

define(FR, f24)  //W*(A-B), real
define(FI, f25)  //"       imag "
define(FRo,f26)
define(FIo,f27)

define(DR, f28)  //Difference of A-B, real part
define(DI, f29)  //" ", imag "
define(WR, f30)  //W (twiddle factor), real part
define(WI, f31)  //" " , imag
define(WRo,f10)  //W (twiddle factor), real part (EXTRA copy)
define(WIo,f11)  //" " , imag

_difstep_::
 ld.l   0(groups),groups   //fix Fortran call-by-reference (indirection)
 ld.l   0(offset),offset   //
 shl    3,offset,offset    //change from elements to bytes
 shl    1,offset,offset2

 fst.q  f8 ,-16(sp)++      //save "local" regs
 fst.q  f12,-16(sp)++      //" "

 adds   -1,groups,groups   //pre-decrement for bnc usage, or bla usage
 adds   -16,r0,decrem      //bla decrement

// We code the last 2 stages as special cases:
//-----------------------
 xor    8,offset,r0        //offset=1, special case, no complex mult
 bc     offset_1           //(ASSUMING offset=1 means wincr=0, and no twiddle used)

 xor    16,offset,r0       //offset=2, special case, no complex mult
 bc     offset_2          //(ASSUMING offset=2 means wincr=N/4)
//-----------------------
 ld.l    0(wincr),wincr
 ld.l    0(wlimit),wlimit

 pfadd.ss f0,f0,f0
 pfadd.ss f0,f0,f0
 pfadd.ss f0,f0,f0          // init A1,A2,A3=0
 pfmul.ss f0,f0,f0
```

```
 pfmul.ss f0,f0,f0
 pfmul.ss f0,f0,f0
//-----------------------
// init pointers:
 shl   3,wincr,wincr  //scale for bytes.
 shl   1,wincr,wind   //init wind =2*wincr

 pfld.d 0 ( wstart),f0
 pfld.d wincr ( wstart),f0
 adds   -8,astart,FEtch
 pfld.d wind (wstart),f0
 adds   wincr,wind,wind //wind now 3*wincr
// here fetch first set of A,B,W before bla-loop
 pfld.d wind (wstart),WR
 adds   wincr,wind,wind
 and    wlimit,wind,wind //modulo-wlimit  the w index
// modulo-addressing on W() keeps the pfld pipeline full.
//  The code never does a W-fetch beyond the end of the table.
// And the modulo-check needs to be done only every 4th pfld, as always
//  we use a multiple of 4 W() factors.

 fld.d  8 (FEtch)++,AR
 fld.d  offset (FEtch),BR
d.r2apl.ss f0,f0,f0  //clear Treg.
 adds -32,offset,somecount // bla counter (predecrement by 4 elements)
// --------------------------------
// Definitions for pipe diagram:
//  (the complex multiply product, F, broken into 4 real mult and 2
//    adds):
//   WR = cos(), WI=-sin().
//   DR = AR - BR; (difference of Real components of A,B)
//   DI = AI - BI; (difference of Imag components)
//   ER = AR + BR;  EI = AI + BI;
//   FR = K - L;  where K= WR*DR, L=WI*DI
//   FI = N + M;  where M= WI*DR, N=WR*DI

// For 1st time thru inner_loop, don't have correct values to store.
// Must do 1 loop before the loop, sans the stores.
first_bfly::  //fill pipe
                         // KR...KI...M1....M2....M3   T   A1 ....A2....A3.... Write
d.r2pt.ss WR,f0,f0      // WR0  -
 pfld.d  wind (wstart),WRo
d.pfsub.ss AR,BR,f0     //            -     -     -     -   DR0   -     -
 fld.d  8 (FEtch)++,ARo
d.ratls2.ss AI,BI,f0  //            -     -     -     -   DI0   DR0   -     -
 fld.d  offset (FEtch),BRo
d.i2st.ss  WI,f0,f0    //      WI0  -     -     -     -     -     DI0   DR0   -
 adds     wincr,wind,wind
d.ratlp2.ss AR,BR,DR  //            K0    -     -     -   ER0   -     DI0   DR0
 nop
d.ialp2.ss AI,BI,DI   //            L0    K0    -         EI0   ER0   -     DI0
```

```
 pfld.d  wind (wstart),WR
d.r2pt.ss WRo,DI,f0   // WR1  -    N0    L0    K0    -     -    EI0   ER0    -
 fld.d  8 (FEtch)++,AR
d.pfsub.ss ARo,BRo,ER //           N0    L0    K0    -    DR1   -     EI0   ER0
 fld.d  offset (FEtch),BR
d.ratls2.ss AIo,BIo,EI//           -     N0    L0    K0   DI1   DR1   -     EI0
 adds     wincr,wind,wind
d.i2st.ss  WIo,DR,f0  //      WI1  M0    -     N0    K0   K-L   DI1   DR1    -
 and      wlimit ,wind,wind

quickstart::
d.ratlp2.ss ARo,BRo,DR//           K1    M0    -     N0   ER1   FR0   DI1   DR1
 bla decrem,somecount,inner_loop //init LCC
d.ialp2.ss AIo,BIo,DI //           L1    K1    M0    N0   EI1   ER1   FR0   DI1
 adds     -16,astart,STore  // ptrs init 16 low, for fst.q instructions
//-----------------------------------------------------
// Each butterfly = 1 complx multiply, 1 complx add, 1 complx subtract
//   =       4 multiply, 3 add,3 subtract
//           3 8-byte fetches (A, B, W)
//           2 8-byte stores (A, B)
//
// 6 cycles per butterfly
//
// inner_loop: iterates "offset/2" times (eg, N/4 for stage 1, N/8 for stage2),
//   for each group. It does 2 butterflies per iteration

inner_loop::           // KR...KI...M1....M2....M3   T    A1....A2....A3....Write
d.r2pt.ss WR,DI,FR     // WR2  -    N1    L1    K1   N0   N+M   EI1   ER1   FR0
 pfld.d  wind (wstart),WRo
d.pfsub.ss AR,BR,ERo  //            N1    L1    K1   N0   DR2   FI0   EI1   ER1
 fld.d  8 (FEtch)++,ARo
d.ratls2.ss AI,BI,EIo //            -     N1    L1   K1   DI2   DR2   FI0   EI1
 fld.d  offset (FEtch),BRo
d.i2st.ss  WI,DR,FI   //       WI2  M1    -     N1   K1   K-L   DI2   DR2   FI0
 fst.q  ER,16(STore)++ //update ER/EI/ERo/EIo
d.ratlp2.ss AR,BR,DR  //            K2    M1    -    N1   ER2   FR1   DI2   DR2
 adds    wincr,wind,wind
d.ialp2.ss AI,BI,DI   //            L2    K2    M1   N1   EI2   ER2   FR1   DI2
//no need for modulo-check ("and") here, as odd num of W's have been fetched.
 pfld.d  wind (wstart),WR
//.................................................................
                       // KR...KI...M1....M2....M3   T    A1....A2....A3....Write
d.r2pt.ss WRo,DI,FRo  // WR3  -    N2    L2    K2   N1   N+M   EI2   ER2   FR1
 adds    wincr,wind,wind
d.pfsub.ss ARo,BRo,ER //           N2    L2    K2   N1   DR3   FI1   EI2   ER2
 fld.d  8 (FEtch)++,AR
d.ratls2.ss AIo,BIo,EI//           -     N2    L2   K2   DI3   DR3   FI1   EI2
 fld.d  offset (FEtch),BR
d.i2st.ss  WIo,DR,FIo //      WI3  M2    -     N2   K2   K-L   DI3   DR3   FI1
 fst.q  FR, offset (STore)
```

```
 //update FR/FI/FRo/FIo
d.ratlp2.ss ARo,BRo,DR//         K3    M2    -    N2   ER3   FR2   DI3    DR3
 bla decrem,somecount, inner_loop
d.ialp2.ss AIo,BIo,DI //         L3    K3    M2   N2   EI3   ER3   FR2    DI3
 and     wlimit,wind,wind //modulo.

end_inner_loop:: //KEEP Pipelines full
// RE-init pointers for fetches
d.fiadd.ss f0,f0,f0
 adds   offset2,astart,astart //bump to next group
     //redo A,B fetches, with proper ptr.
d.fiadd.ss f0,f0,f0
 fld.d  0(astart)  ,AR //get first AR/AI in next group
d.fiadd.ss f0,f0,f0
 fld.d  offset (astart),BR
d.fiadd.ss f0,f0,f0
 adds     0,astart,FEtch

last_bfly:: //do final 2 butterflies, start next group
                      // KR...KI...M1....M2....M3   T    A1....A2....A3....Write
d.r2pt.ss WR,DI,FR    // WR4  -    N3    L3    K3   N2   N+M   EI3   ER3   FR2
 pfld.d  wind (wstart),WRo
d.pfsub.ss AR,BR,ERo  //           N3    L3    K3   N2   DR4   FI2   EI3   ER3
 fld.d  8 (FEtch)++,ARo
d.ratls2.ss AI,BI,EIo //           -     N3    L3   K3   DI4   DR4   FI2   EI3
 fld.d  offset (FEtch),BRo
d.i2st.ss  WI,DR,FI   //     WI4   M3    -     N3   K3   K-L   DI4   DR4   FI2
 fst.q  ER,16(STore)++
d.ratlp2.ss AR,BR,DR  //           K4    M3    -    N3   ER4   FR3   DI4   DR4
 adds    wincr,wind,wind
d.ialp2.ss AI,BI,DI   //           L4    K4    M3   N3   EI4   ER4   FR3   DI4
 pfld.d  wind (wstart),WR
//..............................................................................
                      // KR...KI...M1....M2....M3   T    A1....A2....A3....Write
d.r2pt.ss WRo,DI,FRo  // WR5  -    N4    L4    K4   N3   N+M   EI4   ER4   FR3
 fld.d  8 (FEtch)++,AR
d.pfsub.ss ARo,BRo,ER //           N4    L4    K4   N3   DR5   FI3   EI4   ER4
 adds -32,offset,somecount // reset bla counter
d.ratls2.ss AIo,BIo,EI//           -     N4    L4   K4   DI5   DR5   FI3   EI4
 adds    wincr,wind,wind
d.i2st.ss  WIo,DR,FIo //     WI5   M4    -     N4   K4   K-L   DI5   DR5   FI3
 adds -1,groups,groups
d.fnop
 fld.d  offset (FEtch),BR
d.fnop
 bnc.t quickstart //branch on value of groups
d.fnop
 fst.q  FR, offset (STore)

end_last_bfly::
d.fnop
```

```
 br endit
fiadd.ss f0,f0,f0
 fst.q  FR, offset (STore) //repeated for bnc.t untaken case
 .align   .quad
//============================================================
offset_1::
// want FEtch=0,2,4,6,8,... elements.  ASSUMING wincr=0,
//  and that w=(1,0), so that no complex mult needed, and NO W will be fetched.
//  E=A+B, F=A-B.  (Per double-butterfly loop:  8 pfadd,4 dword fld, 4 fst,
//  1 bla)(fld.q required, to reduce # flds to avoid pipe stalls)
//  Performance = 4 cyc/bfly best case.

//Redefine regs for fld.q,fst.q usage, when A and B adjacent:
define(AR3,f12)  //element A, real component
define(AI3,f13)  // " ", imag
define(BR3,f14)  //element B, real component
define(BI3,f15)
define(AR4,f16)  // extra  A value, for prefetch
define(AI4,f17)
define(BR4,f18)  // extra  A value, for prefetch
define(BI4,f19)
define(ER3, f20) //A+B, real (ER = AR + BR)
define(EI3, f21) // "   imag "
define(FR3, f22) //(A-B), real
define(FI3, f23) // "    imag "
define(ER4,f24)  //A+B, real, extra copy
define(EI4,f25)  // "   imag
define(FR4,f26)
define(FI4,f27)
//========================================
 adds   -16,astart,FEtch
 fld.q  16 (FEtch)++,AR4
 adds   -1,groups,somecount // bla counter (predecremented already by 1)
        //using groups=bla count on the offset_1 loop, intentionally.
 adds   -16,FEtch,STore
//startup the loop:
// ---------------------// A1......A2......A3......Write:
d.pfadd.ss AR4,BR4,f0   // ARn+BRn -       -       -
 fld.q  16 (FEtch)++,AR3
d.pfadd.ss AI4,BI4,f0   // AIn+BIn ERn     -       -
 adds   -2,r0,decrem    //2 bflies per loop
d.pfsub.ss AR4,BR4,f0   // ARn-BRn EIn     ERn     -
 bla decrem,somecount, offset1_loop  //init LCC
d.pfsub.ss AI4,BI4,ER4  // AIn-BIn FRn     EIn     ERnext
 nop
// ---------------------// A1......A2......A3......Write:
offset1_loop::
d.pfadd.ss AR3,BR3,EI4  // AR+BR   FI-     FR-     EI-
 nop
d.pfadd.ss AI3,BI3,FR4  // AI+BI   ER      FI-     FR-
```

```
 fld.q  16 (FEtch)++,AR4
d.pfsub.ss AR3,BR3,FI4  // AR-BR   EI      ER      FI-
 fst.q    ER4,16(STore)++
d.pfsub.ss AI3,BI3,ER3  // AI-BI   FR      EI      ER
 nop
d.pfadd.ss AR4,BR4,EI3  // AR2+BR2 FI      FR      EI
 fld.q  16 (FEtch)++,AR3
d.pfadd.ss AI4,BI4,FR3  // AI2+BI2 ER2     FI      FR
 nop
d.pfsub.ss AR4,BR4,FI3  // AR2-BR2 EI2     ER2     FI
 bla decrem,somecount, offset1_loop
d.pfsub.ss AI4,BI4,ER4  // AI2-BI2 FR2     EI2     ERnext
 fst.q  ER3,16(STore)++
//-------------------------
end_offset1_loop::
d.fiadd.ss f0,f0,f0
 br endit
fiadd.ss f0,f0,f0
  nop
//-------------------------
offset_2::
// want FEtch=0,1;4,5;8,9;12,13;... elements.
// ASSUMING wincr=N/4  (W_addr=0,N/4,0,N/4,0,...). Trivial W() factors.
// USE bla loop, incrementing FEtch by 16 (2*offset).
//  Even-indexed elements identical to offset_1,W=W0, no complex mult.
//    So FReven=(AR-BR), FIeven=(AI-BI).
//  Odd components have W=(0,-1).  So FRodd=(AI-BI), FIodd=(BR-AR).
//  Each fld.q fetches AReven,AIeven,ARodd,AIodd.

//Assume ER,EI,ERo,EIo are 4 contiguous regs.
//Assume FR,FI,FRo,FIo are 4 contiguous regs.

 adds     -16,astart,FEtch
 fld.q  16 (FEtch)++,AR
 fld.q  16 (FEtch)++,BR
 adds     0,groups,somecount //bla counter
//startup the loop:
// ---------------------// A1......A2......A3......Write:
  pfadd.ss AR ,BR ,f0   // AR+BRe                  -
  pfadd.ss AI ,BI ,f0   // AI+BIe  ER              -
d.pfadd.ss ARo,BRo,f0   // ARo+BRo EI      ER      -
 nop
d.pfadd.ss AIo,BIo,ER   // AIo+BIo ERo     EI      ER
 nop
d.pfsub.ss AR ,BR ,EI   // AR-BRe  EIo     ERo     EI
 adds     -1,r0,decrem //2 bflies per loop, but groups are half desired value.
d.pfsub.ss AI ,BI ,ERo  // AI-BIe  FR      EIo     ERo
 adds     -16,astart,STore
d.pfsub.ss AIo,BIo,EIo  // AIo-BIo FI      FR      EIo
```

```
 bla decrem,somecount, offset2_loop  //init LCC
d.pfsub.ss BRo,ARo,FR    // BRo-ARo FRo     FI      FR
 nop
offset2_loop::
d.fnop
 fld.q  16 (FEtch)++,AR //fetch AR,AI,ARo,AIo
d.fnop
 fld.q  16 (FEtch)++,BR //fetch BR,BI,BRo,BIo
// ---------------------// A1......A2......A3......Write:
d.pfadd.ss AR ,BR ,FI    // AR+BRe  FIo     FRo     FI
 nop
d.pfadd.ss AI ,BI ,FRo   // AI+BIe  ER      FIo     FRo
 nop
d.pfadd.ss ARo,BRo,FIo   // ARo+BRo EI      ER      FIo
 fst.q    ER ,16(STore)++  //update ER ,EI ,ERo,EIo
d.pfadd.ss AIo,BIo,ER    // AIo+BIo ERo     EI      ER
 nop
d.pfsub.ss AR ,BR ,EI    // AR-BRe  EIo     ERo     EI
 nop
d.pfsub.ss AI ,BI ,ERo   // AI-BIe  FR      EIo     ERo
 fst.q  FR ,16(STore)++
d.pfsub.ss AIo,BIo,EIo   // AIo-BIo FI      FR      EIo
 bla decrem,somecount,offset2_loop
d.pfsub.ss BRo,ARo,FR    // BRo-ARo FRo     FI      FR
 nop

endit::
// restore regs
fiadd.ss f0,f0,f0 //exit DIM
 fld.q   0(sp),f12
fiadd.ss f0,f0,f0 //last DIM pair
 fld.q   16(sp),f8
adds    32,sp,sp
 bri r1
  nop
//---------------------------------
```

difstepf.f

Fortran equivalent of *difstep.ss*. Included here for clarity.

```
c------------------------------------------
c difstepf.f: do one stage of fft (DIF) butterflies
c  This code is the Fortran equivalent of difstep.ss.
c
c------------------------------------------
c Decimation in Freq, radix-2, inplace, 1-dimen
```

```
c  The "CVD$ " comments are directives to the VAST2(tm) Vectorizer.
c Do one entire stage (n/2 butterflies).  Sample invocation:
c  call difstep(a,w,groups,offset,wincr)

c Inputs:
c   A= complex array of input, single-prec float
c        (complex stored as 4byte real, 4byte imag contiguously)
c   W=  pointer to array of twiddle factors.  Assuming W(k) is
c      CMPLX(cos(2pi*k/N)),-sin(2pi*k/N))  for k=0 to (N/2)-1.
c   offset = distance (in "elements") between
c      the 2 input values for each butterfly
c   groups = number of sub-DFTs this stage is split into.
c    (groups*offset*2 = N)
c   wincr = distance (except for scale-by-8byte sizeof(complex)) between
c      successive w values for successive butterflies
c
c Outputs:
c A= complex butterflied version of input.

        SUBROUTINE difstep(a,w,groups,offset,wincr)
        integer groups,offset,wincr
        integer i,j,index1,iplus
        complex a(groups*offset*2),w(groups*offset),wtemp,temp
c-----------------------------------------------------
c We implement a...
c Special case for offset=1(last stage): no complex multiplies, simple add

c  (Performance enhancement)
        IF (offset .eq. 1) THEN
                DO 8 i = 1,(2*groups),2
                  iplus = i + 1
                  temp = a(iplus)
                  a(iplus) = a(i) - temp
8                 a(i) = a(i) + temp
        ELSE
C----------------------------------
C Special case for offset=2 (next-to-last stage): no complex multiplies,

cc    simple add.  (Performance enhancement)
cc For half the butterflies, W=(1,0).  For the other half, W=(0,-1)
        IF (offset .eq. 2) THEN
                DO 90 i = 1,(4*groups),4
                  iplus = i + 2
                  temp = a(iplus)
                  a(iplus) = a(i) - temp
90                a(i) = a(i) + temp

C  2nd call to i-loop: w=cmplx(0,-1.)
c
c
```

```
       DO 92 i = 2,(4*groups),4
         iplus = i + 2
         temp = a(i) - a(iplus)
         a(i) = a(i) + a(iplus)
92       a(iplus) = CMPLX(AIMAG(temp),-REAL(temp))
        ELSE
C---------------------------------
c "DO 20" index1-loop is "outer loop"
        DO 20 index1 = 1,(2*offset*groups),(2*offset)
               j = 1
               DO 10 i = index1,(index1+offset-1)
                 iplus = i + offset
                 temp = a(i) - a(iplus)
                 a(i) = a(i) + a(iplus)
                 a(iplus) = w(j) * temp
10               j = j + wincr
20      CONTINUE

        ENDIF
        ENDIF
        RETURN
        END
cccccccccccccccccccccccccccccccccc
        subroutine fetch(a,n)
        integer n
        complex a(n),temp
cc Kludge do-nothing prefetch.
        temp = a(1)
        RETURN
        END
cccccccccccccccccccccccccccccccccc
        subroutine bitrev(a,dummy,n)
C Bit-Reverse
C Inputs:
C   A= complex array of input, single-prec float
C   dummy = %val(m).  Not used here.
C   N = number of input points (and output points)

C Output:
C   A = original A data, but in bit-reversed order from A

        integer n,i,j,k,ndiv2
        complex a(n),temp
C----------------------------------
C "DO 7" loop to in-place-bit-reverse-shuffle output
      j=1
      ndiv2 = n / 2
      DO 7  i= 1, n-1
        IF (i .lt. j) THEN
              temp = a(j)
```

```
                a(j) = a(i)
                a(i) = temp
          ENDIF
          k = ndiv2
C       "While (j .gt. k)" /*decrease j by 2**something */
6         IF (j .gt. k) THEN
                j = j-k
                k = k / 2
                GOTO 6
          ENDIF
C       Add next lower power of 2 to j
7       j = j+k
        RETURN
        END
C---------------------------------
```

bitrev.ss

Assembly code to do bit-reversal.

```
//------------------------------------------
// bitrev.ss
//
//   BIT-reversal of 8byte array elements.   IN PLACE.
// (Allows arrays of 8,16,32,64,128,256,512, or 1024 elements)
//====================================================
//  Invocation: (from Fortran)
//call bitrev(a,%VAL(m))
//  Inputs:
//a  = r16 = pointer to array of 8byte elements
//m=r17 (call by value)= base-2 log of total number of elements
//        (2**m = N)
// Outputs:
//      a=  Bit-reversed ordered version of A
//
// Expected best-can-do performance, and measured performance=
//  approx 4*N clocks
//----------------------------------------------------------
define(astart, r16)  //initial input data base address
define(m, r17)
define(logN,r17)
define(dest1,r19)
define(dest2,r20)
define(dest3,r21)
define(dest4,r22)
define(iptr, r23)  //index-array pointer

define(decrem,r24) //bla decrement
```

```
define(count,r25) // bla counter

.text
.align .quad
//=========================================
_bitrev_::
//fetch base address for index table (rbasetab)
// base-addr-table elements = (baseaddr, number_of_swaps-2)
// base-addr-table indexed by logN.
 shl    3,logN,r30  //scale to 8-byte-entry length
 mov    rbasetab,r29
 ld.l   r29(r30), iptr
 addu   4,r29,r29
 ld.l   r29(r30), count //number of swaps required for this value N

 pfld.d 0(iptr),f0 //initiate fetch of first 2 bit-rev indices
 pfld.d 8(iptr)++,f0
 adds   -2,r0,decrem //2 swaps per loop
 pfld.d 8(iptr)++,f0

 bla    decrem,count, revloop  //init LCC
  pfld.d 8(iptr)++,f16   //get 2 indices, but don't cache the indices

revloop:: //2 swaps per loop
 //7.5 cycles consumed for each swap, best case.
 pfld.d 8(iptr)++,f18    //2 more indices
 fxfr f16,dest1  //transfer to integer index regs
 fxfr f17,dest2
 fld.d  dest1 (astart),f24 //fetch 2 elements to swap
 fld.d  dest2 (astart),f26
 fxfr f18,dest3
 fst.d  f24, dest2 (astart)
 fst.d  f26, dest1 (astart)
 fxfr f19,dest4
 fld.d  dest3 (astart),f28
 fld.d  dest4 (astart),f30
 pfld.d 8(iptr)++,f16    //2 more indices
 fst.d  f28, dest4 (astart)
 bla decrem,count, revloop  //
  fst.d f30, dest3 (astart)

 bri    r1
  nop
//---------------------------------------------
// _fetch8_: Touch all 32-byte lines in the 8k data bytes, to get them
//   into dcache. (ASSUMING .lte. 8kBytes and .gte. 4kBytes)
//
//  Invocation= fetch(astart,num8)
//  Inputs=
//    astart=r16=pointer to data which is to be touched.
```

```
//    num8=r17 (passed by VALUE, %VAL(), not by reference)
//-----------------------------------
define(num8,r17)
define(FEtch, r26)

_fetch8_::
_fetch_::

 adds   -4,r0,decrem  //4 8-byte-groups per cache line
 adds   508,r0,count  //512, but pre-decremented for bla usage
 bla    decrem,count,floop
  adds  -32,astart,FEtch
floop::
 bla    decrem,count,floop
  fld.d 32(FEtch)++,f30 //dummy load, to cause cache line fills

 adds   -512,num8,count
 bc     fdone  //if data exhausted, quit

 adds   -8,count,count //predecr for bla
 bla    decrem,count,floop2 //set LCC
  fld.d 32(FEtch)++,f30
floop2::
 bla    decrem,count,floop2
  fld.d 32(FEtch)++,f30 //dummy load.
fdone::
 bri r1
  nop

 .data
//---------------------------------------------
// rbasetab:: (Table of bit-reversed indices for bitrev subroutine)
//  base-addr-table elements = (baseaddr, number_of_swaps-2)
//  base-addr-table indexed by logN.
 .align .quad
rbasetab::
 .long [6]0 //don't bother with log(n)=0,1,2
 .long rev8,   0
 .long rev16,   4
 .long rev32,   10
 .long rev64,   26
 .long rev128,  54
 .long rev256,  118
 .long rev512,  238
 .long rev1024, 494
//====================
//number of swaps=240 for N=512 (ie, 32 symmetrical patterns
//  exist between 0 and 511.)
// rev512: array of bit-reversed indices, for N=512.
```

```
//  Each entry is ("i", and "bit-reversed-i"), shifted left by 3
//    to account for 8-byte-elements.
 .align .quad
rev512::
 .long     8, 2048,    16, 1024
 .long    24, 3072,    32,  512
 .long    40, 2560,    48, 1536
 .long    56, 3584,    64,  256

[etc ... ]
```

fft.f

Fortran FFT algorithm. Generates "correct" answers for comparison against the other code.

```
C file = fft.f
C FFT routine from Rabiner & Gold, 1975, previously published by
C  Cooley, Lewis, Welch
C The CVD$ comments are directives for the VAST2(tm) Vectorizer.
C Decimation in Time, radix-2, inplace, 1-dimen
C Inputs:
C   A= complex array of input, up to 1024 pts, single-prec float
C       M= log of number of pts = (Number of stages of FFT)
C       N = number of points     ie, N= 2**M = number of pts
C
C Outputs:
C       A= complex fft of input A, in NON-bit-reversed order.
C
C  W (twiddle factor) calculated by recursion takes ~15% more
C  operations than keeping entire twiddle array as constants
C  pre-allocated.
C
        subroutine fft(a,m,n)
        integer m,n, i, j,k, ndiv2,powers2(0:10)
        integer iplus,offset, stage, index1, groups
        complex a(n),wtemp(2),w(11),temp

C Init partial twiddle factor array w() with (cos,-sin) of pi,pi/2,pi/4,...
       data w(1) /(-1.0,0.0) /
       data w(2) /(0.0,-1.0) /
       data w(3) /(0.7071068,-0.7071068)/
       data w(4) /(0.9238795,-0.3826834)/
       data w(5) /(0.9807853,-0.1950903)/
       data w(6) /(0.9951847,-0.0980171)/
```

```
      data w(7) /(0.9987955,-0.0490677)/
      data w(8) /(0.9996988,-0.0245412)/
      data w(9) /(0.9999247,-0.0122715)/
      data w(10) /(0.9999812,-0.0061359) /
      data w(11) /(0.9999953,-0.003068) /

      data powers2 /1,2,4,8,16,32,64,128,256,512,1024/

C Setup for bit-reversal loop:
        ndiv2 = n / 2
        j =1
C----------------------------------
C "DO 7" loop to in-place-bit-reverse-shuffle input
        DO 7  i= 1, n-1
          IF (i .lt. j) THEN
                temp = a(j)
                a(j) = a(i)
                a(i) = temp
          ENDIF
          k = ndiv2
C       "While (j .gt. k)" /*decrease j by 2**something */
6         IF (j .gt. k) THEN
                j = j-k
                k = k / 2
                GOTO 6
          ENDIF
C       Add next lower power of 2 to j
7       j = j+k
C----------------------------------
C Special case for stage 1: no complex multiplies, simple add
C  (Performance enhancement)
        groups = 2
        offset = 1
        index1 = 1

C  i-loop iterates N/2 times for 1st stage (and would do twice N/4 x C for 2nd)
CVD$    NODEPCHK
        DO 8 i = 1,n,2
          iplus = i + 1
          temp = a(iplus)
          a(iplus) = a(i) - temp
8         a(i) = a(i) + temp
C----------------------------------
C Special case for stage 2: no complex multiplies, simple add
```

```
C  (Performance enhancement)
        groups = 4
        offset = 2
        index1 = 1

C  i-loop iterates N/4 times for 2nd stage
C  1st call to i-loop,in stage2: index1=1, wtemp(1)=(1,0)
CVD$    NODEPCHK
        DO 90 i = 1,n,4
          iplus = i + 2
          temp = a(iplus)
          a(iplus) = a(i) - temp
90        a(i) = a(i) + temp

C  2nd call to i-loop,in stage2: index1=2, wtemp(1)=cmplx(0,-1.)
      index1 = 2

CVD$    NODEPCHK
        DO 92 i = 2,n,4
          iplus = i + 2
          temp = CMPLX(AIMAG(a(iplus)),-REAL(a(iplus)))
          a(iplus) = a(i) - temp
92        a(i) = a(i) + temp
C---------------------------------
C "DO 20" stage-loop executed once for each of the (m) stages of FFT
C    (Except 1st and 2nd stage)
C    offset gets 4,8,16,32,64,128,256...
        DO 20 stage = 3,m
                groups = powers2(stage)
                offset = groups/2
                wtemp(1) =(1.0, 0.0)
CC              w = cmplx(cos(pi/offset) , -sin(pi/offset))
C  One twiddle seed (W) calc per stage.
C  We pre-allocated w(12)-array with those values, avoid cos/sin C calls

C "DO 20" index1-loop would iterate once for 1st stage, 2x for 2nd, 4x
C  for 3rd
C    stage, 8x for 4th stage, 16x for 5th stage,....
C  It Updates the twiddle factor (wtemp(1))
C-----------------------------------------------------
        DO 20 index1 = 1,offset

C "DO 10" i-loop does each butterfly of each stage, with varying
C twiddles i-loop iterates N/2 times for 1st stage, N/4 x for 2nd,
```

```
C N/8 x for 3rd stage, N/16 x for 4th stage,... 1 time for last
C stage.

CVD$    NODEPCHK
CVD$    ALTCODE
                DO 10 i = index1,n,groups
                   iplus = i + offset
                   temp = a(iplus) * wtemp(1)
                   a(iplus) = a(i) - temp
10                 a(i) = a(i) + temp
20      wtemp(1) = wtemp(1) * w(stage)
        RETURN
        END
C-----------------------------------
```

CHAPTER 11
APPLICATION EXAMPLE: THE 3-D GRAPHICS TRANSFORM

The transform where computations are performed on image data structures, not on the pixels, is an important step in graphics processing. Employing rotation, projection, and other techniques, 3-D images can be synthesized and manipulated using shape and location information. This information can exist in various formats—such as a database of display lists or in polygon vertex information—where polygons can be mapped onto an image. Manipulating data in one of these formats has distinct advantages in speed, capabilities, and storage requirements over manipulating each individual bit of an image. Nevertheless, the computations required for 3-D transforms are significant. This chapter explains representation in the 3-D coordinate system, shows how the different transforms are performed, and gives a programming example for the 3-D graphics transform with the i860 processor.

The 3-D Coordinate System

A point in three-dimensional space is defined by its three coordinates, so that a point P is represented by the vector (x,y,z). The x, y, and z values correspond to the distances along each axis of a coordinate system. The coordinate system and the rotation directions are shown in Figure 11-1, which is a *left-handed* system where the z axis goes into the page. Note that you are probably more familiar with the *right-handed* system taught in high-school geometry where the positive z axis comes out of the page. By convention, the left-handed system is used in graphics. Although the three coordinates are sufficient to represent a point, in graphics programming, it is convenient to represent points by four-value *homogeneous coordinates.* In homogeneous coordinates, a point is defined by a 4-D vector (Wx, Wy, Wz, W). The additional factor, W, is called the scaling, or Weighing factor. To determine the actual coordinates of P, the scaling factor has to be divided out, leaving (x,y,z,1).

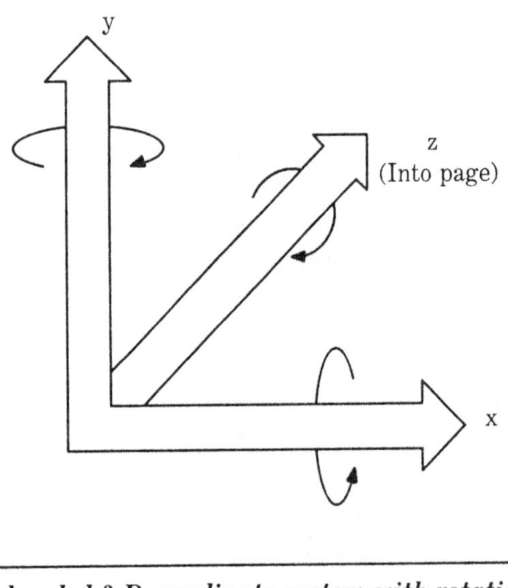

Figure 11-1. Left-handed 3-D coordinate system with rotation directions

The use of homogeneous coordinates has two advantages. First, the range of numbers represented by (x,y,z) can exceed the limits imposed by the processor's data types. Thus using W would be advantageous if, for example, the coordinate data types were 16-bit integers; however, the floating-point data types of the i860 processor provide adequate resolution for high-definition displays without use of the W-factor.

The second advantage is due to the capabilities of a 4 × 4 transform matrix. The 1 × 4 vector of homogeneous coordinates is more conveniently manipulated by the 4 × 4 transform matrix. The 4 × 4 transform matrix can represent all the transformations of a point, while a 3 × 3 matrix cannot. This capability will be discussed in the following section.

The Graphics Transform

The data points that exist in an image's database are manipulated to meet different display requirements. An application may require that an object be transformed in several ways:

- Local scaling—narrow or widen objects in one dimension
- Rotation—move in a circular fashion
- Translation—linear movement
- Perspective—give the impression of depth
- Zooming—move display in or out

Each of these operations can be performed through various matrix multiplications (also called matrix dot products).

The Transform Matrix

The components of a 4 × 4 matrix, when multiplied by a point in homogeneous representation (a 1 × 4 vector), do not all have the same effect on that point. Figure 11-2 shows the various functions of the

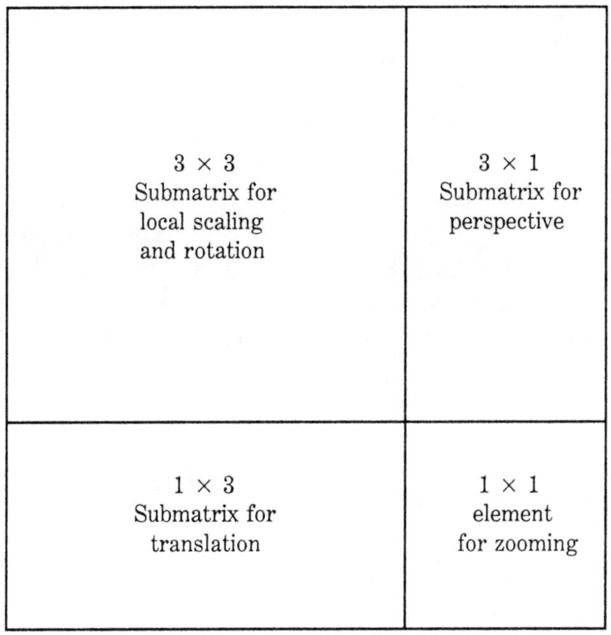

***Figure 11-2.** The 4 × 4 transform matrix with submatrix functions*

matrix. For example, the upper left 3 × 3 submatrix performs scaling and rotation. Figure 11-3 illustrates how to set up the matrix for performing scaling and rotation around the x, y, and z axes. The functions S(x), S(y), and S(z) correspond to the trigonometric sine function for each of the respective angles of rotation. Similarly, C(x), C(y), and C(z) correspond to the cosine of the respective angles of rotation. The operation is performed by multiplying each of the 1 × 4 vectors that correspond to an object's points by the matrix. See Figure 11-4 where the product of a 1 × 4 vector with a 4 × 4 matrix is shown.

In Figure 11-2, the 1 × 3 submatrix in the lower left-hand corner is used for translation. Figure 11-5 gives the translation matrix in which the position change along each of the axes is expressed by Δx, Δy, and Δz. The 3 × 1 submatrix to the upper-right in Figure 11-2 is required for the perspective. Perspective adds realism by making objects that are further from view seem smaller in size. This is shown in the cube example of Figure 11-6 where a single vanishing point is used to add

a.
$$\begin{bmatrix} S(x) & 0 & 0 & 0 \\ 0 & S(y) & 0 & 0 \\ 0 & 0 & S(z) & 0 \\ 0 & 0 & 0 & 1 \end{bmatrix}$$

C( ) is the cosine of the angle of rotation about the x axis.

S( ) is the sine of the angle.

b.
$$\begin{bmatrix} 1 & 0 & 0 & 0 \\ 0 & C(x) & S(x) & 0 \\ 0 & -S(x) & C(x) & 0 \\ 0 & 0 & 0 & 1 \end{bmatrix}$$

c.
$$\begin{bmatrix} C(y) & 0 & -S(y) & 0 \\ 0 & 1 & 0 & 0 \\ S(y) & 0 & C(y) & 0 \\ 0 & 0 & 0 & 1 \end{bmatrix}$$

d.
$$\begin{bmatrix} C(z) & S(z) & 0 & 0 \\ -S(z) & C(z) & 0 & 0 \\ 0 & 0 & 1 & 0 \\ 0 & 0 & 0 & 1 \end{bmatrix}$$

Figure 11-3.* *a. Matrix for scaling, b. Rotation around x axis, c. Rotation around y axis, and d. Rotation around z axis

$$[Vx,\ Vy,\ Vz,\ Vw] * \begin{bmatrix} M11 & M12 & M13 & M14 \\ M21 & M22 & M23 & M24 \\ M31 & M32 & M33 & M34 \\ M41 & M42 & M43 & M44 \end{bmatrix} = [Ux,\ Uy,\ Uz,\ Uw] =$$

$$\begin{bmatrix} (Vx*M11 + Vy*M21 + Vz*M31 + Vw*M41), \\ (Vx*M12 + Vy*M22 + Vz*M32 + Vw*M42), \\ (Vx*M13 + Vy*M23 + Vz*M33 + Vw*M43), \\ (Vx*M14 + Vy*M24 + Vz*M34 + Vw*M44) \end{bmatrix}$$

Figure 11-4.* *Multiplication of 1 × 4 vector with a 4 × 4 matrix

$$\begin{bmatrix} 1 & 0 & 0 & 0 \\ 0 & 1 & 0 & 0 \\ 0 & 0 & 1 & 0 \\ \Delta x & \Delta y & \Delta z & 1 \end{bmatrix}$$

Figure 11-5. Matrix for translation (T)

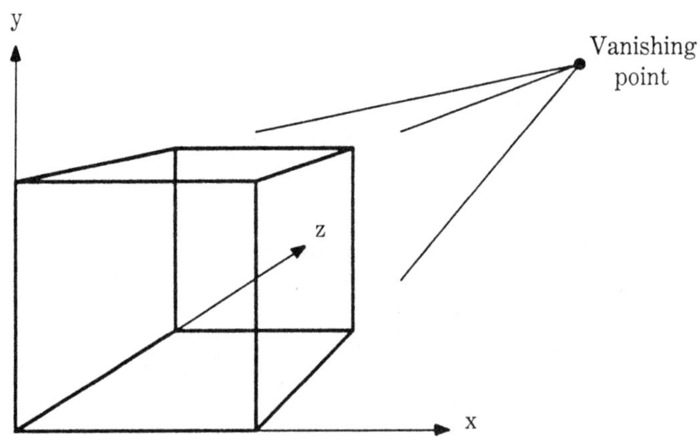

Figure 11-6. Adding perspective to the view of a cube

depth to the view. The 1 × 1 element of the lower-right corner in Figure 11-2 is used for zooming. Each of the five types of matrix operations can be performed separately. If multiple operations are required, the operations can be combined into a single matrix prior to the multiplication.

Transform Code Design

The following transform procedure performs the complete matrix multiplication. Some systems achieve high transformation rates by eliminating some of the matrix capabilities. For example, by eliminating perspective and zooming, the transformation matrix can be reduced to 3 × 3, with translation performed separately as simple additions. The procedure presented here, however, makes no simplifying eliminations.

Clearly, the graphics transformation consists of multiplications followed by additions. The dual-operation instructions of the i860 microprocessor are designed precisely to execute this type of calculation efficiently by using the pipelined adder and multiplier in parallel. For single-precision floating point, the adder and multiplier pipelines both have three stages. The dual-operation floating-point instructions employed for the transform are shown in Table 11-1.

Table 11-1. ***Dual-Operation Floating-Point Instructions Employed for the Transform***

Mnemonic	*Multiplier*	*Adder*	*Register Update*
m12apm	*fsrc1***fsrc2*	Mout+Aout	
m12tpm	*fsrc1***fsrc2*	T+Mout	
m12ttpa	*fsrc1***fsrc2*	T+Aout	T<-- Mout
i2pt	KI**fsrc2*	T+Mout	KI<-- *fsrc1*
i2apt	KI**fsrc2*	T+Aout	KI<-- *fsrc1*, T<-- Mout
i2apl	KI**fsrc2*	*fsrc1*+Aout	T<-- Mout

The row*column dot products are calculated to match the behavior of the floating-point instructions, not in the order you would choose for pencil and paper calculation. Instead of calculating all of row1*column1 (R1C1), followed by row1*column2 (R1C2), the code in Figure 11-7 interleaves R1C1 multiplies with R1C2 and R1C3. Thus, when the third stage of the adder ejects an R1C1 component, another R1C1 component is ready at the output of the multiplier to be immediately added by an instruction that feeds the adder output back into the adder input.

In examining the program in Figure 11-7, note that the adder is used by only 12 of the 16 cycles of `xformloop`, while the multiplier is busy for all 16 cycles. This idle time in the adder occurs because the dot-product operation requires only M−1 adds for M multiplies. The code uses dual-instruction mode, so that loop control and fetching of the vertices can be performed in parallel with the transformation calculations.

To achieve maximum throughput, the next input for the floating-point operation must be fetched before the current one has been completely processed. This is accomplished by alternating between two sets of input registers and by unrolling the loop (that is, by processing two inputs in each loop). The section of code entitled `ODD VERTEX` is identical to the section entitled `EVEN VERTEX` except for the input registers used.

The transform procedure can be called by a C program using the invocation:

```
xform(input_list, matrix, output_list, vertex_count);
```

The same procedure can be used to multiply two 4 × 4 matrices, by calling it as

```
xform(matrix_A, matrix_B, result_matrix, 4);
```

The result_matrix accomplishes the same transformation on a vertex as would multiplying the vertex by matrix_*A* and matrix_*B* in succession.

Transform Performance

At 40 Mhz, the peak transform rate is

$$\frac{\text{40 million clocks/sec}}{\text{16 clocks/xform}} = \text{2.5 million xforms/sec}$$

```
// i860(tm) CPU Code to multiply a list of 3D vertices in homogeneous coordinates
//   by a 4x4 matrix.  The code does (1x4)*(4x4) vector-times-matrix products.

// Parameters
    Vp=r16  // Pointer to single-precision input vertex list
    Mp=r17  // Pointer to single-precision xform matrix M
    Up=r18  // Pointer to single-precision output vertex list
    VN=r19  // Number of vertices (assumed >= 1)
// To call this procedure from C-code:
//     xform (input_list, matrix, output_list, vertex_count);

    XW=f2   // Temporary
// Tranformation matrix M.  Assumes that M is stored row-major, as in C.
    M11=f4;   M12=f5;   M13=f6;   M14=f7    // row 1
    M21=f8;   M22=f9;   M23=f10;  M24=f11   // row 2
    M31=f12;  M32=f13;  M33=f14;  M34=f15   // row 3
    M41=f16;  M42=f17;  M43=f18;  M44=f19   // row 4

// Input vertex V
//   Even    Odd    --  Ping-pong input registers
    Vx=f20; VX=f28  // x component of vertex
    Vy=f21; VY=f29  // y component of vertex
    Vz=f22; VZ=f30  // z component of vertex
    Vw=f23; VW=f31  // w component of vertex

// Transformed (output) vertex U
    Ux=f24; Uy=f25; Uz=f26; Uw=f27

// This procedure modifies all floating-point registers.  Save on the
// stack any floating point registers that the caller assumes preserved.

xform:: ; _xform::
  fld.q  0(Vp), Vx       // Load first even vertex
  fld.q  0(Mp), M11      // Load transformation matrix M, row 1
  fld.q 48(Mp), M41      // Load row 4

// For brevity in pipeline diagrams, let a symbol of the form "apq"
//  represent Va*Mpq.  For example, y21 represents Vy*M21.
```

Figure 11-7. Example transform procedure

```
//                     //        Multiplier        -- Adder ---
//                     //          Stages              Stages
//                     // KR KI *1   *2   *3   T   A1   A2   A3    Rslt  Instr#
d.i2pt.ss   Vy, f0,  f0 // -- y  --   --   --   --  --   --   --    --    (aa)
  fld.q 32(Mp), M31     // Load row 3
d.m12apm.ss Vx, M11, f0 // -- y  x11 --   --   --  --   --   --    --    (01)
  fld.q 16(Mp), M21     // Load row 2
d.m12apm.ss Vw, M41, f0 // -- y  w41 x11 --   --  --   --   --    --    (02)
  adds    -16, Up,  Up  // Compensate for autoincrement store
//                     // KR KI *1   *2   *3   T   A1   A2   A3    Rslt  Instr#
d.m12apm.ss Vx, M12, f0 // -- y  x12 w41 x11 --  --   --   --    --    (03)
  nop
d.m12ttpa.ss Vw,M42, f0 // -- y  w42 x12 w41 x11 --   --   --    --    (04)
  nop
d.m12tpm.ss Vy, M21, f0 // -- y  y21 w42 x12 --  x11+ --   --    --    (05)
  nop                   //                         w41
d.i2apl.ss  f0, M22, f0 // -- y  y22 y21 w42 x12 --   x11+ --    --    (06)
  nop                   //                              w41
d.m12tpm.ss Vx, M13, f0 // -- y  x13 y22 y21 --  x12+ --   x11+ --    (07)
  nop                   //                         w42       w41
d.m12apm.ss Vz, M31, f0 // -- y  z31 x13 y22 --  x11+ x12+ --    --    (08)
  nop                   //                         y21+ w42
                        //                         w41
d.m12ttpa.ss Vw,M43, f0 // -- y  w43 z31 x13 y22 --   x11+ x12+ --    (09)
  nop                   //                              y21+ w42
                        //                              w41
d.m12ttpa.ss Vz,M32, f0 // -- y  z32 w43 z31 x13 x12+ --   x11+ --    (10)
  adds -2, VN, VN       //                         y22+      y21+
  // -1 indicates done  //                         w42       w41
d.m12apm.ss Vx, M14, f0 // -- y  x14 z32 w43 x13 x11+ x12+ --    --    (11)
  fld.d  16(Vp)++, VX   //                         y21+ y22+
  // Next vertex (odd)  //                         z31+ w42
                        //                         w41
d.m12tpm.ss Vy, M23, f0 // -- y  y23 x14 z32 --  x13+ x11+ x12+ --    (12)
  nop                   //                         w43  y21+ y22+
                        //                              z31+ w42
                        //                              w41
d.m12apm.ss Vw, M44, f0 // -- y  w44 y23 x14 --  x12+ x13+ x11+ --    (13)
  bc end_even_xform     //                         y22+ w43  y21+
// Avoid using data     //                         z32+      z31+
// beyond end of list   //                         w42       w41

d.i2apt.ss  VY, M24, Ux // -- Y  y24 w44 y23 x14 --   x12+ x13+ x11+  (14)
  fld.d 8(Vp), VZ       //                              y22+ w43  y21+
  // Rest of vertex     //                              z32+      z31+
                        //                              w42       w41
```

Figure 11-7. Example transform procedure (continued)

```
d.m12apm.ss Vz, M33, f0 // -- Y  z33 y24 w44 x14 x13+ --   x12+ --   (15)
  nop                   //                       y23       y22+
                        //                       w43       z32+
                        //                                 w42
d.m12tpm.ss Vz, M34, Uy // -- Y  z34 z33 y24 --  x14+ x13+ --   x12+ (16)
  nop                   //                       w44  y23+      y22+
                        //                            w43       z32+
                        //                                      w42
```

```
xformloop:: //----------------ODD VERTEX------------------//
//                      // KR KI *1  *2  *3  T   A1   A2   A3   Rslt Instr#
d.m12ttpa.ss VX,M11, f0 // -- Y  X11 z34 z33 y24 --   x14+ x13+ --   (01)
  nop                   //                            w44  y23+
                        //                                 w43
d.m12apm.ss VW, M41, f0 // -- Y  W41 X11 z34 y24 x13+ --   x14+ --   (02)
  nop                   //                       y23+      w44
                        //                       z33+
                        //                       w43
d.m12tpm.ss VX, M12, XW // -- Y  X12 W41 X11 --  y24+ x13+ --   x14+ (03)
  nop                   //                       z34  y23+      w44
                        //                            z33+
                        //                            w43
d.m12ttpa.ss VW,M42, f0 // -- Y  W42 X12 W41 X11 --   y24+ x13+ --   (04)
  nop                   //                            z34  y23+
                        //                                 z33+
                        //                                 w43
d.m12tpm.ss VY, M21, Uz // -- Y  Y21 W42 X12 --  X11+ --   y24+ x13+ (05)
  nop                   //                       W41       z34  y23+
                        //                                      z33+
                        //                                      w43
d.i2apl.ss  XW, M22, f0 // -- Y  Y22 Y21 W42 X12 x14+ X11+ --   --   (06)
  nop                   //                       y24+ W41
                        //                       z34+
                        //                       w44
d.m12tpm.ss VX, M13, f0 // -- Y  X13 Y22 Y21 --  X12+ x14+ X11+ --   (07)
  nop                   //                       W42  y24+ W41
                        //                            z34+
                        //                            w44
d.m12apm.ss VZ, M31, f0 // -- Y  Z31 X13 Y22 --  X11+ X12+ x14+ --   (08)
  nop                   //                       Y21+ W42  y24+
```

Figure 11-7. Example transform procedure **(continued)**

```
                         //                      W41        z34+
                         //                                 w44
d.ml2ttpa.ss VW,M43, Uw // -- Y  W43 Z31 X13 Y22 --    X11+ X12+ x14+  (09)
  fst.q Ux, 16(Up)++     //                            Y21+ W42  y24+
// Store xformed vertex //                             W41       z34+
                         //                                      w44
d.ml2ttpa.ss VZ,M32, f0 // -- Y  Z32 W43 Z31 X13 X12+ --    X11+ --    (10)
  adds -1, VN, VN        //                      Y22+       Y21+
                         //                      W42        W41

d.ml2apm.ss VX, M14, f0 // -- Y  X14 Z32 W43 X13 X11+ X12+ --   --     (11)
  fld.d 16(Vp)++, Vx     //                      Y21+ Y22+
  // Next even vertex    //                      Z31+ W42
                         //                      W41
d.ml2tpm.ss VY, M23, f0 // -- Y  Y23 X14 Z32 --  X13+ X11+ X12+ --     (12)
  nop                    //                      W43  Y21+ Y22+
                         //                           Z31+ W42
                         //                           W41
//                       // KR KI *1  *2  *3  T  A1   A2   A3   Rslt  Instr#
d.ml2apm.ss VW, M44, f0 // -- Y  W44 Y23 X14 --  X12+ X13+ X11+ --     (13)
  bc end_odd_xform       //                      Y22+ W43  Y21+
// Avoid using data      //                      Z32+      Z31+
// beyond end of list    //                      W42       W41

d.i2apt.ss  Vy, M24, Ux // -- y  Y24 W44 Y23 X14 --   X12+ X13+ X11+  (14)
  fld.d 8(Vp), Vz        //                           Y22+ W43  Y21+
  // Rest of vertex      //                           Z32+      Z31+
                         //                           W42       W41
d.ml2apm.ss VZ, M33, f0 // -- y  Z33 Y24 W44 X14 X13+ --   X12+ --     (15)
  nop                    //                      Y23       Y22+
                         //                      W43       Z32+
                         //                                W42
d.ml2tpm.ss VZ, M34, Uy // -- y  Z34 Z33 Y24 --  X14+ X13+ --   X12+  (16)
  nop                    //                      W44  Y23+      Y22+
                         //                           W43       Z32+
                         //                                     W42
```

Figure 11-7. Example transform procedure (continued)

```
//----EVEN VERTEX-------// KR KI *1  *2  *3  T   A1   A2   A3   Rslt  Instr#
d.m12ttpa.ss Vx,M11, f0 // -- y  x11 Z34 Z33 Y24 --   X14+ X13+ --    (01)
  nop                   //                            W44  Y23+
                        //                                 W43
d.m12apm.ss Vw, M41, f0 // -- y  w41 x11 Z34 Y24 X13+ --   X14+ --    (02)
  nop                   //                       Y23+      W44
                        //                       Z33+
                        //                       W43
d.m12tpm.ss Vx, M12, XW // -- y  x12 w41 x11 --  Y24+ X13+ --   X14+  (03)
  nop                   //                       Z34  Y23+      W44
                        //                            Z33+
                        //                            W43
d.m12ttpa.ss Vw,M42, f0 // -- y  w42 x12 w41 x11 --   Y24+ X13+ --    (04)
  nop                   //                            Z34  Y23+
                        //                                 Z33+
                        //                                 W43
d.m12tpm.ss Vy, M21, Uz // -- y  y21 w42 x12 --  x11+ --   Y24+ X13+  (05)
  nop                   //                       w41       Z34  Y23+
                        //                                      Z33+
                        //                                      W43
d.i2apl.ss  XW, M22, f0 // -- y  y22 y21 w42 x12 X14+ x11+ --   --    (06)
  nop                   //                       Y24+ w41
                        //                       Z34+
                        //                       W44
d.m12tpm.ss Vx, M13, f0 // -- y  x13 y22 y21 --  x12+ X14+ x11+ --    (07)
  nop                   //                       w42  Y24+ w41
                        //                            Z34+
                        //                            W44
d.m12apm.ss Vz, M31, f0 // -- y  z31 x13 y22 --  x11+ x12+ X14+ --    (08)
  nop                   //                       y21+ w42  Y24+
                        //                       w41       Z34+
                        //                                 W44
//                      // KR KI *1  *2  *3  T   A1   A2   A3   Rslt  Instr#
d.m12ttpa.ss Vw,M43, Uw // -- y  w43 z31 x13 y22 --   x11+ x12+ X14+  (09)
  fst.q Ux, 16(Up)++    //                            y21+ w42  Y24+
// Store xformed vertex //                            w41       Z34+
                        //                                      W44
```

Figure 11-7. Example transform procedure (continued)

```
d.m12ttpa.ss Vz,M32, f0 // -- y  z32 w43 z31 x13 x12+ --   x11+ --    (10)
  adds -1, VN, VN       //                       y22+      y21+
                        //                       w42       w41
d.m12apm.ss Vx, M14, f0 // -- y  x14 z32 w43 x13 x11+ x12+ --   --    (11)
  fld.d 16(Vp)++, VX    //                       y21+ y22+
  // Next odd vertex    //                       z31+ w42
                        //                       w41
d.m12tpm.ss Vy, M23, f0 // -- y  y23 x14 z32 --  x13+ x11+ x12+ --    (12)
  nop                   //                       w43  y21+ y22+
                        //                            z31+ w42
                        //                            w41
d.m12apm.ss Vw, M44, f0 // -- y  w44 y23 x14 --  x12+ x13+ x11+ --    (13)
  bc end_even_xform     //                       y22+ w43  y21+
// Avoid using data     //                       z32+      z31+
// beyond end of list   //                       w42       w41

d.i2apt.ss  VY, M24, Ux // -- Y  y24 w44 y23 x14 --   x12+ x13+ x11+  (14)
  fld.d 8(Vp), VZ       //                            y22+ w43  y21+
  // Rest of vertex     //                            z32+      z31+
                        //                            w42       w41
d.m12apm.ss Vz, M33, f0 // -- Y  z33 y24 w44 x14 x13+ --   x12+ --    (15)
  br        xformloop   //                       y23       y22+
                        //                       w43       z32+
                        //                                 w42
d.m12tpm.ss Vz, M34, Uy // -- Y  z34 z33 y24 --  x14+ x13+ --   x12+  (16)
  nop                   //                       w44  y23+      y22+
                        //                            w43       z32+
end_even_xform::        //                                      w42
d.i2apt.ss  f0, M24, Ux // -- -- y24 w44 y23 x14 --   x12+ x13+ x11+  (14)
  nop                   //                            y22+ w43  y21+
                        //                            z32+      z31+
                        //                            w42       w41
d.m12apm.ss Vz, M33, f0 // -- -- z33 y24 w44 x14 x13+ --   x12+ --    (15)
  br end_xformloop      //                       y23       y22+
                        //                       w43       z32+
                        //                                 w42
d.m12tpm.ss Vz, M34, Uy // -- -- z34 z33 y24 --  x14+ x13+ --   x12+  (16)
```

Figure 11-7. Example transform procedure (continued)

```
  nop                   //                     w44  y23+      y22+
                        //                          w43       z32+
                        //                                    w42
end_odd_xform::
d.i2apt.ss  f0, M24, Ux // -- -- Y24 W44 Y23 X14 --   X12+ X13+ X11+  (14)
  fld.d 8(Vp), Vz       //                            Y22+ W43  Y21+
  // Rest of vertex     //                            Z32+      Z31+
                        //                            W42       W41
//                      // KR KI *1  *2  *3  T   A1   A2   A3   Rslt  Instr#
d.m12apm.ss VZ, M33, f0 // -- -- Z33 Y24 W44 X14 X13+ --   X12+ --    (15)
  nop                   //                       Y23       Y22+
                        //                       W43       Z32+
                        //                                 W42
d.m12tpm.ss VZ, M34, Uy // -- -- Z34 Z33 Y24 --  X14+ X13+ --   X12+  (16)
  nop                   //                       W44  Y23+      Y22+
                        //                            W43       Z32+
                        //                                      W42
end_xformloop::         // Begin exit from dual-instruction mode
m12ttpa.ss  f0,  f0, f0 // -- -- 0   z34 z33 y24 --   x14+ x13+ --    (01)
  nop                   //                            w44  y23+
                        //                                 w43
m12apm.ss   f0,  f0, f0 // -- -- 0   0   z34 y24 x13+ --   x14+ --    (02)
  nop                   //                       y23+      w44
                        //                       z33+
                        //                       w43
m12tpm.ss   f0,  f0, XW // -- -- 0   0   0   --  y24+ x13+ --   x14+  (03)
                        //                       z34  y23+      w44
                        //                            z33+
                        //                            w43
m12ttpa.ss  f0,  f0, f0 // -- -- 0   0   0   0   --   y24+ x13+ --    (04)
                        //                            z34  y23+
                        //                                 z33+
                        //                                 w43
m12tpm.ss   f0,  f0, Uz // -- -- 0   0   0   0   0    --   y24+ x13+  (05)
```

Figure 11-7. Example transform procedure (continued)

```
                          //                                      z34  y23+
                          //                                           z33+
                          //                                           w43
i2apl.ss     XW,   f0, f0 // -- -- 0   0   0   0   x14+ 0    --   --    (06)
                          //                       y24+
                          //                       z34+
                          //                       w44
ml2tpm.ss    f0,   f0, f0 // -- -- 0   0   0   0   0    x14+ 0    --    (07)
                          //                            y24+
                          //                            z34+
                          //                            w44
ml2apm.ss    f0,   f0, f0 // -- -- 0   0   0   0   0    0    x14+ --    (08)
                          //                                 y24+
                          //                                 z34+
                          //                                 w44
ml2ttpa.ss  f0,    f0, Uw // -- -- 0   0   0   0   0    0    0    x14+  (09)
                          //                                      y24+
                          //                                      z34+
                          //                                      w44
//bri r1                  // Do bri here, if this code is a subroutine
fst.q Ux, 16(Up)++        // Store last xformed vertex
```

Figure 11-7. Example transform procedure **(continued)**

The peak number of floating-point operations per second is

40 million clocks/sec * 28 flops/xform * 1 xform / 16 clocks = 70 MFlops

The latency period from the first floating-point operation to the first result is 27 cycles; thus, the procedure is much more efficient on a list of vertices than on a single one.

Furthermore, these figures are not indicative of total graphics performance, because the transform code is just one part of a graphics system. Transformation of vertex normals, lighting calculations, dividing out W, clipping, and rendering must also be considered. Transform performance will decrease somewhat from the peak values, due to data cache misses and TLB (Translation Look-a-Side Buffer) misses, as in any real algorithm.

Perspective Divide

Sooner or later, W must be divided out of the transformed vertices. This division is called *perspective divide* because W arose from multiplying the 3×1 perspective submatrix by the input vertex. The division serves to reduce the apparent size of objects (for example, X and Y values) that are farther from the viewer.

An algorithm for division is shown in Chapter 6, "Floating-Point Operations." The division code (*pdivide*) shown in Figure 11-8 expands on the basic algorithm by:

1. Performing three divisions (x,y, and z are each divided by W) with one reciprocal calculation (1/W).

2. Exploiting floating-point pipelining and dual-operation instructions.

Pdivide is coded as a stand-alone function operating on a vertex list. The overhead for function entry and exit, for loop setup, and for loading the vertices can be avoided by integrating the perspective divide with another procedure, such as transformation.

```
//  i860(tm) CPU code for PIPELINED DIVIDE FOR 3D GRAPHICS PERSPECTIVE       //
//-------------------------------------------------------------------------//
// Assumes lists of vertices using single-precision floating-point
//    homogeneous coordinates.
//  Calling invocation from C-code: pdivide(input_list,output_list, Length)

Vp  = r16; // Points to list of input vertices, in order x1,y1,z1,w1, x2,y2,...
Up  = r17; // Points to list of output vertices, in the same order
Len = r18; // Number of vertices (assumed >= 3, and a multiple of 3).
//-------------------------------------------------------------------------//
// For each input vertex (x, y, z, w), calculate (x/w, y/w, z/w, 1).
// Because pipelines have three stages, work on three vertices at a time.
//
//-------------------------------------------------------------------------//

G1    = f28; G2    = f29; G3    = f30        // Guesses at reciprocals
W1rcp = f19; W2rcp = f23; W3rcp = f27        // True reciprocals

// Registers to hold coordinates of three vertices:
X1 = f16; Y1 = f17; Z1 = f18; W1 = f19
X2 = f20; Y2 = f21; Z2 = f22; W2 = f23
X3 = f24; Y3 = f25; Z3 = f26; W3 = f27

temp = f31; Dcr  = r19       // Loop decrement
float1 = f8     // Single-precision 1.0
float2 = f9     // Single-precision 2.0
//-------------------------------------------------------------------------//
one:    .float 1.0              // One for normalized W
two:    .float 2.0              // Two for floating-point divide usage

pdivide::  ; _pdivide::
  fld.d one_two, float1
  mov   -3, Dcr                 // Set loop decrement
  addu  -16, Up, Up             // Compensate for autoincrement
  fld.q  0(Vp), X1
  addu  -1, Len, Len
  fld.q 16(Vp)++, X2
  bla  Dcr, Len, pdiv_loop      // Initialize LCC
   fld.q 16(Vp)++, X3
```

Figure 11-8. Example perspective divide

```
pdiv_loop::
// First calculate reciprocals for 3 vertices: 1/W1, 1/W2, 1/W3.
// Pipelined floating-point division with 15 bits of precision in result.
//  (Such precision is plenty, as 1/w used only for creating screen-image
//   coordinates, and screen has less than 2K pixels/dimension.)
// Newton-Raphson formula for divide:  Gnew = Guess*(2-(Guess*W))
  frcp.ss W1, G1                // Guess1  (approx. 1/w1)
  frcp.ss W2, G2                // Guess2  (1/w2)
  frcp.ss W3, G3                // Guess3

  pfmul.ss W1, G1, f0           // Guess1*W1
  pfmul.ss W2, G2, f0
  pfmul.ss W3, G3, f0
  i2s1.ss   float2, f0, f0      // 2-(Guess1*W1)
  i2s1.ss   float2, f0, f0      // 2-(Guess2*W2)
  i2s1.ss   float2, f0, f0      // 2-(Guess3*W3)

  m12apm.ss  G1, temp, temp     // Start calc of Guess*(2-Guess*W1)
  m12apm.ss  G2, temp, temp     // Guess*(2-Guess*W2)
  m12apm.ss  G3, temp, temp     // Guess*(2-Guess*W3)
//If 23-bit precision divide is required, insert the following 9 instructions:
// pfmul.ss  W1, G1, G1;     pfmul.ss  W2, G2, G2;     pfmul.ss W3, G3, G3
// i2s1.ss   float2, f0, f0; i2s1.ss   float2, f0, f0; i2s1.ss float2, f0, f0
// m12apm.ss G1, temp, temp; m12apm.ss G2, temp, temp; m12apm.ss G3, temp, temp

  pfmul.ss  Y1, W1rcp, W1rcp    // Start Y1/W1
  // W1rcp has 1/W1 (15 bits precision)
  pfmul.ss  X1, W1rcp, W2rcp    //       X1/W1
  pfmul.ss  Z1, W1rcp, W3rcp    //       Z1/W1

  pfmul.ss W2rcp, Y2, Y1        // Start Y2/W2
  pfmul.ss W2rcp, X2, X1        //       X2/W2
  pfmul.ss W2rcp, Z2, Z1        //       Z2/W2
  pfmul.ss W3rcp, Y3, Y2        // Start Y3/W3
  pfmul.ss W3rcp, X3, X2        //       X3/W3
  pfmul.ss W3rcp, Z3, Z2        //       Z3/W3
```

Figure 11-8. Example perspective divide (continued)

```
// NOTE: The following 3 multiplies could begin a scaling operation,
// in which case src1 and src2, instead of being f0, would multiply
// a scale factor for screen size by Y1, Y2, and Y3
  pfmul.ss f0, f0, Y3
  pfmul.ss f0, f0, X3
    .align .double
d.pfmul.ss f0, f0, Z3           // Initiate dual-instruction mode
d.fmov.ss  float1, W1
  fmov.ss  float1, W2   ;   fst.q X1, 16(Up)++  // New W value is 1.0
  fmov.ss  float1, W3   ;   fst.q X2, 16(Up)++  // Last dual-mode pair
  fst.q X3, 16(Up)++

  fld.q 16(Vp)++, X1
  fld.q 16(Vp)++, X2
  bla Dcr, Len, pdiv_loop
   fld.q 16(Vp)++, X3
  bri r1
   nop
//--------------- THE END ----------------//
```

Figure 11-8. Example perspective divide **(continued)**

The transform function shown in this chapter is but one of the steps in a graphics application. Following the transform, the graphics system must expand the database of vertices into a display of all of the required pixels. The 3-D rendering instructions detailed in Chapter 7, "Graphics Rendering Instructions," are used for this final step by performing hidden surface elimination, distance interpolation, and shading. Both the pipelined floating-point hardware and the integer graphics pipeline are essential to speed the calculations required for 3-D graphics.

APPENDIX A
INSTRUCTION SET SUMMARY

Key to Abbreviations

isrc1	The first operand of an instruction can be an integer register, or a 16-bit immediate constant or address offset. The immediate value is sign extended for arithmetic instructions and is zero extended for logical instructions. The integer register is encoded as bits 15:11 of the instruction and the 16-bit immediate is encoded as bits 15:0 of the instruction.
isrc2	An integer register. Encoded as bits 25:21 of the instruction. Used as the second operand of integer instructions.
#constA	A 16-bit immediate constant sign extended to 32 bits. Encoded as bits 15:0 of the instruction. Used as the first operand in arithmetic instructions and address calculation.
#constL	A 16-bit immediate constant zero extended to 32 bits. Encoded as bits 15:0 of the instruction. Used as the first operand in logical instructions.
#sconst	A "short" 5-bit immediate constant zero extended to 32 bits. Encoded as bits 15:11 of the instruction. Used as the first operand in compare and branch instructions.
ctrlreg	A control register. One of **psr**, **epsr**, **db**, **dirbase**, **fir**, or **fsr**. Encoded as bits 25:21 of the instruction. Used for **ld.c** and **st.c** only.
fdest	A floating-point register. Encoded as bits 20:16 of the instruction. Used as the destination of floating-point instructions.

freg	A floating-point register. Encoded as bits 20:16 of the instruction. Used as the source operand for floating-point store and pixel store instructions.
fsrc1	A floating-point register. Encoded as bits 15:11 of the instruction. Used as the first operand of floating-point instructions.
fsrc2	A floating-point register. Encoded as bits 25:21 of the instruction. Used as the second operand of floating-point instructions.
idest	An integer register. Encoded as bits 20:16 of the instruction. Used as the destination of integer instructions.
lbroff	A 26-bit, signed, relative branch offset.
mem.*x*[addr]	The data is loaded or stored from/to memory. The address used is **addr** and the size of the load or store is given by *x*. Bits 25 = 0 of the instruction.
PM[i], *fsrc1(i)*, *fsrc2(i)*, *fdest(i)*	Graphics instructions operate on 64 bits of pixels or Z-buffer values at once. The pixel mask, destination, and source operands can be considered as arrays of two, four, or eight elements, depending on the size of the elements. For instance, these arrays have two elements for the 32-bit Z-buffer check instruction **fzchkl**.
sbroff	A 16-bit, signed, relative branch offset encoded as bits 20:16 and 10:0 of the instruction.
target	The address target of a control transfer instruction. The value of *target* is computed by left shifting the offset (either *lbroff* or *sbroff*) two bits, sign extending it to 32 bits, and adding the result to the address of the control-transfer instruction plus four. If this sum exceeds $2^{32} - 4$, the result is undefined.

Key to Size Specifications

`.p`	Precision specification **.ss**, **.sd**, or **.dd** (**.ds** not permitted). Refer to Table 6-2
`.r`	Precision specification **.ss**, **.sd**, **.ds**, or **.dd**. Refer to Table 6-2
`.v`	Precision specification **.sd** or **.dd** (64-bit results)
`.w`	Precision specification **.ss** (32 bits) or **.dd** (64 bits)
`.x`	Size specification **.b** (8 bits), **.s** (16 bits), or **.l** (32 bits)
`.y`	Size specification **.l** (32 bits), **.d** (64 bits), or **.q** (128 bits)
`.z`	Size specification **.l** (32 bits) or **.d** (64 bits)

Key to Symbols

← Receives the results of
6= = if equal, then expression is true
// indicates a comment

Adds — Add Signed Integers — Adds

Operation: *idest* ← *isrc1* + *isrc2*

Syntax:
adds *isrc1, isrc2, idest*
adds *#constA, isrc2, idest*

Description: Add the two source operands using signed binary addition and store the result in the destination register.

CC:	CC ← (*isrc1* + *isrc2*) < 0
OF:	OF ← (bit 31 carry ≠ bit 30 carry)
FSR:	not affected

Instruction Encoding:

```
31 30 29 28 27 26 25 24 23 22 21 20 19 18 17 16 15 14 13 12 11 10  9  8  7  6  5  4  3  2  1  0
1  0  0  1  0  0  --src2---  --dest---  --src1---  0 0 0 0 0 0 0 0 0 0 0
1  0  0  1  0  1  --src2---  --dest---  -------16-bit Immediate--------
```

Instruction Fields:

src1, src2	Specifies any of the integer registers
dest	Specifies any of the integer registers
Immediate	A 16-bit constant, sign extended to 32 bits

Programming Notes:

A one clock freeze occurs on a **bc, bnc, bc.t,** or a **bnc.t** following the **adds** instruction.

Used with **r0** as the destination, the **adds** instruction can be used for doing signed comparison.

Exceptions: None

Addu — Add Unsigned Integers — Addu

Operation: *idest* ← *isrc1* + *isrc2*

Syntax: **addu** *isrc1, isrc2, idest*
addu *#constA, isrc2, idest*

Description: Add the two source operands using unsigned binary addition and store the result in the destination register.

CC: CC ← (bit 31 carry)
OF: OF ← (bit 31 carry)
FSR: not affected

Instruction Encoding:

```
31 30 29 28 27 26 25 24 23 22 21 20 19 18 17 16 15 14 13 12 11 10  9  8  7  6  5  4  3  2  1  0
1 0 0 0 0 0 --src2--- --dest--- --src1--- 0 0 0 0 0 0 0 0 0 0 0
1 0 0 0 0 1 --src2--- --dest--- -------16-bit Immediate--------
```

Instruction Fields:

src1, src2	Specifies any of the integer registers
dest	Specifies any of the integer registers
Immediate	A 16-bit constant, sign extended to 32 bits

Programming Notes:

A one clock freeze occurs on a **bc**, **bnc**, **bc.t**, or a **bnc.t** following the **addu** instruction.

Used with **r0** as the destination, the **addu** instruction can be used for doing unsigned comparison.

Exceptions: None

And — Logical And — And

Operation: *idest* ← *isrc1* AND *isrc2*

Syntax:

```
and isrc1, isrc2, idest
and #constL, isrc2, idest
```

Description: Perform bitwise AND on the two source operands and store the result in the destination register.

CC:	CC ← (result == 0)
OF:	not affected
FSR:	not affected

Instruction Encoding:

```
31 30 29 28 27 26 25 24 23 22 21 20 19 18 17 16 15 14 13 12 11 10  9  8  7  6  5  4  3  2  1  0
1 1 0 0 0 0 --src2--- --dest--- --src1--- 0 0 0 0 0 0 0 0 0 0 0
1 1 0 0 0 1 --src2--- --dest--- -------16-bit Immediate--------
```

Instruction Fields:

src1, src2	Specifies any of the integer registers
dest	Specifies any of the integer registers
Immediate	A 16-bit constant, zero extended to 32 bits

Programming Notes:

Exceptions: None

Andh Logical And High Andh

Operation: *idest* ← (*#constL* left shifted 16 bits) AND *isrc2*

Syntax: **andh** *#constL, isrc2, idest*

Description: Perform bitwise AND on the two source operands and store the result in the destination register. The first source operand is created by using the 16-bit constant as the high 16 bits of the operand and filling the low 16 bits with zeros.

CC:	CC ← (result == 0)
OF:	not affected
FSR:	not affected

Instruction Encoding:

```
31 30 29 28 27 26 25 24 23 22 21 20 19 18 17 16 15 14 13 12 11 10  9  8  7  6  5  4  3  2  1  0
1  1  0  0  1  1 --src2--- --dest--- -------16-bit Immediate--------
```

Instruction Fields:

src2	Specifies any of the integer registers
dest	Specifies any of the integer registers
Immediate	A 16-bit constant, left shifted 16 bits, filled with zeros on the right

Programming Notes:

Exceptions: None

Andnot — Logical And Not — Andnot

Operation: *idest* ← (NOT *src1*) AND *isrc2*

Syntax:

andnot *isrc1, isrc2, idest*
andnot *#constL, isrc2, idest*

Description: Invert the first source operand and then perform bit-wise AND on the two operands, storing the result in the destination register.

CC:	CC ← (result = = 0)
OF:	not affected
FSR:	not affected

Instruction Encoding:

```
31 30 29 28 27 26 25 24 23 22 21 20 19 18 17 16 15 14 13 12 11 10  9  8  7  6  5  4  3  2  1  0
1  1  0  1  0  0  --src2---  --dest---  --src1---  0  0  0  0  0  0  0  0  0  0  0
1  1  0  1  0  1  --src2---  --dest---  -------16-bit Immediate--------
```

Instruction Fields:

src1, src2	Specifies any of the integer registers
dest	Specifies any of the integer registers
Immediate	A 16-bit constant, zero extended to 32 bits

Programming Notes:

Exceptions: None

Andnoth Logical And Not High Andnoth

Operation: *idest* ← NOT(*#constL* left shifted 16 bits) AND *isrc2*

Syntax: **andnoth** *#constL, isrc2, idest*

Description: Invert the first source operand and then perform bitwise AND on the two operands storing the result in the destination register. The first source operand is created by using the 16-bit constant as the high 16 bits of the operand and filling the low 16 bits with zeros.

CC:	CC ← (result = = 0)
OF:	not affected
FSR:	not affected

Instruction Encoding:

```
31 30 29 28 27 26 25 24 23 22 21 20 19 18 17 16 15 14 13 12 11 10  9  8  7  6  5  4  3  2  1  0
1  1  0  1  1  1 --src2--- --dest--- -------16-bit Immediate--------
```

Instruction Fields:

src2	Specifies any of the integer registers
dest	Specifies any of the integer registers
Immediate	A 16-bit constant, left shifted 16 bits, filled with zeros on the right

Programming Notes:

Exceptions: None

Bc — Branch on CC — Bc

Operation:

```
IF ( CC == 1 )
THEN
   Continue execution at target.
ELSE
   Continue execution at next sequential instruction.
FI
```

Syntax: **bc** *lbroff*

Description: If the CC bit is set, then branch to the given target address. The target address is computed from the relative branch offset. **Bc** is not a delayed branch; use **bc.t** for delayed branches.

CC:	not affected
OF:	not affected
FSR:	not affected

Instruction Encoding:

```
31 30 29 28 27 26 25 24 23 22 21 20 19 18 17 16 15 14 13 12 11 10 9 8 7 6 5 4 3 2 1 0
0  1  1  1  0  0  -------26-bit signed relative branch offset--------
```

Instruction Fields:

Relative offset is a signed number of instructions.

Programming Notes:

A one clock freeze occurs on a **bc** that is taken.

Another one clock freeze occurs on a **bc** that immediately follows an **adds, addu, pfeq, pfgt, pfle, subs,** or a **subu** instruction.

Branching beyond the 32-bit addressing range of the i860 microprocessor has undefined results.

Exceptions: None

Bc.t Branch on CC, Taken Bc.t

Operation:

```
IF ( CC == 1 )
THEN
    Execute one more instruction.
    Continue execution at target.
ELSE
    Skip the next sequential instruction.
FI
```

Syntax: **bc.t** *lbroff*

Description: If the CC bit is set, then branch to the target address after executing one more instruction. The target address is computed from the relative branch offset. If the branch is not taken, the next sequential instruction is skipped.

CC:	not affected
OF:	not affected
FSR:	not affected

Instruction Encoding:

```
31 30 29 28 27 26 25 24 23 22 21 20 19 18 17 16 15 14 13 12 11 10  9  8  7  6  5  4  3  2  1  0
0  1  1  1  0  1  -------26-bit signed relative branch offset--------
```

Instruction Fields:

Relative offset is a signed number of instructions.

Programming Notes:

The sequential instruction following **bc.t** must not be a branch, **call**, **calli**, **intovr**, or **trap** instruction, or the target of a branch, **call**, or **calli** instruction.

A one clock freeze occurs on a **bc.t** that is not taken.

Another one clock freeze occurs on a **bc.t** that immediately follows an **adds, addu, pfeq, pfgt, pfle, subs,** or a **subu** instruction.

Branching beyond the 32-bit addressing range of the i860 microprocessor has undefined results.

Exceptions: None

Bla Branch on LCC and ADD Bla

Operation:

LCC_Temp ← (*isrc1* + *isrc2* ≥ 0)
isrc2 ← *isrc1* + *isrc2*
Execute one more sequential instruction.
IF (LCC = = 1)
THEN
  LCC ← LCC_Temp.
  Continue execution at *target*.
ELSE
  LCC ← LCC_Temp.
  Continue execution at the second sequential instruction.
FI

Syntax: **bla** *isrc1, isrc2, sbroff*

Description: If LCC is set, then branch to the target address after executing one more instruction and add the two source operands, storing the result in the second operand register. LCC is subsequently set if the addition results in a nonnegative result. The target address is computed from the relative branch offset. If the branch is not taken, the next sequential instruction is still executed.

CC: not affected
OF: not affected
FSR: not affected

Instruction Encoding:

```
31 30 29 28 27 26 25 24 23 22 21 20 19 18 17 16 15 14 13 12 11 10 9 8 7 6 5 4 3 2 1 0
1  0  1  1  0  1  --src2--- -Offhigh- --src1--- -----Offset Low------
```

Instruction Fields:

src1, src2	Specifies any of the integer registers
Offhigh	The high five bits of the offset *sbroff*
Offset low	The low eleven bits of the offset *sbroff*

Programming Notes:

The sequential instruction following **bla** must not be a branch, **call**, **calli**, **intovr**, or **trap** instruction, or the target of a branch, **call**, or **calli** instruction.

isrc1 must not be the same register as *isrc2*.

A one clock freeze occurs on a **bla** that is not taken.

Branching beyond the 32-bit addressing range of the i860 microprocessor has undefined results.

Programs should avoid calling subroutines while within a **bla** loop, because a subroutine may also use **bla** and change LCC.

Exceptions: If an exception occurs on the **bla** instruction or the next instruction, LCC is not updated. The trap handler must resume execution with the **bla** instruction so the LCC setting is not lost.

Bnc Branch on not CC Bnc

Operation:

```
IF ( CC == 0 )
THEN
    Continue execution at target.
ELSE
    Continue execution at next sequential instruction.
FI
```

Syntax: **bnc** *lbroff*

Description: If the CC bit is not set, then branch to the given target address. The target address is computed from the relative branch offset. Use **bnc.t** for delayed branches.

CC:	not affected
OF:	not affected
FSR:	not affected

Instruction Encoding:

```
31 30 29 28 27 26 25 24 23 22 21 20 19 18 17 16 15 14 13 12 11 10 9 8 7 6 5 4 3 2 1 0
0  1  1  1  1  0  -------26-bit signed relative branch offset--------
```

Instruction Fields:

Relative offset is a signed number of instructions.

Programming Notes:

A one clock freeze occurs on a **bnc** that is taken.

A one clock freeze occurs on a **bnc** that immediately follows an **adds, addu, pfeq, pfgt, pfle, subs,** or a **subu** instruction.

Branching beyond the 32-bit addressing range of the i860 microprocessor has undefined results.

Exceptions: None

Bnc.t — Branch on not CC, Taken — Bnc.t

Operation:

```
IF ( CC == 0 )
THEN
    Execute one more instruction.
    Continue execution at target.
ELSE
    Skip the next sequential instruction.
FI
```

Syntax: **bnc.t** *lbroff*

Description: If the CC bit is not set, then branch to the target address after executing one more instruction. The target address is computed from the relative branch offset. If the branch is not taken, the next sequential instruction is skipped.

CC:	not affected
OF:	not affected
FSR:	not affected

Instruction Encoding:

```
31 30 29 28 27 26 25 24 23 22 21 20 19 18 17 16 15 14 13 12 11 10 9 8 7 6 5 4 3 2 1 0
0  1  1  1  1  1  -------26-bit signed relative branch offset--------
```

Instruction Fields:

Relative offset is a signed number of instructions.

Programming Notes:

The sequential instruction following **bnc.t** must not be a branch, **call**, **calli**, **intovr**, or **trap** instruction, or the target of a branch, **call**, or **calli**, instruction.

A one clock freeze occurs on a **bnc.t** that is not taken.

A one clock freeze occurs on a **bnc.t** that immediately follows an **adds, addu, pfeq, pfgt, pfle, subs,** or a **subu** instruction.

Branching beyond the 32-bit addressing range of the i860 microprocessor has undefined results.

Exceptions: None

Br Branch Direct Unconditionally Br

Operation:

Execute one more sequential instruction.
Continue execution at *target*.

Syntax: **br** *lbroff*

Description: Branch to the target address after executing one more instruction. The target address is computed from the relative branch offset.

CC:	not affected
OF:	not affected
FSR:	not affected

Instruction Encoding:

```
31 30 29 28 27 26 25 24 23 22 21 20 19 18 17 16 15 14 13 12 11 10 9 8 7 6 5 4 3 2 1 0
0  1  1  0  1  0  -------26-bit signed relative branch offset--------
```

Instruction Fields:

Relative offset is a signed number of instructions.

Programming Notes:

The sequential instruction following **br** must not be a branch, **call**, **calli**, **intovr**, or **trap** instruction, or the target of a branch, **call**, or **calli** instruction.

Branching beyond the 32-bit addressing range of the i860 microprocessor has undefined results.

Exceptions: None

Bri Branch Indirect Unconditionally Bri

Operation:

```
Execute one more sequential instruction.
IF( no trap bits in psr are set )
THEN
   Continue execution at the address in isrc1.
ELSE
   Copy PU to U in psr.
   Copy PIM to IM in psr.
   Clear trap bits.
   IF( DS == 0 AND DIM == 0 )
   THEN
     Enter single-instruction mode for next two instructions.
   ELSE IF( DS == 0 AND DIM == 1 )
         THEN
           Enter dual-instruction mode for next two instructions.
         ELSE IF( DS == 1 AND DIM == 0 )
               THEN
                 Enter dual-instruction mode after executing one
                   instruction in single-instruction mode.
               ELSE // ( DS == 1 AND DIM == 1 )
                 Enter single-instruction mode after executing
                   one instruction in dual-instruction mode.
               FI
                 Continue execution at the address in isrc1.
FI
```

Syntax: **bri** *isrc1*

Description: Branch to the address in the source operand after executing one more instruction. This instruction is used to implement a return from a subroutine or a return from a trap.

CC:	not affected
OF:	not affected
FSR:	not affected

Instruction Encoding:

```
31 30 29 28 27 26 25 24 23 22 21 20 19 18 17 16 15 14 13 12 11 10 9 8 7 6 5 4 3 2 1 0
0  1  0  0  0  0  0  0  0  0  0  0  0  0  0  0  --src1---     0  0 0 0 0 0 0 0 0 0 0
```

Instruction Fields:

src1 Specifies any of the integer registers

Programming Notes:

The sequential instruction following **bri** must not be a branch, **call**, **calli**, **intovr**, or **trap** instruction, or the target of a branch, **call**, or **calli** instruction.

When using a **bri** to return from a trap handler, programmers should take care to prevent traps from occurring on that or on the next sequential instruction. IM in the **psr** should be zero (interrupts disabled) when **bri** is executed to return from the trap handler.

bri takes two clocks to execute.

Return from subroutine is implemented by branching to the return address with the **bri** instruction.

Exceptions: None

Bte Branch and Test Equal Bte

Operation:

IF(*isrc1* == *isrc2*)
THEN
  Continue execution at *target*.
ELSE
  Continue execution at next sequential instruction.
FI

Syntax: **bte** *isrc1, isrc2, sbroff*
bte *#sconst, isrc2, sbroff*

Description: If the two source operands are equal, then branch to the target address. The target address is computed from the relative branch offset.

CC: not affected
OF: not affected
FSR: not affected

Instruction Encoding:

```
31 30 29 28 27 26 25 24 23 22 21 20 19 18 17 16 15 14 13 12 11 10 9 8 7 6 5 4 3 2 1 0
0  1  0  1  1  0  --src2--- -Offhigh- --src1--- -----Offset low------
0  1  0  1  1  1  --src2--- -Offhigh- -sconst-- -----Offset low------
```

Instruction Fields:

src1, src2	Specifies any of the integer registers
Offhigh	The high five bits of the offset *sbroff*
Offset low	The low eleven bits of the offset *sbroff*
sconst	A five-bit immediate constant, zero extended to 32 bits

Programming Notes:

A two clock freeze occurs on a **bte** that is taken.

Branching beyond the 32-bit addressing range of the i860 microprocessor has undefined results.

Exceptions: None

Btne Branch and Test Not Equal Btne

Operation:

IF(*isrc1* ≠ *isrc2*)
THEN
  Continue execution at *target*.
ELSE
  Continue execution at next sequential instruction.
FI

Syntax: **btne** *isrc1, isrc2, sbroff*
btne *#sconst, isrc2, sbroff*

Description: If the two source operands are not equal, then branch to the target address. The target address is computed from the relative branch offset.

CC:	not affected
OF:	not affected
FSR:	not affected

Instruction Encoding:

```
31 30 29 28 27 26 25 24 23 22 21 20 19 18 17 16 15 14 13 12 11 10 9 8 7 6 5 4 3 2 1 0
0 1 0 1 0 0 --src2--- -Offhigh- --src1--- -----Offset low------
0 1 0 1 0 1 --src2--- -Offhigh- -sconst-- -----Offset low------
```

Instruction Fields:

src1, src2	Specifies any of the integer registers
Offhigh	The high five bits of the offset *sbroff*
Offset low	The low eleven bits of the offset *sbroff*
sconst	A five-bit immediate constant, zero extended to 32 bits

Programming Notes:

A two clock freeze occurs on a **btne** that is taken.

Branching beyond the 32-bit addressing range of the i860 microprocessor has undefined results.

Exceptions: None

Call — Subroutine Call — Call

Operation:

r1 ← address of the next sequential instruction plus four.
Execute the next sequential instruction.
Continue execution at *target*.

Syntax: `call lbroff`

Description: Branch to the target address after executing one more instruction and save the return address in **r1**. The target address is computed from the relative branch offset.

CC: not affected
OF: not affected
FSR: not affected

Instruction Encoding:

```
31 30 29 28 27 26 25 24 23 22 21 20 19 18 17 16 15 14 13 12 11 10  9  8  7  6  5  4  3  2  1  0
0  1  1  0  1  1 -------26-bit signed relative branch offset--------
```

Instruction Fields:

o

Relative offset is a signed number of instructions.

Programming Notes:

The sequential instruction following **call** must not be a branch, **call**, **calli**, **intovr**, or **trap** instruction, or the target of a branch, **call**, or **calli** instruction.

A one clock freeze occurs if **r1** is a source operand of the next instruction.

Branching beyond the 32-bit addressing range of the i860 microprocessor has undefined results.

Exceptions: None

Calli Indirect Subroutine Call Calli

Operation:

r1 ← address of the next sequential instruction plus four.
Execute the next sequential instruction.
Continue execution at address in *isrc1*.

Syntax: `calli` *isrc1*

Description: Branch to the address in the source operand after executing one more instruction and save the return address in **r1**.

CC: not affected
OF: not affected
FSR: not affected

Instruction Encoding:

```
31 30 29 28 27 26 25 24 23 22 21 20 19 18 17 16 15 14 13 12 11 10 9 8 7 6 5 4 3 2 1 0
0  1  0  0  1  1  0  0  0  0  0  0  0  0  0  0  --src1---     0  0 0 0 0 0 0 0 0 0 1 0
```

Instruction Fields:

src1 Specifies any of the integer registers

Programming Notes:

The sequential instruction following **calli** must not be a branch, **call**, **calli**, **intovr**, or **trap** instruction, or the target of a branch, **call**, or **calli** instruction.

calli takes two clocks to execute.

A one clock freeze occurs if **r1** is a source operand of the next instruction.

Exceptions: None

Fadd.p Floating-Point Add Fadd.p

Operation: *fdest* ← *fsrc1* + *fsrc2*

Syntax: **fadd.p** *fsrc1, fsrc2, fdest*
(**.p** = **.ss**, **.sd**, **.dd**)

Description: Add the two source operands using signed floating-point addition and store the result in the destination register.

CC:	not affected
OF:	not affected
FSR:	AA, AE, AI, AO, AU, RR, SI, SE

Instruction Encoding:

```
31 30 29 28 27 26 25 24 23 22 21 20 19 18 17 16 15 14 13 12 11 10  9  8  7  6  5  4  3  2  1  0
0  1  0  0  1  0  --src2---      --dest---      --src1---      0  D  S  R  0  1  1  0  0  0  0
```

Instruction Fields:

D	Dual-Instruction mode bit
	0 -Single-instruction mode
	1 -Dual-instruction mode
S,R	Source and Result precision
	00 - single, single (**.ss**)
	01 - single, double (**.sd**)
	10 - reserved
	11 - double, double (**.dd**)
src1, src2	Specifies any of the floating-point registers
dest	Specifies any of the floating-point registers

Programming Notes:

Exceptions:

Floating-Point Source
Floating-Point Result

Faddp — Add with Pixel Merge — Faddp

Operation:

fdest ← *fsrc1* + *fsrc2*
Shift and load the MERGE register as defined in Table 7-3.

Syntax: **faddp** *fsrc1, fsrc2, fdest*

Description: Add the two source operands using signed fixed-point addition and storing the result in the destination register. The two sources are expected to contain eight 8-bit, four 16-bit, or two 32-bit pixels, depending on the contents of the PS field of the **epsr**. The MERGE register is shifted and loaded as defined in Table 7-3. This instruction is used for color intensity interpolation.

CC:	not affected
OF:	not affected
FSR:	not affected

Instruction Encoding:

```
31 30 29 28 27 26 25 24 23 22 21 20 19 18 17 16 15 14 13 12 11 10  9  8  7  6  5  4  3  2  1  0
 0  1  0  0  1  0 --src2---   --dest---      --src1---       0  D  1  1  1  0  1  0  0  0  0
```

Instruction Fields:

D	Dual-Instruction mode bit 0 - Single-instruction mode 1 - Dual-instruction mode
src1, src2	Specifies any even (64-bit) floating-point registers
dest	Specifies any even (64-bit) floating-point register

Programming Notes:

A one clock freeze occurs if *fdest* is a source operand of the next instruction.

fsrc1, fsrc2, fdest must be even-numbered floating-point registers.

Exceptions: None

Faddz Add with Z Merge Faddz

Operation:

fdest ← *fsrc1* + *fsrc2*
Shift the MERGE register right 16 bits and load MERGE register bits 63:48 and 31:16 with bits 63:48 and 31:16 of (*fsrc1* + *fsrc2*).

Syntax: **faddz** *fsrc1, fsrc2, fdest*

Description: Add the two source operands using signed, 32-bit, fixed-point addition, storing the result in the destination register. The sources are expected to contain two 32-bit, Z-buffer distance values. The 32-bit Z-buffer values consist of a 16-bit integer and a 16-bit fraction. The 16-bit integer parts of the two 32-bit **adds** are stored in the MERGE register. The MERGE register is shifted right 16 bits before being loaded with the results of the two **adds**. Normally, two **faddz** instructions are executed consecutively resulting in four Z-buffer adds.

CC:	not affected
OF:	not affected
FSR:	not affected

Instruction Encoding:

```
31 30 29 28 27 26 25 24 23 22 21 20 19 18 17 16 15 14 13 12 11 10 9 8 7 6 5 4 3 2 1 0
0  1  0  0  1  0  --src2---     --dest---      --src1---      0  D 1 1 1 0 1 0 0 0 1
```

Instruction Fields:

D	Dual-Instruction mode bit 0 - Single-instruction mode 1 - Dual-instruction mode
src1, src2	Specifies any even (64-bit) floating-point register
dest	Specifies any even (64-bit) floating-point register

Programming Notes:

A one clock freeze occurs if *fdest* is a source operand of the next instruction.

fsrc1, fsrc2, fdest, must be even-numbered floating-point registers.

faddz is intended for use with 16-bit Z-buffers.

Exceptions: None

Famov.r — Floating-Point Adder Move — Famov.r

Operation: *fdest* ← *fsrc1*

Syntax: **famov.r** *fsrc1, fdest*
(**.r** = **.ss**, **.sd**, **.ds**, **.dd**)

Description: Move the floating-point source operand through the floating-point adder, preserving negative zero (−0) and store the value in the destination register.

CC: not affected
OF: not affected
FSR: AI, AO, AU, RE, AA, RR, SI, SE

Instruction Encoding:

31	30	29	28	27	26	25	24	23	22	21	20–16	15–11	10	9	8	7	6	5	4	3	2	1	0
0	1	0	0	1	0	0	0	0	0	0	--dest---	--src1---	0	D	S	R	0	1	1	0	0	1	1

Instruction Fields:

D — Dual-Instruction mode bit
- 0 - Single-instruction mode
- 1 - Dual-instruction mode

S, R — Source and Result precision
- 00 - single, single (**.ss**)
- 01 - single, double (**.sd**)
- 10 - double, single (**.ds**)
- 11 - double, double (**.dd**)

src1 — Specifies any of the floating-point registers
dest — Specifies any of the floating-point registers

Programming Notes:

famov should be used to convert a number from double-precision to single-precision.

Exceptions:

Floating-Point Source
Floating-Point Result

Fiadd.w — Long-Integer Add — Fiadd.w

Operation: *fdest* ← *fsrc1* + *fsrc2*

Syntax: **fiadd.w** *fsrc1, fsrc2, fdest*
(**.w** = **.ss**, **.dd**)

Description: Add the two source operands using signed 32- or 64-bit integer addition and store the result in the destination register.

CC: not affected
OF: not affected
FSR: not affected

Instruction Encoding:

31	30	29	28	27	26	25–21	20–16	15–11	10	9	8	7	6	5	4	3	2	1	0
0	1	0	0	1	0	--src2---	--dest---	--src1---	0	D	S	R	1	0	0	1	0	0	1

Instruction Fields:

D — Dual-instruction mode bit
- 0 - Single-instruction mode
- 1 - Dual-instruction mode

S, R — Source and Result precision
- 00 - 32 bits (**.ss**)
- 01 - reserved
- 10 - reserved
- 11 - 64 bits (**.dd**)

src1, src2 — Specifies any of the floating-point registers
dest — Specifies any of the floating-point registers

Programming Notes:

A one clock freeze occurs if *fdest* is a source operand of the next instruction, and the next instruction is a floating-point or graphics unit instruction.

Exceptions: None

Fisub.w Long-Integer Subtract Fisub.w

Operation: *fdest* ← *fsrc1* − *fsrc2*

Syntax: **fisub.w** *fsrc1, fsrc2, fdest*
(**.w** = **.ss**, **.dd**)

Description: Subtract the second source operand from the first source operand using signed 32- or 64-bit integer subtraction and store the result in the destination register.

CC: not affected
OF: not affected
FSR: not affected

Instruction Encoding:

```
31 30 29 28 27 26 25 24 23 22 21 20 19 18 17 16 15 14 13 12 11 10  9  8  7  6  5  4  3  2  1  0
0  1  0  0  1  0  --src2---    --dest---     --src1---     0  D  S  R  1  0  0  1  1  0  1
```

Instruction Fields:

D	Dual-Instruction mode bit 0 - Single-instruction mode 1 - Dual-instruction mode
S, R	Source and Result precision 00 - 32 bits (**.ss**) 01 - reserved 10 - reserved 11 - 64 bits (**.dd**)
src1, src2	Specifies any of the floating-point registers
dest	Specifies any of the floating-point registers

Programming Notes:

A one clock freeze occurs if *fdest* is a source operand of the next instruction.

Exceptions: None

Fix.v Floating-Point to Integer Conversion Fix.v

Operation:

fdest ← 64-bit value with low-order 32 bits equal to the rounded integer part of *fsrc1* in signed two's complement integer form.

Syntax: **fix.v** *fsrc1, fdest*
(.v = **.sd**, **.dd**)

Description: Convert the source operand to integer by rounding the floating-point number and storing the result in the low-order 32 bits of the destination register pair.

CC: not affected
OF: not affected
FSR: AO, RR, SE

Instruction Encoding:

```
31 30 29 28 27 26 25 24 23 22 21 20 19 18 17 16 15 14 13 12 11 10  9  8  7  6  5  4  3  2  1  0
 0  1  0  0  1  0  0  0  0  0  0 --dest---  --src1---  0  D  S  R  0  1  1  0  0  1  0
```

Instruction Fields:

D Dual-Instruction mode bit
  0 - Single-instruction mode
  1 - Dual-instruction mode
S, R Source and Result precision
  00 - reserved
  01 - single, double (**.sd**)
  10 - reserved
  11 - double, double (**.dd**)
src1 Specifies any of the floating-point registers
dest Specifies any even (64-bit) floating-point register

Programming Notes: Fix will signal an overflow if the integer part of `src1` exceeds the numbers representable by 32-bit 2's complement integers. Underflow and inexact are never signaled.

Exceptions:

Floating-Point Source
Floating-Point Result

Fld.y Floating-Point Load Fld.y

Operation:

fdest ← mem.y[*isrc1* + *isrc2*]
IF(Autoincrement)
THEN
  isrc2 ← *isrc1* + *isrc2*.
FI

Syntax:

fld.y *isrc1(isrc2)++, fdest*
fld.y *#const (isrc2), fdest*
fld.y *isrc1(isrc2)++, fdest*
fld.y *#constA(isrc2)++, fdest*
(**.y** = **.1**, **.d**, **.q**)

Description: Load 32, 64, or 128 bits from memory into the destination register. The address is calculated by adding the two source operands using signed binary addition. For autoincrement addressing, the result of this addition is stored in the second source register.

CC: not affected
OF: not affected
FSR: not affected

Instruction Encoding:

```
31 30 29 28 27 26 25 24 23 22 21 20 19 18 17 16 15 14 13 12 11 10  9  8  7  6  5  4  3  2  1  0
0 0 1 0 0 0 --src2--- --dest--- --src1--- 0 0 0 0 0 0 0 0 -S- A
0 0 1 0 0 1 --src2--- --dest--- -------16-bit Immediate-- -S- A
```

Instruction Fields:

S	Operand Size 00 - 64 bits (**.d**) 01 - 32 bits (**.l**) 10 - 128 bits (**.q**) 11 - 32 bits (**.l**)
A	Autoincrement 0 - No increment 1 - Autoincrement
src1, src2	Specifies any of the integer registers
dest	Specifies any of the floating-point registers
Immediate	A 16-bit constant, sign extended to 32 bits. Bits zero and one of the immediate value are forced to zero to maintain alignment. When bit one of the immediate value is zero, bit two is also forced to zero. Note that the immediate value overlaps the S and A fields above.

Programming Notes:

isrc1 must not be the same register as *isrc2* for the autoincrementing form of **fld**, unless both are **r0**.

A two clock freeze occurs if *fdest* is a source operand of the following instruction, or...

A one clock freeze occurs if *fdest* is a source operand of the second following instruction. (The freezes do not accumulate if *fdest* is used in both following instructions.)

A one clock freeze occurs if the preceding instruction was a store (**st, fst, pst**) that hit the data cache.

Assemblers and compilers must align the immediate address offset to the same boundary as the effective address, because the lower bits of the immediate offset are used to encode operand length information.

If a data-access trap occurs, *isrc2* will have been updated with (*isrc1* + *isrc2*) for the autoincrementing form.

Exceptions: Data-Access Trap

Flush — Cache Flush — Flush

Operation:

Replace the block in the data cache that has address (*#constA* + *isrc2*) and update memory if the contents of that block had been modified.
IF(Autoincrement)
THEN
  isrc2 ← *#constA* + *isrc2*
FI

Syntax: **flush** *#constA (isrc2)*
flush *#constA (isrc2)*++

Description: Flush a line of the cache by loading the address of a reserved area of memory. See Figure 9-6 for a routine that uses the **flush** instruction correctly.

CC:	not affected
OF:	not affected
FSR:	not affected

Instruction Encoding:

```
31 30 29 28 27 26 25 24 23 22 21 20 19 18 17 16 15 14 13 12 11 10  9  8  7  6  5  4  3  2  1  0
0  0  1  1  0  1  --src2---  0  0  0  0  0  -------16-bit Immediate--  0  0  A
```

Instruction Fields:

A	Autoincrement 0 - No increment 1 - Autoincrement
src2	Specifies any of the integer registers

Immediate	A 16-bit constant, sign extended to 32 bits. Bits zero and one of the immediate value are forced to zero to maintain alignment. When bit one of the immediate value is zero, bit two is also forced to zero.

Programming Notes:

Flush is a no-op in user mode; use it only in supervisor mode.

A three clock freeze occurs on a **flush** followed by another **flush**. The freeze is two clocks if there is one instruction between the two **flush** instructions, and only one clock if there are two instructions between the two.

Assemblers and compilers must align the immediate address offset to the same boundary as the effective address, because the lower bits of the immediate offset are used to encode operand length information.

The address *(#constA + isrc2)* must be readable and writable by the user's code, but never used by programmers to contain data, as that 4K block may be written to by the caching mechanism sometime after the **flush**.

Exceptions: None

Fmlow.dd Floating-Point Multiply Low Fmlow.dd

Operation:

fdest ← low-order 53 bits of (*fsrc1* mantissa) × (*fsrc2* mantissa)
fdest bit 53 ← most significant bit of mantissa

Syntax: **fmlow.dd** *fsrc1, fsrc2, fdest*

Description: Multiply the low-order bits of the two 64-bit source operands and store the result in the destination register. The **fmlow** instruction is used for 32-bit integer multiplies by loading the integers into the low-order 32 bits of the source registers. The result will be the low-order 32 bits of the destination register.

CC: not affected
OF: not affected
FSR: not affected

Instruction Encoding:

```
31 30 29 28 27 26 25 24 23 22 21 20 19 18 17 16 15 14 13 12 11 10  9  8  7  6  5  4  3  2  1  0
0  1  0  0  1  0  --src2---      --dest---      --src1---      0  D  1  1  0  1  0  0  0  0  1
```

Instruction Fields:

D Dual-Instruction mode bit
  0 - Single-instruction mode
  1 - Dual-instruction mode
src1, src2 Specifies any even (64-bit) floating-point registers
dest Specifies any even (64-bit) floating-point registers

Programming Notes:

A three clock freeze occurs if the immediately prior operation is scalar and *fsrc1* is the same as the *fdest* of the prior operation.

A two clock freeze occurs if the immediately prior operation is scalar and *fsrc1* is not the same as *fdest* of the prior operation.

A one clock freeze occurs if the immediately prior operation is pipelined and *fsrc1* is the same as the *fdest* of the prior operation.

Exceptions: None

Fmov.r Floating-Point Register-Register Move Fmov.r

Operation: *fdest* ← *fsrc1*

Syntax: **fmov.r** *fsrc1, fdest*
(.r = .ss, .sd, .ds, .dd)

Description: Move a floating-point value from the source register to the destination register. This is not an instruction, but an assembler pseudo operation. See below for how this pseudo operation is encoded.

CC: not affected
OF: not affected
FSR: **fmov.ds** can set AO, AI, AU, AE, AA, SI, SE
fmov.sd can set SE

Instruction Encoding: Assembler pseudo operation encodings:

fmov.ss *fsrc1, fdest*	is encoded as	**fiadd.ss**	*fsrc1,* **f0**, *fdest*
fmov.dd *fsrc1, fdest*	is encoded as	**fiadd.dd**	*fsrc1,* **f0**, *fdest*
fmov.sd *fsrc1, fdest*	is encoded as	**famov.sd**	*fsrc1, fdest*
fmov.ds *fsrc1, fdest*	is encoded as	**famov.ds**	*fsrc1, fdest*

Programming Notes:

Exceptions:

For **fmov.ds**, FP Result exception or FP Source exceptions
For **fmov.sd**, FP Source Exception

Fmul.p Floating-Point Multiply Fmul.p

Operation: *fdest* ← *fsrc1* × *fsrc2*

Syntax: **fmul.p** *fsrc1, fsrc2, fdest*
(.p = .ss, .sd, .dd)

Description: Multiply the two source operands using signed floating-point multiplication and store the result in the destination register.

CC: not affected
OF: not affected
FSR: MA, MI, MO, MU, SI

Instruction Encoding:

```
31 30 29 28 27 26 25 24 23 22 21 20 19 18 17 16 15 14 13 12 11 10 9 8 7 6 5 4 3 2 1 0
0  1  0  0  1  0  --src2---  --dest---  --src1---  0  D  S  R  0  1  0  0  0  0  0
```

Instruction Fields:

D	Dual-Instruction mode bit 0 - Single-instruction mode 1 - Dual-instruction mode
S, R	Source and Result precision 00 - single, single (**.ss**) 01 - single, double (**.sd**) 10 - reserved 11 - double, double (**.dd**)
src1, src2	Specifies any of the floating-point registers
dest	Specifies any of the floating-point registers

Programming Notes:

A three clock freeze occurs if the immediately prior operation is scalar and *fsrc1* is the same as the *fdest* of the prior operation.

A two clock freeze occurs if the immediately prior operation is scalar and *fsrc1* is not the same as *fdest* of the prior operation.

A one clock freeze occurs if the immediately prior operation is pipelined and *fsrc1* is the same as the *fdest* of the prior operation.

A two clock freeze occurs on 1.6% of all data patterns. The freeze is for rounding and is data dependent. This freeze affects only the multiplier and the *fdest*. The freeze will not be seen if two integer operations follow the **fmul**. The data patterns are not symmetric—(3 × 2) will freeze, but (2 × 3) will not.

Exceptions:

Floating-Point Source
Floating-Point Result

Fnop Floating-Point No Operation Fnop

Operation: None

Syntax: `fnop`

Description: No operation is performed and no pipelines are affected. This is not an instruction, but an assembler pseudo operation. See below for how this pseudo operation is encoded.

CC: not affected
OF: not affected
FSR: not affected

Instruction Encoding: Assembler pseudo operation encodings:

`fnop` is encoded as `shrd r0,r0,r0`

Programming Notes: Bit 9 is the Dual-instruction-mode bit.

Exceptions: `d.fnop` cannot be used to initiate entry into Dual-instruction mode.

Form — Or with Merge Register — Form

Operation:

fdest ← *fsrc1* OR MERGE
MERGE ← 0

Syntax: **form** *fsrc1, fdest*

Description: Perform the bitwise OR operation on the source register and the MERGE register and store the result in the destination register. This instruction is used to retrieve pixels/Z-buffer values from the MERGE register.

CC:	not affected
OF:	not affected
FSR:	not affected

Instruction Encoding:

```
31 30 29 28 27 26 25 24 23 22 21 20 19 18 17 16 15 14 13 12 11 10 9 8 7 6 5 4 3 2 1 0
0  1  0  0  1  0  0  0  0  0  0  --dest---      --src1---      0 D 1 1 1 0 1 1 0 1 0
```

Instruction Fields:

D	Dual-Instruction mode bit 0 - Single-instruction mode 1 - Dual-instruction mode
src1	Specifies any even (64-bit) floating-point registers
dest	Specifies any even (64-bit) floating-point registers

Programming Notes:

A one clock freeze occurs if *fdest* is a source operand of the next instruction.

Exceptions: None

Frcp.p — Floating-Point Reciprocal — Frcp.p

Operation: `fdest` ← 1 / `fsrc2` with maximum mantissa error of 2^{-7}

Syntax: **frcp.p** *fsrc2, fdest*
(**.p = .ss, .sd, .dd**)

Description: Take the approximate floating-point reciprocal of the source register and store the result in the destination register.

CC: not affected
OF: not affected
FSR: not affected

Instruction Encoding:

```
31 30 29 28 27 26 25 24 23 22 21 20 19 18 17 16 15 14 13 12 11 10  9  8  7  6  5  4  3  2  1  0
0  1  0  0  1  0 --src2--- --dest--- 0  0  0  0  0  0  D  S  R  0  1  0  0  0  1  0
```

Instruction Fields:

D	Dual-Instruction mode bit 0 - Single-instruction mode 1 - Dual-instruction mode
S, R	Source and Result precision 00 - single, single (**.ss**) 01 - single, double (**.sd**) 10 - reserved 11 - double, double (**.dd**)
src2	Specifies any of the floating-point registers
dest	Specifies any of the floating-point registers

Programming Notes:

An FP source exception occurs if **fsrc2** is 0, or **f0**, or **f1**.

Exceptions:

Floating-Point Source
Floating-Point Result

Frsqr.p Floating-Point Reciprocal Square Root Frsqr.p

Operation:

fdest ← $1 / \sqrt{fsrc2}$ with maximum mantissa error of 2^{-7}

Syntax: **frsqr.p** *fsrc2, fdest*
(**.p** = **.ss, .sd, .dd**)

Description: Take the floating-point reciprocal of the square root of the source register and store the result in the destination register.

CC:	not affected
OF:	not affected
FSR:	not affected

Instruction Encoding:

```
31 30 29 28 27 26 25 24 23 22 21 20 19 18 17 16 15 14 13 12 11 10  9  8  7  6  5  4  3  2  1  0
 0  1  0  0  1  0 --src2--- --dest--- 0  0  0  0  0  0  D  S  R  0  1  0  0  0  1  1
```

Instruction Fields:

D	Dual-Instruction mode bit 0 - Single-instruction mode 1 - Dual-instruction mode
S, R	Source and Result precision 00 - single, single (**.ss**) 01 - single, double (**.sd**) 10 - reserved 11 - double, double (**.dd**)
src2	Specifies any of the floating-point registers
dest	Specifies any of the floating-point registers

Programming Notes:

An FP Source exception occurs if **fsrc2** is zero or negative.

Exceptions:

Floating-Point Source
Floating-Point Result

Fst.y Floating-Point Store Fst.y

Operation:

```
mem.y[ isrc1 + isrc2 ] ← freg
IF(Autoincrement)
THEN
   isrc2 ← isrc1 + isrc2
FI
```

Syntax:

```
fst.y  freg,isrc1(isrc2)
fst.y  freg,#constA(isrc2)
fst.y  freg,isrc1(isrc2)++
fst.y  freg,#constA(isrc2)++
(.y = .l, .d, .q)
```

Description: Store 32, 64, or 128 bits to memory from the *freg* floating-point register. The address is calculated by adding the two source operands using signed binary addition. For autoincrement addressing, the result of this addition is stored in the second source register.

CC:	not affected
OF:	not affected
FSR:	not affected

Instruction Encoding:

```
31 30 29 28 27 26 25 24 23 22 21 20 19 18 17 16 15 14 13 12 11 10  9  8  7  6  5  4  3  2  1  0
0 0 1 0 1 0 --src2--- --dest--- --src1--- 0 0 0 0 0 0 0 0 -S- A
0 0 1 0 1 1 --src2--- --dest--- -------16-bit Immediate-- -S- A
```

Instruction Fields:

S	Operand Size 00 - 64 bits (**.d**) 01 - 32 bits (**.l**) 10 - 128 bits (**.q**) 11 - 32 bits (**.l**)
A	Autoincrement 0 - No increment 1 - Autoincrement
src1, src2	Specifies any of the integer registers
dest	Specifies any of the floating-point registers
Immediate	A 16-bit constant, sign extended to 32 bits with 3 least significant bits recoded as above

Programming Notes:

isrc1 must not be the same register as *isrc2* for the autoincrementing form of **fst**, unless both are **r0**.

A one clock freeze occurs if the **fst** hits the data cache and the following instruction is **fld**, or **ld**.

A one clock freeze occurs when the instruction following **fst** is a pipelined floating-point instruction that overwrites the register being stored.

Assemblers and compilers must align the immediate address offset to the same boundary as the effective address, because the lower three bits of the immediate offset are used to encode operand length information.

Exceptions: Data-Access Trap

Fsub.p — Floating-Point Subtract — Fsub.p

Operation: *fdest* ← *fsrc1* − *fsrc2*

Syntax: **fsub.p** *fsrc1, fsrc2, fdest*
(**.p** = **.ss, .sd, .dd**)

Description: Subtract the second source operand from the first source operand using signed 32- or 64-bit floating-point subtraction and store the result in the destination register.

CC:	not affected
OF:	not affected
FSR:	AA, AE, AI, AO, AU, RR, SI, SE

Instruction Encoding:

```
31 30 29 28 27 26 25 24 23 22 21 20 19 18 17 16 15 14 13 12 11 10  9  8  7  6  5  4  3  2  1  0
 0  1  0  0  1  0 --src2--- --dest--- --src1---  0  D  S  R  0  1  1  0  0  0  1
```

Instruction Fields:

D	Dual-Instruction mode bit 0 - Single-instruction mode 1 - Dual-instruction mode
S, R	Source and Result precision 00 - single, single (**.ss**) 01 - single, double (**.sd**) 10 - reserved 11 - double, double (**.dd**)
src1, src2	Specifies any of the floating-point registers
dest	Specifies any of the floating-point registers

Programming Notes:

Exceptions:

Floating-Point Source
Floating-Point Result

Ftrunc.v Floating-Point to Integer Conversion Ftrunc.v

Operation:

fdest ← 64-bit value with low-order 32 bits equal to truncated integer part of *fsrc1* in two's complement form.

Syntax: **ftrunc.v** *fsrc1, fdest*
(**.v** = **.sd, .dd**)

Description: Convert the source operand to integer by truncating the integer part of the floating-point number and storing the result in the low-order 32 bits of the destination register pair.

CC:	not affected
OF:	not affected
FSR:	AO, RR, SE

Instruction Encoding:

```
31 30 29 28 27 26 25 24 23 22 21 20 19 18 17 16 15 14 13 12 11 10  9  8  7  6  5  4  3  2  1  0
 0  1  0  0  1  0  0  0  0  0  0 --dest--- --src1--- 0  D  S  R  0  1  1  1  0  1  0
```

Instruction Fields:

D	Dual-Instruction mode bit 0 - Single-instruction mode 1 - Dual-instruction mode
S, R	Source and Result precision 00 - reserved 01 - single, double (**.sd**) 10 - reserved 11 - double, double (**.dd**)
src1	Specifies any of the floating-point registers
dest	Specifies any even (64-bit) floating-point register

Programming Notes:

Fix will signal an overflow if the integer part of *src1* exceeds the number representable by 32-bit 2's complement integers. Underflow and inexact are never signaled.

Exceptions:

Floating-Point Source
Floating-Point Result

Fxfr Transfer Floating-Point to Integer Register Fxfr

Operation: `idest ← fsrc1`

Syntax: **fxfr** *fsrc1, idest*

Description: Transfer the value in the floating-point source register to the integer destination register. Do not convert to integer format.

CC: not affected
OF: not affected
FSR: not affected

Instruction Encoding:

```
31 30 29 28 27 26 25 24 23 22 21 20 19 18 17 16 15 14 13 12 11 10  9  8  7  6  5  4  3  2  1  0
 0  1  0  0  1  0  0  0  0  0  0 --dest---    --src1---     0  D  0  0  1  0  0  0  0  0  0
```

Instruction Fields:

D	Dual-Instruction mode bit 0 - Single-instruction mode 1 - Dual-instruction mode
src1	Specifies any of the floating-point registers
dest	Specifies any of the integer registers

Programming Notes:

A one clock freeze occurs if *idest* is a source operand of the next instruction.

The **fxfr** instruction is executed by the graphics unit. When **fxfr** is executed all contents of the graphics pipeline are lost.

In DIM, an **fxfr** cannot transfer to an *idest* used by the companion core operation.

In DIM, the core operation paired with **fxfr** cannot be **ld, ld.c, st, st.c, call, calli, ixfr,** or any operation that updates an integer register.

Exceptions: None

Fzchkl — 32-Bit Z-Buffer Check — Fzchkl

Operation:

Consider *fsrc1*, *fsrc2*, and *fdest* each consisting of two 32-bit fields.
PM ← PM shifted right by 2 bits
FOR i = 0 to 1
DO
   PM[i + 6] ← *fsrc2*(i) ≤ *fsrc1*(i) (unsigned)
   fdest(i) ← smaller of *fsrc2*(i) and *fsrc1*(i)
OD
MERGE ← 0

Syntax: **fzchkl** *fsrc1, fsrc2, fdest*

Description: Compare the two Z-buffer distance values in the first source operand to the two values in the second source operand, storing the smaller two values in the destination register and setting the appropriate PM bits.

CC: not affected
OF: not affected
FSR: not affected

Instruction Encoding:

```
31 30 29 28 27 26 25 24 23 22 21 20 19 18 17 16 15 14 13 12 11 10 9 8 7 6 5 4 3 2 1 0
0  1  0  0  1  0  --src2---  --dest---  --src1---  0  D  1  1  1  0  1  0  1  1
```

Instruction Fields:

D   Dual-Instruction mode bit
      0 - Single-instruction mode
      1 - Dual-instruction mode

src1, src2	Specifies any even (64-bit) floating-point registers
dest	Specifies any even (64-bit) floating-point registers

Programming Notes:

A one clock freeze occurs if *fdest* is a source operand of the next instruction.

Exceptions: None

Fzchks 16-Bit Z-Buffer Check Fzchks

Operation:

Consider *fsrc1*, *fsrc2*, and *fdest* each consisting of 4 16-bit fields.
PM ← PM shifted right by 4 bits
FOR i = 0 to 3
DO
  PM[i + 4] ← *fsrc2*(i) ≤ *fsrc1*(i) (unsigned)
  fdest(i) ← smaller of *fsrc2*(i) and *fsrc1*(i).
OD
MERGE ← 0

Syntax: **fzchks** *fsrc1*, *fsrc2*, *fdest*

Description: Compare the four Z-buffer distance values in the first source operand to the four values in the second source operand, storing the smaller four values in the destination register and setting the appropriate PM bits.

CC: not affected
OF: not affected
FSR: not affected

Instruction Encoding:

```
31 30 29 28 27 26 25 24 23 22 21 20 19 18 17 16 15 14 13 12 11 10  9  8  7  6  5  4  3  2  1  0
 0  1  0  0  1  0 --src2---    --dest---    --src1---   0  D  1  1  1  0  1  1  1  1  1
```

Instruction Fields:

D Dual-Instruction mode bit
  0 - Single-instruction mode
  1 - Dual-instruction mode

src1, src2	Specifies any even (64-bit) floating-point register
dest	Specifies any even (64-bit) floating-point register

Programming Notes:

A one clock freeze occurs if *fdest* is a source operand of the next instruction.

Exceptions: None

I2apl.p Pipelined F-P Add and Multiply I2apl.p

Operation:

fdest ← last stage adder result.
Advance adder pipeline one stage.
Advance multiplier pipeline one stage.
First stage adder pipeline ← *fsrc1* + adder result.
First stage multiplier pipeline ← KI × *fsrc2*.
T ← multiplier result.

Syntax: **i2apl.p** *fsrc1, fsrc2, fdest*
(**.p** = **.ss**, **.sd**, **.dd**)

Description: Add the first source operand to the last stage result of the adder pipeline using signed floating-point addition. Multiply the second source operand by the contents of the KI register using 32- or 64-bit floating-point multiplication. Store the last stage result of the adder pipeline in the destination register. Store the last stage result of the multiplier pipeline in the T register.

CC: not affected
OF: not affected
FSR: AA, AE, AI, AO, AU, MA, MI, MO, MU, SI

Instruction Encoding:

```
31 30 29 28 27 26 25 24 23 22 21 20 19 18 17 16 15 14 13 12 11 10  9  8  7  6  5  4  3  2  1  0
 0  1  0  0  1  0 --src2--- --dest--- --src1--- 1  D  S  R  0  0  0  0  1  1  0
```

Instruction Fields:

D Dual-Instruction mode bit
0 - Single-instruction mode
1 - Dual-instruction mode

S, R	Source and Result precision 00 - single, single (**.ss**) 01 - single, double (**.sd**) 10 - reserved 11 - double, double (**.dd**)
src1, src2	Specifies any of the floating-point registers
dest	Specifies any of the floating-point registers

Programming Notes:

Exceptions:

Floating-Point Source
Floating-Point Result

I2apt.p Pipelined F-P Add and Multiply I2apt.p

Operation:

fdest ← last stage adder result.
Advance adder pipeline one stage.
Advance multiplier pipeline one stage.
First stage adder pipeline ← T + adder result.
First stage multiplier pipeline ← KI × *fsrc2.*
T ← multiplier result.
KI ← *fsrc1*

Syntax: **i2apt.p** *fsrc1, fsrc2, fdest*
(**.p** = **.ss, .sd, .dd**)

Description: Add the contents of the T register to the last stage result of the adder pipeline using signed floating-point addition. Multiply the second source operand by the contents of the KI register using 32- or 64-bit floating-point multiplication. Store the last stage result of the adder pipeline in the destination register. Store the last stage result of the multiplier pipeline in the T register. Load the KI register with the first source operand.

CC:	not affected
OF:	not affected
FSR:	AA, AE, AI, AO, AU, MA, MI, MO, MU, SI

Instruction Encoding:

```
31 30 29 28 27 26 25 24 23 22 21 20 19 18 17 16 15 14 13 12 11 10  9  8  7  6  5  4  3  2  1  0
 0  1  0  0  1  0 --src2--- --dest--- --src1---  1  D  S  R  0  0  0  0  1  1  1
```

Instruction Fields:

D Dual-Instruction mode bit
- 0 - Single-instruction mode
- 1 - Dual-instruction mode

S, R	Source and Result precision 00 - single, single (**.ss**) 01 - single, double (**.sd**) 10 - reserved 11 - double, double (**.dd**)
src1, src2	Specifies any of the floating-point registers
dest	Specifies any of the floating-point registers

Programming Notes:

fsrc1 must not be the same register as *fdest*.

Exceptions:

Floating-Point Source
Floating-Point Result

I2as1.p Pipelined F-P Subtract and Multiply I2as1.p

Operation:

fdest ← last stage adder result.
Advance adder pipeline one stage.
Advance multiplier pipeline one stage.
First stage adder pipeline ← *fsrc1* − adder result.
First stage multiplier pipeline ← KI × *fsrc2*.
T ← multiplier result.

Syntax: **i2as1.p** *fsrc1, fsrc2, fdest*
(**.p** = **.ss, .sd, .dd**)

Description: Subtract the last stage result of the adder pipeline from the first source operand using signed floating-point subtraction. Multiply the second source operand by the contents of the KI register using 32- or 64-bit floating-point multiplication. Store the last stage result of the adder pipeline in the destination register. Store the last stage result of the multiplier pipeline in the T register.

CC: not affected
OF: not affected
FSR: AA, AE, AI, AO, AU, MA, MI, MO, MU, SI, SE

Instruction Encoding:

```
31 30 29 28 27 26 25 24 23 22 21 20 19 18 17 16 15 14 13 12 11 10 9 8 7 6 5 4 3 2 1 0
0  1  0  0  1  0  --src2---    --dest---      --src1---      1  D S R 0 0 1 0 1 1 0
```

Instruction Fields:

D Dual-Instruction mode bit
 0 - Single-instruction mode
 1 - Dual-instruction mode

S, R	Source and Result precision 00 - single, single (**.ss**) 01 - single, double (**.sd**) 10 - reserved. 11 - double, double (**.dd**)
src1, src2	Specifies any of the floating-point registers
dest	Specifies any of the floating-point registers

Programming Notes:

Exceptions:

Floating-Point Source
Floating-Point Result

I2ast.p Pipelined F-P Subtract and Multiply I2ast.p

Operation:

fdest ← last stage adder result
Advance adder pipeline one stage.
Advance multiplier pipeline one stage.
First stage adder pipeline ← T − adder result.
First stage multiplier pipeline ← KI × *fsrc2*.
T ← multiplier result
KI ← *fsrc1*

Syntax: **i2ast.p** *fsrc1, fsrc2, fdest*
(**.p** = **.ss**, **.sd**, **.dd**)

Description: Subtract the last stage result of the adder pipeline from the contents of the T register using signed floating-point subtraction. Multiply the second source operand by the contents of the KI register using 32- or 64-bit floating-point multiplication. Store the last stage result of the adder pipeline in the destination register. Store the last stage result of the multiplier pipeline in the T register. Load the KI register with the first source operand.

CC:	not affected
OF:	not affected
FSR:	AA, AE, AI, AO, AU, MA, MI, MO, MU, SI

Instruction Encoding:

```
31 30 29 28 27 26 25 24 23 22 21 20 19 18 17 16 15 14 13 12 11 10 9 8 7 6 5 4 3 2 1 0
0  1  0  0  1  0  --src2---      --dest---      --src1---      1  D S R 0 0 1 0 1 1 1
```

Instruction Fields:

D	Dual-Instruction mode bit 0 - Single-instruction mode 1 - Dual-instruction mode
S, R	Source and Result precision 00 - single, single (**.ss**) 01 - single, double (**.sd**) 10 - reserved 11 - double, double (**.dd**)
src1, src2	Specifies any of the floating-point registers
dest	Specifies any of the floating-point registers

Programming Notes:

fsrc1 must not be the same register as *fdest*.

Exceptions:

Floating-Point Source
Floating-Point Result

I2p1.p Pipelined F-P Add and Multiply I2p1.p

Operation:

fdest ← last stage adder result.
Advance adder pipeline one stage.
Advance multiplier pipeline one stage.
First stage adder pipeline ← *fsrc1* + multiplier result.
First stage multiplier pipeline ← KI × *fsrc2*.

Syntax: **i2p1.p** *fsrc1, fsrc2, fdest*
(**.p** = **.ss**, **.sd**, **.dd**)

Description: Add the first source operand to the last stage result of the multiplier pipeline using signed floating-point addition. Multiply the second source operand by the contents of the KI register using 32- or 64-bit floating-point multiplication. Store the last stage result of the adder pipeline in the destination register.

CC:	not affected
OF:	not affected
FSR:	AA, AE, AI, AO, AU, MA, MI, MO, MU, SI, SE

Instruction Encoding:

```
31 30 29 28 27 26 25 24 23 22 21 20 19 18 17 16 15 14 13 12 11 10  9  8  7  6  5  4  3  2  1  0
 0  1  0  0  1  0 --src2--- --dest--- --src1---  1  D  S  R  0  0  0  0  1  0  0
```

Instruction Fields:

D Dual-Instruction mode bit
  0 - Single-instruction mode
  1 - Dual-instruction mode

S, R	Source and Result precision 00 - single, single (`.ss`) 01 - single, double (`.sd`) 10 - reserved 11 - double, double (`.dd`)
src1, src2	Specifies any of the floating-point registers
dest	Specifies any of the floating-point registers

Programming Notes:

Exceptions:

Floating-Point Source
Floating-Point Result

I2pt.p Pipelined F-P Add and Multiply I2pt.p

Operation:

fdest ← last stage adder result.
Advance adder pipeline one stage.
Advance multiplier pipeline one stage.
First stage adder pipeline ← T + multiplier result.
First stage multiplier pipeline ← KI × *fsrc2*.
KI ← *fsrc1*.

Syntax: **i2pt.p** *fsrc1, fsrc2, fdest*
(**.p** = **.ss**, **.sd**, **.dd**)

Description: Add the contents of the T register to the last stage result of the multiplier pipeline using signed floating-point addition. Multiply the second source operand by the contents of the KI register using 32- or 64-bit floating-point multiplication. Store the last stage result of the adder pipeline in the destination register. Load the KI register with the first source operand.

CC:	not affected
OF:	not affected
FSR:	AA, AE, AI, AO, AU, MA, MI, MO, MU, SI, SE

Instruction Encoding:

```
31 30 29 28 27 26 25 24 23 22 21 20 19 18 17 16 15 14 13 12 11 10  9  8  7  6  5  4  3  2  1  0
0  1  0  0  1  0  --src2---  --dest---  --src1---  1  D  S  R  0  0  0  0  1  0  1
```

Instruction Fields:

D Dual-Instruction mode bit
 0 - Single-instruction mode
 1 - Dual-instruction mode

S, R	Source and Result precision 00 - single, single (`.ss`) 01 - single, double (`.sd`) 10 - reserved 11 - double, double (`.dd`)
srcl, src2	Specifies any of the floating-point registers
dest	Specifies any of the floating-point registers

Programming Notes:

fsrc1 must not be the same register as *fdest*.

Exceptions:

Floating-Point Source
Floating-Point Result

I2s1.p Pipelined F-P Subtract and Multiply I2s1.p

Operation:

fdest ← last stage adder result.
Advance adder pipeline one stage.
Advance multiplier pipeline one stage.
First stage adder pipeline ← *fsrc1* − multiplier result.
First stage multiplier pipeline ← KI × *fsrc2*.

Syntax: **i2s1.p** *fsrc1, fsrc2, fdest*
(**.p** = **.ss**, **.sd**, **.dd**)

Description: Subtract the last stage result of the multiplier pipeline from the first source operand using signed floating-point subtraction. Multiply the second source operand by the contents of the KI register using 32- or 64-bit floating-point multiplication. Store the last stage result of the adder pipeline in the destination register.

CC:	not affected
OF:	not affected
FSR:	AA, AE, AI, AO, AU, MA, MI, MO, MU, SI, SE

Instruction Encoding:

```
31 30 29 28 27 26 25 24 23 22 21 20 19 18 17 16 15 14 13 12 11 10  9  8  7  6  5  4  3  2  1  0
 0  1  0  0  1  0 --src2--- --dest--- --src1---  1  D  S  R  0  0  1  0  1  0  0
```

Instruction Fields:

D Dual-Instruction mode bit
0 - Single-instruction mode
1 - Dual-instruction mode

S, R	Source and Result precision 00 - single, single (**.ss**) 01 - single, double (**.sd**) 10 - reserved 11 - double, double (**.dd**)
src1, src2	Specifies any of the floating-point registers
dest	Specifies any of the floating-point registers

Programming Notes:

Exceptions:

Floating-Point Source
Floating-Point Result

I2st.p Pipelined F-P Subtract and Multiply I2st.p

Operation:

fdest ← last stage adder result.
Advance adder pipeline one stage.
Advance multiplier pipeline one stage.
First stage adder pipeline ← T − multiplier result.
First stage multiplier pipeline ← KI × *fsrc2*.
KI ← *fsrc1*

Syntax: **i2st.p** *fsrc1, fsrc2, fdest*
(**.p** = **.ss**, **.sd**, **.dd**)

Description: Subtract the last stage result of the multiplier pipeline from the contents of the T register using signed floating-point subtraction. Multiply the second source operand by the contents of the KI register using 32- or 64-bit floating-point multiplication. Store the last stage result of the adder pipeline in the destination register. Load the KI register with the first source operand.

CC:	not affected
OF:	not affected
FSR:	AA, AE, AI, AO, AU, MA, MI, MO, MU, SI, SE

Instruction Encoding:

```
31 30 29 28 27 26 25 24 23 22 21 20 19 18 17 16 15 14 13 12 11 10  9  8  7  6  5  4  3  2  1  0
 0  1  0  0  1  0 --src2--- --dest--- --src1--- 1  D  S  R  0  0  1  0  1  0  1
```

Instruction Fields:

D Dual-Instruction mode bit
0 - Single-instruction mode
1 - Dual-instruction mode

S, R	Source and Result precision 00 - single, single (`.ss`) 01 - single, double (`.sd`) 10 - reserved 11 - double, double (`.dd`)
src1, src2	Specifies any of the floating-point registers
dest	Specifies any of the floating-point registers

Programming Notes:

fsrc1 must not be the same register as *fdest*.

Exceptions:

Floating-Point Source
Floating-Point Result

Ialp2.p Pipelined F-P Add and Multiply Ialp2.p

Operation:

fdest ← last stage adder result.
Advance adder pipeline one stage.
Advance multiplier pipeline one stage.
First stage adder pipeline ← *fsrc1* + *fsrc2*.
First stage multiplier pipeline ← KI × adder result.

Syntax: **ialp2.p** *fsrc1, fsrc2, fdest*
(**.p** = **.ss, .sd, .dd**)

Description: Add the two source operands using signed floating-point addition. Multiply the last stage result of the adder pipeline by the contents of the KI register using 32- or 64-bit floating-point multiplication. Store the last stage result of the adder pipeline in the destination register.

CC: not affected
OF: not affected
FSR: AA, AE, AI, AO, AU, MA, MI, MO, MU, SI, SE

Instruction Encoding:

```
31 30 29 28 27 26 25 24 23 22 21 20 19 18 17 16 15 14 13 12 11 10 9 8 7 6 5 4 3 2 1 0
0  1  0  0  1  0  --src2---      --dest---      --src1---      1  D S R 0 0 0 1 1 1 0
```

Instruction Fields:

D Dual-Instruction mode bit
0 - Single-instruction mode
1 - Dual-instruction mode

S, R	Source and Result precision 00 - single, single (**.ss**) 01 - single, double (**.sd**) 10 - reserved 11 - double, double (**.dd**)
src1, src2	Specifies any of the floating-point registers
dest	Specifies any of the floating-point registers

Programming Notes:

Exceptions:

Floating-Point Source
Floating-Point Result

Ia1s2.p Pipelined F-P Subtract and Multiply Ia1s2.p

Operation:

fdest ← last stage adder result.
Advance adder pipeline one stage.
Advance multiplier pipeline one stage.
First stage adder pipeline ← *fsrc1* − *fsrc2*.
First stage multiplier pipeline ← KI × adder result.

Syntax: **ia1s2.p** *fsrc1, fsrc2, fdest*
(**.p** = **.ss, .sd, .dd**)

Description: Subtract the second source operand from the first source operand using signed floating-point subtraction. Multiply the last stage result of the adder pipeline by the contents of the KI register using 32- or 64-bit floating-point multiplication. Store the last stage result of the adder pipeline in the destination register.

CC:	not affected
OF:	not affected
FSR:	AA, AE, AI, AO, AU, MA, MI, MO, MU, SI, SE

Instruction Encoding:

```
31 30 29 28 27 26 25 24 23 22 21 20 19 18 17 16 15 14 13 12 11 10 9 8 7 6 5 4 3 2 1 0
0  1  0  0  1  0  --src2---  --dest---  --src1---  1 D S R 0 0 1 1 1 1 0
```

Instruction Fields:

D Dual-Instruction mode bit
0 - Single-instruction mode
1 - Dual-instruction mode

S, R	Source and Result precision 00 - single, single (**.ss**) 01 - single, double (**.sd**) 10 - reserved 11 - double, double (**.dd**)
src1, src2	Specifies any of the floating-point registers
dest	Specifies any of the floating-point registers

Programming Notes:

Exceptions:

Floating-Point Source
Floating-Point Result

Iat1p2.p Pipelined F-P Add and Multiply Iat1p2.p

Operation:

fdest ← last stage adder result.
Advance adder pipeline one stage.
Advance multiplier pipeline one stage.
First stage adder pipeline ← *fsrc1* + *fsrc2.*
First stage multiplier pipeline ← KI × adder result.
T ← multiplier result.

Syntax: **iat1p2.p** *fsrc1, fsrc2, fdest*
(**.p** = **.ss**, **.sd**, **.dd**)

Description: Add the two source operands using signed floating-point addition. Multiply the last stage result of the adder pipeline by the contents of the KI register using 32- or 64-bit floating-point multiplication. Store the last stage result of the adder pipeline in the destination register. Store the last stage result of the multiplier pipeline in the T register.

CC:	not affected
OF:	not affected
FSR:	AA, AE, AI, AO, AU, MA, MI, MO, MU, SI, SE

Instruction Encoding:

```
31 30 29 28 27 26 25 24 23 22 21 20 19 18 17 16 15 14 13 12 11 10  9  8  7  6  5  4  3  2  1  0
0  1  0  0  1  0  --src2---  --dest---  --src1---  1  D  S  R  0  0  0  1  1  0  0
```

Instruction Fields:

D Dual-Instruction mode bit
  0 - Single-instruction mode
  1 - Dual-instruction mode

S, R	Source and Result precision 00 - single, single (`.ss`) 01 - single, double (`.sd`) 10 - reserved 11 - double, double (`.dd`)
src1, src2	Specifies any of the floating-point registers
dest	Specifies any of the floating-point registers

Programming Notes:

Exceptions:

Floating-Point Source
Floating-Point Result

Iat1s2.p Pipelined F-P Subtract and Multiply Iat1s2.p

Operation:

fdest ← last stage adder result.
Advance adder pipeline one stage.
Advance multiplier pipeline one stage.
First stage adder pipeline ← *fsrc1* − *fsrc2*.
First stage multiplier pipeline ← KI × adder result.
T ← multiplier result.

Syntax: **iat1s2.p** *fsrc1, fsrc2, fdest*
(**.p** = **.ss**, **.sd**, **.dd**)

Description: Subtract the second source operand from the first source operand using signed floating-point subtraction. Multiply the last stage result of the adder pipeline by the contents of the KI register using 32- or 64-bit floating-point multiplication. Store the last stage result of the adder pipeline in the destination register. Store the last stage result of the multiplier pipeline in the T register.

CC:	not affected
OF:	not affected
FSR:	AA, AE, AI, AO, AU, MA, MI, MO, MU, SI, SE

Instruction Encoding:

```
31 30 29 28 27 26 25 24 23 22 21 20 19 18 17 16 15 14 13 12 11 10  9  8  7  6  5  4  3  2  1  0
0  1  0  0  1  0  --src2---   --dest---   --src1---   1  D  S  R  0  0  1  1  1  0  0
```

Instruction Fields:

D Dual-Instruction mode bit
  0 - Single-instruction mode
  1 - Dual-instruction mode

S, R	Source and Result precision 00 - single, single (**.ss**) 01 - single, double (**.sd**) 10 - reserved 11 - double, double (**.dd**)
src1, src2	Specifies any of the floating-point registers
dest	Specifies any of the floating-point registers

Programming Notes:

Exceptions:

Floating-Point Source
Floating-Point Result

Intovr Software Trap on Integer Overflow Intovr

Operation:

IF(OF == 1)
THEN
  Generate trap with IT set in **psr**.
ELSE
  Continue with next sequential instruction.
FI

Syntax: **intovr**

Description: If the OF bit of **epsr** is set, then generate a software trap with IT set in **psr**.

CC:	not affected
OF:	not affected
FSR:	not affected

Instruction Encoding:

31	30	29	28	27	26	25	24	23	22	21	20	19	18	17	16	15	14	13	12	11	10	9	8	7	6	5	4	3	2	1	0
0	1	0	0	1	1	0	0	0	0	0	0	0	0	0	0	0	0	0	0	0	0	0	0	0	0	0	0	0	1	0	0

Instruction Fields:

Programming Notes:

OF in **epsr** is not a cumulative or sticky flag; thus it changes value with every integer add or subtract.

Exceptions: Instruction Trap

Ixfr Transfer Integer to Floating-Point Register Ixfr

Operation: *fdest* ← *isrc1*

Syntax: `ixfr` *isrc1*, *fdest*

Description: Transfer the 32-bit value in the integer source register to the floating-point destination register. No format conversion is done.

CC: not affected
OF: not affected
FSR: not affected

Instruction Encoding:

31	30	29	28	27	26	25	24	23	22	21	20 19 18 17 16	15 14 13 12 11	10	9	8	7	6	5	4	3	2	1	0
0	0	0	0	1	0	0	0	0	0	0	--dest---	--src1---	0	0	0	0	0	0	0	0	0	0	0

Instruction Fields:

src1 Specifies any of the integer register
dest Specifies any of the floating-point registers

Programming Notes:

A two clock freeze occurs if *fdest* is a source operand of the following instruction, or...

A one clock freeze occurs if *fdest* is a source operand of the second following instruction. (The freezes do not accumulate if *fdest* is used in both following instructions.)

Exceptions: None

Ld.c Load from Control Register Ld.c

Operation: *idest* ← *ctrlreg*

Syntax: **ld.c** *ctrlreg, idest*

Description: Load 32 bits from a control register into the integer destination register.

CC: not affected
OF: not affected
FSR: not affected

Instruction Encoding:

```
31 30 29 28 27 26 25 24 23 22 21 20 19 18 17 16 15 14 13 12 11 10  9  8  7  6  5  4  3  2  1  0
0  0  1  1  0  0  --src2---      --dest---      0  0  0  0  0  0  0  0  0  0  0  0  0  0  0  0
```

Instruction Fields:

src2 Specifies one of the control registers
- 00000 - **fir**
- 00001 - **psr**
- 00010 - **dirbase**
- 00011 - **db**
- 00100 - **fsr**
- 00101 - **epsr**

dest Specifies any of the integer registers

Programming Notes:

A one clock freeze occurs if *idest* is a source operand of the next instruction.

The fault instruction register (**fir**) must be loaded using **ld.c fir,** *idest* for the trap handler to be able to handle subsequent traps.

Saving `fir` any time except the first time after a trap occurs saves the address of the `ld.c` instruction in single-instruction mode, or the address of the floating-point companion to the `ld.c` instruction in dual-instruction mode.

Exceptions: None

Ld.x Load Integer Ld.x

Operation: *idest* ← mem.*x*[*isrc1* + *isrc2*]

Syntax:

```
ld.x isrc1(isrc2),idest
ld.x #constA(isrc2),idest
(.x = .b, .s, .l)
```

Description: Load 8, 16, or 32 bits from memory into the destination register. The address is calculated by adding the two source operands using signed binary addition. 8-bit and 16-bit values are sign extended to 32 bits.

CC: not affected
OF: not affected
FSR: not affected

Instruction Encoding:

```
31 30 29 28 27 26 25 24 23 22 21 20 19 18 17 16 15 14 13 12 11 10 9 8 7 6 5 4 3 2 1 0
0 0 0 L 0 0 --src2--- --dest--- --src1--- 0 0 0 0 0 0 0 0 0 0 S
0 0 0 L 0 1 --src2--- --dest--- -------16-bit Immediate------ S
```

Instruction Fields:

L, S	Length of load 0,0 - 8 bits (**.b**) 0,1 - 8 bits (**.b**) 1,0 - 16 bits (**.s**) 1,1 - 32 bits (**.l**)
src1, src2	Specifies any of the integer registers
dest	Specifies any of the integer registers
Immediate	A 16-bit constant, sign extended to 32 bits. If L (bit 28) is set, bit zero of the immediate value is forced to zero to maintain alignment.

Programming Notes:

A one clock freeze occurs if the preceding instruction was a store (**fst, st**) that hit the data cache.

A one clock freeze occurs if *idest* is a source operand of the next instruction.

Assemblers and compilers must align the immediate address offset to the same boundary as the effective address, because the lower bit of the immediate offset is used to encode operand length information.

Exceptions: Data Access Trap

Lock Begin Interlocked Bus Sequence Lock

Operation:

BL ← 1
Lock the bus on the next load or store that misses the cache.
Disable interrupts until bus is unlocked.

Syntax: **lock**

Description: Set the BL bit and lock the bus, by asserting the LOCK# pin, on the next load or store that misses the cache. Interrupts are disabled from the clock of the **lock** instruction until the bus is unlocked.

CC:	not affected
OF:	not affected
FSR:	not affected

Instruction Encoding:

31	30	29	28	27	26	25	24	23	22	21	20	19	18	17	16	15	14	13	12	11	10	9	8	7	6	5	4	3	2	1	0
0	1	0	0	1	1	0	0	0	0	0	0	0	0	0	0	0	0	0	0	0	0	0	0	0	0	0	0	0	0	0	1

Instruction Fields:

Programming Notes:

The instructions **lock** and **unlock** allow programs running in multiprocessor and multithreaded systems to perform read-modify-write sequences. See Chapter 9, "Operating System Support," for more information.

If any trap occurs during a locked sequence, the IL bit of **epsr** will be set.

An instruction **trap** will occur if there is not both an **unlock** instruction and a load or store subsequent within 30 instructions of the **lock** instruction.

Exceptions: Instruction Trap

M12apm.p Pipelined F-P Add and Multiply M12apm.p

Operation:

fdest ← last stage adder result.
Advance adder pipeline one stage.
Advance multiplier pipeline one stage.
First stage adder pipeline ← adder result + multiplier result.
First stage multiplier pipeline ← *fsrc1* × *fsrc2*.

Syntax: **m12apm.p** *fsrc1, fsrc2, fdest*
(**.p** = **.ss**, **.sd**, **.dd**)

Description: Add the last stage result of the multiplier pipeline to the last stage result of the adder pipeline using signed floating-point addition. Multiply the two source operands using 32- or 64-bit floating-point multiplication. Store the last stage result of the adder pipeline in the destination register.

CC:	not affected
OF:	not affected
FSR:	AA, AE, AI, AO, AU, MA, MI, MO, MU, SI, SE

Instruction Encoding:

```
31 30 29 28 27 26 25 24 23 22 21 20 19 18 17 16 15 14 13 12 11 10  9  8  7  6  5  4  3  2  1  0
0  1  0  0  1  0 --src2--- --dest--- --src1--- 1  D  S  R  0  0  0  1  0  0  1
```

Instruction Fields:

D Dual-Instruction mode bit
0 - Single-instruction mode
1 - Dual-instruction mode

S, R	Source and Result precision 00 - single, single (**.ss**) 01 - single, double (**.sd**) 10 - reserved 11 - double, double (**.dd**)
src1, src2	Specifies any of the floating-point registers
dest	Specifies any of the floating-point registers

Programming Notes:

fsrc1 must not be the same register as *fdest*.

A one clock freeze occurs if the prior operation is pipelined and *fsrc1* is the same register as the *fdest* of the prior operation.

Exceptions:

Floating-Point Source
Floating-Point Result

M12asm.p Pipelined F-P Subtract and Multiply M12asm.p

Operation:

`fdest` ← last stage adder result.
Advance adder pipeline one stage.
Advance multiplier pipeline one stage.
First stage adder pipeline ← adder result − multiplier result.
First stage multiplier pipeline ← `fsrc1` × `fsrc2`.

Syntax: **m12asm.p** *fsrc1, fsrc2, fdest*
(**.p** = **.ss, .sd, .dd**)

Description: Subtract the last stage result of the multiplier pipeline from the last stage result of the adder pipeline using signed floating-point subtraction. Multiply the two source operands using 32- or 64-bit floating-point multiplication. Store the last stage result of the adder pipeline in the destination register.

CC:	not affected
OF:	not affected
FSR:	AA, AE, AI, AO, AU, MA, MI, MO, MU, SI, SE

Instruction Encoding:

```
31 30 29 28 27 26 25 24 23 22 21 20 19 18 17 16 15 14 13 12 11 10  9  8  7  6  5  4  3  2  1  0
0  1  0  0  1  0  --src2---  --dest---  --src1---  1  D  S  R  0  0  1  1  0  0  1
```

Instruction Fields:

D Dual-Instruction mode bit
  0 - Single-instruction mode
  1 - Dual-instruction mode

S, R	Source and Result precision 00 - single, single (**.ss**) 01 - single, double (**.sd**) 10 - reserved 11 - double, double (**.dd**)
src1, src2	Specifies any of the floating-point registers
dest	Specifies any of the floating-point registers

Programming Notes:

fsrc1 must not be the same register as *fdest*.

A one clock freeze occurs if the prior operation is pipelined and *fsrc1* is the same register as the *fdest* of the prior operation.

Exceptions:

Floating-Point Source
Floating-Point Result

M12tpa.p Pipelined F-P Add and Multiply M12tpa.p

Operation:

fdest ← last stage adder result.
Advance adder pipeline one stage.
Advance multiplier pipeline one stage.
First stage adder pipeline ← T + adder result.
First stage multiplier pipeline ← *fsrc1* × *fsrc2*.

Syntax: **m12tpa.p** *fsrc1, fsrc2, fdest*
(**.p** = **.ss**, **.sd**, **.dd**)

Description: Add the contents of the T register to the last stage result of the adder pipeline using signed floating-point addition. Multiply the two source operands using 32- or 64-bit floating-point multiplication. Store the last stage result of the adder pipeline in the destination register.

CC:	not affected
OF:	not affected
FSR:	AA, AE, AI, AO, AU, MA, MI, MO, MU, SI, SE

Instruction Encoding:

```
31 30 29 28 27 26 25 24 23 22 21 20 19 18 17 16 15 14 13 12 11 10  9  8  7  6  5  4  3  2  1  0
 0  1  0  0  1  0 --src2---    --dest---    --src1---    1  D  S  R  0  0  0  1  1  1  1
```

Instruction Fields:

D Dual-Instruction mode bit
0 - Single-instruction mode
1 - Dual-instruction mode

S, R	Source and Result precision 00 - single, single (`.ss`) 01 - single, double (`.sd`) 10 - reserved 11 - double, double (`.dd`)
src1, src2	Specifies any of the floating-point registers
dest	Specifies any of the floating-point registers

Programming Notes:

fsrc1 must not be the same register as *fdest*.

A one clock freeze occurs if the prior operation is pipelined and *fsrc1* is the same register as the *fdest* of the prior operation.

Exceptions:

Floating-Point Source
Floating-Point Result

M12tpm.p Pipelined F-P Add and Multiply M12tpm.p

Operation:

fdest ← last stage adder result.
Advance adder pipeline one stage.
Advance multiplier pipeline one stage.
First stage adder pipeline ← T + multiplier result.
First stage multiplier pipeline ← *fsrc1* × *fsrc2*.

Syntax: **m12tpm.p** *fsrc1, fsrc2, fdest*
(**.p** = **.ss**, **.sd**, **.dd**)

Description: Add the contents of the T register to the last stage result of the multiplier pipeline using signed floating-point addition. Multiply the two source operands using 32- or 64-bit floating-point multiplication. Store the last stage result of the adder pipeline in the destination register.

CC:	not affected
OF:	not affected
FSR:	AA, AE, AI, AO, AU, MA, MI, MO, MU, SI, SE

Instruction Encoding:

```
31 30 29 28 27 26 25 24 23 22 21 20 19 18 17 16 15 14 13 12 11 10  9  8  7  6  5  4  3  2  1  0
 0  1  0  0  1  0 --src2--- --dest--- --src1---  1  D  S  R  0  0  0  1  1  0  1
```

Instruction Fields:

D Dual-Instruction mode bit
 0 - Single-instruction mode
 1 - Dual-instruction mode

S, R	Source and Result precision 00 - single, single (**.ss**) 01 - single, double (**.sd**) 10 - reserved 11 - double, double (**.dd**)
src1, src2	Specifies any of the floating-point registers
dest	Specifies any of the floating-point registers

Programming Notes:

fsrc1 must not be the same register as *fdest*.

A one clock freeze occurs if the prior operation is pipelined and *fsrc1* is the same register as the *fdest* of the prior operation.

Exceptions:

Floating-Point Source
Floating-Point Result

M12tsa.p Pipelined F-P Subtract and Multiply M12tsa.p

Operation:

fdest ← last stage adder result.
Advance adder pipeline one stage.
Advance multiplier pipeline one stage.
First stage adder pipeline ← T − adder result.
First stage multiplier pipeline ← *fsrc1* × *fsrc2*.

Syntax: **m12tsa.p** *fsrc1, fsrc2, fdest*
(**.p** = **.ss, .sd, .dd**)

Description: Subtract the last stage result of the adder pipeline from the contents of the T register using signed floating-point subtraction. Multiply the two source operands using 32- or 64-bit floating-point multiplication. Store the last stage result of the adder pipeline in the destination register.

CC:	not affected
OF:	not affected
FSR:	AA, AE, AI, AO, AU, MA, MI, MO, MU, SE, SI

Instruction Encoding:

```
31 30 29 28 27 26 25 24 23 22 21 20 19 18 17 16 15 14 13 12 11 10  9  8  7  6  5  4  3  2  1  0
0  1  0  0  1  0  --src2---      --dest---      --src1---      1  D  S  R  0  0  1  1  1  1  1
```

Instruction Fields:

D Dual-Instruction mode bit
0 - Single-instruction mode
1 - Dual-instruction mode

S, R	Source and Result precision 00 - single, single (`.ss`) 01 - single, double (`.sd`) 10 - reserved 11 - double, double (`.dd`)
src1, src2	Specifies any of the floating-point registers
dest	Specifies any of the floating-point registers

Programming Notes:

fsrc1 must not be the same register as *fdest*.

A one clock freeze occurs if the prior operation is pipelined and *fsrc1* is the same register as the *fdest* of the prior operation.

Exceptions:

Floating-Point Source
Floating-Point Result

M12tsm.p Pipelined F-P Subtract and Multiply M12tsm.p

Operation:

fdest ← last stage adder result.
Advance adder pipeline one stage.
Advance multiplier pipeline one stage.
First stage adder pipeline ← T − multiplier result.
First stage multiplier pipeline ← *fsrc1* × *fsrc2*.

Syntax: **m12tsm.p** *fsrc1, fsrc2, fdest*
(.p = .ss, .sd, .dd)

Description: Subtract the last stage result of the multiplier pipeline from the contents of the T register using signed floating-point subtraction. Multiply the two source operands using 32- or 64-bit floating-point multiplication. Store the last stage result of the adder pipeline in the destination register.

CC:	not affected
OF:	not affected
FSR:	AA, AE, AI, AO, AU, MA, MI, MO, MU, SE, SI

Instruction Encoding:

```
31 30 29 28 27 26 25 24 23 22 21 20 19 18 17 16 15 14 13 12 11 10  9  8  7  6  5  4  3  2  1  0
0  1  0  0  1  0 --src2--- --dest--- --src1--- 1  D  S  R  0  0  1  1  1  0  1
```

Instruction Fields:

D Dual-Instruction mode bit
0 - Single-instruction mode
1 - Dual-instruction mode

S, R	Source and Result precision 00 - single, single (**.ss**) 01 - single, double (**.sd**) 10 - reserved 11 - double, double (**.dd**)
src1, src2	Specifies any of the floating-point registers
dest	Specifies any of the floating-point registers

Programming Notes:

fsrc1 must not be the same register as *fdest*.

A one clock freeze occurs if the prior operation is pipelined and *fsrc1* is the same register as the *fdest* of the prior operation.

Exceptions:

Floating-Point Source
Floating-Point Result

M12ttpa.p Pipelined F-P Add and Multiply M12ttpa.p

Operation:

fdest ← last stage adder result.
Advance adder pipeline one stage.
Advance multiplier pipeline one stage.
First stage adder pipeline ← T + adder result.
First stage multiplier pipeline ← *fsrc1* × *fsrc2*.
T ← multiplier result.

Syntax: **m12ttpa.p** *fsrc1, fsrc2, fdest*
(**.p** = **.ss**, **.sd**, **.dd**)

Description: Add the contents of the T register to the last stage result of the adder pipeline using signed floating-point addition. Multiply the two source operands using 32- or 64-bit floating-point multiplication. Store the last stage result of the adder pipeline in the destination register. Store the last stage result of the multiplier pipeline in the T register.

CC:	not affected
OF:	not affected
FSR:	AA, AE, AI, AO, AU, MA, MI, MO, MU, SE, SI

Instruction Encoding:

```
31 30 29 28 27 26 25 24 23 22 21 20 19 18 17 16 15 14 13 12 11 10 9 8 7 6 5 4 3 2 1 0
0  1  0  0  1  0  --src2---    --dest---    --src1---    1  D S R 0 0 0 1 0 1 1
```

Instruction Fields:

D Dual-Instruction mode bit
0 - Single-instruction mode
1 - Dual-instruction mode

S, R	Source and Result precision 00 - single, single (**.ss**) 01 - single, double (**.sd**) 10 - reserved 11 - double, double (**.dd**)
src1, src2	Specifies any of the floating-point registers
dest	Specifies any of the floating-point registers

Programming Notes:

fsrc1 must not be the same register as *fdest*.

A one clock freeze occurs if the prior operation is pipelined and *fsrc1* is the same register as the *fdest* of the prior operation.

Exceptions:

Floating-Point Source
Floating-Point Result

M12ttsa.p Pipelined F-P Subtract and Multiply M12ttsa.p

Operation:

fdest ← last stage adder result.
Advance adder pipeline one stage.
Advance multiplier pipeline one stage.
First stage adder pipeline ← T − adder result.
First stage multiplier pipeline ← *fsrc1* × *fsrc2*.
T ← multiplier result.

Syntax: **m12ttsa.p** *fsrc1, fsrc2, fdest*
(.p = .ss, .sd, .dd)

Description: Subtract the last stage result of the adder pipeline from the contents of the T register using signed floating-point subtraction. Multiply the two source operands using 32- or 64-bit floating-point multiplication. Store the last stage result of the adder pipeline in the destination register. Store the last stage result of the multiplier pipeline in the T register.

CC:	not affected
OF:	not affected
FSR:	AA, AE, AI, AO, AU, MA, MI, MO, MU, SE, SI

Instruction Encoding:

```
31 30 29 28 27 26 25 24 23 22 21 20 19 18 17 16 15 14 13 12 11 10 9 8 7 6 5 4 3 2 1 0
0  1  0  0  1  0  --src2---   --dest---   --src1---   1  D S R 0 0 1 1 0 1 1
```

Instruction Fields:

D Dual-Instruction mode bit
0 - Single-instruction mode
1 - Dual-instruction mode

S, R	Source and Result precision 00 - single, single (`.ss`) 01 - single, double (`.sd`) 10 - reserved 11 - double, double (`.dd`)
src1, src2	Specifies any of the floating-point registers
dest	Specifies any of the floating-point registers

Programming Notes:

`fsrc1` must not be the same register as *`fdest`*.

A one clock freeze occurs if the prior operation is pipelined and *`fsrc1`* is the same register as the *`fdest`* of the prior operation.

Exceptions:

Floating-Point Source
Floating-Point Result

Mi2mpl.p Pipelined F-P Multiply with Add Mi2mpl.p

Operation:

fdest ← last stage multiplier result.
Advance adder pipeline one stage.
Advance multiplier pipeline one stage.
First stage adder pipeline ← *fsrc1* + multiplier result.
First stage multiplier pipeline ← KI × *fsrc2*.
T ← multiplier result.

Syntax: **mi2mpl.p** *fsrc1, fsrc2, fdest*
(**.p** = **.ss**, **.sd**, **.dd**)

Description: Add the first source operand to the last stage result of the multiplier pipeline using signed floating-point addition. Multiply the second source operand by the contents of the KI register using 32- or 64-bit floating-point multiplication. Store the last stage result of the multiplier pipeline in the destination register and in the T register.

CC: not affected
OF: not affected
FSR: AA, AE, AI, AO, AU, MA, MI, MO, MU, SE, SI

Instruction Encoding:

```
31 30 29 28 27 26 25 24 23 22 21 20 19 18 17 16 15 14 13 12 11 10  9  8  7  6  5  4  3  2  1  0
0  1  0  0  1  0  --src2---  --dest---  --src1---  0  D  S  R  0  0  0  0  1  1  0
```

Instruction Fields:

D Dual-Instruction mode bit
  0 - Single-instruction mode
  1 - Dual-instruction mode

S, R	Source and Result precision 00 - single, single (**.ss**) 01 - single, double (**.sd**) 10 - reserved 11 - double, double (**.dd**)
src1, src2	Specifies any of the floating-point registers
dest	Specifies any of the floating-point registers

Programming Notes:

This instruction is pipelined although the encoding has P = 0.

Exceptions:

Floating-Point Source
Floating-Point Result

Mi2mpt.p Pipelined F-P Multiply with Add Mi2mpt.p

Operation:

fdest ← last stage multiplier result.
Advance adder pipeline one stage.
Advance multiplier pipeline one stage.
First stage adder pipeline ← T + multiplier result.
First stage multiplier pipeline ← KI × *fsrc2*.
T ← multiplier result.
KI ← *fsrc1*.

Syntax: **mi2mpt.p** *fsrc1, fsrc2, fdest*
(**.p** = **.ss, .sd, .dd**)

Description: Add the contents of the T register to the last stage result of the multiplier pipeline using signed floating-point addition. Multiply the second source operand by the contents of the KI register using 32- or 64-bit floating-point multiplication. Store the last stage result of the multiplier pipeline in the destination register and in the T register. Load the KI register with the first source operand.

CC: not affected
OF: not affected
FSR: AA, AE, AI, AO, AU, MA, MI, MO, MU, SE, SI

Instruction Encoding:

```
31 30 29 28 27 26 25 24 23 22 21 20 19 18 17 16 15 14 13 12 11 10  9  8  7  6  5  4  3  2  1  0
0  1  0  0  1  0  --src2---      --dest---      --src1---      0  D  S  R  0  0  0  0  1  1  1
```

Instruction Fields:

D Dual-Instruction mode bit
0 - Single-instruction mode
1 - Dual-instruction mode

S, R	Source and Result precision 00 - single, single (`.ss`) 01 - single, double (`.sd`) 10 - reserved 11 - double, double (`.dd`)
src1, src2	Specifies any of the floating-point registers
dest	Specifies any of the floating-point registers

Programming Notes:

fsrc1 must not be the same register as *fdest*.
This instruction is pipelined although the encoding has P = 0.

Exceptions:

Floating-Point Source
Floating-Point Result

Mi2ms1.p Pipelined F-P Multiply with Subtract Mi2ms1.p

Operation:

fdest ← last stage multiplier result.
Advance adder pipeline one stage.
Advance multiplier pipeline one stage.
First stage adder pipeline ← *fsrc1* − multiplier result.
First stage multiplier pipeline ← KI × *fsrc2*.
T ← multiplier result.

Syntax: **mi2ms1.p** *fsrc1, fsrc2, fdest*
(**.p = .ss, .sd, .dd**)

Description: Subtract the last stage result of the multiplier pipeline from the first source operand using signed floating-point subtraction. Multiply the second source operand by the contents of the KI register using 32- or 64-bit floating-point multiplication. Store the last stage result of the multiplier pipeline in the destination register and in the T register.

CC:	not affected
OF:	not affected
FSR:	AA, AE, AI, AO, AU, MA, MI, MO, MU, SE, SI

Instruction Encoding:

```
31 30 29 28 27 26 25 24 23 22 21 20 19 18 17 16 15 14 13 12 11 10  9  8  7  6  5  4  3  2  1  0
 0  1  0  0  1  0 --src2--- --dest--- --src1--- 0  D  S  R  0  0  1  0  1  1  0
```

Instruction Fields:

D Dual-Instruction mode bit
0 - Single-instruction mode
1 - Dual-instruction mode

S, R	Source and Result precision 00 - single, single (`.ss`) 01 - single, double (`.sd`) 10 - reserved 11 - double, double (`.dd`)
src1, src2	Specifies any of the floating-point registers
dest	Specifies any of the floating-point registers

Programming Notes:

This instruction is pipelined although the encoding has `P` = 0.

Exceptions:

Floating-Point Source
Floating-Point Result

Mi2mst.p Pipelined F-P Multiply with Subtract Mi2mst.p

Operation:

fdest ← last stage multiplier result.
Advance adder pipeline one stage.
Advance multiplier pipeline one stage.
First stage adder pipeline ← T − multiplier result.
First stage multiplier pipeline ← KI × *fsrc2*.
T ← multiplier result.
KI ← *fsrc1*.

Syntax: mi2mst.p *fsrc1*, *fsrc2*, *fdest*
(.p = .ss, .sd, .dd)

Description: Subtract the last stage result of the multiplier pipeline from the contents of the T register using signed floating-point subtraction. Multiply the second source operand by the contents of the KI register using 32- or 64-bit floating-point multiplication. Store the last stage result of the multiplier pipeline in the destination register and in the T register. Load the KI register with the first source operand.

CC: not affected
OF: not affected
FSR: AA, AE, AI, AO, AU, MA, MI, MO, MU, SE, SI

Instruction Encoding:

```
31 30 29 28 27 26 25 24 23 22 21 20 19 18 17 16 15 14 13 12 11 10  9  8  7  6  5  4  3  2  1  0
 0  1  0  0  1  0 --src2--- --dest--- --src1--- 0  D  S  R  0  0  1  0  1  1  1
```

Instruction Fields:

D Dual-Instruction mode bit
0 - Single-instruction mode
1 - Dual-instruction mode

S, R	Source and Result precision 00 - single, single (`.ss`) 01 - single, double (`.sd`) 10 - reserved 11 - double, double (`.dd`)
src1, src2	Specifies any of the floating-point registers
dest	Specifies any of the floating-point registers

Programming Notes:

fsrc1 must not be the same register as *fdest*.
This instruction is pipelined although the encoding has P = 0.

Exceptions:

Floating-Point Source
Floating-Point Result

Mi2p1.p Pipelined F-P Multiply with Add Mi2p1.p

Operation:

fdest ← last stage multiplier result.
Advance adder pipeline one stage.
Advance multiplier pipeline one stage.
First stage adder pipeline ← *fsrc1* + multiplier result.
First stage multiplier pipeline ← KI × *fsrc2*.

Syntax: **mi2p1.p** *fsrc1, fsrc2, fdest*
(**.p = .ss, .sd, .dd**)

Description: Add the last stage result of the multiplier pipeline to the first source operand using signed floating-point addition. Multiply the second source operand by the contents of the KI register using 32- or 64-bit floating-point multiplication. Store the last stage result of the multiplier pipeline in the destination register.

CC:	not affected
OF:	not affected
FSR:	AA, AE, AI, AO, AU, MA, MI, MO, MU, SE, SI

Instruction Encoding:

```
31 30 29 28 27 26 25 24 23 22 21 20 19 18 17 16 15 14 13 12 11 10  9  8  7  6  5  4  3  2  1  0
0  1  0  0  1  0  --src2---  --dest---  --src1---  0  D  S  R  0  0  0  0  1  0  0
```

Instruction Fields:

D Dual-Instruction mode bit
 0 - Single-instruction mode
 1 - Dual-instruction mode

S, R	Source and Result precision 00 - single, single (**.ss**) 01 - single, double (**.sd**) 10 - reserved 11 - double, double (**.dd**)
src1, src2	Specifies any of the floating-point registers
dest	Specifies any of the floating-point registers

Programming Notes:

This instruction is pipelined although the encoding has P = 0.

Exceptions:

Floating-Point Source
Floating-Point Result

Mi2pt.p Pipelined F-P Multiply with Add Mi2pt.p

Operation:

fdest ← last stage multiplier result.
Advance adder pipeline one stage.
Advance multiplier pipeline one stage.
First stage adder pipeline ← T + multiplier result.
First stage multiplier pipeline ← KI × *fsrc2*.
KI ← *fsrc1*.

Syntax: **mi2pt.p** *fsrc1, fsrc2, fdest*
(**.p** = **.ss, .sd, .dd**)

Description: Add the last stage result of the multiplier pipeline to the contents of the T register using signed floating-point addition. Multiply the second source operand by the contents of the KI register using 32- or 64-bit floating-point multiplication. Store the last stage result of the multiplier pipeline in the destination register. Load the KI register with the first source operand.

CC:	not affected
OF:	not affected
FSR:	AA, AE, AI, AO, AU, MA, MI, MO, MU, SE, SI

Instruction Encoding:

```
31 30 29 28 27 26 25 24 23 22 21 20 19 18 17 16 15 14 13 12 11 10  9  8  7  6  5  4  3  2  1  0
0  1  0  0  1  0  --src2---  --dest---  --src1---  0  D  S  R  0  0  0  0  1  0  1
```

Instruction Fields:

D Dual-Instruction mode bit
  0 - Single-instruction mode
  1 - Dual-instruction mode

S, R	Source and Result precision 00 - single, single (**.ss**) 01 - single, double (**.sd**) 10 - reserved 11 - double, double (**.dd**)
src1, src2	Specifies any of the floating-point registers
dest	Specifies any of the floating-point registers

Programming Notes:

fsrc1 must not be the same register as *fdest*.
This instruction is pipelined although the encoding has P = 0.

Exceptions:

Floating-Point Source
Floating-Point Result

Mi2s1.p Pipelined F-P Multiply with Subtract Mi2s1.p

Operation:

fdest ← last stage multiplier result.
Advance adder pipeline one stage.
Advance multiplier pipeline one stage.
First stage adder pipeline ← *fsrc1* − multiplier result.
First stage multiplier pipeline ← KI × *fsrc2*.

Syntax: **mi2s1.p** *fsrc1, fsrc2, fdest*
(.p = .ss, .sd, .dd)

Description: Subtract the last stage result of the multiplier pipeline from the first source operand using signed floating-point subtraction. Multiply the second source operand by the contents of the KI register using 32- or 64-bit floating-point multiplication. Store the last stage result of the multiplier pipeline in the destination register.

CC: not affected
OF: not affected
FSR: AA, AE, AI, AO, AU, MA, MI, MO, MU, SE, SI

Instruction Encoding:

```
31 30 29 28 27 26 25 24 23 22 21 20 19 18 17 16 15 14 13 12 11 10  9  8  7  6  5  4  3  2  1  0
 0  1  0  0  1  0 --src2--- --dest--- --src1---  0  D  S  R  0  0  1  0  1  0  0
```

Instruction Fields:

D Dual-Instruction mode bit
0 - Single-instruction mode
1 - Dual-instruction mode

S, R	Source and Result precision 00 - single, single (`.ss`) 01 - single, double (`.sd`) 10 - reserved 11 - double, double (`.dd`)
src1, src2	Specifies any of the floating-point registers
dest	Specifies any of the floating-point registers

Programming Notes:

This instruction is pipelined although the encoding has P = 0.

Exceptions:

Floating-Point Source
Floating-Point Result

Mi2st.p Pipelined F-P Multiply with Subtract Mi2st.p

Operation:

fdest ← last stage multiplier result.
Advance adder pipeline one stage.
Advance multiplier pipeline one stage.
First stage adder pipeline ← T − multiplier result.
First stage multiplier pipeline ← KI × *fsrc2*.
KI ← *fsrc1*.

Syntax: **mi2st.p** *fsrc1, fsrc2, fdest*
(**.p** = **.ss, .sd, .dd**)

Description: Subtract the last stage result of the multiplier pipeline from the contents of the T register using signed floating-point subtraction. Multiply the second source operand by the contents of the KI register using 32- or 64-bit floating-point multiplication. Store the last stage result of the multiplier pipeline in the destination register. Load the KI register with the first source operand.

CC:	not affected
OF:	not affected
FSR:	AA, AE, AI, AO, AU, MA, MI, MO, MU, SE, SI

Instruction Encoding:

```
31 30 29 28 27 26 25 24 23 22 21 20 19 18 17 16 15 14 13 12 11 10 9 8 7 6 5 4 3 2 1 0
0  1  0  0  1  0  --src2---      --dest---      --src1---      0  D S R 0 0 1 0 1 0 1
```

Instruction Fields:

D Dual-Instruction mode bit
0 - Single-instruction mode
1 - Dual-instruction mode

S, R	Source and Result precision 00 - single, single (`.ss`) 01 - single, double (`.sd`) 10 - reserved 11 - double, double (`.dd`)
src1, src2	Specifies any of the floating-point registers
dest	Specifies any of the floating-point registers

Programming Notes:

fsrc1 must not be the same register as *fdest*.
This instruction is pipelined although the encoding has P = 0.

Exceptions:

Floating-Point Source
Floating-Point Result

Mim1p2.p Pipelined F-P Multiply with Add Mim1p2.p

Operation:

fdest ← last stage multiplier result.
Advance adder pipeline one stage.
Advance multiplier pipeline one stage.
First stage adder pipeline ← *fsrc1* + *fsrc2*.
First stage multiplier pipeline ← KI × multiplier result.

Syntax: **mim1p2.p** *fsrc1, fsrc2, fdest*
(**.p** = **.ss, .sd, .dd**)

Description: Add the two source operands using signed floating-point addition. Multiply the last stage multiplier result by the contents of the KI register using 32- or 64-bit floating-point multiplication. Store the last stage result of the multiplier pipeline in the destination register.

CC:	not affected
OF:	not affected
FSR:	AA, AE, AI, AO, AU, MA, MI, MO, MU, SE, SI

Instruction Encoding:

```
31 30 29 28 27 26 25 24 23 22 21 20 19 18 17 16 15 14 13 12 11 10  9  8  7  6  5  4  3  2  1  0
 0  1  0  0  1  0 --src2--- --dest--- --src1--- 0  D  S  R  0  0  0  1  1  1  0
```

Instruction Fields:

D Dual-Instruction mode bit
0 - Single-instruction mode
1 - Dual-instruction mode

S, R	Source and Result precision 00 - single, single (`.ss`) 01 - single, double (`.sd`) 10 - reserved 11 - double, double (`.dd`)
src1, src2	Specifies any of the floating-point registers
dest	Specifies any of the floating-point registers

Programming Notes:

This instruction is pipelined although the encoding has P = 0.

Exceptions:

Floating-Point Source
Floating-Point Result

Mim1s2.p Pipelined F-P Multiply with Subtract Mim1s2.p

Operation:

fdest ← last stage multiplier result.
Advance adder pipeline one stage.
Advance multiplier pipeline one stage.
First stage adder pipeline ← *fsrc1* − *fsrc2*.
First stage multiplier pipeline ← KI × multiplier result.

Syntax: **mim1s2.p** *fsrc1, fsrc2, fdest*
(.p = **.ss, .sd, .dd**)

Description: Subtract the second source operand from the first source operand using signed floating-point subtraction. Multiply the last stage multiplier result by the contents of the KI register using 32- or 64-bit floating-point multiplication. Store the last stage result of the multiplier pipeline in the destination register.

CC: not affected
OF: not affected
FSR: AA, AE, AI, AO, AU, MA, MI, MO, MU, SE, SI

Instruction Encoding:

```
31 30 29 28 27 26 25 24 23 22 21 20 19 18 17 16 15 14 13 12 11 10  9  8  7  6  5  4  3  2  1  0
0  1  0  0  1  0  --src2---  --dest---  --src1---  0  D  S  R  0  0  1  1  1  1  0
```

Instruction Fields:

D Dual-Instruction mode bit
0 - Single-instruction mode
1 - Dual-instruction mode

S, R	Source and Result precision 00 - single, single (**.ss**) 01 - single, double (**.sd**) 10 - reserved 11 - double, double (**.dd**)
src1, src2	Specifies any of the floating-point registers
dest	Specifies any of the floating-point registers

Programming Notes:

This instruction is pipelined although the encoding has P = 0.

Exceptions:

Floating-Point Source
Floating-Point Result

Mimt1p2.p Pipelined F-P Multiply with Add Mimt1p2.p

Operation:

fdest ← last stage multiplier result.
Advance adder pipeline one stage.
Advance multiplier pipeline one stage.
First stage adder pipeline ← *fsrc1* + *fsrc2*.
First stage multiplier pipeline ← KI × multiplier result.
T ← multiplier result.

Syntax: **mimt1p2.p** *fsrc1, fsrc2, fdest*
(**.p** = **.ss**, **.sd**, **.dd**)

Description: Add the two source operands using signed floating-point addition. Multiply the last stage multiplier result by the contents of the KI register using 32- or 64-bit floating-point multiplication. Store the last stage result of the multiplier pipeline in the destination register and in the T register.

CC:	not affected
OF:	not affected
FSR:	AA, AE, AI, AO, AU, MA, MI, MO, MU, SE, SI

Instruction Encoding:

```
31 30 29 28 27 26 25 24 23 22 21 20 19 18 17 16 15 14 13 12 11 10  9  8  7  6  5  4  3  2  1  0
0  1  0  0  1  0  --src2---  --dest---  --src1---  0  D  S  R  0  0  0  1  1  0  0
```

Instruction Fields:

D Dual-Instruction mode bit
0 - Single-instruction mode
1 - Dual-instruction mode

S, R	Source and Result precision 00 - single, single (`.ss`) 01 - single, double (`.sd`) 10 - reserved 11 - double, double (`.dd`)
src1, src2	Specifies any of the floating-point registers
dest	Specifies any of the floating-point registers

Programming Notes:

This instruction is pipelined although the encoding has P = 0.

Exceptions:

Floating-Point Source
Floating-Point Result

Mimt1s2.p Pipelined F-P Multiply with Subtract Mimt1s2.p

Operation:

fdest ← last stage multiplier result.
Advance adder pipeline one stage.
Advance multiplier pipeline one stage.
First stage adder pipeline ← *fsrc1* − *fsrc2*.
First stage multiplier pipeline ← KI × multiplier result.
T ← multiplier result.

Syntax: **mimt1s2.p** *fsrc1, fsrc2, fdest*
(**.p** = **.ss, .sd, .dd**)

Description: Subtract the second source operand from the first source operand using signed floating-point subtraction. Multiply the last stage multiplier result by the contents of the KI register using 32- or 64-bit floating-point multiplication. Store the last stage result of the multiplier pipeline in the destination register and in the T register.

CC:	not affected
OF:	not affected
FSR:	AA, AE, AI, AO, AU, MA, MI, MO, MU, SE, SI

Instruction Encoding:

```
31 30 29 28 27 26 25 24 23 22 21 20 19 18 17 16 15 14 13 12 11 10  9  8  7  6  5  4  3  2  1  0
0  1  0  0  1  0  --src2---  --dest---  --src1---  0  D  S  R  0  0  1  1  1  0  0
```

Instruction Fields:

D Dual-Instruction mode bit
0 - Single-instruction mode
1 - Dual-instruction mode

S, R	Source and Result precision 00 - single, single (`.ss`) 01 - single, double (`.sd`) 10 - reserved 11 - double, double (`.dd`)
src1, src2	Specifies any of the floating-point registers
dest	Specifies any of the floating-point registers

Programming Notes:

This instruction is pipelined although the encoding has P = 0.

Exceptions:

Floating-Point Source
Floating-Point Result

Mm12mpm.p Pipelined F-P Multiply with Add Mm12mpm.p

Operation:

fdest ← last stage multiplier result.
Advance adder pipeline one stage.
Advance multiplier pipeline one stage.
First stage adder pipeline ← multiplier result + multiplier result.
First stage multiplier pipeline ← *fsrc1* × *fsrc2*.

Syntax: **mm12mpm.p** *fsrc1, fsrc2, fdest*
(.p = .ss, .sd, .dd)

Description: Add the last stage multiplier result to itself using signed floating-point addition. Multiply the two source operands using 32- or 64-bit floating-point multiplication. Store the last stage result of the multiplier pipeline in the destination register.

CC:	not affected
OF:	not affected
FSR:	AA, AE, AI, AO, AU, MA, MI, MO, MU, SE, SI

Instruction Encoding:

```
31 30 29 28 27 26 25 24 23 22 21 20 19 18 17 16 15 14 13 12 11 10  9  8  7  6  5  4  3  2  1  0
0  1  0  0  1  0  --src2---      --dest---      --src1---      0  D  S  R  0  0  0  1  0  0  1
```

Instruction Fields:

D — Dual-Instruction mode bit
- 0 - Single-instruction mode
- 1 - Dual-instruction mode

S, R — Source and Result precision
- 00 - single, single (.ss)
- 01 - single, double (.sd)

	10 - reserved
	11 - double, double (**.dd**)
src1, src2	Specifies any of the floating-point registers
dest	Specifies any of the floating-point registers

Programming Notes:

fsrc1 must not be the same register as *fdest*.
This instruction is pipelined although the encoding has P = 0.

Exceptions:

Floating-Point Source
Floating-Point Result

Mm12msm.p Pipelined F-P Multiply with Subtract Mm12msm.p

Operation:

fdest ← last stage multiplier result.
Advance adder pipeline one stage.
Advance multiplier pipeline one stage.
First stage adder pipeline ← Multiplier Result − multiplier result.
First stage multiplier pipeline ← *fsrc1* × *fsrc2*.

Syntax: **mm12msm.p** *fsrc1, fsrc2, fdest*
(**.p = .ss, .sd, .dd**)

Description: Subtract the last stage multiplier result from itself using signed floating-point subtraction. Multiply the two source operands using 32- or 64-bit floating-point multiplication. Store the last stage result of the multiplier pipeline in the destination register.

CC:	not affected
OF:	not affected
FSR:	AA, AE, AI, AO, AU, MA, MI, MO, MU, SE, SI

Instruction Encoding:

```
31 30 29 28 27 26 25 24 23 22 21 20 19 18 17 16 15 14 13 12 11 10  9  8  7  6  5  4  3  2  1  0
 0  1  0  0  1  0 --src2--- --dest--- --src1---  0  D  S  R  0  0  1  1  0  0  1
```

Instruction Fields:

D Dual-Instruction mode bit
  0 - Single-instruction mode
  1 - Dual-instruction mode

S, R	Source and Result precision 00 - single, single (`.ss`) 01 - single, double(`.sd`) 10 - reserved 11 - double, double (`.dd`)
src1, src2	Specifies any of the floating-point registers
dest	Specifies any of the floating-point registers

Programming Notes:

fsrc1 must not be the same register as *fdest*.

This instruction is pipelined although the encoding has P = 0.

A programmer can use **mm12msm** to initialize the adder pipeline to zero while multiplying.

Exceptions:

Floating-Point Source
Floating-Point Result

Mm12tpm.p Pipelined F-P Multiply with Add Mm12tpm.p

Operation:

`fdest` ← last stage multiplier result.
Advance adder pipeline one stage.
Advance multiplier pipeline one stage.
First stage adder pipeline ← `T` + multiplier result.
First stage multiplier pipeline ← `fsrc1` × `fsrc2`.

Syntax: **mm12tpm.p** *fsrc1, fsrc2, fdest*
(**.p** = **.ss, .sd, .dd**)

Description: Add the last stage multiplier result to the contents of the `T` register using signed floating-point addition. Multiply the two source operands using 32- or 64-bit floating-point multiplication. Store the last stage result of the multiplier pipeline in the destination register.

CC:	not affected
OF:	not affected
FSR:	AA, AE, AI, AO, AU, MA, MI, MO, MU, SE, SI

Instruction Encoding:

```
31 30 29 28 27 26 25 24 23 22 21 20 19 18 17 16 15 14 13 12 11 10  9  8  7  6  5  4  3  2  1  0
 0  1  0  0  1  0 --src2---  --dest---  --src1---   0  D  S  R  0  0  0  1  1  0  1
```

Instruction Fields:

D	Dual-Instruction mode bit 0 - Single-instruction mode 1 - Dual-instruction mode
S, R	Source and Result precision 00 - single, single (**.ss**) 01 - single, double (**.sd**)

	10 - reserved
	11 - double, double (**.dd**)
src1, src2	Specifies any of the floating-point registers
dest	Specifies any of the floating-point registers

Programming Notes:

fsrc1 must not be the same register as *fdest*.
This instruction is pipelined although the encoding has P = 0.

Exceptions:

Floating-Point Source
Floating-Point Result

Mm12tsm.p Pipelined F-P Multiply with Subtract Mm12tsm.p

Operation:

fdest ← last stage multiplier result.
Advance adder pipeline one stage.
Advance multiplier pipeline one stage.
First stage adder pipeline ← T − multiplier result.
First stage multiplier pipeline ← *fsrc1* × *fsrc2*.

Syntax: **mm12tsm.p** *fsrc1, fsrc2, fdest*
(**.p** = **.ss**, **.sd**, **.dd**)

Description: Subtract the last stage multiplier result from the contents of the T register using signed floating-point subtraction. Multiply the two source operands using 32- or 64-bit floating-point multiplication. Store the last stage result of the multiplier pipeline in the destination register.

CC: not affected
OF: not affected
FSR: AA, AE, AI, AO, AU, MA, MI, MO, MU, SE, SI

Instruction Encoding:

```
31 30 29 28 27 26 25 24 23 22 21 20 19 18 17 16 15 14 13 12 11 10 9 8 7 6 5 4 3 2 1 0
0  1  0  0  1  0  --src2---      --dest---      --src1---      0  D S R 0 0 1 1 1 0 1
```

Instruction Fields:

D Dual-Instruction mode bit
  0 - Single-instruction mode
  1 - Dual-instruction mode

S, R Source and Result precision
  00 - single, single (**.ss**)
  01 - single, double (**.sd**)

	10 - reserved
	11 - double, double (**.dd**)
src1, src2	Specifies any of the floating-point registers
dest	Specifies any of the floating-point registers

Programming Notes:

fsrc1 must not be the same register as *fdest*.
This instruction is pipelined although the encoding has P = 0.

Exceptions:

Floating-Point Source
Floating-Point Result

Mm12ttpm.p Pipelined F-P Multiply with Add Mm12ttpm.p

Operation:

fdest ← last stage multiplier result.
Advance adder pipeline one stage.
Advance multiplier pipeline one stage.
First stage adder pipeline ← T + multiplier result.
First stage multiplier pipeline ← *fsrc1* × *fsrc2*.
T ← multiplier result.

Syntax: **mm12ttpm.p** *fsrc1, fsrc2, fdest*
(**.p = .ss, .sd, .dd**)

Description: Add the last stage multiplier result to the contents of the T register using signed floating-point addition. Multiply the two source operands using 32- or 64-bit floating-point multiplication. Store the last stage result of the multiplier pipeline in the destination register and in the T register.

CC: not affected
OF: not affected
FSR: AA, AE, AI, AO, AU, MA, MI, MO, MU, SE, SI

Instruction Encoding:

```
31 30 29 28 27 26 25 24 23 22 21 20 19 18 17 16 15 14 13 12 11 10  9  8  7  6  5  4  3  2  1  0
0  1  0  0  1  0  --src2---  --dest---  --src1---  0  D  S  R  0  0  0  1  0  1  1
```

Instruction Fields:

D Dual-Instruction mode bit
0 - Single-instruction mode
1 - Dual-instruction mode

S, R	Source and Result precision 00 - single, single (**.ss**) 01 - single, double (**.sd**) 10 - reserved 11 - double, double (**.dd**)
src1, src2	Specifies any of the floating-point registers
dest	Specifies any of the floating-point registers

Programming Notes:

fsrc1 must not be the same register as *fdest*.
This instruction is pipelined although the encoding has P = 0.

Exceptions:

Floating-Point Source
Floating-Point Result

Mm12ttsm.p Pipelined F-P Multiply with Subtract Mm12ttsm.p

Operation:

fdest ← last stage multiplier result.
Advance adder pipeline one stage.
Advance multiplier pipeline one stage.
First stage adder pipeline ← T − multiplier result.
First stage multiplier pipeline ← *fsrc1* × *fsrc2.*
T ← multiplier result.

Syntax: **mm12ttsm.p** *fsrc1, fsrc2, fdest*
(**.p = .ss, .sd, .dd**)

Description: Subtract the last stage multiplier result from the contents of the T register using signed floating-point subtraction. Multiply the two source operands using 32- or 64-bit floating-point multiplication. Store the last stage result of the multiplier pipeline in the destination register and in the T register.

CC:	not affected
OF:	not affected
FSR:	AA, AE, AI, AO, AU, MA, MI, MO, MU, SE, SI

Instruction Encoding:

```
31 30 29 28 27 26 25 24 23 22 21 20 19 18 17 16 15 14 13 12 11 10  9  8  7  6  5  4  3  2  1  0
 0  1  0  0  1  0 --src2---  --dest---  --src1---  0  D  S  R  0  0  1  1  0  1  1
```

Instruction Fields:

D Dual-Instruction mode bit
0 - Single-instruction mode
1 - Dual-instruction mode

S, R	Source and Result precision
	00 - single, single (`.ss`)
	01 - single, double (`.sd`)
	10 - reserved
	11 - double, double (`.dd`)
src1, src2	Specifies any of the floating-point registers
dest	Specifies any of the floating-point registers

Programming Notes:

fsrc1 must not be the same register as *fdest*.
This instruction is pipelined although the encoding has P = 0.

Exceptions:

Floating-Point Source
Floating-Point Result

Mov Integer Register-Register Move Mov

Operation: *idest* ← *isrc2*

Syntax: **mov** *isrc2,idest*

Description: Move a value from the integer source register to the destination register. This is not an instruction, but an assembler pseudo operation. See below for how this pseudo operation is encoded.

CC: not affected
OF: not affected
FSR: not affected

Instruction Encoding: Assembler pseudo operation encodings:

mov *isrc2, idest*	is encoded as	**shl**	**r0,** *isrc2, idest*
mov *#const, idest*	IF (*#const* ≤0x7FFF) THEN **mov** is encoded as	**or**	*#const,* **r0,** *idest*
	ELSE is coded as	**orh**	high part, **r0,** *idest*
		or	low part, **r0,** *idest*
	FI		

Programming Notes:

Exceptions: None

Mr2mp1.p   Pipelined F-P Multiply with Add   Mr2mp1.p

Operation:

fdest ← last stage multiplier result.
Advance adder pipeline one stage.
Advance multiplier pipeline one stage.
First stage adder pipeline ← *fsrc1* + multiplier result.
First stage multiplier pipeline ← KR × *fsrc2*.
T ← multiplier result.

Syntax: **mr2mp1.p** *fsrc1, fsrc2, fdest*
(.p = .ss, .sd, .dd)

Description: Add the last stage multiplier result to the first source operand using signed floating-point addition. Multiply the second source operand by the contents of the KR register using 32- or 64-bit floating-point multiplication. Store the last stage result of the multiplier pipeline in the destination register and in the T register.

CC: not affected
OF: not affected
FSR: AA, AE, AI, AO, AU, MA, MI, MO, MU, SE, SI

Instruction Encoding:

```
31 30 29 28 27 26 25 24 23 22 21 20 19 18 17 16 15 14 13 12 11 10  9  8  7  6  5  4  3  2  1  0
0 1 0 0 1 0 --src2--- --dest--- --src1--- 0 D S R 0 0 0 0 0 1 0
```

Instruction Fields:

D   Dual-Instruction mode bit
0 - Single-instruction mode
1 - Dual-instruction mode

S, R	Source and Result precision 00 - single, single (**.ss**) 01 - single, double (**.sd**) 10 - reserved 11 - double, double (**.dd**)
src1, src2	Specifies any of the floating-point registers
dest	Specifies any of the floating-point registers

Programming Notes:

This instruction is pipelined although the encoding has P = 0.

Exceptions:

Floating-Point Source
Floating-Point Result

Mr2mpt.p Pipelined F-P Multiply with Add Mr2mpt.p

Operation:

fdest ← last stage multiplier result.
Advance adder pipeline one stage.
Advance multiplier pipeline one stage.
First stage adder pipeline ← T + multiplier result.
First stage multiplier pipeline ← KR × *fsrc2.*
T ← multiplier result.
KR ← *fsrc1.*

Syntax: **mr2mpt.p** *fsrc1, fsrc2, fdest*
(**.p** = **.ss, .sd, .dd**)

Description: Add the last stage multiplier result to the contents of the T register using signed floating-point addition. Multiply the second source operand by the contents of the KR register using 32- or 64-bit floating-point multiplication. Store the last stage result of the multiplier pipeline in the destination register and in the T register. Load the KR register with the first source operand.

CC: not affected
OF: not affected
FSR: AA, AE, AI, AO, AU, MA, MI, MO, MU, SE, SI

Instruction Encoding:

```
31 30 29 28 27 26 25 24 23 22 21 20 19 18 17 16 15 14 13 12 11 10 9 8 7 6 5 4 3 2 1 0
0  1  0  0  1  0  --src2---    --dest---      --src1---      0  D S R 0 0 0 0 0 1 1
```

Instruction Fields:

D Dual-Instruction mode bit
0 - Single-instruction mode
1 - Dual-instruction mode

S, R	Source and Result precision 00 - single, single (.ss) 01 - single, double (.sd) 10 - reserved 11 - double, double (.dd)
src1, src2	Specifies any of the floating-point registers
dest	Specifies any of the floating-point registers

Programming Notes:

fsrc1 must not be the same register as *fdest*.
This instruction is pipelined although the encoding has P = 0.

Exceptions:

Floating-Point Source
Floating-Point Result

Mr2ms1.p Pipelined F-P Multiply with Subtract Mr2ms1.p

Operation:

fdest ← last stage multiplier result.
Advance adder pipeline one stage.
Advance multiplier pipeline one stage.
First stage adder pipeline ← *fsrc1* − multiplier result.
First stage multiplier pipeline ← KR × *fsrc2*.
T ← multiplier result.

Syntax: **mr2ms1.p** *fsrc1, fsrc2, fdest*
(**.p** = **.ss**, **.sd**, **.dd**)

Description: Subtract the last stage multiplier result from the first source operand using signed floating-point subtraction. Multiply the second source operand by the contents of the KR register using 32- or 64-bit floating-point multiplication. Store the last stage result of the multiplier pipeline in the destination register and in the T register.

CC:	not affected
OF:	not affected
FSR:	AA, AE, AI, AO, AU, MA, MI, MO, MU, SE, SI

Instruction Encoding:

```
31 30 29 28 27 26 25 24 23 22 21 20 19 18 17 16 15 14 13 12 11 10  9  8  7  6  5  4  3  2  1  0
0  1  0  0  1  0  --src2---  --dest---  --src1---  0  D  S  R  0  0  1  0  0  1  0
```

Instruction Fields:

D Dual-Instruction mode bit
 0 - Single-instruction mode
 1 - Dual-instruction mode

S, R	Source and Result precision 00 - single, single (`.ss`) 01 - single, double (`.sd`) 10 - reserved 11 - double, double (`.dd`)
src1, src2	Specifies any of the floating-point registers
dest	Specifies any of the floating-point registers

Programming Notes:

This instruction is pipelined although the encoding has P = 0.

Exceptions:

Floating-Point Source
Floating-Point Result

Mr2mst.p Pipelined F-P Multiply with Subtract Mr2mst.p

Operation:

fdest ← last stage multiplier result.
Advance adder pipeline one stage.
Advance multiplier pipeline one stage.
First stage adder pipeline ← T − multiplier result.
First stage multiplier pipeline ← KR × *fsrc2*.
T ← multiplier result.
KR ← *fsrc1*.

Syntax: **mr2mst.p** *fsrc1, fsrc2, fdest*
(**.p** = **.ss**, **.sd**, **.dd**)

Description: Subtract the last stage multiplier result from the contents of the T register using signed floating-point subtraction. Multiply the second source operand by the contents of the KR register using 32- or 64-bit floating-point multiplication. Store the last stage result of the multiplier pipeline in the destination register and in the T register. Load the KR register with the first source operand.

CC:	not affected
OF:	not affected
FSR:	AA, AE, AI, AO, AU, MA, MI, MO, MU, SE, SI

Instruction Encoding:

```
31 30 29 28 27 26 25 24 23 22 21 20 19 18 17 16 15 14 13 12 11 10  9  8  7  6  5  4  3  2  1  0
0  1  0  0  1  0  --src2---     --dest---      --src1---       0  D  S  R  0  0  1  0  0  1  1
```

Instruction Fields:

D Dual-Instruction mode bit
0 - Single-instruction mode
1 - Dual-instruction mode

S, R	Source and Result precision 00 - single, single (`.ss`) 01 - single, double (`.sd`) 10 - reserved 11 - double, double (`.dd`)
src1, src2	Specifies any of the floating-point registers
dest	Specifies any of the floating-point registers

Programming Notes:

fsrc1 must not be the same register as *fdest*.
This instruction is pipelined although the encoding has P = 0.

Exceptions:

Floating-Point Source
Floating-Point Result

Mr2p1.p Pipelined F-P Multiply with Add Mr2p1.p

Operation:

fdest ← last stage multiplier result.
Advance adder pipeline one stage.
Advance multiplier pipeline one stage.
First stage adder pipeline ← *fsrc1* + multiplier result.
First stage multiplier pipeline ← KR × *fsrc2*.

Syntax: **mr2p1.p** *fsrc1, fsrc2, fdest*
(**.p** = **.ss**, **.sd**, **.dd**)

Description: Add the last stage multiplier result to the first source operand using signed floating-point addition. Multiply the second source operand by the contents of the KR register using 32- or 64-bit floating-point multiplication. Store the last stage result of the multiplier pipeline in the destination register.

CC: not affected
OF: not affected
FSR: AA, AE, AI, AO, AU, MA, MI, MO, MU, SE, SI

Instruction Encoding:

```
31 30 29 28 27 26 25 24 23 22 21 20 19 18 17 16 15 14 13 12 11 10  9  8  7  6  5  4  3  2  1  0
0  1  0  0  1  0  --src2---      --dest---      --src1---      0  D  S  R  0  0  0  0  0  0  0
```

Instruction Fields:

D Dual-Instruction mode bit
0 - Single-instruction mode
1 - Dual-instruction mode

S, R	Source and Result precision 00 - single, single (`.ss`) 01 - single, double (`.sd`) 10 - reserved 11 - double, double (`.dd`)
src1, src2	Specifies any of the floating-point registers
dest	Specifies any of the floating-point registers

Programming Notes:

This instruction is pipelined although the encoding has P = 0.

Exceptions:

Floating-Point Source
Floating-Point Result

Mr2pt.p Pipelined F-P Multiply with Add Mr2pt.p

Operation:

fdest ← last stage multiplier result.
Advance adder pipeline one stage.
Advance multiplier pipeline one stage.
First stage adder pipeline ← T + multiplier result.
First stage multiplier pipeline ← KR × *fsrc2.*
KR ← *fsrc1.*

Syntax: **mr2pt.p** *fsrc1, fsrc2, fdest*
(**.p** = **.ss**, **.sd**, **.dd**)

Description: Add the last stage multiplier result to the contents of the T register using signed floating-point addition. Multiply the second source operand by the contents of the KR register using 32- or 64-bit floating-point multiplication. Store the last stage result of the multiplier pipeline in the destination register. Load the KR register with the first source operand.

CC:	not affected
OF:	not affected
FSR:	AA, AE, AI, AO, AU, MA, MI, MO, MU, SE, SI

Instruction Encoding:

```
31 30 29 28 27 26 25 24 23 22 21 20 19 18 17 16 15 14 13 12 11 10  9  8  7  6  5  4  3  2  1  0
 0  1  0  0  1  0 --src2---  --dest---  --src1---   0  D  S  R  0  0  0  0  0  1
```

Instruction Fields:

D Dual-Instruction mode bit
0 - Single-instruction mode
1 - Dual-instruction mode

S, R	Source and Result precision 00 - single, single (`.ss`) 01 - single, double (`.sd`) 10 - reserved 11 - double, double (`.dd`)
src1, src2	Specifies any of the floating-point registers
dest	Specifies any of the floating-point registers

Programming Notes:

fsrc1 must not be the same register as *fdest*.
This instruction is pipelined although the encoding has P = 0.

Exceptions:

Floating-Point Source
Floating-Point Result

Mr2s1.p Pipelined F-P Multiply with Subtract Mr2s1.p

Operation:

fdest ← last stage multiplier result.
Advance adder pipeline one stage.
Advance multiplier pipeline one stage.
First stage adder pipeline ← *fsrc1* − multiplier result.
First stage multiplier pipeline ← KR × *fsrc2*.

Syntax: **mr2s1.p** *fsrc1*, *fsrc2*, *fdest*
(.p = .ss, .sd, .dd)

Description: Subtract the last stage multiplier result from the first source operand using signed floating-point subtraction. Multiply the second source operand by the contents of the KR register using 32- or 64-bit floating-point multiplication. Store the last stage result of the multiplier pipeline in the destination register.

CC:	not affected
OF:	not affected
FSR:	AA, AE, AI, AO, AU, MA, MI, MO, MU, SE, SI

Instruction Encoding:

```
31 30 29 28 27 26 25 24 23 22 21 20 19 18 17 16 15 14 13 12 11 10  9  8  7  6  5  4  3  2  1  0
0  1  0  0  1  0  --src2---  --dest---  --src1---  0  D  S  R  0  0  1  0  0  0  0
```

Instruction Fields:

D Dual-Instruction mode bit
 0 - Single-instruction mode
 1 - Dual-instruction mode

S, R	Source and Result precision 00 - single, single (`.ss`) 01 - single, double (`.sd`) 10 - reserved 11 - double, double (`.dd`)
src1, src2	Specifies any of the floating-point registers
dest	Specifies any of the floating-point registers

Programming Notes:

This instruction is pipelined although the encoding has P = 0.

Exceptions:

Floating-Point Source
Floating-Point Result

Mr2st.p Pipelined F-P Multiply with Subtract Mr2st.p

Operation:

fdest ← last stage multiplier result.
Advance adder pipeline one stage.
Advance multiplier pipeline one stage.
First stage adder pipeline ← T − multiplier result.
First stage multiplier pipeline ← KR × *fsrc2*.
KR ← *fsrc1*.

Syntax: **mr2st.p** *fsrc1, fsrc2, fdest*
(**.p** = **.ss**, **.sd**, **.dd**)

Description: Subtract the last stage multiplier result from the contents of the T register using signed floating-point subtraction. Multiply the second source operand by the contents of the KR register using 32- or 64-bit floating-point multiplication. Store the last stage result of the multiplier pipeline in the destination register. Load the KR register with the first source operand.

CC: not affected
OF: not affected
FSR: AA, AE, AI, AO, AU, MA, MI, MO, MU, SE, SI

Instruction Encoding:

```
31 30 29 28 27 26 25 24 23 22 21 20 19 18 17 16 15 14 13 12 11 10  9  8  7  6  5  4  3  2  1  0
 0  1  0  0  1  0 --src2---  --dest---  --src1---  0  D  S  R  0  0  1  0  0  0  1
```

Instruction Fields:

D Dual-Instruction mode bit
0 - Single-instruction mode
1 - Dual-instruction mode

S, R	Source and Result precision 00 - single, single (`.ss`) 01 - single, double (`.sd`) 10 - reserved 11 - double, double (`.dd`)
src1, src2	Specifies any of the floating-point registers
dest	Specifies any of the floating-point registers

Programming Notes:

fsrc1 must not be the same register as *fdest*.
This instruction is pipelined although the encoding has P = 0.

Exceptions:

Floating-Point Source
Floating-Point Result

Mrm1p2.p Pipelined F-P Multiply with Add Mrm1p2.p

Operation:

fdest ← last stage multiplier result.
Advance adder pipeline one stage.
Advance multiplier pipeline one stage.
First stage adder pipeline ← *fsrc1* + *fsrc2*.
First stage multiplier pipeline ← KR × multiplier result.

Syntax: **mrm1p2.p** *fsrc1, fsrc2, fdest*
(**.p** = **.ss**, **.sd**, **.dd**)

Description: Add the two source operands using signed floating-point addition. Multiply the last stage multiplier result by the contents of the KR register using 32- or 64-bit floating-point multiplication. Store the last stage result of the multiplier pipeline in the destination register.

CC: not affected
OF: not affected
FSR: AA, AE, AI, AO, AU, MA, MI, MO, MU, SE, SI

Instruction Encoding:

```
31 30 29 28 27 26 25 24 23 22 21 20 19 18 17 16 15 14 13 12 11 10  9  8  7  6  5  4  3  2  1  0
0  1  0  0  1  0  --src2---  --dest---  --src1---  0  D  S  R  0  0  0  1  0  1  0
```

Instruction Fields:

D Dual-Instruction mode bit
0 - Single-instruction mode
1 - Dual-instruction mode

S, R Source and Result precision
00 - single, single (**.ss**)
01 - single, double (**.sd**)

	10 - reserved
	11 - double, double (**.dd**)
src1, src2	Specifies any of the floating-point registers
dest	Specifies any of the floating-point registers

Programming Notes:

This instruction is pipelined although the encoding has P = 0.

Exceptions:

Floating-Point Source
Floating-Point Result

Mrm1s2.p Pipelined F-P Multiply with Subtract Mrm1s2.p

Operation:

fdest ← last stage multiplier result.
Advance adder pipeline one stage.
Advance multiplier pipeline one stage.
First stage adder pipeline ← *fsrc1* − *fsrc2*.
First stage multiplier pipeline ← KR × multiplier result.

Syntax: **mrm1s2.p** *fsrc1, fsrc2, fdest*
(.p = .ss, .sd, .dd)

Description: Subtract the second source operand from the first source operand using signed floating-point subtraction. Multiply the last stage multiplier result by the contents of the KR register using 32- or 64-bit floating-point multiplication. Store the last stage result of the multiplier pipeline in the destination register.

CC: not affected
OF: not affected
FSR: AA, AE, AI, AO, AU, MA, MI, MO, MU, SE, SI

Instruction Encoding:

```
31 30 29 28 27 26 25 24 23 22 21 20 19 18 17 16 15 14 13 12 11 10  9  8  7  6  5  4  3  2  1  0
 0  1  0  0  1  0 --src2--- --dest--- --src1--- 0  D  S  R  0  0  1  1  0  1  0
```

Instruction Fields:

D Dual-Instruction mode bit
0 - Single-instruction mode
1 - Dual-instruction mode

S, R	Source and Result precision 00 - single, single (.ss) 01 - single, double (.sd) 10 - reserved 11 - double, double (.dd)
src1, src2	Specifies any of the floating-point registers
dest	Specifies any of the floating-point registers

Programming Notes:

This instruction is pipelined although the encoding has P = 0.

Exceptions:

Floating-Point Source
Floating-Point Result

Mrmt1p2.p Pipelined F-P Multiply with Add Mrmt1p2.p

Operation:

fdest ← last stage multiplier result.
Advance adder pipeline one stage.
Advance multiplier pipeline one stage.
First stage adder pipeline ← *fsrc1* + *fsrc2*.
First stage multiplier pipeline ← KR × multiplier result.
T ← multiplier result.

Syntax: **mrmt1p2.p** *fsrc1, fsrc2, fdest*
(**.p** = **.ss**, **.sd**, **.dd**)

Description: Add the two source operands using signed floating-point addition. Multiply the last stage multiplier result by the contents of the KR register using 32- or 64-bit floating-point multiplication. Store the last stage result of the multiplier pipeline in the destination register and in the T register.

CC:	not affected
OF:	not affected
FSR:	AA, AE, AI, AO, AU, MA, MI, MO, MU, SE, SI

Instruction Encoding:

```
31 30 29 28 27 26 25 24 23 22 21 20 19 18 17 16 15 14 13 12 11 10 9 8 7 6 5 4 3 2 1 0
0  1  0  0  1  0  --src2---   --dest---   --src1---   0 D S R 0 0 0 1 0 0 0
```

Instruction Fields:

D Dual-Instruction mode bit
  0 - Single-instruction mode
  1 - Dual-instruction mode

S, R	Source and Result precision 00 - single, single (`.ss`) 01 - single, double (`.sd`) 10 - reserved 11 - double, double (`.dd`)
src1, src2	Specifies any of the floating-point registers
dest	Specifies any of the floating-point registers

Programming Notes:

This instruction is pipelined although the encoding has P = 0.

Exceptions:

Floating-Point Source
Floating-Point Result

Mrmt1s2.p Pipelined F-P Multiply with Subtract Mrmt1s2.p

Operation:

fdest ← last stage multiplier result.
Advance adder pipeline one stage.
Advance multiplier pipeline one stage.
First stage adder pipeline ← *fsrc1* − *fsrc2*.
First stage multiplier pipeline ← KR × multiplier result.
T ← multiplier result.

Syntax: **mrmt1s2.p** *fsrc1, fsrc2, fdest*
(**.p** = **.ss**, **.sd**, **.dd**)

Description: Subtract the second source operand from the first source operand using signed floating-point subtraction. Multiply the last stage multiplier result by the contents of the KR register using 32- or 64-bit floating-point multiplication. Store the last stage result of the multiplier pipeline in the destination register and in the T register.

CC:	not affected
OF:	not affected
FSR:	AA, AE, AI, AO, AU, MA, MI, MO, MU, SE, SI

Instruction Encoding:

```
31 30 29 28 27 26 25 24 23 22 21 20 19 18 17 16 15 14 13 12 11 10  9  8  7  6  5  4  3  2  1  0
 0  1  0  0  1  0 --src2--- --dest--- --src1---  0  D  S  R  0  0  1  1  0  0  0
```

Instruction Fields:

D Dual-Instruction mode bit
0 - Single-instruction mode
1 - Dual-instruction mode

S, R	Source and Result precision 00 - single, single (`.ss`) 01 - single, double (`.sd`) 10 - reserved 11 - double, double (`.dd`)
src1, src2	Specifies any of the floating-point registers
dest	Specifies any of the floating-point registers

Programming Notes:

This instruction is pipelined although the encoding has P = 0.

Exceptions:

Floating-Point Source
Floating-Point Result

Nop Integer No Operation Nop

Operation: None

Syntax: `nop`

Description: No operation is performed. This is not an instruction, but an assembler pseudo operation. See below for how this pseudo operation is encoded.

CC: not affected
OF: not affected
FSR: not affected

Instruction Encoding: Assembler pseudo operation encodings:

`nop` is encoded as `shl r0, r0, r0`

Programming Notes:

Exceptions: None

Or — Logical OR — Or

Operation: *idest* ← *isrc1* OR *isrc2*

Syntax:

```
or isrc1, isrc2, idest
or #constL, isrc2, idest
```

Description: Perform bitwise OR on the two source operands and store the result in the destination register.

CC: CC ← (result == 0)
OF: not affected
FSR: not affected

Instruction Encoding:

```
31 30 29 28 27 26 25 24 23 22 21 20 19 18 17 16 15 14 13 12 11 10 9 8 7 6 5 4 3 2 1 0
1 1 1 0 0 0 --src2--- --dest--- --src1--- 0 0 0 0 0 0 0 0 0 0 0
1 1 1 0 0 1 --src2--- --dest--- -------16-bit Immediate--------
```

Instruction Fields:

src1, src2	Specifies any of the integer registers
dest	Specifies any of the integer registers
Immediate	A 16-bit constant, zero extended to 32 bits

Programming Notes:

Exceptions: None

Orh Logical OR High Orh

Operation: *idest* ← (*#constL* shifted left 16 bits) OR *isrc2*

Syntax: **orh** *#constL, isrc2, idest*

Description: Perform bitwise OR on the two source operands and store the result in the destination register. The first source operand is created by using the 16-bit constant as the high 16 bits of the operand and filling the low 16 bits with zeros.

CC: CC ← (result = = 0)
OF: not affected
FSR: not affected

Instruction Encoding:

```
31 30 29 28 27 26 25 24 23 22 21 20 19 18 17 16 15 14 13 12 11 10 9 8 7 6 5 4 3 2 1 0
1  1  1  0  1  1  --src2--- --dest--- -------16-bit Immediate--------
```

Instruction Fields:

src2	Specifies any of the integer registers
dest	Specifies any of the integer registers
Immediate	A 16-bit constant, left shifted 16 bits, filled with zeros on the right.

Programming Notes:

Exceptions: None

Pfadd.p Pipelined Floating-Point Add Pfadd.p

Operation:

fdest ← last stage adder result.
Advance adder pipeline one stage.
First stage adder pipeline ← *fsrc1* + *fsrc2*.

Syntax: **pfadd.p** *fsrc1, fsrc2, fdest*
(**.p** = **.ss**, **.sd**, **.dd**)

Description: Add the two source operands using signed floating-point addition. Store the last stage result of the adder pipeline in the destination register.

CC:	not affected
OF:	not affected
FSR:	AA, AE, AI, AO, AU, SE, SI

Instruction Encoding:

```
31 30 29 28 27 26 25 24 23 22 21 20 19 18 17 16 15 14 13 12 11 10  9  8  7  6  5  4  3  2  1  0
 0  1  0  0  1  0 --src2--- --dest--- --src1---  1  D  S  R  0  1  1  0  0  0  0
```

Instruction Fields:

D	Dual-Instruction mode bit 0 - Single-instruction mode 1 - Dual-instruction mode
S, R	Source and Result precision 00 - single, single (**.ss**) 01 - single, double (**.sd**) 10 - reserved 11 - double, double (**.dd**)
src1, src2	Specifies any of the floating-point registers
dest	Specifies any of the floating-point registers

Programming Notes:

Exceptions:

Floating-Point Source
Floating-Point Result

Pfaddp Pipelined Add with Pixel Merge Pfaddp

Operation:

fdest ← last stage graphics result.
Last stage graphics pipeline ← *fsrc1* + *fsrc2.*
Shift and load MERGE register as defined in Table 7-3.

Syntax: **pfaddp** *fsrc1, fsrc2, fdest*

Description: Add the two source operands using signed fixed-point addition. Store the last stage result of the graphics pipeline in the destination register. The two sources are expected to contain eight 8-bit, four 16-bit, or two 32-bit pixels, depending on the contents of the PS field of the **psr**. The MERGE register is shifted and loaded as defined in Table 7-3. This instruction is used for color intensity interpolation.

CC: not affected
OF: not affected
FSR: not affected

Instruction Encoding:

```
31 30 29 28 27 26 25 24 23 22 21 20 19 18 17 16 15 14 13 12 11 10 9 8 7 6 5 4 3 2 1 0
0  1  0  0  1  0  --src2---  --dest---  --src1---  1  D  1  1  1  0  1  0  0  0  0
```

Instruction Fields:

D	Dual-Instruction mode bit 0 - Single-instruction mode 1 - Dual-instruction mode
src1, src2	Specifies any even (64-bit) floating-point register
dest	Specifies any even (64-bit) floating-point register

Programming Notes:

If *fdest* is not **f0**, *fsrc1* and *fsrc2* must not be the same register as *fdest*.

A one clock freeze occurs if *fdest* is a source operand of the next instruction .

Exceptions: None

Pfaddz Pipelined Add with Z Merge Pfaddz

Operation:

fdest ← last stage graphics result.
Last stage graphics pipeline ← *fsrc1* + *fsrc2*.
Shift the MERGE register right 16 bits and load MERGE register bits 63:48 and 31:16 with bits 63:48 and 31:16 of (*fsrc1* + *fsrc2*).

Syntax: **pfaddz** *fsrc1, fsrc2, fdest*

Description: Add the two source operands using signed, 32-bit, fixed-point addition. Store the last stage result of the graphics pipeline in the destination register. The sources are expected to contain two 32-bit, Z-buffer distance values. The 32-bit Z-buffer values consist of a 16-bit integer and a 16-bit fraction. The 16-bit integer parts of the two 32-bit **add**s are stored in the MERGE register. The MERGE register is shifted right 16 bits before being loaded with the results of the two **add**s. Normally, two **pfaddz** instructions are executed consecutively resulting in four Z-buffer **add**s.

CC:	not affected
OF:	not affected
FSR:	not affected

Instruction Encoding:

```
31 30 29 28 27 26 25 24 23 22 21 20 19 18 17 16 15 14 13 12 11 10  9  8  7  6  5  4  3  2  1  0
0  1  0  0  1  0  --src2---      --dest---      --src1---      1  D  1  1  1  0  1  0  0  0  1
```

Instruction Fields:

D Dual-Instruction mode bit
0 - Single-instruction mode
1 - Dual-instruction mode

src1, src2	Specifies any even (64-bit) floating-point register
dest	Specifies any even (64-bit) floating-point register

Programming Notes:

If *fdest* is not **f0**, *fsrc1* and *fsrc2* must not be the same register as *fdest*.

A one clock freeze occurs if *fdest* is a source operand of the next instruction.

fsrc1, fsrc2, fdest, must all be even numbered floating-point registers

pfaddz is intended for use with 16-bit Z-buffers.

Exceptions: None

Pfamov.r Pipelined Floating-Point Adder Move Pfamov.r

Operation:

fdest ← last stage adder result.
Advance adder pipeline one stage.
First stage adder pipeline ← *fsrc1*.

Syntax: **pfamov.r** *fsrc1, fdest*
(**.r = .ss, .sd, .ds, .dd**)

Description: Move the floating-point source operand through the floating-point adder preserving negative zero (−0). Store the last stage result of the adder pipeline in the destination register.

CC:	not affected
OF:	not affected
FSR:	AA, AE, AI, AO, AU

Instruction Encoding:

```
31 30 29 28 27 26 25 24 23 22 21 20 19 18 17 16 15 14 13 12 11 10 9 8 7 6 5 4 3 2 1 0
0  1  0  0  1  0  0  0  0  0  0  --dest---      --src1---       1  D S R 0 1 1 0 0 1 1
```

Instruction Fields:

D Dual-Instruction mode bit
- 0 - Single-instruction mode
- 1 - Dual-instruction mode

S, R Source and Result precision
- 00 - single, single (**.ss**)
- 01 - single, double (**.sd**)
- 10 - double, single (**.ds**).
- 11 - double, double (**.dd**)

src1	Specifies any of the floating-point registers
dest	Specifies any of the floating-point registers

Programming Notes:

pfamov should be used to convert a number from double-precision to single-precision.

Exceptions:

Floating-Point Source
Floating-Point Result

Pfeq.w Pipelined Floating-Point Equal Compare Pfeq.w

Operation:

fdest ← last stage adder result.
Advance adder pipeline one stage.
First stage adder pipeline is undefined.

Syntax: **pfeq.w** *fsrc1, fsrc2, fdest*
(.w = .ss, .dd)

Description: Compare the two source operands using a signed floating-point comparison and set CC if the two operands are equal. Store the last stage result of the adder pipeline in the destination register. The adder result of the comparison operands is undefined, but will not cause floating-point result exceptions.

CC:	CC ← (*fsrc1* = = *fsrc2*)
OF:	not affected
FSR:	SE

Instruction Encoding:

```
31 30 29 28 27 26 25 24 23 22 21 20 19 18 17 16 15 14 13 12 11 10 9 8 7 6 5 4 3 2 1 0
0  1  0  0  1  0  --src2---      --dest---      --src1---      1  D S 0 0 1 1 0 1 0 1
```

Instruction Fields:

D Dual-Instruction mode bit
0 - Single-instruction mode
1 - Dual-instruction mode

S Precision
0 - single (.ss)
1 - double (.dd)

src1, src2	Specifies any of the floating-point registers
dest	Specifies any of the floating-point registers

Programming Notes:

A one clock freeze occurs on a **bc, bnc, bc.t,** or a **bnc.t** following the **pfeq** instruction.

There is no scalar floating-point compare.

In DIM, **pfeq** cannot be paired with or follow **bc, bc.t, bnc,** or **bnc.t**.

Exceptions: Floating-Point Source

Pfgt.w Pipelined Floating-Point Greater-Than Compare Pfgt.w

Operation:

fdest ← last stage adder result.
Advance adder pipeline one stage.
First stage adder pipeline is undefined.

Syntax: **pfgt.w** *fsrc1, fsrc2, fdest*
(**.w** = **.ss**, **.dd**)

Description: Compare the two source operands using a signed floating-point comparison and set CC if the first operand is greater than the second operand. Store the last stage result of the adder pipeline in the destination register. The adder result of the comparison operands is undefined, but will not cause floating-point result exceptions.

CC: CC ← (*fsrc1* > *fsrc2*)
OF: not affected
FSR: SE

Instruction Encoding:

```
31 30 29 28 27 26 25 24 23 22 21 20 19 18 17 16 15 14 13 12 11 10 9 8 7 6 5 4 3 2 1 0
0  1  0  0  1  0  --src2---   --dest---   --src1---   1  D  S  0 0 1 1 0 1 0 0
```

Instruction Fields:

D Dual-Instruction mode bit
  0 - Single-instruction mode
  1 - Dual-instruction mode

S Precision
  0 - single (**.ss**)
  1 - double (**.dd**)

src1, src2	Specifies any of the floating-point registers
dest	Specifies any of the floating-point registers

Programming Notes:

A one clock freeze occurs on a **bc, bnc, bc.t**, or a **bnc.t** following the **pfgt** instruction.

There is no scalar floating-point compare.

In DIM, **pfgt** cannot be paired with or follow **bc, bc.t, bnc,** or **bnc.t**.

Exceptions: Floating-Point Source

Pfiadd.w Pipelined Long-Integer Add Pfiadd.w

Operation:

fdest ← last stage graphics result.
Last stage graphics pipeline ← *fsrc1* + *fsrc2*.

Syntax: **pfiadd.w** *fsrc1, fsrc2, fdest*
(**.w** = **.ss, .dd**)

Description: Add the two source operands using signed 32- or 64-bit integer addition. Store the last stage result of the graphics pipeline in the destination register.

CC: not affected
OF: not affected
FSR: not affected

Instruction Encoding:

```
31 30 29 28 27 26 25 24 23 22 21 20 19 18 17 16 15 14 13 12 11 10  9  8  7  6  5  4  3  2  1  0
 0  1  0  0  1  0 --src2--- --dest--- --src1---  1  D  S  R  1  0  0  1  0  0  1
```

Instruction Fields:

D	Dual-Instruction mode bit 0 - Single-instruction mode 1 - Dual-instruction mode
S, R	Source and Result precision 00 - 32 bits (**.ss**) 01 - reserved 10 - reserved 11 - 64-bits (**.dd**)
src1, src2	Specifies any of the floating-point registers
dest	Specifies any of the floating-point registers

Programming Notes:

If *fdest* is not **f0**, *fsrc1* and *fsrc2* must not be the same register as *fdest*.

A one clock freeze occurs if *fdest* is a source operand of the next instruction.

Exceptions: None

Pfisub.w — Pipelined Long-Integer Subtract — Pfisub.w

Operation:

fdest ← last stage graphics result.
Last stage graphics pipeline ← *fsrc1* − *fsrc2*.

Syntax: **pfisub.w** *fsrc1, fsrc2, fdest*
(**.w = .ss, .dd**)

Description: Subtract the second source operand from the first source operand using signed 32- or 64-bit integer subtraction. Store the last stage result of the graphics pipeline in the destination register.

CC:	not affected
OF:	not affected
FSR:	not affected

Instruction Encoding:

```
31 30 29 28 27 26 25 24 23 22 21 20 19 18 17 16 15 14 13 12 11 10  9  8  7  6  5  4  3  2  1  0
0  1  0  0  1  0  --src2---    --dest---      --src1---      1  D  S  R  1  0  0  1  1  0  1
```

Instruction Fields:

D	Dual-Instruction mode bit 0 - Single-instruction mode 1 - Dual-instruction mode
S, R	Source and Result precision 00 - 32 bits (**.ss**) 01 - reserved 10 - reserved 11 - 64-bits (**.dd**)
src1, src2	Specifies any of the floating-point registers
dest	Specifies any of the floating-point registers

Programming Notes:

If *fdest* is not **f0**, *fsrc1* and *fsrc2* must not be the same register as *fdest*.

A one clock freeze occurs if *fdest* is a source operand of the next instruction.

Exceptions: None

Pfix.v Pipelined F-P to Integer Conversion Pfix.v

Operation:

fdest ← last stage adder result.
Advance adder pipeline one stage.
First stage adder pipeline ← 64-bit value with low-order 32 bits equal to the rounded integer part of *fsrc1* in signed two's complement integer form.

Syntax: **pfix.v** *fsrc1, fdest*
(**.v** = **.sd**, **.dd**)

Description: Convert the source operand to integer by rounding the floating-point number. Store the last stage result of the adder pipeline in the low-order 32 bits of the destination register pair.

CC:	not affected
OF:	not affected
FSR:	AO, SE

Instruction Encoding:

```
31 30 29 28 27 26 25 24 23 22 21 20 19 18 17 16 15 14 13 12 11 10 9 8 7 6 5 4 3 2 1 0
0 1 0 0 1 0 0 0 0 0 0 --dest--- --src1--- 1 D S R 0 1 1 0 0 1 0
```

Instruction Fields:

D	Dual-Instruction mode bit 0 - Single-instruction mode 1 - Dual-instruction mode
S, R	Source and Result precision 00 - reserved 01 - single, double (**.sd**) 10 - reserved 11 - double, double (**.dd**)

src1	Specifies any of the floating-point registers
dest	Specifies any even (64-bit) floating-point register

Programming Notes:

Fix will signal an overflow if the integer part of `src1` exceeds the numbers representable by 32-bit 2's complement integers. Underflow and inexact are never signaled.

Exceptions:

Floating-Point Source
Floating-Point Result

Pfld.z Pipelined Floating-Point Load Pfld.z

Operation:

fdest ← mem.*z*[third previous **pfld**'s (*isrc1* + *isrc2*)].
(where .*z* is precision of third previous **pfld.z**)
IF(Autoincrement)
THEN
  isrc2 ← *isrc1* + *isrc2*.
FI

Syntax:

pfld.z *isrc1 (isrc2), fdest*
pfld.z *#constA (isrc2), fdest*
pfld.z *isrc1 (isrc2)++, fdest*
pfld.z *#constA (isrc2)++, fdest*
(**.z = .l, .d**)

Description: Load 32 or 64 bits from memory. Store the last stage data of the three-stage load pipeline in the destination register. The address is calculated by adding the two source operands using signed binary addition. For autoincrement addressing, the result of this addition is stored in the second source register.

CC:	not affected
OF:	not affected
FSR:	not affected

Instruction Encoding:

```
31 30 29 28 27 26 25 24 23 22 21 20 19 18 17 16 15 14 13 12 11 10 9 8 7 6 5 4 3 2 1 0
0 1 1 0 0 0 --src2--- --dest--- --src1--- 0 0 0 0 0 0 0 0 -S- A
0 1 1 0 0 1 --src2--- --dest--- -------16-bit Immediate-- -S- A
```

Instruction Fields:

S	Operand Size. 00 - 64-bits (`.d`) 01 - 32 bits (`.l`) 10 - reserved 11 - 32 bits (`.l`)
A	Autoincrement 0 - No increment 1 - Autoincrement
src1, src2	Specifies any of the integer registers
dest	Specifies any of the floating-point registers
Immediate	A 16-bit constant, sign extended to 32 bits. Bits zero and one of the immediate value are forced to zero to maintain alignment. When bit one of the immediate value is zero, bit two is also forced to zero.

Programming Notes:

isrc1 must not be the same register as *isrc2* for the autoincrementing form of **pfld**, unless both are **r0**.

A two clock freeze occurs if *fdest* is a source operand of the following instruction, or...

A one clock freeze occurs if *fdest* is a source operand of the second following instruction. (The freezes do not accumulate if *fdest* is used in both following instructions.)

A freeze occurs on **pfld** when there are three outstanding **pfld**s. The freeze is one plus the number of clocks until the data is returned for the first of the three **pfld**s.

The **pfld** instruction does not cache data. Use this instruction for data that will be kept in a register, or for data that will not be used frequently.

A freeze occurs on **pfld** when it hits the data cache. The freeze is two clocks plus the number of clocks to finish all outstanding bus cycles.

Assemblers and compilers must align the immediate address offset to the same boundary as the effective address, because the lower bits of the immediate offset are used to encode operand length information.

If a data-access trap occurs, *isrc2* will have been updated with (*isrc1* + *isrc2*), for the autoincrementing form.

Exceptions: Data-Access Trap

Pfle.w Pipelined F-P Less-Than or Equal Compare Pfle.w

Operation:

fdest ← last stage adder result.
Advance adder pipeline one stage.
First stage adder pipeline is undefined, but no result exception is reported.

Syntax: **pfle.w** *fsrc1, fsrc2, fdest*
(**.w** = **.ss**, **.dd**)

Description: Compare the two source operands using a signed floating-point comparison and clear CC if the first operand is less than or equal to the second operand. Store the last stage result of the adder pipeline in the destination register. The adder result of the comparison operands is undefined, but will not cause floating-point result exceptions.

CC:	CC ← NOT(*fsrc1* ≤ *fsrc2*)
OF:	not affected
FSR:	SE

Instruction Encoding:

```
31 30 29 28 27 26 25 24 23 22 21 20 19 18 17 16 15 14 13 12 11 10 9 8 7 6 5 4 3 2 1 0
0  1  0  0  1  0  --src2---      --dest---      --src1---      1  D S 1 0 1 1 0 1 0 0
```

Instruction Fields:

D Dual-Instruction mode bit
  0 - Single-instruction mode
  1 - Dual-instruction mode

S Precision
  0 - single (**.ss**)
  1 - double (**.dd**)

src1, src2	Specifies any of the floating-point registers
dest	Specifies any of the floating-point registers

Programming Notes:

A one clock freeze occurs on a **bc, bnc, bc.t,** or a **bnc.t** following the **pfle** instruction.

There is no scalar floating-point compare.

In DIM, **pfle** cannot be paired with or follow **bc, bc.t, bnc,** or **bnc.t**.

This instruction performs the same function as the **pfgt** instruction.

Exceptions: Floating-Point Source

Pfmov.r Pipelined Floating-Point Move Pfmov.r

Operation:

For **.sd** and **.ds**:
fdest ← last stage adder result.
Advance adder pipeline one stage.
First stage adder pipeline ← *fsrc1*.

For **.ss** and **.dd**:
fdest ← last stage graphics result.
First stage graphics pipeline ← *fsrc1*.

Syntax: **pfmov.r** *fsrc1, fdest*
(**.r** = **.ss, .sd, .ds, .dd**)

Description: Move a floating-point value from the source register to the destination register of a later instruction. Store the last stage result of the adder or graphics pipeline in the destination register. This is not an instruction, but an assembler pseudo operation. See below for how this pseudo operation is encoded.

CC:	not affected
OF:	not affected
FSR:	SE (**.sd** and **.ds** only)

Instruction Encoding: Assembler pseudo operation encodings:

pfmov.ss *fsrc1, fdest*	is encoded as	**pfiadd.ss** *fsrc1*, **f0**, *fdest*
pfmov.dd *fsrc1, fdest*	is encoded as	**pfiadd.dd** *fsrc1*, **f0**, *fdest*
pfmov.sd *fsrc1, fdest*	is encoded as	**pfamov.sd** *fsrc1, fdest*
pfmov.ds *fsrc1, fdest*	is encoded as	**pfamov.ds** *fsrc1, fdest*

Programming Notes:

Note that the pipeline is the three-stage adder pipeline for **pfmov.sd** and **pfmov.ds**, but the one-stage graphics pipeline for **pfmov.ss** and **pfmov.dd**.

Exceptions: F-P Source, F-P Result (**.sd** and **.ds** only)

Pfmul.p Pipelined Floating-Point Multiply Pfmul.p

Operation:

fdest ← last stage multiplier result.
Advance multiplier pipeline one stage.
First stage multiplier pipeline ← *fsrc1* × *fsrc2*.

Syntax: **pfmul.p** *fsrc1, fsrc2, fdest*
(**.p** = **.ss**, **.sd**, **.dd**)

Description: Multiply the two source operands using signed floating-point multiplication. Store the last stage result of the multiplier pipeline in the destination register.

CC:	not affected
OF:	not affected
FSR:	MA, MI, MO, MU, SE, SI

Instruction Encoding:

```
31 30 29 28 27 26 25 24 23 22 21 20 19 18 17 16 15 14 13 12 11 10 9 8 7 6 5 4 3 2 1 0
0  1  0  0  1  0  --src2---   --dest---   --src1---   1  D  S  R  0  1  0  0  0  0  0
```

Instruction Fields:

D	Dual-Instruction mode bit 0 - Single-instruction mode 1 - Dual-instruction mode
S, R	Source and Result precision 00 - single, single (**.ss**) 01 - single, double (**.sd**) 10 - reserved 11 - double, double (**.dd**)

src1, src2	Specifies any of the floating-point registers
dest	Specifies any of the floating-point registers

Programming Notes:

If *fdest* is not **f0**, *fsrc1* must not be the same register as *fdest*.

A three clock freeze occurs if the prior operation is scalar and *fsrc1* is the same as the *fdest* of the prior operation.

A two clock freeze occurs if the prior operation is scalar and *fsrc1* is not the same as *fdest* of the prior operation.

A one clock freeze occurs if the prior operation is pipelined and *fsrc1* is the same as the *fdest* of the prior operation.

A two clock freeze occurs on 1.6% of all data patterns. The freeze is for rounding and is data dependent. This freeze only affects the multiplier and the *fdest*. The freeze will not be seen if at least two integer operations follow the **pfmul**.

See Chapter 6, "Floating Point Operations," for restrictions and hints on single- to double- and double- to single-precision transitions using **pfmul**.

Exceptions:

Floating-Point Source
Floating-Point Result

Pfmul3.dd Three-Stage Pipelined F-P Multiply Pfmul3.dd

Operation:

fdest ← last stage multiplier result.
Advance three-stage multiplier pipeline one stage.
First stage multiplier pipeline ← *fsrc1* × *fsrc2*.

Syntax: **pfmul3.dd** *fsrc1, fsrc2, fdest*

Description: Multiply the two source operands using signed floating-point multiplication and forcing a three-stage pipeline. Store the last stage result of the multiplier pipeline in the destination register.

CC:	not affected
OF:	not affected
FSR:	MO, MU, MI, MA, SE, SI

Instruction Encoding:

```
31 30 29 28 27 26 25 24 23 22 21 20 19 18 17 16 15 14 13 12 11 10  9  8  7  6  5  4  3  2  1  0
0  1  0  0  1  0  --src2---      --dest---      --src1---       1  D  1  1  0  1  0  0  1  0  0
```

Instruction Fields:

D	Dual-Instruction mode bit 0 - Single-instruction mode 1 - Dual-instruction mode
src1, src2	Specifies any even (64-bit) floating-point register
dest	Specifies any even (64-bit) floating-point register

Programming Notes:

If *fdest* is not **f0**, *fsrc1* must not be the same register as *fdest*.

The **pfmul3.dd** instruction is primarily used by trap handlers in restoring pipeline contents (see Chapter 9, "Operating System Support"). It should not be mixed in instruction sequences with other pipelined multiplier instructions.

Exceptions:

Floating-Point Source
Floating-Point Result

Pform Pipelined OR with Merge Register Pform

Operation:

fdest ← last stage graphics result.
Last stage graphics pipeline ← *fsrc1* OR MERGE.
MERGE ← 0.

Syntax: **pform** *fsrc1, fdest*

Description: Logically perform the OR operation on the 64-bit source register with the MERGE register. Store the last stage result of the graphics pipeline in the destination register. This instruction is used to retrieve pixels or Z-buffer values from the MERGE register.

CC:	not affected
OF:	not affected
FSR:	not affected

Instruction Encoding:

```
31 30 29 28 27 26 25 24 23 22 21 20 19 18 17 16 15 14 13 12 11 10  9  8  7  6  5  4  3  2  1  0
 0  1  0  0  1  0  0  0  0  0  0 --dest---     --src1---       1  D  1  1  1  0  1  1  0  1  0
```

Instruction Fields:

D	Dual-Instruction mode bit 0 - Single-instruction mode 1 - Dual-instruction mode
src1	Specifies any even (64-bit) floating-point register
dest	Specifies any even (64-bit) floating-point register

Programming Notes:

If *fdest* is not **f0**, *fsrc1* must not be the same register as *fdest*.

A one clock freeze occurs if *fdest* is a source operand of the next instruction.

Exceptions: None

Pfsub.p Pipelined Floating-Point Subtract Pfsub.p

Operation:

fdest ← last stage adder result.
Advance adder pipeline one stage.
First stage adder pipeline ← *fsrc1* − *fsrc2*.

Syntax: **pfsub.p** *fsrc1, fsrc2, fdest*
(**.p** = **.ss**, **.sd**, **.dd**)

Description: Subtract the second source operand from the first source operand using signed 32- or 64-bit floating-point subtraction. Store the last stage result of the adder pipeline in the destination register.

CC: not affected
OF: not affected
FSR: AO, AE, AU, AI, SI, SE

Instruction Encoding:

```
31 30 29 28 27 26 25 24 23 22 21 20 19 18 17 16 15 14 13 12 11 10  9  8  7  6  5  4  3  2  1  0
0  1  0  0  1  0  --src2---  --dest---  --src1---  1  D  S  R  0  1  1  0  0  0  1
```

Instruction Fields:

D Dual-Instruction mode bit
  0 - Single-instruction mode
  1 - Dual-instruction mode
S, R Source and Result precision
  00 - single, single (**.ss**)
  01 - single, double (**.sd**)
  10 - reserved
  11 - double, double (**.dd**)

src1, src2	Specifies any of the floating-point registers
dest	Specifies any of the floating-point registers

Programming Notes:

Exceptions:

Floating-Point Source
Floating-Point Result

Pftrunc.v Pipelined F-P to Integer Conversion Pftrunc.v

Operation:

fdest ← last stage adder result.
Advance adder pipeline one stage.
First stage adder pipeline ← 64-bit value with low-order 32 bits equal to the truncated integer part of *fsrc1* in signed two's complement integer form.

Syntax: **pftrunc.v** *fsrc1, fdest*
(**.v** = **.sd, .dd**)

Description: Convert the source operand to 32-bit integer format by truncating the integer part of the floating-point number using the adder pipeline. No rounding is done. Store the last stage result of the adder pipeline in the destination register.

CC: not affected
OF: not affected
FSR: AO, SE

Instruction Encoding:

```
31 30 29 28 27 26 25 24 23 22 21 20 19 18 17 16 15 14 13 12 11 10  9  8  7  6  5  4  3  2  1  0
 0  1  0  0  1  0  0  0  0  0  0 --dest--- --src1---  1  D  S  R  0  1  1  1  0  1  0
```

Instruction Fields:

D Dual-Instruction mode bit
 0 - Single-instruction mode
 1 - Dual-instruction mode

S, R Source and Result precision
 00 - reserved.
 01 - single, double (**.sd**)

	10 - reserved
	11 - double, double (`.dd`)
srcl	Specifies any of the floating-point registers
dest	Specifies any even floating-point register

Programming Notes:

Fix will signal overflow if the integer part of *scr1* exceeds the numbers representable by 32-bit 2's complement integers. Underflow and inexact are never signaled.

Exceptions:

Floating-Point Source
Floating-Point Result

Pfzchkl Pipelined 32-Bit Z-Buffer Check Pfzchkl

Operation:

Consider *fsrc1*, *fsrc2*, and *fdest* each consisting of two 32-bit fields.
fdest ← last stage graphics result.
PM ← PM shifted right by 2 bits.
FOR i = 0 to 1
DO
PM[i + 6] ← *fsrc2(i)* ≤ *fsrc1(i)* (unsigned).
Last stage graphics pipeline ← smaller of *fsrc2(i)* and *fsrc1(i)*.
OD
MERGE ← 0.

Syntax: **pfzchkl** *fsrc1, fsrc2, fdest*

Description: Compare the two Z-buffer distance values in the first source operand to the two values in the second source operand. Put the smaller two values in the graphics pipeline setting the appropriate PM bits. Store the last stage result of the graphics pipeline in the destination register.

CC: not affected
OF: not affected
FSR: not affected

Instruction Encoding:

```
31 30 29 28 27 26 25 24 23 22 21 20 19 18 17 16 15 14 13 12 11 10 9 8 7 6 5 4 3 2 1 0
0  1  0  0  1  0  --src2---  --dest---  --src1---  1  D  1  1  1  0  1  0  1  1  1
```

Instruction Fields:

D Dual-Instruction mode bit
0 - Single-instruction mode
1 - Dual-instruction mode

src1, src2	Specifies any even (64-bit) floating-point register
dest	Specifies any even (64-bit) floating-point register

Programming Notes:

A one clock freeze occurs if *fdest* is a source operand of the next instruction.

Exceptions: None

Pfzchks Pipelined 16-Bit Z-Buffer Check Pfzchks

Operation:

Consider *fsrc1, fsrc2,* and *fdest* each consisting of four 16-bit fields.
fdest ← last stage graphics result.
PM ← PM shifted right by 4 bits.
FOR i = 0 to 3
DO
  PM[i + 4] ← *fsrc2(i)* ≤ *fsrc1(i)* (unsigned).
  Last stage graphics pipeline ← smaller of *fsrc2(i)* and *fsrc1(i).*
OD
MERGE ← 0.

Syntax: **pfzchks** *fsrc1, fsrc2, fdest*

Description: Compare the four Z-buffer distance values in the first source operand to the four values in the second source operand. Put the smaller four values in the graphics pipeline setting the appropriate PM bits. Store the last stage result of the graphics pipeline in the destination register.

CC: not affected
OF: not affected
FSR: not affected

Instruction Encoding:

```
31 30 29 28 27 26 25 24 23 22 21 20 19 18 17 16 15 14 13 12 11 10  9  8  7  6  5  4  3  2  1  0
 0  1  0  0  1  0 --src2--- --dest--- --src1---  1  D  1  1  1  0  1  1  1  1  1
```

Instruction Fields:

D Dual-Instruction mode bit
  0 - Single-instruction mode
  1 - Dual-instruction mode

src1, src2	Specifies any even (64-bit) floating-point register
dest	Specifies any even (64-bit) floating-point register

Programming Notes:

A one clock freeze occurs if *fdest* is a source operand of the next instruction, and the next instruction.

Exceptions: None

Pst.d — Pixel Store — Pst.d

Operation:

For pixels enabled in the low-order bits of PM:
   mem.*d*[*#constA* + *isrc2*] ← *freg.*
Shift PM right by the number of pixels in 8 bytes, based on PS
IF(Autoincrement)
THEN
   isrc2 ← *#constA* + *isrc2.*
FI

Syntax: **pst.d** *freg, #constA (isrc2)*
pst.d *freg, #constA (isrc2)++*

Description: Store up to 64 bits to memory from the source register. The address is calculated by adding the two source operands using signed binary addition. For autoincrement addressing, the result of this addition is stored in the second source register. The bits that are stored to memory are assumed to be pixels with a length given by PS in **psr**. The instruction stores pixels if there is a bit set in PM that corresponds to the pixel. Pixels that correspond to unset bits are not stored.

CC: not affected
OF: not affected
FSR: not affected

Instruction Encoding:

```
31 30 29 28 27 26 25 24 23 22 21 20 19 18 17 16 15 14 13 12 11 10  9  8  7  6  5  4  3  2  1  0
0  0  1  1  1  1  --src2---  --dest---  -------16-bit Immediate--  0  0  A
```

Instruction Fields:

A Autoincrement
0 - No increment
1 - Autoincrement

src2	Specifies any of the integer registers
dest	Specifies any even (64-bit) floating-point register
Immediate	A 16-bit constant, sign extended to 32 bits. Bits zero and one of the immediate value are forced to zero to maintain alignment. When bit one of the immediate value is zero, bit two is also forced to zero.

Programming Notes:

Assemblers and compilers must align the immediate address offset to the same boundary as the effective address, because the lower bits of the immediate offset are used to encode operand length information.

The **pst** instruction is normally used in Z-buffer hidden surface elimination. See Chapter 7, "Graphics Rendering Instructions," for more information.

Exceptions: Data-Access Trap

R2apl.p Pipelined F-P Add and Multiply R2apl.p

Operation:

fdest ← last stage adder result.
Advance adder pipeline one stage.
Advance multiplier pipeline one stage.
First stage adder pipeline ← *fsrc1* + adder result.
First stage multiplier pipeline ← KR × *fsrc2*.
T ← multilplier result.

Syntax: **r2apl.p** *fsrc1, fsrc2, fdest*
(**.p** = **.ss, .sd, .dd**)

Description: Add the first source operand to the last stage result of the adder pipeline using signed floating-point addition. Multiply the second source operand by the contents of the KR register using 32- or 64-bit floating-point multiplication. Store the last stage result of the adder pipeline in the destination register. Store the last stage result of the multiplier pipeline in the T register.

CC:	not affected
OF:	not affected
FSR:	AA, AE, AI, AO, AU, MA, MI, MO, MU, SE, SI

Instruction Encoding:

```
31 30 29 28 27 26 25 24 23 22 21 20 19 18 17 16 15 14 13 12 11 10  9  8  7  6  5  4  3  2  1  0
 0  1  0  0  1  0 --src2--- --dest--- --src1--- 1  D  S  R  0  0  0  0  0  1  0
```

Instruction Fields:

D Dual-Instruction mode bit
0 - Single-instruction mode
1 - Dual-instruction mode

S, R	Source and Result precision 00 - single, single (**.ss**) 01 - single, double (**.sd**) 10 - reserved 11 - double, double (**.dd**)
src1, src2	Specifies any of the floating-point registers
dest	Specifies any of the floating-point registers

Programming Notes:

Exceptions:

Floating-Point Source
Floating-Point Result

R2apt.p Pipelined F-P Add and Multiply R2apt.p

Operation:

fdest ← last stage adder result.
Advance adder pipeline one stage.
Advance multiplier pipeline one stage.
First stage adder pipeline ← T + adder result.
First stage multiplier pipeline ← KR × *fsrc2.*
T ← multiplier result.
KR ← *fsrc1.*

Syntax: **r2apt.p** *fsrc1, fsrc2, fdest*
(**.p** = **.ss, .sd, .dd**)

Description: Add the contents of the T register to the last stage result of the adder pipeline using signed floating-point addition. Multiply the second source operand by the contents of the KR register using 32- or 64-bit floating-point multiplication. Store the last stage result of the adder pipeline in the destination register. Store the last stage result of the multiplier pipeline in the T register. Load the KR register with the first source operand.

CC:	not affected
OF:	not affected
FSR:	AA, AE, AI, AO, AU, MA, MI, MO, MU, SE, SI

Instruction Encoding:

```
31 30 29 28 27 26 25 24 23 22 21 20 19 18 17 16 15 14 13 12 11 10  9  8  7  6  5  4  3  2  1  0
0  1  0  0  1  0  --src2---      --dest---      --src1---      1  D  S  R  0  0  0  0  0  1  1
```

Instruction Fields:

D	Dual-Instruction mode bit 0 - Single-instruction mode 1 - Dual-instruction mode
S, R	Source and Result precision 00 - single, single (`.ss`) 01 - single, double (`.sd`) 10 - reserved 11 - double, double (`.dd`)
src1, src2	Specifies any of the floating-point registers
dest	Specifies any of the floating-point registers

Programming Notes:

fsrc1 must not be the same register as *fdest*.

Exceptions:

Floating-Point Source
Floating-Point Result

R2as1.p Pipelined F-P Subtract and Multiply R2as1.p

Operation:

fdest ← last stage adder result.
Advance adder pipeline one stage.
Advance multiplier pipeline one stage.
First stage adder pipeline ← *fsrc1* − adder result.
First stage multiplier pipeline ← KR × *fsrc2*.
T ← multiplier result.

Syntax: **r2as1.p** *fsrc1, fsrc2, fdest*
(**.p** = **.ss**, **.sd**, **.dd**)

Description: Subtract the last stage result of the adder pipeline from the first source operand using signed floating-point subtraction. Multiply the second source operand by the contents of the KR register using 32- or 64-bit floating-point multiplication. Store the last stage result of the adder pipeline in the destination register. Store the last stage result of the multiplier pipeline in the T register.

CC: not affected
OF: not affected
FSR: AA, AE, AI, AO, AU, MA, MI, MO, MU, SE, SI

Instruction Encoding:

```
31 30 29 28 27 26 25 24 23 22 21 20 19 18 17 16 15 14 13 12 11 10  9  8  7  6  5  4  3  2  1  0
0  1  0  0  1  0  --src2---     --dest---      --src1---      1  D  S  R  0  0  1  0  0  1  0
```

Instruction Fields:

D Dual-Instruction mode bit
0 - Single-instruction mode
1 - Dual-instruction mode

S, R	Source and Result precision 00 - single, single (`.ss`) 01 - single, double (`.sd`) 10 - reserved 11 - double, double (`.dd`)
src1, src2	Specifies any of the floating-point registers
dest	Specifies any of the floating-point registers

Programming Notes:

Exceptions:

Floating-Point Source
Floating-Point Result

R2ast.p Pipelined F-P Subtract and Multiply R2ast.p

Operation:

fdest ← last stage adder result.
Advance adder pipeline one stage.
Advance multiplier pipeline one stage.
First stage adder pipeline ← T − adder result.
First stage multiplier pipeline ← KR × *fsrc2*.
T ← multiplier result.
KR ← *fsrc1*.

Syntax: **r2ast.p** *fsrc1, fsrc2, fdest*
(**.p** = **.ss, .sd, .dd**)

Description: Subtract the last stage result of the adder pipeline from the contents of the T register using signed floating-point subtraction. Multiply the second source operand by the contents of the KR register using 32- or 64-bit floating-point multiplication. Store the last stage result of the adder pipeline in the destination register. Store the last stage result of the multiplier pipeline in the T register. Load the KR register with the first source operand.

CC: not affected
OF: not affected
FSR: AA, AE, AI, AO, AU, MA, MI, MO, MU, SE, SI

Instruction Encoding:

```
31 30 29 28 27 26 25 24 23 22 21 20 19 18 17 16 15 14 13 12 11 10 9 8 7 6 5 4 3 2 1 0
0  1  0  0  1  0  --src2---      --dest---      --src1---      1  D S R 0 0 1 0 0 1 1
```

Instruction Fields:

D	Dual-Instruction mode bit 0 - Single-instruction mode 1 - Dual-instruction mode
S, R	Source and Result precision 00 - single, single (**.ss**) 01 - single, double (**.sd**) 10 - reserved 11 - double, double (**.dd**)
src1, src2	Specifies any of the floating-point registers
dest	Specifies any of the floating-point registers

Programming Notes:

fsrc1 must not be the same register as *fdest*.

Exceptions:

Floating-Point Source
Floating-Point Result

R2p1.p Pipelined F-P Add and Multiply R2p1.p

Operation:

fdest ← last stage adder result.
Advance adder pipeline one stage.
Advance multiplier pipeline one stage.
First stage adder pipeline ← *fsrc1* + multiplier result.
First stage multiplier pipeline ← KR × *fsrc2*.

Syntax: **r2p1.p** *fsrc1, fsrc2, fdest*
(**.p** = **.ss**, **.sd**, **.dd**)

Description: Add the first source operand to the last stage result of the multiplier pipeline using signed floating-point addition. Multiply the second source operand by the contents of the KR register using 32- or 64-bit floating-point multiplication. Store the last stage result of the adder pipeline in the destination register.

CC:	not affected
OF:	not affected
FSR:	AA, AE, AI, AO, AU, MA, MI, MO, MU, SE, SI

Instruction Encoding:

```
31 30 29 28 27 26 25 24 23 22 21 20 19 18 17 16 15 14 13 12 11 10  9  8  7  6  5  4  3  2  1  0
0  1  0  0  1  0  --src2---  --dest---  --src1---  1  D  S  R  0  0  0  0  0  0  0
```

Instruction Fields:

D Dual-Instruction mode bit
 0 - Single-instruction mode
 1 - Dual-instruction mode

S, R	Source and Result precision 00 - single, single (`.ss`) 01 - single, double (`.sd`) 10 - reserved 11 - double, double (`.dd`)
src1, src2	Specifies any of the floating-point registers
dest	Specifies any of the floating-point registers

Programming Notes:

Exceptions:

Floating-Point Source
Floating-Point Result

R2pt.p Pipelined F-P Add and Multiply R2pt.p

Operation:

fdest ← last stage adder result.
Advance adder pipeline one stage.
Advance multiplier pipeline one stage.
First stage adder pipeline ← T + multiplier result.
First stage multiplier pipeline ← KR × *fsrc2.*
KR ← *fsrc1.*

Syntax: **r2pt.p** *fsrc1, fsrc2, fdest*
(**.p** = **.ss, .sd, .dd**)

Description: Add the contents of the T register to the last stage result of the multiplier pipeline using signed floating-point addition. Multiply the second source operand by the contents of the KR register using 32- or 64-bit floating-point multiplication. Store the last stage result of the adder pipeline in the destination register. Load the KR register with the first source operand.

CC: not affected
OF: not affected
FSR: AA, AE, AI, AO, AU, MA, MI, MO, MU, SE, SI

Instruction Encoding:

31	30	29	28	27	26	25–21	20–16	15–11	10	9	8	7	6	5	4	3	2	1	0
0	1	0	0	1	0	--src2---	--dest---	--src1---	1	D	S	R	0	0	0	0	0	0	1

Instruction Fields:

D Dual-Instruction mode bit
0 - Single-instruction mode
1 - Dual-instruction mode

S, R	Source and Result precision 00 - single, single (**.ss**) 01 - single, double (**.sd**) 10 - reserved 11 - double, double (**.dd**)
src1, src2	Specifies any of the floating-point registers
dest	Specifies any of the floating-point registers

Programming Notes:

fsrc1 must not be the same register as *fdest*.

Exceptions:

Floating-Point Source
Floating-Point Result

R2s1.p Pipelined F-P Subtract and Multiply R2s1.p

Operation:

fdest ← last stage adder result.
Advance adder pipeline one stage.
Advance multiplier pipeline one stage.
First stage adder pipeline ← *fsrc1* − multiplier result.
First stage multiplier pipeline ← KR × *fsrc2*.

Syntax: **r2s1.p** *fsrc1, fsrc2, fdest*
(**.p** = **.ss**, **.sd**, **.dd**)

Description: Subtract the last stage result of the multiplier pipeline from the first source operand using signed floating-point subtraction. Multiply the second source operand by the contents of the KR register using 32- or 64-bit floating-point multiplication. Store the last stage result of the adder pipeline in the destination register.

CC: not affected
OF: not affected
FSR: AA, AE, AI, AO, AU, MA, MI, MO, MU, SE, SI

Instruction Encoding:

```
31 30 29 28 27 26 25 24 23 22 21 20 19 18 17 16 15 14 13 12 11 10  9  8  7  6  5  4  3  2  1  0
 0  1  0  0  1  0 --src2---  --dest---   --src1---   1  D  S  R  0  0  1  0  0  0  0
```

Instruction Fields:

D Dual-Instruction mode bit
0 - Single-instruction mode
1 - Dual-instruction mode

S, R	Source and Result precision 00 - single, single (`.ss`) 01 - single, double (`.sd`) 10 - reserved 11 - double, double (`.dd`)
src1, src2	Specifies any of the floating-point registers
dest	Specifies any of the floating-point registers

Programming Notes:

Exceptions:

Floating-Point Source
Floating-Point Result

R2st.p Pipelined F-P Subtract and Multiply R2st.p

Operation:

fdest ← last stage adder result.
Advance adder pipeline one stage.
Advance multiplier pipeline one stage.
First stage adder pipeline ← T − multiplier result.
First stage multiplier pipeline ← KR × *fsrc2.*
KR ← *fsrc1.*

Syntax: **r2st.p** *fsrc1, fsrc2, fdest*
(**.p** = **.ss, .sd, .dd**)

Description: Subtract the last stage result of the multiplier pipeline from the contents of the T register using signed floating-point subtraction. Multiply the second source operand by the contents of the KR register using 32- or 64-bit floating-point multiplication. Store the last stage result of the adder pipeline in the destination register. Load the KR register with the first source operand.

CC:	not affected
OF:	not affected
FSR:	AA, AE, AI, AO, AU, MA, MI, MO, MU, SE, SI

Instruction Encoding:

```
31 30 29 28 27 26 25 24 23 22 21 20 19 18 17 16 15 14 13 12 11 10  9  8  7  6  5  4  3  2  1  0
0  1  0  0  1  0  --src2---  --dest---  --src1---  1  D  S  R  0  0  1  0  0  0  1
```

Instruction Fields:

D Dual-Instruction mode bit
0 - Single-instruction mode
1 - Dual-instruction mode

S, R	Source and Result precision 00 - single, single (.ss) 01 - single, double (.sd) 10 - reserved 11 - double, double (.dd)
src1, src2	Specifies any of the floating-point registers
dest	Specifies any of the floating-point registers

Programming Notes:

fsrc1 must not be the same register as *fdest*.

Exceptions:

Floating-Point Source
Floating-Point Result

Ra1p2.p Pipelined F-P Add and Multiply Ra1p2.p

Operation:

fdest ← last stage adder result.
Advance adder pipeline one stage.
Advance multiplier pipeline one stage.
First stage adder pipeline ← *fsrc1* + *fsrc2*.
First stage multiplier pipeline ← KR × adder result.

Syntax: **ra1p2.p** *fsrc1, fsrc2, fdest*
(**.p** = **.ss, .sd, .dd**)

Description: Add the two source operands using signed floating-point addition. Multiply the last stage result of the adder pipeline by the contents of the KR register using 32- or 64 bit floating-point multiplication. Store the last stage result of the adder pipeline in the destination register.

CC: not affected
OF: not affected
FSR: AA, AE, AI, AO, AU, MA, MI, MO, MU, SE, SI

Instruction Encoding:

```
31 30 29 28 27 26 25 24 23 22 21 20 19 18 17 16 15 14 13 12 11 10  9  8  7  6  5  4  3  2  1  0
0  1  0  0  1  0  --src2---  --dest---  --src1---  1  D  S  R  0  0  0  1  0  1  0
```

Instruction Fields:

D Dual-Instruction mode bit
0 - Single-instruction mode
1 - Dual-instruction mode

S, R	Source and Result precision 00 - single, single (`.ss`) 01 - single, double (`.sd`) 10 - reserved 11 - double, double (`.dd`)
src1, src2	Specifies any of the floating-point registers
dest	Specifies any of the floating-point registers

Programming Notes:

Exceptions:

Floating-Point Source
Floating-Point Result

Ra1s2.p Pipelined F-P Subtract and Multiply Ra1s2.p

Operation:

fdest ← last stage adder result.
Advance adder pipeline one stage.
Advance multiplier pipeline one stage.
First stage adder pipeline ← *fsrc1* − *fsrc2*.
First stage multiplier pipeline ← KR × adder result.

Syntax: **ra1s2.p** *fsrc1, fsrc2, fdest*
(**.p** = **.ss**, **.sd**, **.dd**)

Description: Subtract the second source operand from the first source operand using signed floating-point subtraction. Multiply the last stage result of the adder pipeline by the contents of the KR register using 32- or 64-bit floating-point multiplication. Store the last stage result of the adder pipeline in the destination register.

CC:	not affected
OF:	not affected
FSR:	AA, AE, AI, AO, AU, MA, MI, MO, MU, SE, SI

Instruction Encoding:

```
31 30 29 28 27 26 25 24 23 22 21 20 19 18 17 16 15 14 13 12 11 10 9 8 7 6 5 4 3 2 1 0
0  1  0  0  1  0  --src2---   --dest---     --src1---     1  D S R 0 0 1 1 0 1 0
```

Instruction Fields:

D Dual-Instruction mode bit
0 - Single-instruction mode
1 - Dual-instruction mode

S, R	Source and Result precision 00 - single, single (`.ss`) 01 - single, double (`.sd`) 10 - reserved 11 - double, double (`.dd`)
src1, src2	Specifies any of the floating-point registers
dest	Specifies any of the floating-point registers

Programming Notes:

Exceptions:

Floating-Point Source
Floating-Point Result

Rat1p2.p Pipelined F-P Add and Multiply Rat1p2.p

Operation:

fdest ← last stage adder result.
Advance adder pipeline one stage.
Advance multiplier pipeline one stage.
First stage adder pipeline ← *fsrc1* + *fsrc2*.
First stage multiplier pipeline ← KR × adder result.
T ← multiplier result.

Syntax: **rat1p2.p** *fsrc1, fsrc2, fdest*
(**.p** = **.ss**, **.sd**, **.dd**)

Description: Add the two source operands using signed floating-point addition. Multiply the last stage result of the adder pipeline by the contents of the KR register using 32- or 64-bit floating-point multiplication. Store the last stage result of the adder pipeline in the destination register. Store the last stage result of the multiplier pipeline in the T register.

CC:	not affected
OF:	not affected
FSR:	AA, AE, AI, AO, AU, MA, MI, MO, MU, SE, SI

Instruction Encoding:

```
31 30 29 28 27 26 25 24 23 22 21 20 19 18 17 16 15 14 13 12 11 10  9  8  7  6  5  4  3  2  1  0
 0  1  0  0  1  0 --src2--- --dest--- --src1---  1  D  S  R  0  0  0  1  0  0  0
```

Instruction Fields:

D Dual-Instruction mode bit
0 - Single-instruction mode
1 - Dual-instruction mode

S, R	Source and Result precision 00 - single, single (`.ss`) 01 - single, double (`.sd`) 10 - reserved 11 - double, double (`.dd`)
src1, src2	Specifies any of the floating-point registers
dest	Specifies any of the floating-point registers

Programming Notes:

Exceptions:

Floating-Point Source
Floating-Point Result

Rat1s2.p Pipelined F-P Subtract and Multiply Rat1s2.p

Operation:

fdest ← last stage adder result.
Advance adder pipeline one stage.
Advance multiplier pipeline one stage.
First stage adder pipeline ← *fsrc1* − *fsrc2*.
First stage multiplier pipeline ← KR × adder result.
T ← multiplier result.

Syntax: **rat1s2.p** *fsrc1*, *fsrc2*, *fdest*
(.p = .ss, .sd, .dd)

Description: Subtract the second source operand from the first source operand using signed floating-point subtraction. Multiply the last stage result of the adder pipeline by the contents of the KR register using 32- or 64-bit floating-point multiplication. Store the last stage result of the adder pipeline in the destination register. Store the last stage result of the multiplier pipeline in the T register.

CC: not affected
OF: not affected
FSR: AA, AE, AI, AO, AU, MA, MI, MO, MU, SE, SI

Instruction Encoding:

```
31 30 29 28 27 26 25 24 23 22 21 20 19 18 17 16 15 14 13 12 11 10 9 8 7 6 5 4 3 2 1 0
0  1  0  0  1  0  --src2---     --dest---      --src1---      1  D S R 0 0 1 1 0 0 0
```

Instruction Fields:

D Dual-Instruction mode bit
0 - Single-instruction mode
1 - Dual-instruction mode

S, R	Source and Result precision 00 - single, single (`.ss`) 01 - single, double (`.sd`) 10 - reserved 11 - double, double (`.dd`)
src1, src2	Specifies any of the floating-point registers
dest	Specifies any of the floating-point registers

Programming Notes:

Exceptions:

Floating-Point Source
Floating-Point Result

Shl — Shift Left — Shl

Operation:

idest ← *isrc2* shifted left by *isrc1* bits

Syntax: **shl** *isrc1, isrc2, idest*
shl *#constL, isrc2, idest*

Description: Logically shift the second source operand left, filling with zeros and storing the result in the destination register. The first source operand gives the number of bits to shift.

CC: not affected
OF: not affected
FSR: not affected

Instruction Encoding:

```
31 30 29 28 27 26 25 24 23 22 21 20 19 18 17 16 15 14 13 12 11 10  9  8  7  6  5  4  3  2  1  0
1 0 1 0 0 0 --src2--- --dest--- --src1--- 0 0 0 0 0 0 0 0 0 0 0
1 0 1 0 0 1 --src2--- --dest--- -------16-bit Immediate--------
```

Instruction Fields:

src1, src2	Specifies any of the integer registers
dest	Specifies any of the integer registers
Immediate	A 16-bit constant, whose lower five bits give the shift count.

Programming Notes:

The shift left instruction is used for integer register to register moves and core null operations because it does not affect the condition code bit. See the instructions **mov** and **nop**.

Exceptions: None

Shr — Shift Right — Shr

Operation:

idest ← *isrc2* shifted right by *isrc1* bits
SC ← *isrc1*

Syntax: **shr** *isrc1, isrc2, idest*
shr *#constL, isrc2, idest*

Description: Logically shift the second source operand right, filling with zeros and storing the result in the destination register. The first source operand gives the number of bits to shift. This number is also stored in the SC field of **psr**.

CC:	not affected
OF:	not affected
FSR:	not affected

Instruction Encoding:

```
31 30 29 28 27 26 25 24 23 22 21 20 19 18 17 16 15 14 13 12 11 10 9 8 7 6 5 4 3 2 1 0
1  0  1  0  1  0  --src2---    --dest---    --src1---    0 0 0 0 0 0 0 0 0 0 0
1  0  1  0  1  1  --src2---    --dest---    -------16-bit Immediate--------
```

Instruction Fields:

src1, src2	Specifies any of the integer registers
dest	Specifies any of the integer registers
Immediate	A 16-bit constant, whose lower five bits give the shift count.

Programming Notes:

Exceptions: None

Shra — Shift Right Arithmetic — Shra

Operation:

idest ← *isrc2* shifted right arithmetically by *isrc1* bits.

Syntax: **shra** *isrc1, isrc2, idest*
shra *#constA, isrc2, idest*

Description: Shift the second source operand right, filling in the left with sign bits and storing the result in the destination register. The first source operand gives the number of bits to shift.

CC: not affected
OF: not affected
FSR: not affected

Instruction Encoding:

```
31 30 29 28 27 26 25 24 23 22 21 20 19 18 17 16 15 14 13 12 11 10  9  8  7  6  5  4  3  2  1  0
1 0 1 1 1 0 --src2--- --dest--- --src1--- 0 0 0 0 0 0 0 0 0 0 0
1 0 1 1 1 1 --src2--- --dest--- -------16-bit Immediate--------
```

Instruction Fields:

src1, src2	Specifies any of the integer registers
dest	Specifies any of the integer registers
Immediate	A 16-bit constant, whose lower five bits give the shift count.

Programming Notes:

Exceptions: None

Shrd Shift Right Double Shrd

Operation:

idest ← low-order 32 bits of *isrc1:isrc2* shifted right by SC bits.

Syntax: **shrd** *isrc1, isrc2, idest*

Description: Logically shift a 64-bit value right and store the result in the destination register. The SC field of **psr** gives the number of bits to shift. The 64-bit value is formed by using the first source operand as the most significant 32 bits and the second source operand as the least significant 32 bits.

CC:	not affected
OF:	not affected
FSR:	not affected

Instruction Encoding:

```
31 30 29 28 27 26 25 24 23 22 21 20 19 18 17 16 15 14 13 12 11 10 9 8 7 6 5 4 3 2 1 0
1  0  1  1  0  0  --src2---  --dest---  --src1---  0 0 0 0 0 0 0 0 0 0 0
```

Instruction Fields:

src1, src2	Specifies any of the integer registers
dest	Specifies any of the integer registers

Programming Notes:

The shift right double instruction is used for floating-point no operations because it does not affect the condition code bit or the floating-point pipelines. See the **fnop** instruction.

A rotate is implemented by a **shr** count, **r0,r0** followed by **shrd** *isrc1, isrc1, idest*.

Exceptions: None

St.c Store to Control Register St.c

Operation:

ctrlreg ← *isrc1*

Syntax: **st.c** *isrc1, ctrlreg*

Description: Store 32 bits from the source register to the control register. Some control registers have user mode protected bits (see Chapter 4, "Machine Organization") that **st.c** cannot change when in user mode.

CC:	updated by **st.c psr**
OF:	updated by **st.c epsr**
FSR:	updated by **st.c fsr**

Instruction Encoding:

```
31 30 29 28 27 26 25 24 23 22 21 20 19 18 17 16 15 14 13 12 11 10 9 8 7 6 5 4 3 2 1 0
0  0  1  1  1  0  --src2---      0  0  0  0  0  --src1---      0 0 0 0 0 0 0 0 0 0 0
```

Instruction Fields:

src2 Specifies one of the control registers
- 00000 - **fir**
- 00001 - **psr**
- 00010 - **dirbase**
- 00011 - **db**
- 00100 - **fsr**
- 00101 - **epsr**

src1 Specifies any of the integer registers

Programming Notes:

st.c takes three clocks to execute.

After a scalar floating-point operation, a **st.c** to **fsr** must avoid changing the value of RR, RM, or FZ until the point at which result exceptions are reported. See Chapter 4, "Machine Organization," for more details.

Only a trap handler should use the instruction **st.c** to set the trap bits IT, IN, IAT, DAT, or FT of the **psr**.

Programmers must not change the BL bit of the **dirbase** register. Use the **lock** and **unlock** instructions to implement bus locking.

Exceptions: None

St.x Integer Store St.x

Operation:

mem.*x*[*#constA* + *isrc2*] ← *isrc1*

Syntax: **st.x** *isrc1, #constA(isrc2)*
(**.x** = **.b**, **.s**, **.l**)

Description: Store 8, 16, or 32 bits to memory from the first source register. The address is calculated by adding the immediate constant to the second source operand using signed binary addition.

CC:	not affected
OF:	not affected
FSR:	not affected

Instruction Encoding:

```
31 30 29 28 27 26 25 24 23 22 21 20 19 18 17 16 15 14 13 12 11 10  9  8  7  6  5  4  3  2  1  0
0 0 0 L 1 1 --src2--- -Offhigh- --src1--- -----Offset low---- S
```

Instruction Fields:

L, S	Length of store. 0,0 - 8 bits (**.b**) 0,1 - 8 bits (**.b**) 1,0 - 16 bits (**.s**) 1,1 - 32 bits (**.l**)
src1, src2	Specifies any of the integer registers
Offhigh	The high five bits of the offset *#constA*
Offset low	The low eleven bits of the offset *#constA.* If L (bit 28) is set, bit zero of the immediate value is forced to zero to maintain alignment.

Programming Notes:

A one clock freeze occurs if the **st** hits the data cache and the following instruction is **fld**, or **ld**.

Assemblers and compilers must align the immediate address offset to the same boundary as the effective address, because the lower bits of the immediate offset are used to encode operand length information.

Exceptions: Data-Access Trap

Subs — Integer Signed Subtract — Subs

Operation: *idest* ← *isrc1* − *isrc2*

Syntax:
subs *isrc1, isrc2, idest*
subs *#constA, isrc2, idest*

Description: Subtract the second source operand from the first source operand using signed binary subtraction and store the result in the destination register.

CC:	CC ← (*isrc1* ≠ *isrc2* < 0)
OF:	OF ← (bit 31 carry ≠ bit 30 carry)
FSR:	not affected

Instruction Encoding:

```
31 30 29 28 27 26 25 24 23 22 21 20 19 18 17 16 15 14 13 12 11 10  9  8  7  6  5  4  3  2  1  0
1  0  0  1  1  0 --src2--- --dest--- --src1--- 0 0 0 0 0 0 0 0 0 0 0
1  0  0  1  1  1 --src2--- --dest--- -------16-bit Immediate--------
```

Instruction Fields:

src1, src2	Specifies any of the integer registers
dest	Specifies any of the integer registers
Immediate	A 16-bit constant, sign extended to 32 bits

Programming Notes:

A one clock freeze occurs on a **bc, bnc, bc.t,** or a **bnc.t** following the **subs** instruction.

Use the **subs** −1,*isrc2, idest* instruction to get the one's complement of *isrc2*.

Exceptions: None

Subu Integer Unsigned Subtract Subu

Operation:

idest ← *isrc1* − *isrc2*

Syntax: **subu** *isrc1, isrc2, idest*
subu *#constA, isrc2, idest*

Description: Subtract the second source operand from the first source operand using unsigned binary subtraction and store the result in the destination register.

CC:	CC ← (bit 31 carry)
OF:	OF ← NOT(bit 31 carry)
FSR:	not affected

Instruction Encoding:

```
31 30 29 28 27 26 25 24 23 22 21 20 19 18 17 16 15 14 13 12 11 10  9  8  7  6  5  4  3  2  1  0
1  0  0  0  1  0 --src2--- --dest--- --src1--- 0 0 0 0 0 0 0 0 0 0 0
1  0  0  0  1  1 --src2--- --dest--- -------16-bit Immediate--------
```

Instruction Fields:

src1, src2	Specifies any of the integer registers
dest	Specifies any of the integer registers
Immediate	A 16-bit constant, sign extended to 32 bits

Programming Notes:

A one clock freeze occurs on a **bc, bnc, bc.t,** or a **bnc.t** following the **subu** instruction.

Exceptions: None

Trap — Software Trap — Trap

Operation:

IT ← 1.
Generate trap.

Syntax: **trap** *isrc1, isrc2, idest*

Description: Generate a software trap with the IT bit of **psr** set. See Chapter 9, "Operating System Support," for more details on traps and interrupts.

CC:	not affected
OF:	not affected
FSR:	not affected

Instruction Encoding:

```
31 30 29 28 27 26 25 24 23 22 21 20 19 18 17 16 15 14 13 12 11 10  9  8  7  6  5  4  3  2  1  0
0  1  0  0  0  1  --src2---  --dest---  --src1---  0  0  0  0  0  0  0  0  0  0  0
```

Instruction Fields:

src1, src2	Specifies any of the integer registers
dest	Specifies any of the integer registers

Programming Notes:

The **trap** instruction can be used to implement supervisor calls and code breakpoints. The *src1* and *src2* fields can be used to encode the type of trap.

The destination of the **trap** instruction should be **r0**, because its contents are undefined after the operation.

Exceptions: Instruction Trap

Unlock — End Interlocked Bus Sequence — Unlock

Operation:

BL ← 0.
Unlock the bus on the next load or store.
Enable interrupts when bus is unlocked.

Syntax: `unlock`

Description: Unset the BL bit, unlock the bus on the next load or store, and enable interrupts when the bus is unlocked.

CC:	not affected
OF:	not affected
FSR:	not affected

Instruction Encoding:

31	30	29	28	27	26	25	24	23	22	21	20	19	18	17	16	15	14	13	12	11	10	9	8	7	6	5	4	3	2	1	0
0	1	0	0	1	1	0	0	0	0	0	0	0	0	0	0	0	0	0	0	0	0	0	0	0	0	0	0	0	1	1	1

Instruction Fields:

Programming Notes:

The instructions **lock** and **unlock** allow programs running in multiprocessor and multithreaded systems to perform read-modify-write sequences. See Chapter 9, "Operating System Support," for more information.

An instruction **trap** will occur if there is no **unlock** instruction within 30 instructions of the **lock** instruction.

Exceptions: Instruction Trap

Xor — Logical Exclusive OR — Xor

Operation:

idest ← *isrc1* XOR *isrc2*

Syntax: **xor** *isrc1, isrc2, idest*
xor *#constL, isrc2, idest*

Description: Perform bitwise exclusive OR on the two source operands and store the result in the destination register.

CC:	CC ← (*idest* == 0)
OF:	not affected
FSR:	not affected

Instruction Encoding:

```
31 30 29 28 27 26 25 24 23 22 21 20 19 18 17 16 15 14 13 12 11 10 9 8 7 6 5 4 3 2 1 0
1  1  1  1  0  0  --src2---  --dest---  --src1---  0 0 0 0 0 0 0 0 0 0 0
1  1  1  1  0  1  --src2---  --dest---  -------16-bit Immediate--------
```

Instruction Fields:

src1, src2	Specifies any of the integer registers
dest	Specifies any of the integer registers
Immediate	A 16-bit constant, zero extended to 32 bits

Programming Notes:

Exceptions: None

Xorh — Logical Exclusive OR High — Xorh

Operation:

idest ← (*#constL* shifted left 16 bits) XOR *isrc2*

Syntax: **xorh** *#constL, isrc2, idest*

Description: Perform bitwise exclusive OR on the two source operands and store the result in the destination register. The first source operand is created by using the 16-bit constant as the high 16 bits of the operand and filling the low 16 bits with zeros.

CC:	CC ← (result == 0)
OF:	not affected
FSR:	not affected

Instruction Encoding:

```
31 30 29 28 27 26 25 24 23 22 21 20 19 18 17 16 15 14 13 12 11 10  9  8  7  6  5  4  3  2  1  0
1  1  1  1  1  1 --src2--- --dest--- -------16-bit Immediate--------
```

Instruction Fields:

src2	Specifies any of the integer registers
dest	Specifies any of the integer registers
Immediate	A 16-bit constant, left shifted 16 bits, filled with zeros on the right

Programming Notes:

Exceptions: None

APPENDIX B
INSTRUCTION FORMAT AND ENCODING

All instructions are 32 bits long and begin on a four-byte boundary. When operands are registers, the encodings shown in Table B-1 are used.

Among the core instructions, there are two general formats: REG-format and CTRL-format. Within the REG-format there are several variations. REG-format instructions are outlined in Figure B-1.

In core instructions, the *src2* field selects one of the 32 integer registers (most instructions) or one of the control registers (**st.c** and **ld.c**). *dest* selects one of the 32 integer registers (most instructions) or floating-point registers (**fld**, **fst**, **pfld**, **pst**, **ixfr**). For instructions where *src1* is optionally an immediate constant or address offset, bit 26 of the opcode (I-bit) indicates whether *src1* is immediate. If bit 26 is clear, an integer register is used; if bit 26 is set, *src1* is contained in the low-order 16 bits, except for **bte** and **btne** instructions. For **bte** and **btne**, the five-bit immediate constant is contained in the *src1* field. For **st**, **bte**, **btne**, and **bla**, the upper five bits of the *offset* or branch *broffset* are contained in the *dest* field instead of *src1*, and the lower 11 bits of *offset* are the lower 11 bits of the instruction.

Table B-1. Register Encoding

Register	*Encoding*
r0	0
.	.
.	.
.	.
r31	31
f0	0
.	.
.	.
.	.
f31	31
Fault instruction	0
Processor status	1
Directory base	2
Data breakpoint	3
Floating-point status	4
Extended processor status	5

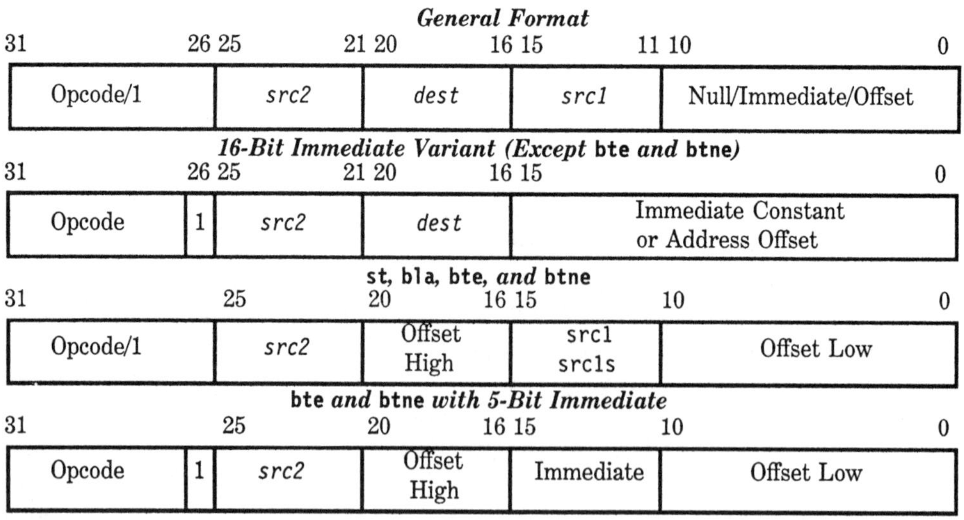

Figure B-1. REG-Format instructions

Table B-2. `ld` *and* `st` *Operand Size*

Bit 28	*Bit 0*	*Operand Size*
0	0	8-bits
0	1	8-bits
1	0	16-bits
1	1	32-bits

For **ld** and **st**, bits 28 and zero determine operand size according to Table B-2. When *src1* is immediate and bit 28 is set, bit zero of the immediate value is forced to zero.

For **fld**, **fst**, **pfld**, **pst** and **flush**, bit 0 selects autoincrement addressing if set. Bits one and two select the operand size according to Table B-3.

When *src1* is immediate, bits zero and one of the immediate value are forced to zero to maintain alignment. When bit one of the immediate value is clear, bit two is also forced to zero.

Table B-3. `fld`, `fst`, `pfld`, `pst` *and* `flush` *Operand Size*

Bit 1	*Bit 2*	*Operand Size*
0	0	64-bits
0	1	128-bits
1	0	32-bits
1	1	32-bits

REG-Format Opcodes

Mnemonic	Description	31	30	29	28	27	26
ld.x	Load Integer	0	0	0	L	0	I
st.x	Store Integer	0	0	0	L	1	1
ixfr	Integer to F-P Reg Transfer	0	0	0	0	1	0
	(reserved)	0	0	0	1	1	0
fld.x, fst.x	Load/Store F-P	0	0	1	0	LS	I
flush	Flush	0	0	1	1	0	1
pst.d	Pixel Store	0	0	1	1	1	1
ld.c, st.c	Load/Store Control Register	0	0	1	1	LS	0
bri	Branch Indirect	0	1	0	0	0	0
trap	Trap	0	1	0	0	0	1
	(Escape for F-P Unit)	0	1	0	0	1	0
	(Escape for Core Unit)	0	1	0	0	1	1
bte, btne	Branch Equal or Not Equal	0	1	0	1	E	I
pfld.y	Pipelined F-P Load	0	1	1	0	0	I
	(CTRL-Format Instructions)	0	1	1	x	x	x
addu, adds, subu, subs,	Add/Subtract	1	0	0	SO	AS	I
shl, shr	Logical Shift	1	0	1	0	LR	I
shrd	Double Shift	1	0	1	1	0	0
bla	Branch LCC and Add	1	0	1	1	0	1
shra	Arithmetic Shift	1	0	1	1	1	I
and(h)	AND	1	1	0	0	H	I
andnot(h)	ANDNOT	1	1	0	1	H	I
or(h)	OR	1	1	1	0	H	I
xor(h)	XOR	1	1	1	1	H	I
	(reserved)	1	1	x	x	1	0

L Integer Length
0 -8 bits
1 -16 or 32 bits (selected by bit 0)

LS Load/Store
0 -Load
1 -Store

SO Signed/Ordinal
0 -Ordinal
1 -Signed

H High
0 -**and, or, andnot, xor**
1 -**andh, orh, andnoth, xorh**

AS Add/Subtract
0 -Add
1 -Subtract

LR Left/Right
0 -Left Shift
1 -Right Shift

E Equal
0 -Branch on Not Equal
1 -Branch on Equal

I Immediate
0 -*src1* is register
1 -*src1* is immediate

Core Escape Instructions

31–26	25–16	15–11	10–5	4–0
010011	reserved	*src1*	reserved	Opcode

Core Escape Opcodes

		4	3	2	1	0
	(reserved)	0	0	0	0	0
lock	Begin interlocked sequence	0	0	0	0	1
calli	Indirect subroutine call	0	0	0	1	0
	(reserved)	0	0	0	1	1
intovr	Trap on integer overflow	0	0	1	0	0
	(reserved)	0	0	1	0	1
	(reserved)	0	0	1	1	0
unlock	End interlocked sequence	0	0	1	1	1
	(reserved)	0	1	x	x	x
	(reserved)	1	0	x	x	x
	(reserved)	1	1	x	x	x

CTRL-Format Instructions

31	28	25–0
011	OPC	*broffset*

CTRL-Format Opcodes

		28	27	26
br	Branch Direct	0	1	0
call	Call	0	1	1
bc(.t)	Branch on CC Set	1	0	T
bnc(.t)	Branch on CC Clear	1	1	T

T Taken
0 -**bc** or **bnc**
1 -**bc.t** or **bnc.t**

Floating-Point Instruction Encoding

31–26	25–21	20–16	15–11	10	9	8	7	6–0
010010	*src2*	*dest*	*src1*	P	D	S	R	Opcode

src1, src2 -Source; one of 32 floating-point registers
dest -Destination register
(instructions other than **fxfr**) one of 32 floating-point registers
(**fxfr**) one of 32 integer registers

P Pipelining
1 -Pipelined instruction mode
0 -Scalar instruction mode*

D Dual-Instruction Mode
1 -Dual-instruction mode
0 -Single instruction mode

S Source Precision
1 -Double-precision source operands
0 -Single-precision source operands

R Result Precision
1 -Double-precision result
0 -Single-precision result

*The exceptions to P-bit encoding are the pipelined **pfmam** and **pfmsm** instructions, which have P=0.

Floating-Point Opcodes

		6	5	4	3	2	1	0
pfam	Add and Multiply*	0	0	0	DPC			
pfmam	Multiply with Add*	0	0	0				
pfsm	Subtract and Multiply*	0	0	1	DPC			
pfmsm	Multiply with Subtract*	0	0	1				
(p)fmul	Multiply	0	1	0	0	0	0	0
fmlow	Multiply Low	0	1	0	0	0	0	1
frcp	Reciprocal	0	1	0	0	0	1	0
frsqr	Reciprocal Square Root	0	1	0	0	0	1	1
pfmul3.dd	3-Stage Pipelined Multiply	0	1	0	0	1	0	0
(p)fadd	Add	0	1	1	0	0	0	0
(p)sub	Subtract	0	1	1	0	0	0	1
(p)fix	Convert to Integer	0	1	1	0	0	1	0
(p)famov	Adder Move	0	1	1	0	0	1	1
pfgt/pfle**	Greater Than	0	1	1	0	1	0	0
pfeq	Equal	0	1	1	0	1	0	1
(p)ftrunc	Truncate	0	1	1	1	0	1	0
fxfr	Transfer to Integer Register	1	0	0	0	0	0	0
(p)fiadd	Long-Integer Add	1	0	0	1	0	0	1
(p)fisub	Long-Integer Subtract	1	0	0	1	1	0	1
(p)fzchkl	Z-Check Long	1	0	1	0	1	1	1
(p)fzchks	Z-Check Short	1	0	1	1	1	1	1
(p)faddp	Add with Pixel Merge	1	0	1	0	0	0	0
(p)faddz	Add with Z Merge	1	0	1	0	0	0	1
(p)form	**OR** with MERGE Register	1	0	1	1	0	1	0

*__pfam__ and __pfsm__ have P-bit set; __pfmam__ and __pfmsm__ have P-bit clear.
**__pfgt__ has R bit cleared; __pfle__ has R bit set.

APPENDIX C
INSTRUCTION TIMING AND CHARACTERISTICS

Instruction Timings

All i860 microprocessor instructions take one clock to execute unless a freeze condition occurs. Freeze conditions and their associated delays are shown in the following table. Freezes due to multiple simultaneous cache misses result in a delay that is the sum of the delays for processing each miss by itself. Other multiple freeze conditions usually add only the delay of the longest individual freeze.

Freeze Condition	*Delay (beyond the default one clock)*
Instruction-cache miss	Number of clocks to read instruction (from ADS# clock to first READY# clock), plus time to last READY# of block when jump or freeze occurs during miss processing, plus two clocks if data cache being accessed when instruction-cache miss occurs.

Freeze Condition	*Delay (beyond the default one clock)*
Reference to destination of **ld** instruction that misses	One plus number of clocks to read data (from ADS# clock to first READY# clock), minus number of instructions executed since load (not counting instruction that references load destination)
fld miss	One plus number of clocks until first READY# returned (for 64-bit read cycles) or until second READY# returned (for 128-bit **fld.q** read cycles)
call, **calli**, **ixfr**, **fxfr**, **ld.c**, or **st.c** and data cache load miss processing in progress	One plus number of clocks until first READY# returned (for 64-bit read cycles) or until second READY# returned (for 128-bit **fld.q** read cycles)
ld, **st**, **pfld**, **fld**, **fst**, or **ixfr** and data cache load miss processing in progress	One plus number of clocks until last READY# returned
Reference to *dest* of **ld**, **call**, **calli**, **fxfr**, or **ld.c** in the next instruction (*dest* of **call** and **calli** is **r1**)	One clock
Reference to *dest* of **fld**, **pfld**, or **ifxr** in the next two instructions	Two clocks in the first instruction; or one in the second instruction
bc, **bnc**, **bc.t**, or **bnc.t** following **addu**, **adds**, **subu**, **subs**, **pfeq**, **pfle**, or **pfgt**	One clock
fsrc1 of multiplier operation refers to result of previous operation (either scalar or pipelined)	One clock
Floating-point operation or graphics-unit instruction or **fst** and scalar operation in progress other than **frcp** or **frsqr**	If the scalar operation is **fadd**, **fix**, **fmlow**, **fmul.ss**, **fmul.sd**, **ftrunc**, or **fsub**, two minus the number of instructions (or dual-mode pairs) executed after the scalar operation. If the scalar operation is **fmul.dd**, three minus the number of instructions (or dual-mode pairs) executed after it. Add one if one or both of the following situations occur

Freeze Condition	*Delay (beyond the default one clock)*
Floating-point or graphics instruction or **fst** and scalar operation in progress other than **frcp** or **frsqr** (*continued*)	a. There is an overlap between the result register(s) of the previous scalar operation, and the source of the floating-point operation, and the destination precision of the scalar operation is different from the source precision of the floating-point operation. b. The floating-point operation is pipelined and its destination is not **f0**. If the sum of the above terms is negative, there is no delay.
Multiplier operation preceded by a double-precision multiply	One clock
TLB miss	Five plus the number of clocks to finish two reads, plus the number of clocks to set A-bits (if necessary)
pfld when three **pfld**'s are outstanding	One plus the number of clocks to READY# from first **pfld**
pfld hits in the data cache	Two plus the number of clocks to the last READY# for all outstanding accesses
Store pipe full (two store miss cycles pending or a 256-bit writeback cycle pending plus external bus pipeline full) and **st**, **pst**, or **fst** miss, **ld** miss, or **flush**	One plus the number of clocks until READY# active on next 64-bit write cycle or second READY# of next 128-bit write cycle
Address pipe full (two internal bus cycles pending plus external bus pipeline full) and **ld**, **fld**, **pfld**, **st**, **fst**, **pst**	Number of clocks until next nonrepeated address can be issued (i.e., an address which is not the second-fourth cycle of a cache fill, or the second-eighth cycle of a CS8 mode instruction fetch, or the second cycle of a 128-bit write)
ld or **fld** following **st**, **pst**, or **fst** hit	One clock
Delayed branch not taken	One clock
Nondelayed branch taken:	
bc, **bnc**	One clock
bte, **btne**	Two clocks

Freeze Condition	*Delay (beyond the default one clock)*
Branch indirect **bri**, **call**, or **calli**	One clock
st.c	Two clocks
Result of graphics-unit instruction (other than **fmov.dd** or **fmov.ss**) used in next instruction when the next instruction is an adder or multiplier instruction	One clock
Result of graphics-unit instruction used in next instruction when the next instruction is a graphics-unit instruction	One clock
flush followed by **flush**	Three clocks minus the number of instructions between the two **flush** instructions
pst or **fst** followed by pipelined floating-point operation that overwrites the register being stored	One clock
Some multiplies, depending on data pattern and instruction sequence. This freeze, which applies to both single- and double-precision data and to both pipelined and scalar operations, occurs for less than 2% of all data patterns and is in addition to any other freeze involving the multiplier unit.	Up to two clocks

Instruction Characteristics

The following table lists some of the characteristics of each instruction. These characteristics are

- Which processing unit executes the instruction. The codes for processing units are as follows:

A Floating-point adder unit
E Core execution unit
G Graphics unit
M Floating-point multiplier unit

- Whether the instruction is pipelined or not. A *P* indicates that the instruction is pipelined.
- Whether the instruction is a delayed branch instruction. A *D* marks the delayed branches.
- Whether the instruction changes the condition code `CC`. A *`CC`* marks those instructions that change `CC`.
- Which faults can be caused by the instruction. The following codes are used for exceptions:

IT	Instruction Fault
SE	Floating-Point Source Exception
RE	Floating-Point Result Exception, including overflow, underflow, inexact result
DAT	Data Access Fault

Note that this is not the same as specifying at which instructions faults may be reported. A RE-fault is reported on the subsequent floating-point instruction plus **pst**, **fst**, and sometimes **fld**, **pfld**, and **ixfr**.

The instruction access fault `IAT` and the interrupt trap `IN` are not shown in the table because they can occur for any instruction.

- Performance notes. These comments regarding optimum performance are recommedations only. If these recommendations are not followed, the i860 microprocessor automatically waits the necessary number of clocks to satisfy internal hardware requirements. The following notes define the numeric codes that appear in the instruction table:

  1. The following instruction should not be a conditional branch (**bc**, **bnc**, **bc.t**, or **bnc.t**).
  2. The destination should not be a source operand of the next two instructions.

3. A load should not directly follow a store that is expected to hit in the data cache.

4. When the prior instruction is scalar, *src1* should not be the same as the *dest* of the prior operation.

5. The *freg* should not reference the destination of the next instruction if that instruction is a pipelined floating-point operation.

6. The destination should not be a source operand of the next instruction.

7. When the prior operation is scalar and multiplier *op1* is *fsrc1*, *fsrc2* should not be the same as the *fdest* of the prior operation.

8. When the prior operation is scalar, *src1* and *src2* of the current operation should not be the same as *dest* of the prior operation.

9. A **pfld** should not immediately follow a **pfld**.

- Programming restrictions. These indicate combinations of conditions that must be avoided by programmers, assemblers, and compilers. The following notes define the alphabetic codes that appear in the instruction table:

a. The sequential instruction following a delayed control-transfer instruction may not be another control-transfer instruction, nor a **trap** instruction, nor the target of a control-transfer instruction.

b. When using a **bri** to return from a trap handler, programmers should take care to prevent traps from occurring on that or on the next sequential instruction. IM should be zero (interrupts disabled) when the **bri** is executed.

c. If *dest* is not zero, *fsrc1* must not be the same as *dest*.

d. When *fsrc1* goes to multiplier *op1* or to KR or KI, *fsrc1* must not be the same as *rdest*.

e. If *dest* is not zero, *src1* and *src2* must not be the same as *dest*.

f. *isrc1* must not be the same register as *isrc2* for the autoincrementing form of this instruction.

Instruction	Execution Unit	Pipelined? Delayed?	Sets CC	Faults	Performance Notes	Programming Restrictions
adds	E		CC		1	
addu	E		CC		1	
and	E		CC			
andh	E		CC			
andnot	E		CC			
andnoth	E		CC			
bc	E					
bc.t	E	D				a
bla	E	D				a,f
bnc	E					
bnc.t	E	D				a
br	E	D				a
bri	E	D				a,b
bte	E					
btne	E					
call	E	D			6	a
calli	E	D			6	a
fadd.p	A			SE,RE		
faddp	G				8	
faddz	G				8	
famov.r	A			SE		
fiadd.w	G				8	
fisub.w	G				8	
fix.p	A			SE,RE		
fld.y	E			DAT	2,3	f
flush	E					
fmlow.dd	M				4	
fmul.p	M			SE,RE	4	
form	G				8	
frcp.p	M			SE,RE		
frsqr.p	M			SE,RE		
fst.y	E			DAT	5	f
fsub.p	A			SE,RE		
ftrunc.p	A			SE,RE		
fxfr	G				6,8	
fzchkl	G				8	
fzchks	G				8	

Instruction	Execution Unit	Pipelined? Delayed?	Sets CC	Faults	Performance Notes	Programming Restrictions
`intovr`	E			IT		
`ixfr`	E				2	
`ld.c`	E					
`ld.x`	E			DAT	6	
`lock`	E			IT*		
`or`	E		CC			
`orh`	E		CC			
`pfadd.p`	A	P		SE,RE		
`pfaddp`	G	P			8	e
`pfaddz`	G	P			8	e
`pfamov.r`	A	P		SE		
`pfam.p`	A&M	P		SE,RE	7	d
`pfeq.p`	A	P	CC	SE	1	
`pfgt.p`	A	P	CC	SE	1	
`pfiadd.w`	G	P			8	e
`pfisub.w`	G	P			8	e
`pfix.p`	A	P		SE,RE		
`pfld.z`	E	P		DAT	2,9	f
`pfle.p`	A	P	CC	SE	1	
`pfmam.p`	A&M	P		SE,RE	7	d
`pfmsm.p`	A&M	P		SE,RE	7	d
`pfmul.p`	M	P		SE,RE	4	c
`pfmul3.dd`	M	P		SE,RE	4	c
`pform`	G	P			8	e
`pfsm.p`	A&M	P		SE,RE	7	d
`pfsub.p`	A	P		SE,RE		
`pftrunc.p`	A	P		SE,RE		
`pfzchkl`	G	P			8	
`pfzchks`	G	P			8	
`pst.d`	E			DAT		f
`shl`	E					
`shr`	E					
`shra`	E					
`shrd`	E					
`st.c`	E					
`st.x`	E			DAT		

Instruction	Execution Unit	Pipelined? Delayed?	Sets cc	Faults	Performance Notes	Programming Restrictions
subs	E		CC		1	
subu	E		CC		1	
trap	E			IT		
unlock	E			IT*		
xor	E		CC			
xorh	E		CC			

*Lack of an **unlock** instruction within 30 instructions after **lock** can cause IT faults.

TRADEMARKS

CRAY 1®	Cray Research Incorporated
DEC®	Digital Equipment Corporation
i486™	Intel Corporation
i860™	Intel Corporation
IBM®	International Business Machines Corporation
System/370™	International Business Machines Corporation
Intel®	Intel Corporation
Intel 386™	Intel Corporation
Microsoft®	Microsoft Corporation
Motorola®	Motorola Incorporated
R2000™	MIPS Computer Systems Incorporated
SPARC™	Sun Microsystems
UNIX®	AT&T
VAX®	Digital Equipment Corporation

INDEX

D

E

F

G

H

I

K

L

M

N

R

S

T

U

V

W

X

Z

The manuscript for this book was prepared and submitted
to Osborne/McGraw-Hill in electronic form.
The acquisitions editor for this project was Elizabeth Fisher,
the technical reviewer was Mark Atkins,
and the project editor was Janis Paris.

Text design by Marcela Hancik and Deborra Knotts,
using Century Expanded for text body and
Avant Garde bold for display.

Cover art by Graphic Eye, Inc. Photo courtesy of Intel
Corporation. Color separation by Phoenix Color Corporation.
Screens produced with InSet, from Inset Systems, Inc.
Book printed and bound by R.R. Donnelley & Sons
Company, Crawfordsville, Indiana.